Deleuze and the Unconscious

Continuum Studies in Continental Philosophy:

Deconstruction and Democracy, Alex Thomson

Deleuze and Guattari's Philosophy of History, Jay Lampert

Deleuze and the Meaning of Life, Claire Colebrook

Derrida and Disinterest, Sean Gaston

Husserl's Phenomenology, Kevin Hermberg

Sartre's Ethics of Engagement, T. Storm Heter

Wittgenstein and Gadamer, Chris Lawn

Deleuze and the Unconscious

Christian Kerslake

continuum

Continuum
The Tower Building, 11 York Road, London SE1 7NX
80 Maiden Lane, Suite 704, New York NY 10038

British Library Cataloguing-in-Publication Data
A catalogue record for this book is available from the British Library.

ISBN-10: HB: 0-8264-8488-3
ISBN-13: HB: 978-0-8264-8488-8

Library of Congress Cataloging-in-Publication Data
A catalog record for this book is available from the Library of Congress.

Typeset by Kenneth Burnley, Wirral, Cheshire
Printed and bound in Great Britain by Biddles Ltd, King's Lynn, Norfolk

Contents

Acknowledgements vii
Abbreviations ix

Introduction 1

1 **The Pathologies of Time: The Unconscious Before Freud** 5

Bergson and Duration 8
Duration and Intensity 10
The Past 16
The Actual and the Virtual 25
Paramnesia and the Transcendental Synthesis of Memory 28
Neurosis and the Unconscious 34
Repetition and Eternal Return 36
Leibniz, Locke and the Theatre of the Unconscious 38
Personal Identity and the Metempsychotic Unconscious 43

2 **The Wasp's Sympathy for the Caterpillar: The Somnambulist Theory of Instinct** 49

Bergson and the Theory of Instinct 53
The Somnambulist Theory of the Unconscious 57
The Wasp's Sympathy for the Caterpillar 61
Ruyer's Defence of Bergson's Theory of Instinct 62
Instinctual Consciousness 65
How to Love the Marvellous 67

3 **Deleuze and the Jungian Unconscious** 69

Jung, Psychosis and the Transformation of Libido 70
Neurosis and Psychosis 79
Jung on the Unconscious 82
Jung's Theory of Instinct 86
Biological Models of Archetypes 88
Instincts and the Imagination 91

Kant, Jung and Sub-Representative Intuition 92
Kant, Jung and Super-Representative Ideas 94
Birth, Death and Sexual Difference 100

4 The World as Symbol: Kant, Jung and Deleuze 103

Jung on Symbolism 105
Kant's Theory of Symbolism 111
Schema and Symbol 120
Symbolism and Esoteric Mathesis 124
The Sexual Act of the Divine Hermaphrodite 134

5 Jung, Leibniz and the Differential Unconscious 138

Synchronicity: Acausal Synthesis 141
Schopenhauer and the Lines of Fate 146
Synchronicity, Immanence and Possible Worlds 150
Leibnizianism after the Speculative Death of God 152
Synchronicity and Repetition in Jung and Freud 154

6 The Occult Unconscious: Sympathy and the Sorcerer 159

Sorcery and the Difference between Human and Animal 161
Becoming-Animal 170
Sorcery of Capitalism 173
Vampires, Intoxication and Night-Consciousness 175
The Somniacal Imagination 186

Notes on Sources 189
Bibliography 228
Index 241

Acknowledgements

This book was written during a Leverhulme Early Career Research Fellowship at the Centre for Research in Modern European Philosophy at Middlesex University in 2002–4, and completed while Research Fellow at Middlesex during 2004–6. The Leverhulme Trust also generously supported a research trip to Paris in 2004.

I would like to acknowledge my gratitude to Peter Osborne, who has encouraged research in the further reaches in contemporary European philosophy at CRMEP at Middlesex over the last few years. Without his support, this book would not have been written. I would like to thank Philippe Van Haute, Tomas Geyskens, and Andreas de Block at Leuven and Nijmegen, for their intelligence and humour during the research-process. I have benefited from some valuable conversations with Daniel W. Smith. Janet Low of CFAR, Sarah Wood, Sonu Shamdasani and William Schupbach of the Wellcome Institute for the History of Medicine, all helped at various points. The staff of the British Library were always helpful and tolerant. Thanks most of all to Ruth Blue and our daughter Eva, for their love and patience.

Abbreviations

AO	*Anti-Oedipus* (1972) (with Félix Guattari)
ATP	*A Thousand Plateaus* (with Félix Guattari)
B	*Bergsonism* (1966)
C2	*Cinema 2* (1985)
CC	*Essays Critical and Clinical* (1993)
DI	*Desert Islands and Other Texts* (texts, 1953–74)
DR	*Difference and Repetition* (1968)
F	*The Fold: Leibniz and the Baroque* (1988)
I & I	*Instincts and Institutions* (ed.) (1953)
KCP	*Kant's Critical Philosophy* (1963)
LS	*Logic of Sense* (1969)
M	*Coldness and Cruelty* (1967)
N	*Negotiations* (texts, 1972–90)
PS	*Proust and Signs* (1964)
SM	'From Sacher-Masoch to Masochism' (1961)
SPE	*Expressionism in Philosophy: Spinoza* (1968)
TRM	*Two Regimes of Madness* (texts, 1975–95)
WP	*What is Philosophy?* (1991) (with Félix Guattari)

Lectures and seminars by Deleuze can be found on the internet at Webdeleuze.com

SE *Standard Edition of the Complete Psychological Works of Sigmund Freud*, ed. J. Strachey (London: Hogarth Press, 1953–74), 24 vols.

CW *The Collected Works of C. G. Jung*, ed. Sir Herbert Read, *et al.*, trans. R. F. C. Hull (New York & Princeton, Bollingen Series 20, 1953–83), 21 vols.

Introduction

For a period of twenty-five years before the publication of the first volume of his controversial masterpiece *Capitalism and Schizophrenia* (1972, co-authored with Félix Guattari), Gilles Deleuze explored a number of different theories of the unconscious. He appears to have inhabited a vanishing niche in French intellectual culture where Pierre Janet's psychology of the unconscious still had some parity with Sigmund Freud's. Deleuze went potholing in a number of obscure places, out of sight of the daylight concerns of his culture and times: Bergson's theories of instinct and memory, Jungianism, symbolism, Bachofen, esotericism (Johann Malfatti and Hoëne Wronski), Gustav Fechner's philosophical fantasy of the three ages of human consciousness, Ludwig Binswanger's theory of schizophrenia, drug experimentation, *sorcery* . . . anything but Freud.[1] He ransacked every forgotten cranny in modern thought in search of theories of the unconscious that restore dimensions, passages, syntheses and dramas of the mind occluded by Freudian psychoanalysis. While it is still unclear to me whether he ever emerged with a single theory of the unconscious, the written records of his excursions do offer us an unusually vivid glimpse inside some of the forgotten warehouses of the nineteenth- and twentieth-century philosophy of the unconscious. The single idea that unites these disparate theories is the belief that there is such a thing as unconscious *mentality*; the unconscious is never merely the physiological. Other than that, though, one is just as likely to find werewolves, sorcerers, drug-addicts, artists, hermaphrodites, vampires, centaurs, perhaps even salamanders and sylphs (not to mention that peculiar class of people known as 'schizophrenics') in Deleuze's galleries of the unconscious as one is to find obsessional neurotics and hysterics.

With *Anti-Oedipus*, the first volume of *Capitalism and Schizophrenia*, Deleuze (and Guattari) certainly played a role, however minor, in the demise of Freudian psychoanalysis in intellectual and therapeutic culture. But unlike other critics of Freud, Deleuze had always intended to replace the Freudian theory of the unconscious with another, more powerful theory of the unconscious. He did not want to naturalize or reduce it, or replace it with 'cognitive science'. To experience a 'fractured "I"' (DR 88–91) is to be threatened by psychosis, and the logic of the psychotic voyage cannot be approached with such means. The novel thing about the contemporary world, according to Deleuze, is that we are waking up to the destination of the human mind, 'the madness of the subject' (CC 30) that Kant had first inadvertently uncovered in the *Critique of Pure Reason* (and which found a furtive, explosive expression in Hölderlin's description of the tragic Oedipus (DR 58, 89). What Deleuze rejected in psychoanalysis was its ongoing inability to deal with the phenomena of psychosis, and in the psychotic phenomena that punctuate neurosis and the course of individuation in general. In one respect at least, the 'Anti-Oedipus' is the being that emerges after the shattering of 'Oedipus'. For Lacan (moving beyond Freud), the Oedipus complex consummates itself in the dissolution and depersonalization of Oedipus at Colonus. 'Oedipus says: Am I made man in the hour when I cease to be? That is the end of Oedipus's psychoanalysis – the psychoanalysis of Oedipus is only completed at Colonus, when he tears his face apart. That is the essential moment, which gives his story its meaning' (Lacan 1954–5: 214). Slavoj Žižek writes of the 'horror' of Oedipus at Colonus, who 'found himself reduced to a kind of soap bubble burst asunder – a scrap of the real, the leftover of a formless slime without any support in the symbolic order' (Žižek 2001: 21). For Lacanian psychoanalysis, the 'Real' must be forever kept at a distance, on the other side of the symbolic order. What must be avoided at all costs is the slide into psychosis, which is characterized as the total collapse of self-reflexive subjectivity. For Žižek, Hegel was right to describe madness as a withdrawal into the 'night of the world', although 'he all too quickly conceives of this withdrawal as a "regression" to the level of the "animal soul" still embedded in its natural environs and determined by the rhythm of nature' (Žižek 1998: 258). Deleuze takes a completely different view of psychosis, derived from Jung, and closer to Hegel's own view:

> What regression brings to the surface certainly seems at first sight to be slime from the depths; but if one does not stop short at a superficial evaluation and refrains from passing judgment on the basis of a preconceived dogma, it will be found that this 'slime' contains not merely incompatible and rejected remnants of everyday life, or inconvenient and objectionable tendencies, but also germs of new life and vital possibilities for the future. (CW 8: 34)

In an early piece, Deleuze endorses Jung's view that 'Freudian methodologies are appropriate mainly for young neurotics whose disorders are related to personal reminiscences and whose problems are about reconciling themselves with the *real* (loving, making oneself lovable, adapting, etc.), without regard for the role of any interior conflicts' (SM 133). The kind of psychopathologies analysed by Freud are thus primarily disorders of adaptation, and he refused to countenance that 'there are neuroses of quite another type which are nearer to psychosis' (ibid.). For Jung and Deleuze, all processes of individuation involve a fundamental psychotic moment: 'The whole course of individuation is dialectical, and the so-called "end" is the confrontation of the ego with the "emptiness" of the centre. Here the limit of the possible experience is reached: the ego dissolves as the reference-point of cognition' (Jung 1975: 259).

The message of Deleuze's and Guattari's *Capitalism and Schizophrenia* is unsettling: we have arrived at a historical point where we no longer have religious or moral protection against the madness that is inherent to the human mind. The two volumes of *Capitalism and Schizophrenia*, which are necessarily extravagant and delirious, are attempts to map out this new space, in order to learn to navigate and control it for a higher purpose. Although the human being is not the 'king of creation', it is 'the being who is in intimate contact with the profound life of all forms or all types of beings, who is responsible for even the stars and animal life . . . the eternal custodian of the machines of the universe' (AO 4). Deleuze is connected to a tradition of thought about the unconscious which is older than Freud's, and more rooted in the philosophical tradition. For Leibniz and Schelling, the task of the human being was to pass through the unconscious in order to assume full consciousness. At one level, this process takes place during what Leibniz, Jung and Deleuze all call 'individuation'. But at another level, it occurs across human culture, in areas we have been conditioned (by the success of psychoanalysis in the twentieth century) not to see as sites of unconscious activity. The encounter with the unconscious is continually to be felt pushing from the other side of modern culture, not just in psychopathology, but in the cinema of the post-war period, in modern music, in occultism and in drug-exploration. The unconscious has not vanished at all, we are still lost in its jungle, perhaps even more than before. New approaches to the unconscious are needed to perceive the full range of its inhabitants.

What follows is no more than a series of attempted raids on Deleuze's hive of ideas about the unconscious. I have left as many gates open, and laid out as many different options for interpretation, as possible. The book could serve as a source book for a reading of Deleuze on the unconscious, although there are plenty of omissions and probably lots of oversights too. I have ended up treating this as inevitable given the subject, which is a fascinating and complex one, and I hope other, better books are written on it before too long. A lot of attention is paid here to Deleuze's early work and influences, upon which much light still needs to be shed. The doctrines of *Anti-Oedipus* are mostly omitted, partly because a clear account of the work is already available in Eugene Holland's *Introduction to Anti-Oedipus* (Holland 1999), and partly because the book attempts to uncover the theoretical background to that work and its sequel, *A Thousand Plateaus*.

The book is not a general introduction to Deleuze (or even to Deleuze and the unconscious), and there is unfortunately also little of clinical relevance here, in part because Deleuze's approaches to the unconscious are not restricted to pathology, but include 'active' approaches to the unconscious (art, intoxication, magic).[2] The chapters are written from a philosophical, not a 'health-care' perspective – although there is certainly work to be done about Deleuze's and Guattari's 'schizoanalysis' from the latter perspective. The aims of philosophy and psychiatry are different, and there is no reason why this should not be so in the case of the unconscious, which has its own history in philosophical thought. Nevertheless, readers will see for themselves that I have not always been able to separate the 'critical' from the 'clinical', nor always been able to tell when Deleuze is speaking as a philosopher, as a 'doctor' of civilization, or as a 'patient' of it.[3] I did attempt to keep my philosopher's wig on throughout my voyages into the more floridly esoteric domains favoured by Deleuze, but I confess that the wig may have slipped on occasion, out of stupefied fascination as much as carelessness. With Deleuze more than any other recent French philosopher, we are forced to suspend our norms about what constitutes 'philosophy', even that sort of philosophy done in that thoroughly dubious field known as 'continental'. Here I have been obliged to work not just as a 'philosopher', but more specifically as a detective, a paid fool, on the trail of an enigmatic, slightly preposterous figure, rather dandified by all accounts, with long fingernails (cf. N 5), whose name everybody seems to know, but about whom curiously very little has yet been established.

Chapter 1

The Pathologies of Time: The Unconscious Before Freud

In the wake of the successes of Darwinism and modern physiological and physical science at the turn of the twentieth century, many efforts were under way to see how far the physiological and biological approaches to consciousness could go. The theories of the unconscious arrived at independently and simultaneously by Bergson and Freud also emerged out of attempts to push the physiological and biological frameworks to their limits, albeit in radically opposing ways. Bergson's *Matter and Memory* was published in 1896, a year after Freud wrote his unpublished 'psychology for neurologists', *Project for a Scientific Psychology*. Both works begin with a basic physiological framework – the reflex arc – and proceed from there to an account of the evolutionary advantages and disadvantages of complex nervous systems. But both works result in conclusions that set their authors apart from the mainstream of naturalizing theories of the mind.

Both authors discover that the process that should really be given a privilege in the mind is not consciousness at all, but the unconscious. It is the unconscious that gives rise to the real split between human beings and the rest of nature, not consciousness. For Freud, this insight led to the abandonment of neurophysiology, as the laws of the unconscious processes appeared to have a logic of their own (displacement, condensation, repression, etc.) which deserved analysis in its own terms rather than in directly physical terms. Freud accepted that it was impossible to directly match wishes, desires and sense-bearing phenomena with physiological states, so he put off the project for a 'scientific psychology'. For Bergson, the insight into the importance of the unconscious came through his realization that memory cannot be approached as a purely physiological process, because the human awareness of time and, in particular, the past, introduces a new kind of process into the brain. Memories cannot be explained in terms of the brain; rather the human brain is shaped or moulded around the pure memories that constitute the past. Memories for the most part are unconscious, and so the most characteristic aspect of human cognition is unconscious. Deleuze takes Bergson's discovery as a challenge to transcendental philosophy: from now on, rather than focusing on consciousness, the transcendental philosopher must explore syntheses of time which are unconscious.

From our vantage point a century later, it is striking how the influence of the Bergson–Janet tradition appears to have been somehow abruptly extinguished by the Second World War. If this tradition evokes any associations for the English-speaking reader today, it is with a peculiar lost Victorian and Edwardian world, a world in which journals of psychology and philosophy were filled with cases and analyses of mediums, somnambulism, hypnosis and spiritualistic phenomena. Now, it is almost as if this period never happened. We seem to have more in common with the period of the 1860s, with the emergence of evolutionary theory in Darwin and Spencer. The motivations of this weird 'spiritualist' interregnum seem ever more inexplicable. But in the early decades of the twentieth century, Bergson's theory of time, based on the concepts of duration (*durée*) and memory, had enjoyed extraordinary popularity in the wider culture. In Paris, Bergson had been a prime mover in the conversion of fin-de-siècle *decadence* into an affirmation of creativity and novelty at the personal and political levels, as well as at the level of life itself (through Bergson's return to biological vitalism). In psychology, Bergsonism was understood by many to have provided a consistent philosophical and metaphysical framework for the empirical work of Pierre Janet (1859–1947) and others.[1] In 1914, Freud wrote that in Paris, 'the conviction still seems to reign (to which Janet himself gave eloquent expression at the [17th International Medical] Congress in London in 1913) that everything good in psychoanalysis is a repetition of Janet's views with insignificant modifications, and that everything else in it is bad' (SE 14: 32). If Freud had to struggle to get his theories recognized at the beginning of the twentieth century, it was because a theory of the unconscious already existed and was widely known in both the academic and psychiatric worlds. Jung's view of the unconscious, as we will see, also originated in the Janet–Bergson school, and his involvement with Freud can be seen as an *interruption* of his development of that school's ideas, rather than a decisive influence.[2]

But after the Second World War Bergson's philosophy of duration and memory was radically eclipsed in France by the existentialist theory of time developed by Sartre from the materials of Heidegger's *Being and Time*. In a landscape of ruins and an atmosphere of shock, the urgent desire to completely renew society, from its foundations upward, perhaps made the Bergsonian emphasis on the continual accumulation of the past in the present unwelcome.[3] In psychology too, Bergson and Janet were eclipsed by the increasing popularity of psychoanalysis and the turn to existential phenomenology. Bergson and Janet continued to influence the phenomenological tradition; Eugène Minkowski's *Lived Time* was strongly indebted to Bergson and Janet, and later influenced Deleuze. But for reasons that are still not entirely clear, the whole Bergson–Janet tradition faded into history. There ceased to be two competing theories of the unconscious and psychopathology, descended from radically different traditions; rather, attempts to make good the absence of a theory of subjectivity and consciousness in Freudian psychoanalysis tended to involve an *incorporation* into psychoanalysis of existentialist theories of subjectivity (Lacan is the most prominent example). The tradition elaborated by Bergson and Janet seemed to be mysteriously cut off, isolated and sealed in pre-war amber.

The peculiar Bergsonian psychology of memory that dominated the beginning of the twentieth century might therefore now appear to be nothing more than a curious anomaly that mainly begs for treatment by intellectual historians. However, the startling fact is that it is fundamental to the psychological thought of Deleuze, who tends to be thought of as one of the most 'contemporary' of French philosophers. Deleuze began writing on Bergson in the early 1950s and Bergson's theory of time remains fundamental to all of his philosophical work. His fullest statement of what is living in Bergson's philosophy is his *Bergsonism* of 1966, although the *Cinema* books of the 1980s are also explicitly developed within a detailed Bergsonian framework. In returning to Bergson, Deleuze ran against the tide, and in 1972 he remarks that 'people . . . laugh at me simply for having written about Bergson at all' (N 6). However, Deleuze's return to Bergson was a return to aspects in Bergson's theory that fell outside the caricatural view of it as an affirmation of Heraclitean flux or novelty. For Deleuze, it was not the well-known theory of duration that is Bergson's most significant contribution to the philosophy of time, but his theory of memory. This theory, which is incredibly baroque and counter-intuitive, and remains so in Deleuze, provides Deleuze with the basis for his own theory of the unconscious. There are also key references to Janet and Jung in Deleuze's work. For Deleuze, the notion of the unconscious cannot be adequately treated outside of an account of the temporal syntheses that characterize human cognition. Deleuze develops and elaborates Bergson's and Janet's theses on memory and arrives at a theory that is distinctive, but recognizably indebted to the early French theory of the unconscious. It is therefore not surprising that Deleuze's first approach to the notion of the unconscious is through Jung rather than Freud.

What was the essential difference between the French and Viennese notions of the unconscious? In 1898, Freud wrote to Fliess, 'I opened a recently published book by Janet, *Hystérie et idées fixes*, with a pounding heart and put it aside again with my pulse calmed. He has no inkling of the key' (Letter of 10 March 1898, Masson 1985: 302). The key, of course, is sexuality. Freud acknowledged that memories were the most obvious examples of unconscious psychic states, but he argued that appealing to memory itself does not give us the key to why certain of these memories are dynamically repressed. For an account of the dynamic relation of the unconscious to consciousness, one needs to venture outside the theory of human cognition and into the theory of sexual development. What is truly unconscious – that is, *blocked* from consciousness – is what is *incompatible* with the ego's conception of itself. Drawing on the sexual traits that therapy shows to be behind many neurotic symptoms, Freud inferred that it was sexual content itself which formed the bedrock of the unconscious.

It might seem surprising to place Deleuze, who is known as a philosopher of 'desire', in the Bergson–Janet tradition of conceptualizing the unconscious and psychopathology in terms of the framework of memory and time, rather than that of sexuality. However, as we will see, the difference between 'desire' and 'sexuality' was key for Jung, whose theories Deleuze explicitly affirmed in 1961. In *Difference and Repetition,* Deleuze develops a theory of the 'synthesis of memory' which he holds is also a 'synthesis of Eros'. In it, Deleuze implies that Freud was a victim of an illusion about the sexual aetiology of psychopathology. Sexual content is so important in many neuroses because it is necessarily fixed upon during the process of a deeper shift that occurs at a particularly crucial stage of psychological development (adolescence). It is not the *cause* of psychopathology (or, indeed, of the unconscious). The synthesis of memory by itself assumes, almost as a by-product, a specific 'erotic' function during the process of individual psychological development. Elsewhere he points out that many other disorders, such as schizophrenia, manic-depression, or the neuroses of people in their thirties and above, are not caused by sexual problems, although sexuality might play a role in them. Deleuze's account of sexuality is non-Freudian from the beginning. Moreover, Deleuze's first work on sexuality occurred in the context of theories of *instinct,* and his main influences were Bergson and Jung, in conjunction with anthropological theories from Malinowski and Hume. Freudians have gone to great lengths to distinguish *Trieb* (drive) from instinct, but in the beginning Deleuze squarely situates himself on the side of instinct. From the outset Deleuze seems to have seen the potential in Bergsonism for a non-Freudian reformulation of the basic themes of psychoanalysis.

Bergson and Duration

The simplest way to begin to dissolve the apparent aberration involved in Deleuze's return to Bergson is to begin with the fact that what is usually taken to be most central to 'Bergsonism' – the notion of duration, expounded in Bergson's first book, the *Essay on the Immediate Data of Consciousness* (translated as *Time and Free Will*) – is actually the mere portal to a much more interesting and profound theory of memory. Deleuze's decision to entitle his book *Bergsonism* is thus polemical, insofar as he redefines what is of central interest in Bergson.

> Bergsonism has often been reduced to the following idea: duration is subjective, and constitutes our internal life. And it is true that Bergson had to express himself in this way, at least at the outset. But increasingly, he came to say something quite different: the only subjectivity is time, non-chronological time grasped in its foundation, and it is we who are internal to time, not the other way round. (C2 82)

Deleuze's depiction of the framework towards which Bergson moved is not exactly pellucid here, but it is enough to say that the 'non-chronological time' referred to concerns memory: for Bergson, our memories *coexist* with our present, and acts of memory must be taken as discontinuous sorties into a preserved past composed of its own stratified formations. Bergson's bizarre but compelling theory of memory leads towards a very different, much more complex, theory of time than the notion of duration.

> In the *Essay on the Immediate Data of Consciousness*, duration is really defined by succession, coexistences referring back to space, and by the power of novelty, repetition referring back to Matter. But, more profoundly, duration is only succession relatively speaking (we have seen in the same way that it is only indivisible relatively). Duration is indeed real succession, but it is so only because, more profoundly, it is *virtual coexistence*: the coexistence with itself of all the levels, all the tensions, all the degrees of contraction and relaxation. (B 60)

Deleuze by no means ignores the notion of duration, but he sees it as the gateway to Bergson's philosophy rather than its centre. Before it leads to memory, it first leads to what will be the key concept of Deleuze's revision of Kant's Transcendental Aesthetic, the notion of 'intensive difference'. It is true, as Bergson says in the *Essay*, that taking duration seriously means that we must abandon any theory of mind which conceives of mental content in terms of discrete, spatialized representations which are indifferent to temporal change. The conscious mind (in Kantian terms 'inner sense') is fundamentally durational, and its contents are therefore mischaracterized if represented spatially. But what this means is that, insofar as the mind is durational, it is host to a specifically intensive – as opposed to extensive – form of developmental differentiation. From childhood to adulthood, the mind passes through intensive thresholds that each time entail re-organization of its mnemic content and practical aims. Hence it makes sense to begin our investigation with Deleuze's reformulation of Bergsonian duration. In his second book, *Matter and Memory* (1896), Bergson completely reconceptualizes his notion of duration so that it now testifies to an *unconscious* weight of memory, while the role of consciousness becomes almost exclusively practical and focused on the *present*. In the *Essay on the Immediate Data of Consciousness*, however, duration is simply identified as the fundamental medium of psychological life. Duration is identified with consciousness in general, to the extent that Bergson denies that duration is a feature of the objective world. A rough general sketch of the position can be given, before we qualify it in certain crucial respects. Mental life is not composed of discrete representations. The way mental representations appear is fundamentally affected by the form of their appearance. The form of their appearance is temporal duration, in which representations are never discrete and homogeneous, but blend into each other, in a 'heterogeneous continuity' (Bergson 1889: 128). Mental representations must appear as part of a developing mental whole, which is in one respect enduring (it prolongs the experiences of the past), and in another respect, open to novelty (the accumulation of the past in the present means that one tends to bring an increasingly complex mental background to what one experiences now, which makes experience of repeated events qualitatively different to their past occurrences).

Duration and Intensity

Bergson's theory of duration is built on his critique of 'psychophysics' in the first chapter of his first book, the *Essay on the Immediate Data of Consciousness*, and we should recount this critique here, as this chapter is an absolutely fundamental building block both in Bergson's theory in general, and in his speculations about the unconscious. In the history of psychology, Fechner's psychophysics is often held to be the first attempt at a genuinely experimental psychology. A properly quantitative account of mental events becomes possible for the first time, in which mental events can be mathematically correlated with physical stimuli. By attacking psychophysics, Bergson was attacking experimental psychology as it existed at the time.

Bergson's main targets are Gustav Fechner (1801–87) and Joseph Delboeuf (1831–96), but we will focus here on the former. In his *Elements of Psychophysics* (1860), Fechner had defined psychophysics (*Psychophysik*) as 'the exact science of the functionally dependent relations of body and soul or, more generally, of the material and the mental, of the physical and the psychological worlds' (Fechner 1860: I, 7). Fechner arrives at his aim of providing a mathematical account of the correlations between physical stimuli and mental events by affirming a *parallelism* of mental and physical events, rather than attempting a reduction of sensations to physical events, as had been attempted by the Enlightenment materialists. By *reducing* psychological sensations to physical events, the early modern materialists had left sensations as mere appearances or epiphenomena, and hence without any status of their own. On this view a mathematical relationship between stimulus and sensation was neither possible nor necessary. Fechner's investigations in psychophysics were therefore intimately related to his affirmation of psychophysical parallelism. We will explore the consequences of this when we have cause to turn to Fechner's metaphysics.

Fechner argued that while an increase in the intensity of a physical *stimulus* does not produce a one-to-one increase in mental *sensation*, there is instead a logarithmic relationship between the two: one series increases geometrically, and the other arithmetically. A logarithmic relationship between two quantitative series allows for increases in the second series to be proportionally relative to the quantities that already exist in the first series. Thus if the aural stimulus of one ringing bell is added to another, the increase in sensation is greater than if one bell is added to ten already ringing bells.

Now, measuring intensive increases in objective stimuli (for instance, the measurement of sound or weight) poses no particular problem, if appropriate and sensitive instruments are available. Fechner bases himself on a law which he attributes to one of his teachers, E. H. Weber, according to which a difference between two stimuli is always perceived as equal if its ratio to the stimuli remains the same, regardless of changes in the absolute size. 'For example, an addition of 1 unit to a stimulus expressed as having a magnitude of 100 units is perceived the same as an addition of 2 to a stimulus of 200 units, of 3 to a stimulus of 300 units, and so on' (Fechner 1860: I, 112; cf. Bergson 1889: 60). The audacity of Fechner's proposal lies in his extension of this law to the relation between stimuli and sensations.

The problem, as Fechner is already completely aware, is how the second series, the series of psychical sensation, is to be measured. What are the 'units' of sensation? Fechner suggested two methods for identifying the minima of a change in sensation: first one must find the *absolute threshold* of a sensation, and then go on to isolate its *differential threshold*. An absolute threshold identifies the point at which a summation of stimuli breaks through to conscious awareness. By increasing the volume of a sound starting from zero, one can locate the point at which it becomes audible. But the absolute threshold only gives one value of a sensation – the lowest intensity of a stimulus at which a sensation is felt (for example, the point at which pain is first felt on the insertion of a pin into the hand). To quantitatively relate two series of intensities, one must be able to show a whole range of correlations. Fechner suggested that this could be done if one discovered the differential threshold of sensation – the minimal unit of change which could give rise to a sensation (Fechner 1860: 202). One therefore must start with the identification of the absolute threshold, and then go back and identify the minimum physical pressure required for a difference to be sensed.

It then becomes possible to use these minima as the way to articulate the series of sensation. To quote Bergson:

> For if we treat as a quantity the difference perceived by consciousness between the two sensations which succeed one another in the course of a continuous increase of stimulus, if we call the first sensation S, and the second ΔS, we shall have to consider every sensation as a sum, obtained by the addition of the minimum differences through which we pass before reaching it. (Bergson 1889: 65)

With the identification of minimal differences of sensation, a mathematical relationship can apparently be established between the series of stimuli and the series of sensations. Each quantitative change in stimulus produces a correlative quantitative change in the series of sensation.

Of course, it is intuitively correct that the sensation of heat will alter in line with the increase in temperature, but Bergson argues that there are basic problems with taking a mathematical view of this correlation. Although we can always gauge when we are getting hotter or colder, it would seem that the correspondences we make between our sensations of warmth and the degree of temperature rest on convention. Moreover, are 'degrees' of sensation really of the same kind as degrees of physical stimulus, such as temperature? I do not pass through two separate successive sensations, but rather through *states* of sensation which flow into one another. 'The mistake which Fechner made . . . was that he believed in an interval between two successive sensations S and S'', when there is simply a *passing* from one to the other and not a *difference* in the arithmetical sense of the word' (Bergson 1889: 68). Thus sensations just do not seem to be measurable in the way that stimuli are. However, 'the novel feature in Fechner's treatment is that he did not consider this difficulty insurmountable. Taking advantage of the fact that sensation varies by sudden jumps while the stimulus increases continuously, he did not hesitate to call these differences of sensation by the same name: they are all, he says, *minimum* differences, since each corresponds to the smallest perceptible increase in the external stimulus' (Bergson 1889: 64). But why should the determination of the differential threshold of a sensation yield a minimum difference which can go on to be applied homogeneously throughout the series of sensation? In 1874 Jules Tannery began to publish a series of objections to Fechner's psychophysics which already contain certain aspects of Bergson's critique. He writes:

> The essential characteristic of directly mensurable dimensions is *homogeneity*: whatever is added, such that something increases, is of the same exact kind as that which was already there: length, surface and time are dimensions of this kind. If we add one length to another, both of them are of the same kind and essence and their sums are also of the same kind. Directly measurable dimensions necessarily have this quality, because measurement itself requires that dimensions of the same kind be comparable. (Tannery 1875: 1019)

But, objects Tannery, if one is holding a warm object in one's hand and its heat increases, then the original sensation of heat is going to be of a different kind to the later sensation of pain (Heidelberger 2004: 209). The fact that the mere increase in stimulus activates different nerves introduces heterogeneity into the series of sensations. Homogeneity in the series of stimuli should therefore not automatically be projected upon the series of sensations.

Bergson cites Tannery's objections (which also include the objection that sensation differentials are merely conventional) but goes on to develop criticisms of his own. He asks us to consider the sensation of pain caused by a pinprick (Bergson 1889: 35ff.). On the hypothesis of psychophysical parallelism, we should predict that if we apply a slowly but continuously increasing amount of force on the pin, then we will feel a pain that increases in parallel. But what happens is that at certain points thresholds are reached, when the pain goes from being, for instance, merely noticeable, to being rather irksome, to being alarming and then excruciating. There are qualitative leaps in the feeling of pain, thresholds of transformation, where a change in nature comes about in the quality of the pain. This may indicate that the series of sensation has its *own* thresholds, which are relatively autonomous of the stimuli-series. The scale of sensations of pain, for instance, may have internal, relative thresholds which cannot be deduced from physiological stimulation. The pain we are feeling at any one point cannot be simply analysed into the addition of homogeneous quantities of pain, all stacked up indifferently upon each other. Now this could be explained (as Tannery suggests) through appeal to different nerve centres and functions in the body. But Bergson also suggests – and this is his original contribution – that the quality of the sensation is also crucially influenced by *how long* we've been enduring the pain. He suggests, against Tannery, that time in fact should *not* be treated as a homogeneous magnitude, but rather that it should be considered to be at the root of the heterogeneity found in the series of sensations. Time, or *duration*, makes a difference to sensation. For instance, sometimes we do not even have to increase the force of the pin to make the pain unbearable, we can just let the same quantity go on for a while longer, and the threshold of alarm is reached. This indicates that the way the pain feels after five minutes will be coloured by the fact of my having *endured* the pain for so long, which thus influences the moment of transformation at which the pain becomes unbearable.

Bergson goes on to make three important inferences at this juncture, which in fact contribute towards a definition of 'duration'. First, each sensation of pain implies the traversal of a preceding series, which must be endured in order to get to the present pain. We cannot miss out any of the stages. A sensation in time of increasing pain is *indivisible*, in the strict sense that it is experienced as a whole, and must include all its phases. The pain is 'swollen by the whole of its past' (Bergson 1889: 153). A boiling point cannot be reached at once; a certain speed cannot be reached without passing through all the other speeds, however quickly. Second, every series of changes is punctuated at various points by *thresholds*, at which a transformation occurs. So we could indeed plot a series of changes during which there are only regular, quantitative changes that can be plotted on a graph. But these would only be differences of *degree*, whereas what Fechner has not accounted for are the possible differences in *kind* or *nature* between sensations. While water is coming to the boil the degrees of temperature can be measured quantitatively from 0 to 100 degrees centigrade; but at 100 degrees, an 'event' happens: the water *changes in nature* and starts to turn into steam. Similarly, the descent of the temperature of water to 0 degrees signifies a change in nature: freezing. Deleuze will call these distinctive points *singularities*. The third characteristic of duration follows from the first two. Once such a plateau has been reached, there is a complete change in the way the elements involved relate to one another. The whole situation changes at 0 and 100 degrees. Ice, liquid and steam all behave in different ways, even if the same substance is involved, water. Thus after each transformation, there is a change *in the whole*, meaning that what happens next happens on new terms.

These attributes of duration suggest a new conception of *time* in general, which Bergson will now argue should be measured and divided up differently to space. The classic dyad between space and time is misleading, as it persuades us that there is something in common between the two. Kant, for instance, thought space and time shared exactly the same formal characteristics: actual infinity and homogeneity (Kant 1782/1787: A23/B38). Bergson, on the other hand, is saying that the forms of time and space should be completely distinguished. By ascribing a special kind of 'heterogeneous continuity' to time, Bergson is not just saying that there are no boundaries between each temporal segment (Kant would agree, and say that the same goes for space as an infinite, homogeneous magnitude). His point is that the type of differentiation appropriate to things insofar as they *endure* must be distinct from the kind of differentiation appropriate to things insofar as they are understood purely spatially and timelessly. By not recognizing the role of duration in sensation, psychophysics gives an abstract, spatialised account of sensation. This, for Bergson, is the real cause of the inadequacy of psychophysics.

Deleuze's emphasis on the passing of intensive thresholds clarifies Bergson's insistence on the 'indivisibility' of duration and therefore of human experience. Bergson sometimes talks in a Romantic way about the 'indivisibility' of duration (thus placing the durational account of human experience in an abstract opposition with the scientific one, which 'murders to dissect').[4]

In the *Essay*, Bergson's conclusion is that the realms of physical quantity and sensate quality are entirely separate: 'the fact is that there is no point of contact between the unextended and the extended, between quality and quantity' (Bergson 1889: 70). The idea proposed by Kant, that there is a special kind of 'intensive magnitude', where sensations can be more or less intense, is rejected by Bergson. If 'we distinguish two kinds of quantity, the one intensive, which admits only of a "more or less", the other extensive, which lends itself to measurement, we are not far from siding with Fechner and the psychophysicists. For, as soon as a thing is acknowledged to be capable of increase and decrease, it seems natural to ask by how much it decreases or by how much it increases . . . Either, then, sensation is pure quality, or, if it is a magnitude, we ought to try to measure it' (72). The notion of intensity is a confused concept, 'situated at the junction of two streams' (73), extensive quantity and the kind of sensed multiplicity we experience in consciousness.

Deleuze's analysis shows that duration is more strictly 'relatively indivisible' (B 60; cf. DR 237), in that each *single* crossing over a threshold involves a change in nature (and therefore is indivisible), but that there may nevertheless be many traversals of thresholds.[5] Deleuze wants to show, after the event, how Bergson did not fully understand the implications of the conception of duration he was bringing into existence; the job of the commentator is to make these implications explicit. In the *Essay on the Immediate Data of Consciousness* Bergson himself had couched his critique of psychophysical parallelism as a *critique* of the notion of intensity, which he takes to imply changes in degree, measured in homogeneous quantity. In the scholastic notion of intensity, still active in Kant's philosophy, degrees of intensity are said to be continuous and homogeneous. Time is not held to make any difference to the gradual increase in intensity of the colour red. But for Deleuze, Bergson's notion of duration helps in fact to indicate the true form and nature of intensity (DR 239). If we follow through Bergson's line of thought, we 'rediscover at the heart of duration the implicated order of intensity' (DR 239). The form of differentiation revealed by duration shows that intensity must itself be thought on the threshold model of intensive *difference.* To say that 'the expression "difference of intensity" is a tautology' (DR 222) is an exaggeration, because Deleuze himself also spells out other, ideal, forms of difference – but nevertheless he shows that duration and intensity are intimately related and produce the basic form of differentiation for any theory of sensation.

Now, although Bergson sometimes seems to suggest (particularly at the start of *Creative Evolution*) that *each moment,* by virtue of taking place in duration, involves something new (or, in Deleuzian terms, that *any* repetition involves a difference), Deleuze sees that it is not necessary to commit oneself to this extreme position. There are stretches of experience when nothing much happens (in the *Cinema* books he calls these 'any-instants-whatever', *instants quelconques*). The strong point of Bergson's argument about duration is that enduring a sensation or experience can *at some point* give rise to a change in nature, and that this property requires that we abandon any notion of time articulated in terms of the accretion of discrete, homogeneous intervals (e.g. clock time).[6] Such thresholds of transformation are fairly frequent in experience, and in the *Essay* Bergson gives a number of descriptions of thresholds that punctuate emotions (e.g. explosions of desire and anger). However, these thresholds are obviously not encountered at every moment (which would be incoherent, as it would preclude the *endurance* of a particular state). In Deleuzian terms, the repetition of a type of event does not *always* involve difference. Furthermore, if this is the reason that duration generates the new, then this modifies the standard, over-simplistic interpretation of Bergson's insistence that duration implies novelty. It is not that the new is ceaselessly produced by the mere fact of duration.[7] It is rather that the new is produced *because duration is the vehicle for intensive differences.*

Duration has the property of *bearing* intensive thresholds of transformation, but each instance of such a threshold seems to refer us back to the thing that is being sensed or experienced. The intensive properties of the experience refer back to properties of the thing, which are *intensive* in the sense that they are internal or intrinsic, as opposed to external or secondary. For instance, the experience of being trapped in a yellow room would thus have singularities particular *to it*: it might be optically stimulating at first, but at a certain point I might start to feel nauseous. In the *Cinema* books Deleuze refers a few times to Goethe's theory of colour, which states that when the intensities of colours are increased, they often produce a transformation: yellow gets rings of red around it. So there might be all sorts of optical effects produced by being stuck in a yellow room long enough. There would thus be differential thresholds proper to the exclusive reception of the colour yellow. Repeated stimulation by the colour yellow would have its own set of singularities. After having been locked in a yellow room once in my life, the *repetition* at a later point of the experience might generate anxiety, and then, depending on how many times it was repeated, panic. Although these intensities would be generated within my body in the room, they are more properly attributed to the room itself. A Yellow Room therefore has its own intensive field, different in kind to the intensities generated by a White Room. Deleuze explicitly takes the concept of duration to give access to 'things themselves' (see, for instance, DI 23), and consciously plays on the multiple meanings of the word 'intensity': metaphysical, durational and affective.

We already see Deleuze engineering a compromise between Bergson and Fechner. Bergsonian duration is shown to conceal precisely the differential thresholds identified by Fechner, but now extracted from their abstract, homogeneous framework. Thus, although thresholds – whether they be of pain or sensory qualities – are embodied in material bodies, these thresholds are only reached on condition that their transformations are *endured.* If, as Kant says in the First Analogy, the passage of time can only be measured by assuming a permanent substance as the backdrop to changes in property, Bergson shows how the nature of physical substances can be modulated by time as duration.

It was Bergson's realization that duration implies the preservation of the past which forced him to modify his identification of duration with *consciousness.* If duration is only possible on condition that the past is preserved, then, Bergson realizes, he must radically modify his theory that consciousness is the primary site of duration. The past is preserved by memory, but at any one time, the vast majority of memories must reside outside consciousness. But if duration is the prolongation of the past into the present, and yet memories are most of the time not conscious, then the durational nature of the mind only indirectly concerns consciousness. Memory, the site of unconscious mental representations, now bears the weight of duration. From now on, the role of consciousness will be restricted and will in fact not be directly connected with duration at all. The function of consciousness is rather to fix itself to *the present,* that is, to the *actual.* Here we begin to see the convergence, albeit quite accidental and via a completely independent route, with Freud: consciousness now becomes a *superficial* phenomenon, concerned with the 'exigencies of life', which conspires to conceal the deeper, unconscious roots proper to the human mind. Bergson plunges into 'the ambiguities which surround the problem of the unconscious', and he emerges arguing that 'the idea of an *unconscious representation* is clear, despite current prejudice' (Bergson 1896: 142).

The Past

When we are indoors, we assume that the world outside carries on existing unperceived. We assume that there is an objective series of events occurring in the external world, which has nothing to do with us. However, Bergson suggests that it is not enough to close the curtains and windows, to detach oneself from the everyday environment to which one spends one's daylight hours trying to adapt, to succeed in escaping 'reality'. We close ourselves off from external, objective reality only for another, inner curtain to open. Once the world of the senses is diminished, one encounters that *other* external world, the past. In Bergson's gothic philosophy of memory, the past is at least as real as the external world. There is no more reason to say 'that the past effaces itself as soon as perceived than there is to suppose that material objects cease to exist when we cease to perceive them' (Bergson 1896: 142). The unperceived external world is analogous to the unperceived past. More strongly, Bergson goes so far as to claim that it is the past that truly *is*. Past events may appear sterile and powerless, while our present seems malleable and open to continual redirection. But once an event is done, it is fixed. It is photographed, and if it can change its significance due to future interpretations, it nevertheless cannot be erased; the past has the attribute of permanence which thinkers since Plato have attributed to the notion of 'being'. The present, on the other hand, is so fleeting and impossible to pin down that it does not have the right to be said to *be*.

Led by the logic of the concept of duration, Bergson is led to the same conclusion that haunted a number of the most significant thinkers of the day, among them Freud and Nietzsche: 'in the mental realm, there is no annihilation' (cf. Nietzsche 1911: # 588). Perhaps it is the vertiginous fascination with this thought that separates our age so radically from Bergson's. Nothing that was ever in the human mind can ever leave it. Part of the reason why Bergson and Nietzsche are more important than Freud for Deleuze is that the former two stay truest to this thought, to the point of delirium. Bergson's theory of the past, and Nietzsche's theory of the eternal return, both express in their different (and, Deleuze contends, ultimately complementary) ways, the implications at both the psychological and ethical levels, of this one thought: that if experiences are lost to our present, the past is not lost to the mind. Deleuze's contribution is to identify Bergson as the philosopher who provided the most powerful arguments to back up that thought; this is why *Matter and Memory* is the central statement of Bergsonian philosophy for Deleuze. Furthermore, if the 'greatest weight' that Nietzsche encounters in the thought of the eternal return is the thought that *all* the past is preserved, then Deleuze's project seems to be to show how Bergson's arguments about the past also help to increase this 'weight' – to the point that liberation from the burden of the past through the affirmation of the eternal return becomes a necessity.

Bergson's theory of memory is the strangest, most counter-intuitive part of his philosophy, and for the casual reader of Deleuze (perhaps introduced to his work through *Anti-Oedipus*), it cannot but be surprising to find a contemporary philosopher defending it so energetically. But Deleuze carries on defending the theory well after *Anti-Oedipus*, and it forms the backbone of *Cinema 2* (1985).[8] The proposition that the past is as real as the external world is already enough to give us a jolt. Reality appears to spill out over the confines of the present moment; surely a fallacy is afoot? Yes, of course the present is *actual*, Bergson reassures us – but that does not mean it has a monopoly on *reality*, which might be something quite different. Is it *a priori* true that only what is actually happening can be said to have reality? Is the past then nothing but a figment of the imagination? But, we want to insist, the past is dead and gone; there is nothing we can *do* about it. Bergson responds: it may be dead, but it is not gone. Without the preservation of the past, there would be no intelligent action in the present, nor the ability to distinguish mere imagination from memory. The past is completely real, says Bergson; in fact, reality might be ascribed with greater assurance to the past than to the present, which is forever in flight, always eclipsed by its imminent negation. Why, then, we protest at this ethereal Frenchman, does not the past flood into the present, incapacitating and choking it, if it is more real than the present? Bergson is unflappable: well, in fact it *does* sometimes in certain pathological cases, and if it does not for most others, that is because they are able to *inhibit* their awareness of the past. The past, Bergson concludes, is unconscious.

The route of Bergson and Janet into the notion of the unconscious was through the notion of memory. The more they had reflected on the conditions for memory, the more they saw psychopathology as resulting from failures in the inhibition of memory. It was this line of research which made them impervious to Freud's sexual repression theory of the unconscious when it appeared. Although Freud is often held to have most radically changed the self-image of humanity through his discovery of the unconscious, for Deleuze, the Bergsonian discovery of the reality of the past is more far-reaching in its transformation of our self-image as human subjects. As a philosopher, Bergson's reconception of subjectivity encompasses a total vision of the human mind which is inevitably wider in scope than Freud's work, which remains necessarily tethered to its origins in the study of psychopathology. But it is not just that Freud does not happen to be a philosopher by training or vocation. The *methods* by which Bergson and Freud discover their separate theories of the unconscious are completely distinct. Freud discovers the unconscious by inferring its existence on the basis of the theory of *repression* he constructs after observing patients exhibiting 'excessively intense' ideas in his clinic. Freud's method goes from dynamic repression to the unconscious; the shape of the unconscious is inferred from the effects of repression. His notion of the unconscious is thus 'relative' to the process of repression and the criterion of what must be repressed from consciousness. If Freud can discover what the cause of repression is, then, it follows, he will know the nature of the unconscious.

Bergson, on the other hand, discovers his own theory of the unconscious – based on the notion of the 'pure past' or 'pure memory' – through philosophy. After reconstructing the implications of the preservation of the past in memory, he is then led to deduce from there that the real, yet virtual, 'pure memories' must in turn be 'repressed' in normal psychology; if they are not, then psychopathology must result. Thus Bergson's discovery of the unconscious proceeds in the reverse direction from Freud's. Whereas Freud goes from psychopathology to the postulation of the unconscious, Bergson goes from the philosophical postulate of the unconscious to psychopathology. In *Bergsonism* Deleuze suggests that this procedure allows Bergson to discover a dimension of the unconscious which is occluded from Freud's vision, proceeding as he does from the concept of repression (or defence in his early writings) to that of the unconscious. Bergson ultimately isolates two different conceptions of the unconscious, one of which can claim to be ontological, the other psychological. After stating that in Bergson there is a 'psychological unconscious, distinct from the ontological unconscious' (B 71), Deleuze says that 'there is no contradiction between these two descriptions of two distinct unconsciousnesses' (B 72). Whether Deleuze is saying here that there are two kinds of unconscious which exist separately, or, on the other hand, that there are different 'levels' of the same unconscious, we will have to examine later. In this chapter we will be focusing on the 'ontological unconscious' which Deleuze claims that Bergson uncovers in his theory of memory. This unconscious 'corresponds to a memory that is pure, virtual, impassive, inactive, *in itself* (ibid.). Like Jung's archetypal unconscious, this Bergsonian ontological unconscious has an autonomy of its own, and is not produced through repression.

In *Matter and Memory* (1896) Bergson stated that truth about 'latent' mental states is that they are *virtual, past* states. There are two types of memories: mechanical habit 'memories' and proper memories of individual events.[9] If a mind can retain mental traces of past events, then it remains permanently at the risk of the capricious reproduction of these traces, whenever it encounters something resembling or contiguous with its former perceptions. There is a 'spontaneity' that must be attributed to the memory trace, which 'is as capricious in reproducing as it is faithful in preserving' (Bergson 1896: 88). By threatening, moreover, to mingle past images with present ones, or load the mind with painful images, memory risks unbalancing the mind when all the latter needs to do, practically speaking, is to perform its functions for the purpose of adaptation, and retain 'attention to life' (Bergson 1896: 175). The difference in kind between perception and memory can thus be identified in terms of the presence or absence of 'activity'. 'The *actuality* of our perception lies in its *activity*, in the movements which prolong it, and not in its greater intensity: the past is only idea, the present is ideo-motor . . . The past is essentially *that which acts no longer* . . . By misunderstanding this characteristic of the past, [we] become incapable of making a real distinction between it and the present, i.e., *that which is acting*' (68–9).

In examining this theory, and Deleuze's own use of it, we will be faced with some difficult interpretative choices. The first choice concerns the status of the theory. What kind of theory is it? Deleuze explicitly broaches this question, but it turns out that his suggestions raise more problems than they answer. As we have mentioned already, Deleuze describes pure memory as 'ontological', as opposed to 'psychological'. His main characterization of the difference between ontology and psychology occurs in this passage:

> What Bergson calls 'pure memory' [*souvenir pur*] has no psychological existence. This is why it is called *virtual*, inactive, and unconscious. All these words are dangerous, in particular, the word 'unconscious' which, since Freud, has become inseparable from an especially effective and active

> psychological existence. We will have occasion to compare the Freudian unconscious with the Bergsonian, since Bergson himself made the comparison. We must nevertheless be clear at this point that Bergson does not use the word 'unconscious' to denote a psychological reality outside consciousness, but to denote a non-psychological reality – being as it is in itself. Strictly speaking, the psychological is the present. Only the present is 'psychological'; but the past is pure ontology; pure memory has only ontological significance. (B 56)

The claim to ontological status appears to rest on two attributes of 'pure memories'. First, Bergson is arguing that we must make a distinction between 'pure memories' [*souvenirs purs*], that is, memories as they are in themselves prior to their being brought to consciousness, and memories as they are 'actualized' and brought to consciousness in the process of memory itself; these latter are 'memory-images' [*images-souvenirs*]. Hence pure memories have an *independence*, an 'in-itself' status, unlike 'memory-images', which, as we will see, are *relative* to the context in which they are actualized. But this is not sufficient to make them 'ontological' in any substantial sense of the term.[10] Hence the second attribute of pure memories would seem to be the key one: that, as past, these pure memories have a permanence which is granted to no other phenomena. As Deleuze says, 'the only equivalent thesis is Plato's notion of Reminiscence. Reminiscence also affirms a pure being of the past, a being in itself of the past, an ontological Memory that is capable of serving as the foundation for the unfolding of time. Yet again, a Platonic inspiration makes itself profoundly felt in Bergson' (B 59).

Deleuze's actual explanation of how this 'ontological memory' is possible will appeal to transcendental grounds, rather than ontological claims in the strict sense.[11] By the time of *Difference and Repetition*, Deleuze is explicitly describing Bergson's theory of memory in terms of 'transcendental synthesis': 'What do we mean in speaking of a pure, *a priori* past, the past in general or as such? If *Matter and Memory* is a great book, it is perhaps because Bergson profoundly explored the domain of this transcendental synthesis of a pure past and discovered all its constitutive paradoxes' (DR 81). The danger of taking Deleuze at his word when he describes the past as 'ontological' is that if we take this thought to its conclusion we will end up with a weird spiritualist Platonism, with pure memories as ontologically fundamental entities. But there seems to be something more complicated going on, even in Janet's strange dream of a paleoscope which would allow one to 'travel' into the past.[12]

For Bergson and Janet, the human being is an organism that happens to have become complex enough to open up a 'zone of indetermination' (Bergson 1896: 32) in its brain, which permits the suspension of habitual reaction and the appeal to past experience. This cerebral zone of indetermination becomes the 'gap' or 'interval' through which duration enters, proceeding to take charge of the organism, turning it inside out. Time surges into the brain, changing everything, so that now it is the brain which becomes shaped around an ever-accumulating ontological memory, rather than vice versa. Wherever interiorized duration arises, time pushes through and inverts the fabric of the universe, so that matter must now be taken as the envelope of temporal becoming, rather than time being dependent on matter. In *Difference and Repetition*, Deleuze makes the Kantian point that 'a succession of instants does not constitute time any more than it causes it to disappear; it indicates only its constantly aborted moment of birth. Time is constituted only in the originary synthesis which operates on the repetition of instants' (DR 70). At the moment that the material universe inverts itself and interiorizes itself virtually, it (starting with the brain) becomes shaped around time, rather than vice versa. There is an ascent, through the involution of virtuality, to an entirely new order of validity, beyond the order of actual fact.

The emergence of memory through the zone of indetermination opens up a process of interiorized *differentiation* which proceeds to evolve in tension with the more generalizing tendencies of intelligence. According to Deleuze, the issue here is not ultimately whether memories can or cannot be localized in the brain. Even if they could be localized in neuronal connections, that would still leave aside the fact that with the *interiorization* of difference (the particular memories), a new relationship arises which *must* be articulated in terms of virtuality and actuality. Memories are preserved *in the mind*, and must therefore somehow coexist with the attention to present reality that absorbs my consciousness. *This* relationship requires a different framework for analysis than does the evolutionary process in general.

In the twentieth century, many philosophers in the post-Kantian tradition, Sartre perhaps being the great example, insisted on treating the mind as a 'for itself' because of the *transcendence of consciousness* beyond the realm of the physical. Following Kant, consciousness must be taken as implicitly self-conscious. In *The Phenomenology of Spirit*, Hegel says that consciousness is implicitly self-conscious because acts of conscious cognition implicitly appeal to criteria which allow us to know that we are knowing, think that we are thinking, etc. 'Hence', Hegel says, 'it is something that goes beyond limits, and since these limits are its own, it is something that goes beyond itself' (Hegel 1807: 51). This double transcendence (to objects and to self) means that consciousness must be taken as fundamentally *for-itself*. In effect, Sartre goes on to radicalize Hegel's claim about the relation between consciousness and transcendence. Sartre infers that this means that consciousness *is* only as *negativity*; 'being for-itself' is a pure 'lack of being' [*manque d'être*] (Sartre 1943: 85).[13] On the other side of the subject there is being *in-itself*, the world of non-conscious objects or physical states, in and for which there is no transcendence. In this sense, then, being is pure immanence; it 'is what it is', as opposed to transcendence, which 'is what it is not and is not what it is'. Human beings thus cannot be treated in strictly evolutionary terms because of their capacity for consciousness.

But in *The Evolution of Memory* (published five years before Sartre's *Being and Nothingness*) Janet argues that the explanation for the absence or nothingness that distinguishes human consciousness is to be sought, quite specifically, in memory, not in consciousness in general. 'The goal of memory is to triumph over absence and it is this struggle against absence which characterises memory' (Janet 1928: 221). The appeal to memory at this point is more complex than the appeal to consciousness, as memory itself is a complex function, having *both* conscious *and* unconscious aspects. Bergson, Janet and Deleuze are performing a delicate balancing act here. Like Freud, they think it is wrong to distinguish human beings from animals on the basis of the consciousness of the former. Consciousness itself is not what distinguishes us from animals; the post-Kantian psychological tradition (led by Wundt) had already succeeded in whittling down consciousness to attention. But for Deleuze and his own tradition, Freud in turn is wrong to assume that a theory of mind must therefore commit itself to 'the task of tracing all the *qualities* of our sensations back to *external quantities*' (SE 1: 308–9). Rather, the notion of the unconscious should be explained in another way. 'The idea of an *unconscious representation* is clear, despite current prejudice' (Bergson 1896: 142). What has been missed by both Freud and the post-Kantian tradition is how it is the *relationship between memory and conscious attention* which separates human beings from the rest of the animal world. On the one hand, memories *interiorize* the developments that take place in duration, and become potentially accessible for consciousness. But on the other hand, consciousness – as an adaptive function – now gains a new function, as it must now *actualize or inhibit* these virtually subsistent memories. The consequence of the interiorization of the past is the emergence of a new relationship between actual and virtual. Deleuze articulates this relationship in terms of the concepts of 'difference' and 'repetition'.

From Deleuze's perspective, then, Bergson misinterprets his own results. As we have seen, Deleuze himself sometimes looks ambivalent about the real status of Bergson's theory: he says that his method is at once 'more than a description of experience and less (in appearance) than a transcendental analysis' (DI 36/46). In *Bergsonism* and *Difference and Repetition*, however (more so than the 1956 articles, which are still under the spell of Bergson's theory of organic memory and instinct), Deleuze's effort is to convert Bergsonism into a transcendental philosophy. Thus the issue is not about whether memories can *actually* (or 'ontologically') subsist outside of the brain. Bergson believes that 'contemporary psychology is seeking to get away from . . . anatomical schemes' (Bergson 1908: 116). However, if one adheres to a transcendental reading of Bergson, one can in fact avoid potential conflict with neuroscience. The point becomes not to defend the immateriality of pure memories, but to show how the complex brain becomes organized around a particular 'problem' which can no longer even be reduced to a problem of adaptation. In Bergsonism, the problem of temporal synthesis develops into a more complex problem: how the virtual and actual are to coexist in the same biological entity. His most powerful point is that the relationship of virtuality and actuality must have its own, autonomous form, and cannot be reduced to material causality. In this sense, his theory is compatible with Janet's evolutionary account, and even with tendencies in Nietzsche's work. In a note from 1886–7, Nietzsche makes the remark that memory must be a 'late' phenomenon, 'insofar as here the drive to make equal seems already to have been subdued: differentiation is preserved' (Nietzsche 1967: # 501). The point is the same as Bergson's: the differentiation of memories is necessarily in tension with other fundamental biological tendencies in the human organism. Even if the differentiation of memories can be counted on its own terms as an adaptive function, an equally important question concerns the compensations and adjustments that would arise as a consequence *within* the mind.[14] The Bergsonian–Deleuzian hypothesis is that a new threshold is reached with the interiorization of memory, and that the mind undergoes a change in nature.

Once the evolutionary path towards the preservation of differentiated memories is taken, a new, fundamental self-relationship is permitted to arise within the mind. This self-relationship is not *in principle* one of inhibition or repression (as on the Freudian model), but is primarily one of *actualization*. The need for repression may arise as a *consequence* of the primary turn towards the actualization of the virtual in 'psychic repetition'. It is the 'interiorization' of memory that becomes possible in complex organisms that sets them apart from other animals. 'The more complex a system, the more the *values peculiar to implication* appear within it' (DR 255). Memory, for Deleuze, is an example – perhaps the privileged example – of how the physical and physiological *intensive* constitution of living beings can become radically 'interiorized'. 'Complex systems increasingly tend to interiorise their constitutive differences . . . The more the difference on which the system depends is interiorised in the phenomenon, the more repetition finds itself interior, the less it depends on external conditions which are supposed to ensure the reproduction of the "same" differences' (DR 256). The 'interiorization' involved in memory is the fundamental condition of the development of 'psychic systems', because repetition only becomes truly 'interior' on condition that memory is possible. The difference between 'material' and 'spiritual' repetition depends on the presence of memory: 'Between the two repetitions, the material and the spiritual, there is a vast difference. The former is a repetition of successive independent elements or instants; the latter is a repetition of the Whole on diverse coexisting levels . . . Spiritual repetition unfolds in the being in itself of the past' (DR 84).

Repression does not produce the unconscious, no more than it is the final form of the relationship between actual and virtual. On this point, Deleuze first of all suggests that the process of individuation comprises an 'unconscious apprenticeship' (PS 14) which culminates in a final integration of consciousness and the unconscious. But by virtue of its 'interiorization of difference', the individuation of mind is also understood as the vehicle for the coming to self-consciousness of the whole of life. In a remarkable passage from *Bergsonism* (to which we return in chapter 6), Deleuze describes how

> in man, and only in man, the actual becomes adequate to the virtual. It could be said that man is capable of rediscovering all the levels, all the degrees of expansion [*détente*] and contraction that coexist in the virtual Whole. As if he were capable of all the frenzies and brought about in himself successively everything that, elsewhere, can only be embodied in different species . . . man is capable of scrambling the planes, of going beyond his own plane as his own condition, in order finally to express naturing Nature. (B 106)

It is completely to miss the point to be put off by the word 'man' or 'human' here; none of this is 'anthropomorphic'. 'Humanity' just happens to be the species in our world that has internalized time through the development of memory. Other species could do the same under certain conditions, and probably have done and will do the same, in different regions of the universe. It is futile to think that complex life forms on other worlds will live substantially different (better?) lives than our own. The problems they encounter will be more or less the same, because the synthesis of time is a fundamental, universal invariant, with a finite set of modes. This is not to say that modifications in the theory of temporal synthesis will not always be possible – Deleuze is preoccupied with just such modifications – but what makes Kant's Copernican revolution so monumental is his uncovering of a level of fundamental, transcendental analysis which holds *for any finite being*. Any being which both has senses and thinks will have to organize their data through normative articulations which function *for* that being through the synthesis of time. Wherever there is intelligent life, it will be organized in temporal syntheses.

Perhaps more than any other recent philosopher, Deleuze has insisted on demonstrating the full extent to which the Copernican revolution has turned the universe inside out. It is not just that time becomes grounded in the subject: 'Time is not the interior in us, but just the opposite, the interiority in which we are, in which we move, live and change. Bergson is much closer to Kant than he himself thinks: Kant defined time as the form of interiority, in the sense that we are internal to time' (C2 82). Bergson opens up memory's Pandora's box, the contents flying out to occupy the entire mind, vanishing into depths of mental life which were hitherto unknown. By virtue of opening up the domain of memory so that it now threatens to dwarf the present, Bergson in turn ratchets up the ethico-temporal problem, making Kierkegaard's and Nietzsche's problems all the more uncircumventable. How can *all that* be re-willed?

It has already been noted that the idea that the past is preserved in its entirety had become something of an occult obsession in *fin-de-siècle* Europe. The fact that the same idea appears in Nietzsche, Freud and Bergson at more or less the same time suggests that an unconscious, collective current was at work during this period, being picked up on by thinkers from many intellectual traditions. It is not immediately clear what historical or sociological methodology would be adequate for articulating this unconscious current. Moreover, a theoretical overdetermination necessarily results from these multiple receptions of the same idea. Freud began by making the distinction between memory and perception in purely neurological terms, only going on to remove this material basis after *The Interpretation of Dreams*. For Nietzsche the thought of the preservation of the past was both a mystical and an ethical thought. The thought of the eternal return first appeared as a mystical intuition of the preservation and return of the past an infinite number of times, but Nietzsche immediately extracted the ethical significance of this thought: the thought that the past is preserved and will return becomes 'the greatest weight', which demands that we reassess our capacities for *willing*. Can the past be re-willed? Deleuze suggests that the synthesis of time internally points towards the problem that he calls 'repetition', which he represents as a kind of ordeal, an experience of terror and freedom (DR 19). Deleuze copes with the charges made against Bergson's theories of time by the existentialists by contending that if Bergson's theory of time does not have a completely theorized account of the role of death, then it nevertheless provides an important new basis for a re-thinking of human finitude. The finitude implied in human temporality remains obscure without a full account of how human memory preserves the past, and Deleuze shows that Bergson's theory of memory might even provide the clearest basis to understand the full stakes implied in the existentialist theme of repetition. For Kierkegaard and Heidegger, repetition is the act that allows a human being to embrace the fact that his actions are not determined, whether by an essential nature or by the past. We finally confront the emptiness of the future and our responsibility for our actions only by affirming our past as radically contingent. Whatever happened to me in the past, I accept it as my responsibility. I can do otherwise now, and therefore I could have done otherwise then. I now sanctify the realization of the contingency of my past by an affirmation of its contingency. In Nietzsche's terms, repetition is a 'willing backwards' (Nietzsche 1884, 'Of Redemption'), that finally frees one to will forwards.

If Deleuze is right, then as the process of interiorization continues in the evolution of culture, the pressure of time might well intensify correspondingly. It is no wonder, then, that many today want to abandon ship, to affirm crude forms of materialism or Darwinism, and simply turn their backs on the demands of temporality. But as the parable says, what if, some day or night, a demon were to steal after them into their loneliest loneliness and say to them: 'This life as you now live it and have lived it, you will have to live once more and innumerable times more . . .' (Nietzsche 1882: # 341). So there is no real alternative: we must construct the paleoscope.

The Actual and the Virtual

In Deleuze, the distinction between the actual and the virtual tends to take over from the distinction between consciousness and the unconscious. This distinction goes back to Leibniz's *New Essays on the Human Understanding*, his critique of Lockean empiricism. Its first target is Locke's idea that the mind is born as a *tabula rasa*. Leibniz attempts to defend the doctrine of innate ideas by appealing to a different image: the mind is like a veined block of marble. Veins and shapes are present on the surface, as well as within the depths of the marble, but these can only be discovered by being chiselled at and exposed to the light. Depending on where one begins chiselling and how one proceeds, different veins will come to the surface, while others may remain entirely latent. Thus the shape of Hercules can only be said to be innate in a block of marble on condition that there are *virtual* veins which outline his shape; but even if his shape is virtually present, that does not mean that it is like a *potentiality* in the Aristotelian sense, which rather *drives* the process of actualization (the seed being the example here). It is innate, but it has no power over whether it gets actualized or not. Thus Leibniz says: 'This is how ideas and truths are innate in us – as inclinations, dispositions, habitudes or natural virtualities [*virtualités*], and not as actions, although these virtualities are always accompanied by certain actualities, often insensible ones, which correspond to them' (Leibniz 1765: 52, trans. modified). There is a clear analogy between Bergsonian pure memories and Leibnizian marble veins, in that neither can properly be described as 'potentialities'. Another term, virtuality, must be used of both. We will return to Leibniz at the end of the chapter, as for the moment our goal is to establish the virtuality of memories, rather than 'innate ideas'.

In themselves, pure recollections are sterile, useless, inactive. The time may come when they are recalled *for* a particular purpose, but in the meantime, they have an opposite status to the present objects of the living being. All memory is a withdrawal to some extent: 'to call up the past in the form of an image, we must be able to withdraw ourselves from the action of the moment, we must have the power to value the useless, we must have the will to dream' (Bergson 1896: 82–3). In fact, memory and dreaming are not so far from each other: dream is the pole of memory which is most opposed to the impersonal, adaptive demands of the present. We should not regard less complete memories as ones that are less complex, but as 'a recollection less *dreamed*, more impersonal, nearer to action, and therefore, more capable of molding itself – like a ready-made garment – upon the new character of the present situation' (241). If a memory is particularly intense, this does not mean that it has been more indelibly imprinted in the brain, but that one is able to detach oneself sufficiently from the demands of the present to be able to effectively revive the memory in a cognitive state that approaches a dream. We become absent from the present, 'absent-minded'. An intense memory is often described as a reverie; it is like a dream, but more fragile. Bergson remarks that 'the extraordinary development of spontaneous memory in most children is due to the fact that they have not yet persuaded their memory to remain bound up with their conduct . . . The apparent diminution of memory, as intellect develops, is then due to the growing organisation of recollections with acts' (153–4). When a child remembers, it is not so far from an adult dreaming; they are completely absorbed in the memory of the specific event, and can remember details which adults cannot. Their exemption from the primary tasks of adaptation no doubt accounts for the human child's ability to get lost in daydream and memory.

The dreamlike character of memory, which is most marked in children, leads Bergson to conceive of memory in terms of *repetition* (162, 241). If recollections subsist in the mind unconsciously, then due to their virtuality we are forced to think of them as awaiting the chance to be revived, or reincarnated in the present. Each present situation is like a shaft of light which breaks through the ceiling of the underworld of memory, illuminating one or two of its denizens. 'Spontaneous' memories are continually evoked by resemblances and contiguities with present perceptions, and which memories are stirred in this way depends on the degree to which the recollector is active or dreaming. The more 'relaxed' (*détendu*) the consciousness is, the deeper and more individual the memories which rise to the surface. The past emerges 'with the assistance' of the present, just as Homer's ghosts sought out new living blood for their reincarnation.

> The sensori-motor apparatus furnishes to ineffective, that is unconscious, memories, the means of taking on a body, of materialising themselves, in short of becoming present. For, that a recollection should appear in consciousness, it is necessary that it should descend from the heights of pure memory down to the precise point where *action* is taking place. In other words, it is from the present that the appeal to which memory responds comes, and it is from the sensori-motor elements of present action that a memory borrows the warmth which gives it life. (153)

Memory, as underworld, is thus home to thousands of bloodless, inactive spirits, which look up whenever a ray of light pierces through a crack in the present. Hence consciousness must set aside all those past images which cannot be coordinated with the present perception and are unable to form with it a *useful* combination. 'Almost the whole of our past is hidden from us because it is inhibited by the necessities of present action' (154). If the 'psychological tension' involved in keeping one's attention focused on the present is left to slacken, then the remembered past could end up crowding out the present.[15] There is thus a primary *inhibition*, or as Deleuze calls it, a repression [*refoulement*] (B 72), which ensures that only what can throw light on the present situation is accepted from the preserved past. There is a 'veil' over the past: 'Fortunate are we to have this obstacle, infinitely precious to us is the veil! The brain is what secures to us this advantage. It keeps our attention fixed on life; and life looks forward; it looks back only in the degree to which the past can aid it to illumine and prepare the future' (Bergson 1912: 57). These virtualities are real – in some ways even more real than the passing present – but are impassive, inactive, they no longer act. 'The cerebral mechanism is arranged just so as to drive back into the unconscious almost the whole of this past, and to admit beyond the threshold only that which can cast light on the present situation or further the action now being prepared – in short, only that which can give *useful* work' (Bergson 1907: 5).

Paramnesia and the Transcendental Synthesis of Memory

But Deleuze's reconstruction of a Bergsonian theory of mind is more complex, and it does not rest ultimately on the foregoing account of the psychic inhibition of the past. Deleuze attempts to bring Bergsonian theory into closer contact with the Kantian and post-Kantian transcendental conception of mind, which foregrounds an epistemic approach to the fundamental *syntheses* of the mind.

> A succession of instants does not constitute time any more than it causes it to disappear; it indicates only its constantly aborted moment of birth. Time is constituted only in the originary synthesis which operates on the repetition of instants . . . The rule of discontinuity or instantaneity in repetition tells us that one instance does not appear unless the other has disappeared – hence the status of *mens momentanea.* (DR 70)[16]

Without the ability to *reproduce* a previous moment that has passed(Kant 1782/87: A99f.) the passing of time could not be registered; it would, as Deleuze says, be 'constantly aborted'. Kant makes the first explicit attempt to derive the structure of the mind from the act of temporal synthesis, in the *Critique of Pure Reason.* . Kant argues that both a 'synthesis of apprehension' and a 'synthesis of reproduction' are necessary in order to be able to 'recognize' something in the present. For in order to be reproduced *as* absent, the content of the previous moment requires a synthesis by a mind able to hold the past and present in a unity, and to be able to class the contents of the two moments under the same concept (no matter how general). In *Difference and Repetition,* Deleuze begins from this premise, but immediately draws our attention to a paradox in the very notion of an ideal reproduction or repetition. On the one hand, if an event is repeated in the mind, then it should reappear as self-identical. But on the other hand, repetition 'does change something in the mind which contemplates it' (DR 70), as a *synthesis* is now present in the mind. 'Does not the paradox of repetition lie in the fact that one can speak of repetition only by virtue of the change or difference that it introduces into the mind which contemplates it? By virtue of a difference that the mind *draws from* repetition' (DR 70). Deleuze roots his discussion here in an analysis of Hume, but Kierkegaard is the first to explicitly deal with the notion of repetition as an intrinsically contradictory notion. Kierkegaard was first to articulate the basic form of temporal synthesis as *repetition,* and Deleuze takes up and vastly elaborates upon Kierkegaard's suggestion. Oddly, Deleuze never explicitly refers to the key text, from Kierkegaard's *Johannes Climacus.* This text presents the most directly 'epistemological' of the interpretations Kierkegaard gives to the notion of repetition, as usually he takes repetition to be an aesthetic concept (in the book *Repetition* itself) or religious concept (e.g. in *Fear and Trembling,* where Abraham acts in order to 'get back' Isaac). There is some evidence to suggest that *Johannes*

Climacus was the first of Kierkegaard's great flow of texts in 1843 (Kierkegaard 1843a: x). In the text, Kierkegaard attempts to identify 'repetition' as the basic category for dealing with the relation between ideality and reality:

> In reality as such, there is no repetition. This is not because everything is different, not at all. If everything in the world were completely identical, in reality there would be no repetition, because reality is only in the moment. If the world, instead of being beauty, were nothing but equally large unvariegated boulders, there would still be no repetition. Throughout eternity, in every moment, I would see a boulder, but there would be no question as to whether it was the same one I had seen before. (Kierkegaard 1843a: 171)

Repetition occurs neither in reality nor ideality, taken in themselves. There is no repetition in reality not because reality is already differentiated (according to the principle of sufficient reason), but because a synthesizer is needed for repetition to take place. However, on the other hand, 'in ideality alone there is no repetition, for the idea is and remains the same, and as such it cannot be repeated' (universals have their own validity, regardless of their instantiation). In neither reality nor ideality by themselves does anything like a repetition exist; but when the two come together, a repetition is possible.

> When ideality and reality touch each other, then repetition occurs. When, for example, I see something in the moment, ideality enters in and will explain that it is a repetition. Here is the contradiction, for that which is, is also in another mode. That the external is, that I see, but in the same instant I bring it into relation with something that also is, something that is the same and that also will explain that the other is the same. Here is a redoubling; here it is a matter of repetition. Ideality and reality therefore collide – in what medium? In time? That is indeed an impossibility. In eternity? That is indeed an impossibility. In what then? In consciousness – there is the contradiction. (ibid.)

Where can this 'collision' take place? It cannot take place in time, because the repetition is the very condition of possibility of apprehending time. But it cannot also take place in eternity, as there would be no *repetition* in eternity; in effect, we would be back with the boulders floating in space, except the boulders would now exist as monads in an eternal order. The concept of 'repetition' thus denotes a paradoxical time-effect, an ontological kink or fold, invaginated (as we saw earlier) in the human brain.

But if the concept of *repetition* is going to be the fundamental synthesis of time, then there seems to be a problem, as the presence of a repetition implies that an original moment is being repeated. But if repetition is supposed to be the basic synthesis of time, then it is contradictory to posit a first moment 'in time' before the synthesis itself. We seem to be back with the problem implicit in Kant's 'synthesis of apprehension': it is both necessary and impossible to conceive of a first manifold or multiplicity 'in itself'. This problem can be solved if we posit that the first moment is *already a repetition.* The notion of repetition would only become consistent if the second moment could be a repetition of the first, while simultaneously the first moment itself would be conceived as a future repetition, due to its preservation. There must be a first moment, a synthesis of preservation, where events are preserved independently of their immediate reproduction. By giving priority to the notion of repetition, it is as if Deleuze is charging Kant with having omitted a more originary moment from this account of the synthesis of 'reproduction'. For if a reproduction is to be possible, then that requires that the first moment must have been *preserved.* Before the synthesis of reproduction, there must be a synthesis of preservation. How can a reproduction recall *that* vanished past moment unless the moment was already prepared for preservation at the point of its vanishing?

In order for a past moment to be reproduced, it must have been recorded *for* reproduction at the moment of its passing. For Deleuze, Bergson is the one contemporary thinker who has taken up this thought, and submitted to its consequences: that 'all consciousness, then, is memory – conservation and accumulation of the past in the present' (Bergson 1919: 5). In many of his early works (and beyond), Deleuze is to be found wrestling with a very deep problem, a properly philosophical problem: how does the present pass into the past? How is the past constituted *as* past? Deleuze proceeds to find this problem in Nietzsche, Proust and Freud, among others. But as we have seen, Bergson is the philosopher who goes into the question of the relation of the past and present in most detail.

It is not enough, he charges, to say that the past is constituted as such *after* a new present has taken its place, as then the scope of that past would be restricted to what it signified for the following present:

> According to the point of view in which I am placed, or the centre of interest which I choose, I divide yesterday differently, discovering several very different series of situations or states in it. . . . Scores of systems of carving are possible, no system corresponds with joints of reality. What right have we, then, to suppose that memory chooses one particular system, or that it divides psychical life into definite periods and awaits the end of each period in order to rule up its accounts with perception? (Bergson 1908: 129)

Now, because the content of each present cannot simply be delimited as soon as the moment has passed, and because it must remain open for future reinterpretation while not ceasing to be identified as *that* past, we are forced to assume that the past is somehow formed 'alongside' the present. Bergson's paradoxical resolution, according to Deleuze, is that 'no present would ever pass were it not past "at the same time" as it is present . . . The past is contemporaneous with the present that it *was*' (DR 81). Or as Bergson himself puts it:

> I hold that the *formation of recollection is never posterior to the formation of perception; it is contemporaneous with it.* For suppose recollection is not created at the same moment as perception: At what moment will it begin to exist? . . . The more we reflect, the more impossible it is to imagine any way in which the recollection can arise if it is not created step by step with the perception itself. (Bergson 1908: 128; cited in B 125)

In other words, each actual present is somehow doubled by a virtual 'shadow' of itself, which enables it to be re-actualized as the past it will have been. Each actual image, he says, must be taken to have *its own* virtual afterimage, which enables it to be re-actualized as the past of that actual moment.

> If we take this direction to its limit, we can say that the actual image itself has a virtual image which corresponds to it like a double or a reflection. In Bergsonian terms, the real object is reflected in a mirror-image as in the virtual object which, from its side and simultaneously, envelops or reflects the real: there is a 'coalescence' between the two. There is a formation of an image with two sides, actual *and* virtual. It is as if an image in a mirror, a photo or a postcard came to life, assumed independence and passed into the actual, even if this meant that the actual image returned into the mirror and resumed its place in the postcard or the photo, following a double movement of liberation and capture. (C2 68)

Deleuze presents this argument a number of times, and a detailed analysis of his various presenatations would be desirable, but cannot be made here.[17] The metaphor of the photograph is helpful, though. It is as if a photograph is taken by memory, a luminous imprint of reality, whose content can only be analysed and interpreted later. Events can happen which will have significance for us at some point in the future, but we are *unconscious* of this significance in and directly after the present. Nevertheless, the event has happened, and that *it happened* will haunt us when we realize later what it meant. Sometimes a magnifying glass will be necessary in order to discern the signs of future fate in the photograph. But, after the event, we are condemned to analyse these photographs for traces of an unconscious line of fate, which has only become conscious later, when it is too late. In his first article on Bergson, Deleuze makes explicit the role of the *unconscious* in the constitution of the past: 'If the past had to wait to be no more, if it were not immediately and henceforth past, "*past* in general", it would never be able to become what it is, it would never be *this* past. The past is therefore the in-itself, the unconscious, or more precisely, as Bergson says, the *virtual*' (DI 29).

Bergson's model seems to be a kind of generalized model of *Nachträglichkeit* or 'deferred action', rooted in the constitution of time itself. Freud turned to the model of trauma in order to understand why it was sexual representations in particular which were repressed into the unconscious. 'If [a] sexual experience occurs during the period of sexual immaturity and the memory of it is aroused during or after maturity, then the memory will have a far stronger excitatory effect than the experience did at the time it happened; and this is because in the meantime puberty has immensely increased the capacity of the sexual apparatus for reaction' (SE 3: 167). Thus infantile sexual trauma had a 'deferred effect', because at the time of the trauma, sexuality was in an undeveloped form, so the sexual significance of the event was not understood; but once puberty had been passed, the subject belatedly realizes the significance of the memory, and now becomes besieged by a memory it is powerless to abreact. Freud was forced to abandon this model for a while once he had begun to affirm the existence of infantile sexuality, which undermined it; nevertheless it returns in the case of the *Wolf Man*, with the Oedipus complex as the mediating conductor that allows the deferred event to assume a more powerful affect. What is striking about Bergson's generalized model of deferred action is that the requirement for a specific mediating conductor appears to vanish. Because Bergson has no axe to grind for any specific aetiological agent in psychopathology (such as sexuality in Freud), in effect he does not need an account of how specific events assume a belated toxicity. The comparison with *Nachträglichkeit* is thus ultimately misleading. For Bergson, psychopathology cannot be explained on the basis of the deferred action of particular early events. Although his colleague Janet will stress the role of actual traumatic events, (in line with the early Freud of the 'seduction theory', but without his restriction to sexual trauma), the *pathology* of trauma is rooted in the ensuing dislocation in the temporal structure of the mind. Indeed, even if there is no actual trauma, there is a pathological orientation built into the structure of temporality. Bergson introduces a theory of *paramnesia* which Deleuze takes up as the foundation for a theory of the autonomous *pathos* of the mind: 'a pathology of repetition' (DR 290).

The pure layer of the past must itself be immediately 'forgotten', as the needs of the present are entirely pragmatic. In the short term, we only need to remember what is of immediate use in the subsequent moments. Under normal circumstances, therefore, this 'double inscription' of past and present is not experienced as such, because our attention is directed towards the future. But if this latter condition is suspended (due to failures in attending to the present), then a certain, paradoxical 'memory of the present' takes place: déjà vu. We experience this present as already *past* (Bergson 1908). Déjà vu, Bergson suggests, only makes sense if we assume that the past is constituted as past at the same time as the present. The Bergsonian notion of déjà vu provides Deleuze with a paradigmatic example of 'transcendental empiricism'. Transcendentally speaking, 'our actual existence . . . whilst it is unrolled in time, duplicates itself all along with a virtual existence, a mirror-image. Every moment of our life presents two aspects, it is actual and virtual, perception on the one side and memory on the other. Each moment of life is split up as and when it is posited. Or rather, it consists in this very splitting' (Bergson 1908: 135). But if the future-oriented direction of cognition is suspended, 'we can become conscious of this duplicating', and experience what Deleuze calls a 'direct or transcendental presentation of time'. Déjà vu thus testifies to a truth at the transcendental level: that 'each present goes back to itself [or returns to itself] as past' (B 59).

Deleuze goes on to suggest that the experience of déjà vu is in fact one of the conditions for the emergence of autonomous thought. Like Hegel, Deleuze does not believe that thought is something natural or proper to human beings; rather something must first force us to think. First an intensive difference is sensed which 'moves the soul, "perplexes" it – in other words, forces it to pose a problem' (DR 140). An intensive threshold is reached and we cannot appeal to previous experience to help decipher it, because crossing the threshold takes us beyond habitual patterns of sensation. But because there are no empirical memories or concepts to help us, Deleuze suggests that what happens first is that we are thrown back on the very ground of our ability to synthesize experience: the pure past. The pure past presses in on our state of cognitive indeterminacy. There is thus an immediate tendency to identify problems or questions 'with singular objects of a transcendental Memory' (DR 140).

Deleuze suggests that Platonic anamnesis or recollection might have its transcendental ground here. In the *Meno*, Plato suggests that what is described as 'learning' is really the recollection of truths that have been forgotten, because one can neither learn what one already knows, nor learn what one does not already know (for how could one recognize its validity, or even know what to look for?). Knowing is therefore recollection. Insofar as the eternal Ideas are only partially figured in any empirical object we encounter, the Platonic experience of knowing must be somewhat akin to an experience of déjà vu. The Platonist will experience their own cognitive activity as a recollection of a previous contemplation of an eternal Idea. Deleuze is suggesting that this Platonizing moment is in fact a necessary detour in the movement that goes from intensity to thought. We think: *I have been here before*, but I can't remember when, it's out of reach . . . What Deleuze calls a 'transcendental memory' now emerges, precisely because of the structure of the preservation of the past just outlined:

> Transcendental memory . . . grasps that which from the outset can only be recalled, even the first time: not a contingent past, but the being of the past as such and the past of every time. In this manner, the forgotten thing appears in person to the memory which essentially apprehends it. It does not address memory without addressing the forgetting within memory. The memorandum here is both unrememberable and immemorial. Forgetting is no longer a contingent incapacity separating us from a memory which is itself contingent: it exists within essential memory as though it were the 'nth' power of memory with regard to its own limit or to that which can only be recalled. (DR 140)

This recollective moment in the passage from intensity to thought retains a strong power over the subject of the transcendental experience. It is always possible that one can get stuck at the stage of recollection, and not make the move to thought. Kierkegaard's entire contribution to the theory of repetition arises from the diagnosis of problems internal to a life of memory or *reminiscence.*

> Say what you will, this question will play a very important role in modern philosophy, for *repetition* is a crucial expression for what 'recollection' was to the Greeks. Just as they taught that all life is a recollecting, modern philosophy will teach that all life is a repetition. (Kierkegaard 1983: 131)

For Kierkegaard, to take one's experience 'recollectively' is to rob oneself of agency or of the thought that whether and how one acts in the present moment matters. Recollection is pathos, and the only action that can overcome the pathology of time is repetition. The effect of overwhelming action with pathos is produced by theories of determinism and reminiscence alike. Recollection, in the modern epoch, must ultimately be understood as an act of defection from the higher task of repetition. If there is a *destination* of active repetition, then failures to meet that destination can retrospectively be interpreted in the light of that destination. Recollection becomes a *mode* of inhabiting the fundamentally repetitive nature of time. When I take a 'recollective' attitude to my actions, I take them as subject to a *fate* over which I have no control. I have been here before, everything has already been decided, it was meant to be. Kierkegaard says enigmatically that recollection must be taken as an *inverted repetition*: 'Repetition and recollection are the same movement, except in opposite directions, for what is recollected has been, is repeated backward, whereas genuine repetition is recollection forward' (Kierkegaard 1843: 131).

Neurosis and the Unconscious

In *Nietzsche and Philosophy* (1962), Deleuze suggests it is not repressed sexuality, but memory itself which provides the basis for neurosis. He combines Nietzsche's account of *ressentiment* with Freud's model of memory as detailed in *Beyond the Pleasure Principle.* Freud was right to insist that memory is a separate system to perception; Bergson had also done this in *Matter and Memory.*[18] But for Freud, more importantly memory expresses 'the pure passive impossibility of escaping from the impression once it is received' (NP 112; cf. SE 18: 25). In other words, Freud is onto something here only because he has touched on the 'vital' problem, diagnosed by Bergson and Janet, that attends the retention of the past.

Memory and repetition are the sickness of humanity, according to Nietzsche. Given memory, it is surprising that anything gets done at all. Nietzsche is much more sensitive to the ethical implications of the preservation of the past. However, he also identifies another memory which is

> no longer a function of the past, but a function of the future. It is not the memory of sensibility, but of the will. It is not the memory of traces but of words. It is the faculty of promising, commitment to the future, memory of the future itself. Remember the promise that has been made is not recalling that it was made at a particular past moment, but that one must hold to it at a future moment. This is precisely the selective object of culture: forming a man capable of promising and thus of making use of the future, a free and powerful man. (NP 134)

The neurotic, it would seem, is the one who remains unable to turn the passive memory into an 'active' memory. Deleuze makes it clear that he does not believe that this symptom of *ressentiment* emerges as the necessary result of an external trauma. 'There is no need for him to have experienced an excessive excitation. This may happen, but it is not necessary' (NP 115). This appears to make the distinction between the man of *ressentiment* and the sovereign individual a matter of constitution. One either 'suffers from reminiscences' or one can 'actively forget'.

> The man of *ressentiment* in himself is a being full of pain: the sclerosis or hardening of his consciousness, the rapidity with which every excitation sets and freezes within him, the weight of the traces that invade him are so many cruel sufferings. And more deeply, *the memory of traces is full of hatred in itself and by itself.* It is venomous and depreciative because it blames the object in order to compensate for its own inability to escape from the traces of the corresponding excitation. (NP 116)

In *Nietzsche and Philosophy,* Deleuze's account of psychological pain comes to rest on the assumption of a disposition to weakness in the cognitive faculty of memory. In a significant reference to Jung, Deleuze suggests that his 'typological' approach to *ressentiment,* guilt and psychopathology is modelled on Jung's typological approach (NP 212). The psychopathology in *Nietzsche and Philosophy* could be described as a vitalized, Nietzscheanized version of Jung's distinction between introversion and extroversion.

From the beginning Jung had more in common with Bergson and Janet than with Freud. But if Jung does indeed side with Janet in giving explanatory primacy to dissocation rather than repression, then we also should not overlook the Bergsonian aspects in Janet's position that might have filtered through to Jung. The most important for us is Janet's Bergsonian conception of the *temporal* structure of dissociation. For Bergson, Janet and Deleuze, the foundation for pathology is latent in the very temporal conditions of experience. If there is a 'split', a *Spaltung* in the subject, as Lacanians claim, then for Bergsonism, the faultline is inherent to the constitution of time itself:

> Our actual existence . . . whilst it is unrolled in time, duplicates itself all along with a virtual existence, a mirror-image. Every moment of our life presents two aspects, it is actual and virtual, perception on the one side and memory on the other. Each moment of life is split up as and when it is posited. Or rather, it consists in this very splitting. (Bergson 1908: 135)

The past and present are contemporaneous, although they absolutely retain their difference in nature; one is virtual and the other is actual. 'Time has to split at the same time as it . . . unfolds itself: it splits into two dissymmetrical jets, one of which makes all the present pass on, while the other preserves all the past' (C2 81). For the Frenchmen, it is as if the subject is first of all split down a line that is intrinsically temporal: the past and the future-oriented present, Deleuze's two 'jets' of time. At the extreme poles of each direction of time lie action and dream. Jung can be read as renaming these two poles as *extraversion* and *introversion*. 'The only difference' between those who tend towards these poles, he says in 'The Stages of Life', 'is that the one has estranged himself from the past and the other from the future' (CW 8: 392).[19]

Repetition and Eternal Return

There are two ethical forms of repetition. Repetition is first a liberation from recollection by the ascription of contingency to the past. It is only once one has come to terms with the past and is given freedom in relation to it (by witnessing its contingency), that one is free to act now. Thus repetition must first involve the ability to re-will my past actions. The imperative asks: 'Can you scan over all your past and will it again?' Only once this re-willing is done can another sort of re-willing come into being, in which I ask myself whether I can will the present actions I am about decide again in the future. This is the second form. 'Can you will this action that you are about to do again'? Thus in Kierkegaard as well as Nietzsche, the gateway called 'repetition' thus leads in two directions: backwards and forwards. You must be able to re-will past events, or will backwards. But you must also be able to 're-will' forwards. The problem is that both of these forms of re-willing give rise to interconnected paradoxes.

With regard to the first form, the way to free oneself from a recollective view of the past is to say 'I willed it thus'. But, the 'I' who wills the past must be different from the 'I' who took themselves to be determined by the past. By rediscovering agency in previous acts where one believed there was none, the re-willing subject undergoes a *transformation* in one's relation to the past. The psychoanalytic treatment provides the best example of this process. But this transformation in the willing agent obviously precludes the presence of a 'self-identical' autonomy (in which the autonomous self-binding underwrites continuity of past, present and future): with the notion of repetition we seem to move *beyond* autonomy (i.e. not backwards to 'before' autonomy).[20]

With regard to the second form, however, the idea that I can commit myself to re-will my present actions seems to depend on the projection of an identical self into the future. But matters are not so simple. Although in his 1962 interpretation of Nietzsche, Deleuze affirms a Kantian, ethical notion of eternal return, Deleuze has to wait for Klossowski to point out that the eternal return implies the dissolution of the identical subject in the future as well.[21] Eternal return implies that if I am going to re-will a previous action, I will only be able to do so by taking it as the act of another, someone with whom I can no longer identify myself. Klossowski reminds us that Nietzsche's first encounter with the thought of the eternal return involves a kind of anamnesis (Klossowski 1969: 57). Nietzsche experiences an uncanny *Stimmung* in which he feels as if he has been here before. However, Nietzsche's experience of the thought of eternal return goes beyond déjà vu. The demon that alights on Nietzsche's shoulder that day on the mountain in 1882 says to him: what if you have not only been here before, but been here before infinite times? For Klossowski, the really insidious thought about the eternal return is not that one's experience of déjà vu might be only the latest in an infinite line, but rather an implication of that hypothesis. For if you have been returning to this spot infinite times, then that means you have in the meantime *forgotten* your presence here. And the logic dictates that you will forget it again.

But then once this necessary presence of forgetting is introduced, the thought of eternal return begins to exert more power. The implication now strengthens the premise. For forgetting is something that is out of my conscious control. Anamnesis or recollection already involves forgetting: when I know something on the model of recollection, I remember something that I have forgotten. But if I have forgotten it once, then I might have forgotten it a number of times. My ego seems to have absolutely no power over forgetting. But if a *series* of rememberings and forgettings is possible, then the anamnesiac's problem changes: the problem of isolating some privileged, originary moment when the truth was given (an original reception of the Ideas, another world beyond the river of Lethe) disappears. The anamnesiac loses their transcendence. Deleuze stresses that 'if there is, in Greece or elsewhere, a genuine knowledge of eternal return, it is a cruel and esoteric knowledge which must be sought in another dimension, more mysterious and more uncommon than that of astronomical or qualitative cycles and their generalities' (DR 242). Towards the end of the book we will see how important 'esoteric' conceptions of the human mind were to Deleuze. In the Hermetic writings of third-century Alexandria, the birthplace of Neoplatonism and the Cabbala, one finds the idea that the human being's true 'identity' is discovered when it sees itself as a 'microcosm'. In Deleuze's esoteric rendering of the eternal return, the anamnesiac loses their connection to an actual transcendence, instead, in the words of the first document in the *Corpus Hermeticum*, 'being made god' (Copenhaver 1992: 6). This *immanence* can only be realized through the encounter with a higher, interior Other, the unconscious.

Leibniz, Locke and the Theatre of the Unconscious

In his 1980 lectures on Leibniz, Deleuze says that 'it is Leibniz who first proposed this great idea, this first great theory of this differential unconscious, and it has never gone away since. There is a very long tradition of this differential conception of the unconscious based on minute perceptions and minute appetitions' (Third Leibniz lecture, 12). We will hear more about this curious tradition (which perhaps only exists in Deleuze's mind) in chapter 5, but this opening chapter will conclude with a brief introduction to Leibniz's philosophy of the unconscious, in which the Hermetic tradition meets with modern philosophy.[22]

Leibniz expounds his notion of unconscious perceptions in most detail in the *New Essays on Human Understanding*, his critique of Lockean empiricism, written in the form of a dialogue between 'Philatheles' and 'Theophilus', who represent Locke and Leibniz respectively.[23] Locke claims that we are tabula rasa or blank surface at the moment of birth, but as the child begins to accommodate itself to its surroundings, it realizes it is in fact in a camera obscura: 'External and internal sensation are the only passages that I can find, of knowledge, to the understanding. These alone, as far as I can discover, are the windows by which light is let into this *dark room*. For, methinks, the understanding is not much unlike a closet wholly shut from light, with only some little openings left, to let in external visible resemblances, or ideas of things without' (Locke 1690: II, 11.17). Theophilus, Leibniz's spokesman in the *New Essays*, replies that the understanding is indeed rather like a dark room, but if Philatheles examined it a little more closely, he would see that the contours of this room reveal it to be something different again from a camera obscura. First, 'we should have to postulate that there is a screen in this dark room' (Leibniz 1765: 144). The camera obscura is fitted with a small candle that sheds a small amount of light (Locke 1690: I, 1.5), so we can imagine Philatheles wandering about with this candle, and then accepting that one of the walls might well serve as a screen, but only for the projection of shadows. The thing is, this screen, Theophilus then continues, 'is not uniform'. No, this screen is 'diversified by folds representing items of innate knowledge; and, what is more, this screen or membrane, being under tension, has a kind of elasticity or active force, and indeed it acts (or reacts) in ways which are adapted both to past folds and to new ones coming from the impressions'. The reaction of Philatheles, Locke's spokesman in the *New Essays*, to this hallucinatory reverie is not presented, but one can imagine him saying (with a Lockean *unease*), 'so, it's a screen for images, but also a sort of pullulating *membrane*, and it has folds, more like a theatre curtain than a screen, in fact . . .' Yes, Theophilus continues, and 'this action would consist in certain vibrations or oscillations, like those we see when a cord under tension is plucked and gives off something of a musical sound. For not only do we receive images and traces in the brain, but we form new ones from them when we bring "complex ideas" to mind; and so the screen which represents our brain must be active and plastic. This analogy would explain reasonably well what goes on in the brain' (ibid.).

It is easy to see why Deleuze begins his late book on Leibniz, *The Fold*, with a description of Leibniz's baroque makeover of Locke's camera obscura. Everything about this scene in the *New Essays* brings to mind that peculiar affect which seems to reside at the core of Deleuze's work, and is manifest most clearly in *Difference and Repetition*: the sense of existence as a theatre where the dream-like spectacle that unfolds before one is always threatening to turn into a corporeal, directly felt nightmare, where the red curtains that part before the stage are revealed, on closer inspection, to be made from living flesh, where hallucinatory dread is continually blending with a mysterious elation. Somehow, we are back in 'the theatre of repetition', where 'we experience pure forces, dynamic lines in space which act without intermediary upon the spirit, and link it directly with nature and history . . . with gestures which develop before organised bodies . . . with spectres and phantoms before characters – the whole apparatus of repetition as a "terrible power"' (DR 10). This passage on the theatre of repetition in *Difference and Repetition* is reminiscent of Hegel's famous 'Man, that Night' fragment (Hegel 1805–6: 87); both are shot through with the same conceptual obscurity and yet bloodshot emotional clarity. One senses that for Deleuze, Leibniz is the philosopher who is closest to this atmosphere. In his hallucinatory transformation of the camera obscura, it is impossible not to recall descriptions of the weird dread that attends an impending psychotic break. A dark room unaccountably begins to pulsate with an impersonal, inhuman life. Leibniz is the discoverer of the unconscious, but the undecidable oscillation of reason and madness with which he approaches it is closer to that of the psychotic rather than the neurotic. If there is one thing common to the great modern speculative philosophers, Leibniz, Hegel and Deleuze, it is the risk that re-animating the universe with a non-organic life might make it altogether uninhabitable for sane human beings. Leibniz's hallucinatory, metamorphic theatres, Hegel's Night and Deleuze's theatre of terror each seem to signal a moment full of dread before the attainment of absolute self-differentiation: the moment of fear that the absolute Subject capable of incarnating or 'bearing' absolute difference might be, in fact, completely insane. In Deleuze's work, most powerfully in *Difference and Repetition*, this fear is never far from the surface, and in a sense one could say that, after Leibniz and Hegel, it has *become conscious* in Deleuze. His ultimate problem, perhaps, is how to cope with the possibility that the absolute subject, in and for itself, is mad, a permanently fractured 'I'.

In the *New Essays* the notion of the unconscious is introduced as a special domain of *thought* (i.e. as more than a description of the mental status of physiological events such as breathing). The notion of the unconscious emerges out of Leibniz's attempt to find a response to Locke's empiricist extrapolation of Descartes' notion of consciousness. Locke takes up Descartes's idea that every mental state must be available to consciousness, and then puts it to anti-Cartesian ends. Thus, following Descartes, he asserts that ''tis altogether as intelligible to say, that a body is extended without parts, as that any thing *thinks without being conscious of it*, or perceiving, that it does so' (Locke 1690: II, 1.19). To suggest that there can be mental states without consciousness is absurd; if something is in the mind, then it is conscious. 'Whatever Idea was never perceived by the mind, was never in the mind' (ibid.: II.4.20). However, to infer from this, as Descartes does, that the contents of the mind are completely transparent to us, and that we know our minds better than our bodies, is mistaken. The problem lies with Descartes's insistence that the mind is a substance in its own right. If it has the independent, self-sufficient and permanent status of a substance, and if all its contents are available to consciousness, then Cartesian consciousness must be insomniac to the point of delirium. Here, Locke suggests, some empiricist common sense is necessary. The empiricist starting point is that the mind is a tabula rasa: the mind is 'furnished' in the course of experience (Locke 1690: II, 1.2). But in that case, Locke suggests, 'I see no reason therefore to believe, that the *soul thinks before the senses have furnished it with ideas* to think on' (ibid.: II, 1.20). It is fine to say, with Descartes, that all mental content is conscious by definition, but whether there is actually anything going on *in* the mind at any given point is another question entirely. There may be nothing at all, or there may be just whatever happens to be occupying the senses at that moment. But whatever *is* present in the mind must be conscious.

In Leibniz's response we witness the birth of the concept of the unconscious. As a rationalist in the Cartesian tradition, he is completely resistant to the Lockean doctrine that 'there is nothing in the soul which does not come from the senses'. Defending the independence of the sphere of the mental from the sphere of sensation, Leibniz's famous riposte is that there is indeed nothing in the soul which does not come from the senses – apart from the soul itself: for 'the soul includes being, substance, one, same, cause, perception, reasoning, and many other notions which the senses cannot provide' (Leibniz 1765: 111). The objection anticipates Kant's insistence on the difference in kind between sensation and the understanding. But at the same time, Leibniz sees the force of Locke's critique of the Cartesian theory of mind. If one is going to suggest that there is more in the mind than what is coming from the senses, then it is indeed absurd to say that such an extended domain of mental content must be conscious. Hence there is one way out: introduce the concept of unconscious mental content. Leibniz's way of expanding the mind beyond consciousness is through the notion of perception. As Nicholas Jolley puts it: 'For Leibniz, perception is a genus of which the thought or consciousness recognised by Descartes and Locke is a species; and thus he wants to admit a class of minute or unconscious perceptions (*petites perceptions, perceptions insensibles*) which are not available to consciousness' (Jolley 1984: 107). In fact, it is an interesting quirk of the history of philosophy that Leibniz coins the term 'apperception' to distinguish between unconscious and conscious perceptions. In 'Principles of Nature and Grace', he puts it as follows:

> It is good to distinguish between *perception*, which is the internal state of the monad representing external things, and *apperception*, which is *consciousness*, or the reflective knowledge of this internal state, something not given to all souls, nor at all times to a given soul. Moreover, it is because they lack this distinction that the Cartesians failed, disregarding the perceptions that we do not apperceive, in the same way that people disregard imperceptible bodies. (Leibniz 1714: 208)

Remaining close to Leibniz's text here permits us to bring about some subtle shifts in our usual conceptions of the unconscious. For just as Leibniz is suggesting that there is a layer of consciousness beneath apperception, so also his own term – perceptions *insensibles* – suggests the specificity of his own notion of the 'unconscious'. Could the 'insensible' even be *conscious*, albeit in some non-representational manner?

Leibniz goes on to press that Locke's doctrine is indefensible from an empirical psychological point of view. If Locke has forced Cartesians to acknowledge the absurdity of their account of mind, he has also forced himself into an opposite corner, for now he is stuck with an account of mind that, strictly speaking, only allows what is *actually* consciously present in the mind to count as mental. It is at this point that Leibniz introduces the notion of the unconscious, through the mediation of the concept of the *virtual*:

> Our gifted author seems to claim that there is nothing *virtual* [*virtuel*] in us. But he cannot hold strictly to this; otherwise his position would be too paradoxical, since . . . we are not always aware of our acquired dispositions, or the contents of our memory, and they do not even come to our aid whenever we need them, though they often come readily to mind when some idle circumstance reminds us of them, as when hearing the opening words of a song is enough to bring back the rest. (Ibid., trans. modified)

Here Leibniz introduces habits and latent memories as examples of mental content which must subsist virtually, but without actual consciousness; from there he moves to memories which resist being pulled up into consciousness, but which are later proven to have been subsistent in the mind nevertheless. Such arguments for the existence of the unconscious persist in Freud (cf. SE 12: 261). It is interesting to observe how phenomena of memory only start to become a philosophical issue in the wake of this particular dispute between Cartesians and empiricists. Perhaps it takes this dispute for future observations of the resistance of memory to consciousness to go on to acquire a new, far-reaching significance. In effect, the concept of the unconscious first emerges through a kind of dialectic between rationalist and empiricist accounts of consciousness. Hence Leibniz's privileged position, as a post-Lockean rationalist (Descartes and Spinoza were dead well before the publication of Locke's *Essay*).

In the same passage Leibniz goes on to acknowledge that Locke sometimes 'limits his thesis to the statement that there is nothing in us of which we have not at least previously been aware' (ibid.). This restriction allows Locke, in theory, to deal with the above objections. However, he is still obliged to account for how latent memories are possible on his own official theory of consciousness. He does not do this, so the restricted thesis perhaps goes to show that he is aware of the consequences of his official theory. Nevertheless, it is interesting that Leibniz continues the attack despite this. After all, this restricted thesis is completely compatible with the Freudian doctrine of the unconscious, so we might be surprised to see Leibniz continuing the attack. He counters this limited thesis with an argument that tests our own limits, with regard to how far we are prepared to follow the rationalist's commitment to reason: 'But no one can establish by reason alone how far our past and now perhaps forgotten apperceptions may have extended, especially if we accept the Platonist's doctrine of recollection which, through sheer myth, is entirely consistent with unadorned reason' (ibid., trans. modified). These comments do also point forward to modern conceptions of the unconscious, but they are not Freudian. Bergson suggests that the form taken by the preserved past introduces effects into memory which do not derive from the mere recording of previous sensations; Kierkegaard shows how Platonic recollection makes sense for us moderns, and Jung attempts to defend the idea of the preservation of an impersonal past. As Leibniz continues, 'Furthermore, why must we acquire everything through apperceptions of outer things and not be able to unearth anything from within ourselves' (ibid.)? Leibniz's own microcosmic conception of unconscious perception is presented most vividly in the following passage:

> These minute perceptions . . . are more effective in their results than has been recognised. They constitute that *je ne sais quoi*, those flavours, those images of sensible qualities, vivid in the aggregate but confused as to the parts, those impressions which are made on us by the bodies around us and which involve the infinite; that connection that each being has with all the rest of the universe. It can even be said that by virtue of these minute perceptions the present is big with the future and burdened with the past, that all things harmonize – *sympnoia panta*, as Hippocrates put it – and that eyes as piercing as God's could read in the lowliest substance the universe's whole sequence of events – 'What is, what was, and what will soon be brought in the future' [Virgil]. (Leibniz 1765: 54–5)

The present is both pregnant with the future and 'burdened with the past'. This double burden appears in the form of unconscious perceptions. Leibniz claims that 'these insensible perceptions' are also responsible for the preservation of past experiences in the individual, 'even when the individual himself has no sense of the previous states, i.e. no longer has any explicit memory of them' (Leibniz 1765: 55). Here unconscious memories are now properly unconscious – i. e. more than merely latent and readily retrievable – because they are states that have become 'implicated' or 'enveloped' once more, and no longer belong to the unfolding of the present. As we have seen, Leibniz takes it as an empirical fact that it is possible for memories to elude retrieval, and this is one of his reasons for claiming the existence of unconscious perceptions. But it is not just that previous conscious experiences are retained as unconscious perceptions. Striking a blow against the Lockean restriction of mental activity to consciousness, Leibniz contends that I can consciously remember things now of which I was *not* conscious at the time. The present moment is burdened with unconscious virtual memories which have not yet been explicated, as well as registering events that are 'not consciously attended to at the time of [their] occurrence' (Jolley 1984: 139).

Now, although these unconscious perceptions may be relegated to a flickering, virtual subsistence, Leibniz then insists that they can also in turn go on to 'be known by a superior mind'. The 'superior mind' might simply be thought to be God, were it not for the ensuing suggestion that the superior mind is one's own mind, now capable of recollecting these forgotten, currently unconscious perceptions. Leibniz argues that 'those [unconscious] perceptions also provide the means for recovering this memory at need, as a result of successive improvements which one may eventually undergo' (ibid.). Now, 'improvements' in the plural here cannot refer to the resurrection, as that is supposed to be a singular event. So these improvements appear to refer to the expansion of the capability to be affected, leading to some sort of intuitive intellect.

Personal Identity and the Metempsychotic Unconscious

Leibniz's introduction of the unconscious has very specific consequences with regard to the issue of personal identity. As we have seen Leibniz defends the Cartesian notion of thinking substance against Locke's empiricism, by having recourse to the notion of unconscious thought. But in the process of criticizing Descartes, Locke also develops a powerful and influential critique of Descartes's notion of the identity of the thinking subject. Descartes has a 'substantialist' or noumenal notion of identity (Jolley 1984: 126). We can chart this development in the concept of personal identity from Descartes, Locke to Leibniz by reference to David Lynch's *Lost Highway* (1996), which develops the same theme. For Descartes, the protagonist of the film, Pete, would be the same person as Fred if they share the same immaterial substance. The problem with Descartes's view is that this identification can only ever be made by an omniscient God and there is no way for us to judge whether identity of substance is indeed conserved. In *Lost Highway*, the only omniscient presence is the demonic Mystery Man, who is not forthcoming about whether Pete and Fred are the same immaterial soul. As observers, all we have to go on is the body of the other; and Pete and Fred are played by different actors in the film. But Descartes himself admits that the material alteration of the properties of the substance does not affect its 'substantial' identity, otherwise, with the recycling of skin and organs throughout the life-cycle, we would pass through a series of different identities. So, from the Cartesian point of view, it is perfectly conceivable that Pete and Fred may be different 'shells' of the same substance, if we are prepared to accept that the possibility that some radical physical transformation of Fred's body has somehow happened overnight. Moreover, if we (as psychoanalytic film theorists suggest) are *identifying* with Fred as the protagonist of the film, we feel just as unable to offer any criteria for identity if we take up his standpoint and attempt to see things from his perspective. Foreshadowing Kant in the Paralogisms, Descartes admits that we do not perceive substance directly, but only 'know a substance by one of its attributes' (Descartes 1644: 210). And consequently, extrapolating from Fred to us, there are no internal criteria either for assessing whether our identity is continuous. Hence the malevolent Mystery Man in the film is permitted to intercede, as a demon, between us and the 'truth' about Fred's/Pete's identity, and to exploit our anxieties about the potential discontinuity of the self.

In the *Essay*, Locke sees clearly that a substantialist notion of personal identity is untenable, and offers no defence against demonic forces at all. If the substance is material, then our identities change with our bodies; if the substance is immaterial, then there are no epistemic criteria for deciding whether substances exist continuously, or whether 'we' are in fact composed of discontinuous substances; in any case Locke has already mounted a celebrated critique against the notion of immaterial substance (which he satirizes as nothing more than an 'I know not what' that is held to be behind appearances). There is, in fact, nothing in the Cartesian view which does anything to hold at bay 'those philosophers who allow of transmigration, and of the opinion that the souls of men may, for their miscarriages, be detruded into the bodies of beasts, as fit habitations, with organs suited to the satisfaction of their brutal inclinations' (Locke 1690: II.27.6). Locke believes that the absurdity of such a view makes itself clear when we reflect that 'nobody, could he be sure that the soul of Heliogabalus were in one of his hogs, would yet say that hog were a *man* or Heliogabalus' (ibid.). That way madness lies. So Locke contends that personal identity is in fact not dependent on the permanence of substance at all, but on the continuity of our consciousness over time. The preservation of substantial identity is not the relevant criterion for personal identity. 'Since consciousness always accompanies thinking, and 'tis that, that makes every one to be, what he calls a *self*; and thereby distinguishes himself from all other thinking beings, in this alone consists *personal Identity*' (Locke 1690: II.27.9). For Locke, a *person* is 'a thinking intelligent being, that has reason and reflection, and can consider itself as itself, the same thinking thing at different times and places'; a *man*, on the other hand, is the body inhabited by the person. On Locke's argument, if I remember previous events as having happened to me, then I am identical with the person who lived those events. 'As far as this consciousness can be extended backwards to any past Action or Thought, so far reaches the Identity of that *Person*; it is the same *self* now as it was then; and 'tis by the same *self* with this present one that now reflects on it, that that Action was done' (ibid.). This is one of Locke's most revolutionary ideas: he gets beyond the idea that identity is rooted in the permanence of some inaccessible substance, and by emphasizing continuity of consciousness over time, rescues personal identity from the threat of demonic interference. However, in doing so, he also tries to be very careful to allow for the coherence of the doctrine of the Resurrection. If we are resurrected, and we *do* happen to remember our previous life, then the resurrected person is the same as the formerly dead person, despite being presented with a new, post-apocalyptic, glorious body. So identity is saved, and Resurrection too remains possible. But at this point, the demons find a crack and creep back in. Locke also recognizes that an odd result of his argument is to admit the possibility of the transmigration of souls, *on condition that the past lives are remembered.* So if Heliogabalus emerged from his voyage through the circuit of births and rebirths, and was able to remember his past lives, whether in Rome or in the pigsty, then we could quite legitimately say that Heliogabalus had been the same 'person' throughout his travails.

Theophilus agrees with Philatheles on this point. 'If there were no connection by way of memory between the different *personae* . . . there would not be enough moral identity to say that this was a single person. And if God wished a human soul to pass into the body of a hog and to forget the man and perform no rational acts, it would not constitute a man' (Leibniz 1765: 233). As hogs are not able to speak, write or paint pictures, we might never learn of the hog's true identity (this would perhaps only become clear when the wheel of births had been traversed). Nevertheless, Theophilus recalls that in *The Golden Ass* Lucius is forced to wander from master to master in the skin of an ass until he is restored to his former shape. (Fiction, Leibniz tells us, can show how such transformations can be wrought in one life, but, as Leibniz no doubt knew, Apuleius's *Golden Ass*, the original title of which is the *Transformations of Lucius Apuleius of Madaura*, is no ordinary fiction, as it is held to contain an authentic account of initiation into an oriental cult.)

Theophilus also acknowledges certain of Philatheles's points about the importance of having *phenomenal* criteria for identity, based in the continuity of memory and consciousness for personal identity. In fact, he adds a further phenomenal criterion: the persistence of regular and consistent appearances in the external world, verifiable through the testimony of others in the outer world (ibid.). At one point Theophilus even concedes that real identity could be altered by God in some extraordinary manner, while personal identity would be preserved (ibid.: 237). But then Theophilus objects that Philatheles's theory is too strong as it follows from it that we are not the same person as we were when we were infants: 'I would not wish to deny . . . that "personal identity" and even the "self" persist in us and that I am that I who was in the cradle merely on the grounds that I can no longer remember anything that I did at that time' (ibid.: 236). Childhood or clinical amnesia provides examples of how the loss of memory is not equivalent to the loss of personal identity. I am still the same individual that I was in the cradle; in fact there may have been events or patterns of experience in my childhood which have influenced my current state, but which are not currently accessible at all. It seems absurd to exclude them from my identity. What is more, 'if I forgot my whole past

. . . I could still learn from others about my life during my preceding state; and similarly, I would have retained my rights without having to be divided into two persons and made to inherit from myself' (Leibniz 1765: 237). The subsistence of my past should not be excluded from my identity even if it is out of reach of my personal, conscious acts of memory.[24]

According to some commentators, Leibniz eventually just reverts to the position that Locke is attacking: that noumenal or substantial identity is essential to personal identity. Indeed, he does say that 'an identity which is apparent to the person concerned . . . presupposes a real identity obtaining through each immediate [temporal] transition' (ibid.: 236; Jolley 1984: 134–7). But according to Jolley, Leibniz accepts Locke's criterion of personal identity, and 'even adopts a stronger and cruder form of the criterion than Locke's own, for whereas Locke argues only for potential memory – that a person could remember an event under certain conditions – Leibniz is committed to a form of actual memory. At every moment in his history a person is unconsciously 'remembering' every previous state, as well as anticipating all his future experiences' (Jolley 1984: 140). It is indeed true that Leibniz's monadology allows him to be a substantialist about identity without being a materialist. But it is as if, just at the moment that something interesting appears in Leibniz's thought, he is seen to retreat with a flourish, uttering absurd theological mumbo-jumbo as he goes. Exit Leibniz from the history of the philosophy of the unconscious. The problem is that these conclusions overlook what is probably the most important thing: Leibniz's distinction between the virtual and the actual (Leibniz 1765: 52). As preserved, memory is not actual at all, but rather virtual; the existence of virtuality does not depend on its actualization.[25]

Perhaps Theophilus's hesitations at this point are symptomatic of an internal breakdown in the dialogue. There is no real dialogue between Leibniz and Locke at this point. Locke died in 1705 while Leibniz was finishing the *New Essays*, and thus never got to hear about unconscious perceptions. Leibniz imagined that for Locke, the question of the unconscious would have been primarily a moral one. The ability to maintain personal identity is essential for moral reasons: '*Person* . . . is a forensic term' (Locke 1690: II.27.26). Personality is required not just for accountability in this life, but for accountability at the Last Judgement. If somebody is to be held accountable for their actions, then they must be able to remember them, or else any punishment arising will be unjust. This means, however, that acts committed in drugged or drunken states, or in sleepwalking, cannot be punished, no more than acts committed before an onset of amnesia. Even if the first two examples are voluntary and the latter involuntary, the problem remains of how to isolate the blameworthy action. A drugged murderer is not held accountable for murder because he voluntarily took drugs, but because he committed murder – but the intention to murder and its consummation occurred in a state of derangement.

Unconscious memory is virtual, and preserved in a state different in kind from actual states, which are indeed imputable. We can imagine Leibniz at this point, peering with Theophilus over the edge of consciousness, hesitating before the vision of a universe composed of inferior and superior consciousnesses, each enveloping the same world from their own perspective, and according to their own speed. There will have to be a revolution in forensics in order to deal with this influx of psychic life. If there are 'superior consciousnesses', they must have undergone some transformation, by which their dominant monads have broken into a 'greater theatre' (Leibniz 1714b: 223, # 75, trans. modified). With the images of Theophilus and Philatheles frozen on the membrane-screen in his camera obscura, Leibniz reflects further, succumbing to somniacal reveries. 'Souls, in general, are living mirrors or images of the universe of creatures' in that they express their relations with the rest of the universe through perception and memory of it. But in turn 'minds are also images of divinity itself . . . capable of knowing the system of the universe' (Leibniz 1714b: 223, # 83). Spiritual beings can unfold or develop their relations to the universe and attempt to understand why it is organized in the way it is. By rationally reconstructing the order of the universe, they can ultimately pose the question of whether it *has* to be organized in this particular way. The spiritual being, accommodating itself to its 'more subtle theatre' is capable not only of knowing the system of the universe, but of 'imitating something of it through their schematic representations of it, each mind being like a little divinity in its own realm' (Leibniz 1714b: 223, # 83).

But what of the innumerable 'inferior consciousnesses', enveloped in darker and darker obscurity? Leibniz murmurs that 'not only souls, but also animals cannot be generated and cannot perish. They are only developed, enveloped, reclothed, unclothed, and transformed' (Leibniz 1714a: 209). He is insisting that this is no barbaric affirmation of the transmigration of souls (or 'metempsychosis'). Since 'souls never entirely leave their body, and do not pass from one body into another that is entirely new to them . . . there is therefore no *metempsychosis,* but there is *metamorphosis*' (ibid.). While it may not be strict metempsychosis, however, this could be called metempsychosis in a limited sense, insofar as souls still journey through successive bodies; whereas they dominate over the body in one lifetime, in the next, they may be relegated to some inferior function, stripped of the power to dominate.

What could all this mean? In *The Fold* Deleuze provides a précis of Fechner's *Little Book of Life after Death,* which he takes to illustrate this conception.[26] Fechner suggests that our view of life after death should be compared to the unborn infant's view of life after birth. For the unborn child, its imminent birth signals the collapse of the amniotic haven in which it has come to consciousness. When the waters break, it has no clue that it is about to emerge into a wider life. Fechner says that 'the relation of the first stage to the second recurs in a higher degree in the relations of the second to the third. Our whole action and will in this world is exactly calculated to procure for us an organism, which, in the next world, we shall perceive and use as our Self' (Fechner 1836: 27–8). In the third age of man, as well as corporeality, it is more specifically sensible intuition [*Anschauung*] which is cast off, leaving only the 'spiritual' essence behind, because 'every cause retains its effects as an eternal possession'.[27] In the following chapters on instinct and occultism we will see that Deleuze takes the esoteric dictum that the 'world is an egg' unusually seriously.[28] The entire process of ontogenesis may be understood as the flight of an embryo through the phases of infancy, childhood, youth, etc. These are the molar intensive transformations that make up the process of individuation. But if, with Leibniz and Bergson, we take the Hermetic view that the human being is a microcosm, then we must be prepared to become aware of a vaster set of 'molecular' intensive transformations. In that case Fechner's psychophysics, contrary to what we may have expected at the beginning, even becomes 'inseparable from the spiritual mechanisms of the monadic soul' (F 97). Leibniz 'substitute[s] the notion of "metaschematism" for that of metempsychosis, meaning by this that a soul never changes bodies, but that its body could be re-enveloped or re-implicated in order to enter other fields of individuation, thereby returning to a "more subtle theatre"' (DR 254; cf. DR 83).[29] It is not that an immortal soul is able to change bodies, but rather that the body is capable of intensive transformations which permit the crossing of thresholds of consciousness.

Chapter 2

The Wasp's Sympathy for the Caterpillar: The Somnambulist Theory of Instinct

Freud's theory of sexuality concerns not the sexual instinct, but the sexual *drives*. Many texts have been written attempting to warn English readers of the translation error in the *Standard Edition* of Freud's works, where *Trieb* (drive) is translated as 'instinct'. Even in France, psychoanalysts such as Lacan were sufficiently disturbed by the English translation error to make repeated references to the difference in kind between the notion of instinct and Freud's notions of wish or drive. Whichever model of instinct is used (we will see that there are several), in each case instinct presents us with a 'pre-established harmony', in which 'the animal fits into its environment' (Lacan 1954–5: 86). The object of psychoanalysis differs in two fundamental respects. First, the human wish (or 'desire', as the French translate *Wunsch*) is a repetition of earlier experiences of satisfaction, but their emergence occurs strictly on the ontogenetic rather than phylogenetic level. There are therefore no pre-given instinctual desires; rather desire is something constructed in the experience of the infant. Second, Freud's analysis in 'Drives and their Vicissitudes' clearly shows that the fully formed sexual drive is the fixated product of a complex developmental trajectory that is subject to numerous contingencies.

But what if this distinction between instinct and drive, which has become a dogma in Lacanian psychoanalysis, does not cover the full set of possibilities latent in the concept of instinct? The concept of instinct has had an extremely interesting history, full of conflicts, and, on closer inspection, it proves impossible to compress this history into a unified narrative. For Freudians and Lacanians, instinct is simply what is biologically given, as opposed to what is constructed in the course of childhood (drive). The processes of displacement of aims, objects, erogeneous zones, and quantitative libidinal thresholds (SE 14: 122) introduce so much variation into early child development that the notion of instinct is made redundant. But in Schopenhauer, Bergson and Deleuze (as well as Raymond Ruyer, another influence on Deleuze), there is a consciousness that can already be attributed to instinct. My challenge here is to show that instinct already has a psychic complexity, and that it is not the mute biological given it is taken to be. If that is right, the distinction between instinct and drive becomes less clear cut.

After a brief period of publication in 1945–7 (articles in literary journals and prefaces to books, devoted to intensely sexual and esoteric or religious themes), Deleuze lapsed into silence until 1953, which is when the 'official'

French biography of his writings starts.[1] For a period of fifteen years, up until the publication of his landmark book, *Difference and Repetition*, Deleuze was to publish many studies in the history of philosophy and literature. His first publications in the early 1950s were devoted to Hume and Bergson. Explicit discussion of the unconscious was rare in these works. In his first article on Bergson, Deleuze had affirmed Bergson's theory (in *Matter and Memory*) that 'The past is the in-itself, the unconscious or, precisely, as Bergson says, the *virtual*' (DI 29). This identification of memory with the unconscious was already profoundly non-Freudian, in that the unconscious was not primarily characterized as the repository of particular repressed (sexual) representations, but instead denoted the retained past *as a whole*, in its relation to the living present. On this theory, what is repressed is first of all the past itself, not particular memories; whereas Freud took little interest in latent memories, they were the key to the notion of the unconscious for Bergson. Bergson developed his psychology in close contact with Pierre Janet. For Bergson and Janet, what makes one ill is not the repression of particular noxious memories, but the state of dissociation from present activity.[2] Bergson and Janet insisted that psychopathology often has temporal (and spatial) aspects which cannot be reduced to repressed wishes. Deleuze will adhere to this fundamentally temporal conception of the unconscious up until *Difference and Repetition*, where he argues that the unconscious is constituted by three syntheses of time (DR 150).

But during the 1950s Deleuze was also paying a lot of attention to what was perhaps Bergson's most notorious theory, the theory of instinct in *Creative Evolution*, which has a more complicated relationship with the concept of the unconscious. In 1953 Deleuze published a volume entitled *Instincts and Institutions*, an edited collection of sixty-six extracts on the eponymous themes and their relationships.[3] Deleuze provides an illuminating preface to the volume (reprinted in *Desert Islands*) which suggests that the text is not simply to be read as a 'Reader' or anthology, but as promoting a particular line of thought. It cannot be denied that there is some degree of ventriloquism in Deleuze's editorial approach to *Instincts and Institutions*, as his selection is very specific and idiosyncratic, and their sequencing also seems to embody an argument, which promotes a particular set of conclusions. What cannot but strike the contemporary reader is that, despite being published two years after the appearance of Tinbergen's landmark book *The Study of Instinct*, Deleuze's volume contains no references to the ethology of Tinbergen or Lorenz. In fact, there is not even an extract from Deleuze's favourite ethologist, Jakob von Uexküll.[4] Instead, the collection is haunted by the 'clairvoyant' or 'somnambulist' theory of instinct, which has a long tradition behind it (as the extracts in the volume show), and which seems to climax in Bergson's reworking of it in *Creative Evolution* (1907). The first extract on the theme of instinct is from Cuvier, for whom the instinctive animal is 'a species of somnambulist' who pursues 'a sort of dream or vision' (I & I: 18). Other citations from Schopenhauer, Jean-Henri Fabre and Bergson take up and pursue further this model of instinct. The problem of instinct is presented through a series of texts on entomology, which illustrate the battle between Darwinians and disciples of Fabre, whom Deleuze describes as 'the Anti-Darwin' (ibid.: 82). Deleuze's selection seems intended to show that the somnambulist model not only predated the Darwinian conception of instinct, but also survived it.

In 1859, Darwin suggested that instinct should be understood as an evolved mechanism like any other, evolving through 'slow and gradual accumulation of numerous, slight, yet profitable, variations' (Darwin 1859: 256). But despite the success of Darwinism in other areas, strangely his explanation of instinct met with only qualified acceptance. At the beginning of the twentieth century, the notion of instinct became a touchstone for debates about the range of the theory of evolution in the late nineteenth century. Bergson's complaint against Darwin in *Creative Evolution* was concentrated around the question of instinct. His main problem was this: if instincts involve very complex, integrated physiological sequences of events, then how can they evolve gradually? Bergson felt entitled to revive the somnambulist model proposed earlier by Cuvier, Schopenhauer and Fabre, claiming against Darwin that instinct must involve more than a set of motor mechanisms and must be taken as a kind of knowledge, implying a peculiar kind of mentality. Just as the somnambulist is perfectly conscious of *what* they are doing, but is unconscious of *why* they are doing it, instinctual activity involves a kind of consciousness which is intellectually unaware of its purpose.

A whole school of 'instinct-theorists' also appeared in the English-speaking world from the late 1890s to 1920s – for instance, Conwy Lloyd Morgan, W. H. R. Rivers and William McDougall, and although only some of them were explicitly sympathetic to Bergson, all also argued that instinct should be conceived on the model of knowledge.[5] In his 1917 survey of these trends and their philosophical origins, *Instinct in Man*, James Drever notes the similarity between Bergson's idea of instinct and the hypothesis put forward by Eduard von Hartmann in his *Philosophy of the Unconscious* (1869) that instinct is manifested through a type of 'clairvoyant intuition' (Drever 1917: 101, 66). Deleuze does not refer to the British instinct-theorists, but it is this general intellectual milieu that he inhabits in *Instincts and Institutions*. On three separate occasions, Bergson's somnambulistic instinct theory is given a prime position in the debate. But Bergson's theory of 'instinctual sympathy' – whose privileged example is that of the wasp which paralyses the caterpillar in order to provide its larvae with a living larder – is probably the most bizarre element in Bergson's philosophy. Reviewing the contributions of Fabre and Bergson in his *Analysis of Mind*, Bertrand Russell remarked on how 'love of the marvellous may mislead even so careful an observer as Fabre and so eminent a philosopher as Bergson' (Russell 1921: 56). From 1920 onwards, a vehement reaction flared up against the theoretical excesses of contemporary instinct theory, and behaviourism made an aggressive attempt to reduce all instincts to reflexes.[6] The instinct-theorists were swiftly forgotten, and if Bergson's theory survived it was only due to the accident of having been proposed by a great philosopher, whose work was preserved for other reasons (the same was true for Schopenhauer's theory).

It is usually held that the concept of instinct only became acceptable again as a result of the emergence of Lorenz's and Tinbergen's ethology in the 1950s. Both ethologists stressed the compatibility of their theories with Darwinism. Deleuze's *Instincts and Institutions* project was therefore a rather unusual one and probably appeared anachronistic even when it was published. His preference for von Uexküll and Buytendijk in any case suggests that his conception of ethology is quite at variance with what became the dominant version of ethology proposed by Lorenz and Tinbergen, which completely rules out appeal to the subjectivity of the organism. Uexküll's original proposal to replace anthropomorphic language in the description of animal behaviour with more neutral terminology was not originally targeted against the ascription of subjective properties to animals. Rather he proposed that 'receptor', for instance, should replace 'sense organ', because an animal's perception of its environment is *selective* and *species-specific*, which implies that, for instance, since animals do not necessarily 'see' in the way that humans do, the most one can infer from the presence of eyes in animals is that they are receptive of light (Burkhardt 2005: 155). For Uexküll, the campaign against anthropomorphism was fully consistent with the ascription of subjective qualities to organisms. 'According to the behaviorists, man's own sensations and will are mere appearance, to be considered, if at all, only as disturbing static . . . We [on the other hand] no longer regard animals as mere machines, but as subjects whose essential activity consists of perceiving and acting' (Uexküll 1934: 6).

In his *Theoretical Biology*, Uexküll makes clear his debt to Kant, and explicitly focuses on the question of how the world *appears* to the animal (Uexküll 1926). The later ethologists rejected Uexküll's emphasis on subjectivity. Tinbergen took Uexküll's earlier critique of anthropomorphic terminology one step further by stating the methodological principle that 'because subjective phenomena cannot be observed objectively in animals, it is idle either to claim or to deny their existence' (Tinbergen 1951: 4). Tinbergen and Lorenz object against Uexküll that it is quite possible to conceive of a selective *Umwelt* carved out of the wider environment without making reference to subjectivity. The tick's behaviour, for instance, can be seen as a sequence of evolved subroutines in the service of its reproductive function. As is well known, in *A Thousand Plateaus* and 'Spinoza and Us' in *Spinoza: Practical Philosophy*, Deleuze appeals to Spinoza's psychophysical parallelism in order to defend Uexküllian ethology from this charge (Ansell Pearson 1999: 179).

But his approach to animal subjectivity in his early writings appears to be rooted in a preference for Bergsonian instinct theory. If we take into consideration the importance ascribed to Bergson's theory of instinct in *Instincts and Institutions* and in other places in his work, then it becomes clear just how unorthodox Deleuze's approach to ethology was. Uexküll certainly would have baulked at some of Bergson's inferences about animal subjectivity. But the somnambulist theory of instinct appears to have profoundly preoccupied Deleuze during what he describes as an 'eight-year hole' in his life, from 1953 to 1961, when he published very little.[7]

Bergson and the Theory of Instinct

Deleuze begins his chapter on instinct in *Instinct and Institutions* with a quote from Cuvier: 'One can only get a clear idea of instinct by admitting that animals have innate and constant images or sensations in their sensorium, which determine them to act, just as ordinary and accidental sensations determine them. It is always a sort of dream or vision which they pursue; in everything that has to do with instinct, one should see them as a species of somnambulist' (I & I: 18). The ensuing extract from Fabre does not take up this theoretical analysis, but does seem to be intended to illustrate it. Fabre gives a description of one of the most disturbing behaviours found in the order of hymenoptera, the paralysing attacks of the *Ammophila Hirsuta* wasp. Although Deleuze cites a number of texts from Fabre in *Instincts and Institutions*, it is likely that he selected the description of the *Ammophila* because Bergson also refers to it in his pages on instinct in *Creative Evolution* (Bergson 1907: 172–4). Solitary nest-building wasps had been the focus of debate about instinct at the end of the nineteenth century. The solitary character of the wasps clearly precludes the learning of nest-building or hunting behaviours. The *Ammophila* wasp hunts caterpillars, sometimes weighing fifteen times as much as itself, as food for its larvae. The larvae do not accept corpses, however, so the wasp paralyses its prey and presents it to them immobile and alive. Fabre describes how the wasp, in a series of swift and precise operations, puts the main locomotor centres of the caterpillar out of action. What is astonishing about the paralysing wasps, he says, is that they specifically target the motor ganglia, *as if they knew* that stinging other ganglia might cause death and therefore putrefaction. The *Ammophila* stings no less than nine of the locomotor centres of the caterpillar, just sufficient to immobilize it. It then squeezes the head of the caterpillar with its mandibles, again with enough force to cause paralysis but not death. After the attack is over, the *Ammophila* grabs the caterpillar by the throat, dragging it back to its shaft in the earth. Astride the paralysed segments of the caterpillar, the newly hatched grub now has continual access to a larder of food which is preserved from putrefaction because it is still alive. During the whole operation, says Fabre, the wasp proceeds with 'surgical precision', as if it knew intimately the facts of her victim's complex nervous system (I & I: 19; Fabre 1920: 38–40). It was this kind of complex, integrated behaviour that persuaded Fabre to affirm the fixity of species, against Darwinism.

Fabre's wasp and caterpillar provide the set piece of Bergson's account of instinct in *Creative Evolution*. In turn, Deleuze's and Guattari's fascination with the 'a-parallel evolution' of the wasp and the orchid is pre-dated by Deleuze's earlier fascination with the funereal dance of the wasp and caterpillar in Fabre and Bergson. What is happening here, says Bergson (moving far beyond Fabre's observations), is an example of a divinatory *sympathy* that flows throughout nature. In its time and after, this suggestion caused confusion to everyone (Jankélévitch 1959: 152). What sympathy! How does Bergson arrive at such a fantastical hypothesis, so radically opposed to current mainstream views of instinctual behaviour that it is hard to imagine now that anyone could have taken it seriously? The problem of the anachronism of Deleuze's return to Bergson's theory of instinct is dwarfed by the uncertain zone of *occult biology* implied by Bergson's proposal. What are the rules that govern this obscure region of thought?

Bergson begins by approaching instinct through a contrast with intelligence as the capacity to use tools. Whereas 'intelligence perfected is the faculty of making and using unorganised instruments', 'instinct perfected is a faculty of using and even of constructing organised instruments' (Bergson 1907: 140). Instincts are thus the direct 'continuation of the work of organisation' (ibid.: 139). For both Bergson and Darwin, the instinct to suck at the breast is not different in kind to the evolution of the mammary glands themselves, in terms of adaptive function. The social instincts of insects are directly correlated with their anatomy, as shown by the worker bees in a hive, which have a different anatomical structure to the others. We cannot tell where the activity of instinct begins and where that of nature ends (ibid.). Nevertheless, Bergson claims that something stops us from reducing instinct to physiological and causal mechanisms, in conformity with a Darwinian account of adaptation. Something distinguishes the activity of instinct from, on the one hand, mechanical reflexes, and on the other hand, from intelligent, conscious behaviour. This is the role of *the unconscious* in instinctual activity.

In *Instincts and Institutions* at the conclusion of the chapter devoted to instinct, Deleuze cites a passage from Bergson's *Creative Evolution* which distinguishes between 'two types of unconsciousness' (Bergson 1907: 143; I & I 28). On the one hand, there is an unconscious 'in which consciousness is *absent*'; the stone is unconscious because it never was nor could have been conscious. But on the other hand, there is an unconscious 'in which consciousness is *nullified*'.[8] A stone may have zero consciousness of its fall, just as an instinct may have zero consciousness. But the two zeros are not the same, as one is the result of a suppression. With the notion of the suppression of consciousness, we seem to be close to Freud. But this impression turns out to be misleading. This is the passage, cited by Deleuze, in which Bergson introduces his version of the somnambulistic model of instinct:

> When we mechanically perform an habitual action, when the somnambulist automatically acts his dream, unconsciousness may be absolute; but this is merely due to the fact that the representation of the act is held in check by the performance of the act itself, which resembles the idea so perfectly, and fits it so exactly, that consciousness is unable to find room between them. *Representation is stopped up by action.* The proof of this is, that if the

> accomplishment of the act is arrested or thwarted by an obstacle, consciousness may reappear. It was there, but neutralised by the action which fulfilled and thereby filled the representation. The obstacle creates nothing positive; it simply makes a void, removes a stopper. This inadequacy of act to representation is precisely what we here call consciousness. (Bergson 1907: 144)

This passage is impossible to understand if one is expecting the 'suppression' of consciousness to be similar to the Freudian model of repression. There is also a difficulty here because Bergson is in the process of moving beyond the functionalist account of consciousness he maintains in *Matter and Memory*. In that text, consciousness is primarily treated as a function of intelligence. One would expect therefore that Bergson would go on to deny consciousness to instinct (which is the opposite of intelligence). It appears that it is a condition of consciousness that there is some (minimal or maximal) choice in relation to the object. Consciousness only 'lights up' when there is a multiplicity of courses of action that might be taken, when *attention* to the situation is required. It is, moreover, by definition never 'adequate' to its object (there is always a 'distance between act and idea'; ibid.: 145), since by its nature it involves appeal to past experiences, to generalizations, and to abstractions that have a strictly pragmatic value in the present situation. In this passage, however, Bergson has gone beyond the identification of consciousness with attention. Intelligent consciousness does not exhaust the genus of consciousness, and we are given reasons for assuming the existence of a consciousness 'by right' which is quite independent of the function of intelligence (ibid.: 179).

> We might suppose that consciousness, even in the most rudimentary animal, covers by right an enormous field, but is compressed in fact in a kind of vise: each advance of the nervous centres, by giving the organism a choice between a larger number of actions, calls forth the potentialities that are capable of surrounding the real, thus opening the vise wider and allowing consciousness to pass more freely. In this second hypothesis . . . it is more true to say that action is the instrument of consciousness . . . It is as if a broad current of consciousness had penetrated matter, loaded, as all consciousness is, with an enormous multiplicity of interwoven potentialities. (Bergson 1907: 179–81)

Deleuze will call this type of consciousness 'pure consciousness'.[9] On top of the perfectly functional explanation of consciousness as an effect of the need to solve practical problems, Bergson goes on to suggest that 'we must also point out that things would go on in just the same way if consciousness, instead of being the effect, were the cause'. Rather than being an effect in the nervous system, the nervous system is *organized around* a more primary, pure consciousness.

This pure consciousness appears to be identical to what Bergson calls 'intuition'. Is instinct the most 'involuted' form of intuition, as Bergson tends to say in his more theosophical moments, or is intuition rather the most 'evolved' form of instinct? This question will be approached in the following section. For the moment, we should just note that Bergson believes intuition to be the form of consciousness appropriate to instinct. Instinct discerns a situation 'from within, quite otherwise than by a process of knowledge – by an intuition (*lived* rather than *represented*)' (ibid.: 175). Instincts are '*felt* rather than *thought*' (172). In instinctual activity there is *no* distance between act and idea. Instinctual intuition even appears to be a kind of 'adequate idea', in which the act perfectly corresponds to a pre-existing idea, or 'fulfils' the idea. Bergson is therefore aware that this intuitive aspect of instinct cannot be thought as 'unconscious' in the sense of 'repressed altogether from consciousness'. If there is no consciousness at all in intuition, then it would be absurd to talk of an 'adequacy of act to idea'. How can an idea be adequate if it is absolutely unconscious? The intuitive aspect of instinct is impossible to divorce from *some* sort of consciousness.

In his defence of Bergson's theory of instinct, 'Bergson et la Sphex Ammophile', Raymond Ruyer argues that Bergson's error in this passage is to 'make "consciousness" the synonym of "representation"' (Ruyer 1959: 177).[10] When he claims that instinct involves a 'suppression' of consciousness, he must mean that it involves a suppression of conscious *representation*, or intelligent consciousness, with its efforts of attention and appeal to conceptual norms. He says clearly that 'although instinct is not within the domain of intelligence, it is not situated beyond the limits of mind' (Bergson 1907: 175), but in the crucial passage in question, it is made less than clear that he is talking about the repression of intelligent consciousness. But this is the only way of making sense of his position. Instinct must not be thought of as 'absolutely' unconscious in the manner of the falling stone (for then it would not be intuitive), but rather as unconscious *relative* to intelligence. But far from being unconscious, instinct in that case might turn out to be *absolutely* conscious. insofar as it involves the adequacy of act to idea. Bergson's distinction between two types of unconsciousness should have been augmented with a distinction between two types (or perhaps poles) of consciousness. What may be unconscious to empirical, representational consciousness, may be intensely conscious to instinctual consciousness.[11]

With this in mind, we might be able to make sense of a peculiar statement in *Difference and Repetition*, where Deleuze bluntly inverts the Freudian notion that the unconscious (along with the affects and compulsive repetitions it produces) is a result of repression. 'I do not repeat because I repress', but 'I repress because I repeat, I forget because I repeat. I repress, because I can live certain things or certain experiences only in the mode of repetition. I am determined to repress whatever would prevent me from living them thus: in particular, the representation which mediates the lived by relating it to the form of a similar or identical object' (DR 18). Instincts would be the first 'repetitions', the first syntheses of consciousness, but in a field of consciousness which is not yet necessarily human. Bergson's theory points us towards an instinctual consciousness native to animal life in general, and which may, under some modified form, also distribute itself in human collectivities.

The Somnambulist Theory of the Unconscious

Noting the increasing popularity of the psychology of the unconscious at the *fin de siècle,* the Kantian psychologist Wilhelm Wundt launched an attack on the notion, which he pointedly associated with mysticism and the 'Schelling school' (Wundt 1908–11: III, 636). In his *Outlines of Psychology* he contended that

> any psychical element that has disappeared from consciousness is to be called unconscious in the sense that we assume the possibility of its renewal, that is, its reappearance in the actual interconnection of psychical processes. Our knowledge of an element that has become unconscious does not extend beyond the possibility of its renewal . . . Assumptions as to the state of the 'unconscious' or as to 'unconscious processes' of any kind . . . are entirely unproductive for psychology. (Wundt 1896: 227–8)

In later, twentieth-century editions of his major work, the *Grundzüge der physiologischen Psychologie* (*Principles of Physiological Psychology,* first published in 1874), Wundt asserts that 'for hypothetical unconscious processes we could substitute actually demonstrable or at any rate less hypothetical conscious processes' (Wundt 1908–11: III, 110).[12]

For Freud and Bergson alike the problem of the unconscious does indeed concern the subsistence of unconscious *mental* states. The idea that there are physiological movements which are beneath the threshold of conscious perception is entirely uncontroversial, and Wundt himself wrote in great detail about lower-order physiological processes in the brain. We are unconscious of digestion, the movements of the autonomous nervous system and the circulation of the blood. The idea that there is an unconscious *mind* raises major philosophical perplexities. How do unconscious states subsist before and after they are conscious? If they finally come to consciousness, does that mean there is no longer an unconscious? How does the ego 'recognize' them, in order to keep them out of consciousness (Sartre's problem of the 'censor')? What is the nature of the dynamic relation between consciousness and the unconscious?

Many philosophical proponents of the unconscious today are still sensitive to Wundt's Kantian rejection of the notion of the unconscious. We will return to it in chapter 3, where we discuss Jung's response to it. Wundt's position remains powerful in a philosophical climate split by the dualism between naturalistic and normative approaches to the mind. Anglo-American philosophical defenders of Freud overcome Wundt's objection by arguing that unconscious mental states cannot be reduced to physiological states precisely because they *do* make implicit appeal to the normative conditions of conscious belief and desire (Hopkins 1982: xvii-xx; Cavell 1993: 31–3). Freud talks of unconscious *wishes*, and to have a wish or a desire is an intentional state, which in turn requires the having of beliefs about the desired object (Gardner 1991). All this is *normative* and cannot be reduced to the naturalistic order of physiology. Defending Freud from such a reduction, David Buller distinguishes a properly 'personal unconscious' from these 'subpersonal unconscious processes' which are '*subdoxastic*, 'inferentially isolated' from the sorts of information that figure in the contents of the conscious motives and beliefs of personal psychology' (Buller 1999: 101). It is subdoxastic processes that are involved in the estimation of depth from binocular vision, or in parsing sentences of our mother tongue. Buller suggests that the kind of subconscious 'homuncular' mechanisms identified by Daniel Dennett in his book *Consciousness Explained* are generally of this type. Unconscious wishes, on the other hand, are not 'inferentially isolated', but are repressed self-deceptively precisely because of the *sense* they carry, and the meaningful implications with which they are bound.

Bergson would agree that the infant's instinct to suck (for instance) is not unconscious in the sense that the growing of mammary glands is unconscious. It is not a physiological event, but nor is it a distorted product of the norms of conceptual representation either. Contemporary normativist attempts to salvage the unconscious remain hampered by one of Freud's key assumptions. If there is any truth in the idea that Freud was the discoverer of the unconscious, then it is perhaps because he is the first to create a strictly 'molar' opposition between consciousness and the unconscious. Freud transformed the philosophy of the unconscious by putting it in an abstract relation of mutual exclusion with consciousness. Either a representation is unconscious or it is not: unconscious, repressed 'representations' are *inferred* from their derivative, conscious representations. The unconscious is the non-conscious, and all pathological states are conscious derivatives of this radically unconscious state. But Freud's opposition misses the distinction between two kinds of consciousness: not all consciousness is dominated by the function of intelligence. Models influenced by Freud assume this false disjunction: either *intelligent* consciousness (means–end actions, conceptual representation), or no consciousness at all.

But there is another tradition of thought about the unconscious: the 'somnambulist' tradition, for which it was the *dissociation* of consciousness which was the primary clinical fact. The somnambulist model of the unconscious prevailed for a period longer than the reign of psychoanalysis. In late seventeenth-century Europe, the practice of hypnosis was confined to circuses and theatres, and its theory was non-existent, but starting in the late eighteenth century with Mesmer and continuing throughout most of the nineteenth century, natural somnambulism (instinct) and artificial somnambulism (hypnosis) played an important role in psychology as a theoretical and practical model and tool. Mesmer's original idea was hatched in his dissertation in medicine at the University of Vienna, which was devoted to the influence of the moon and planets on pathological processes. The sun and moon not only raised the tides of the seas on the earth, but also contributed to 'atmospheric tides', which in turn have an effect on the 'humours' of the body. He refers to the monthly 'tides' of menstruation. After graduating and entering private practice, Mesmer encountered a young woman who had been suffering from delirium, mania, convulsions, fainting and mysterious aches and pains. Miss Oesterline agreed to subject herself to Mesmer's experiments in applying magnetic force to produce 'artificial tides' in her body, compensating for her disequilibrium with the natural cosmic tides. After experiencing some burning pains, Mesmer decided that he must have engineered a magnetic influence. But then for some reason he started to magnetize material objects such as bread or stones, and found that these substances produced the same effect. Mesmer was truly baffled. Then it dawned upon him: the magnetism was emanating from him. There was such a thing as 'animal magnetism', which went quite beyond mere mineral magnetism, which did not affect nervous tissues. Besides Bergson and Schopenhauer, other thinkers important to Deleuze but not cited in *Instincts and Institutions* also had a deep interest in somnambulism, both natural and artificial. Schelling was obsessed by 'clairvoyance' (in *Clara* and the *Stuttgart Seminars*, for instance), while in 1817 the mysterious Johann Malfatti was sent by the Viennese court to investigate animal magnetism in the clinic of K. C. Wolfart, a follower of Mesmer who had set up a state-subsidized clinic in Berlin for the magnetic treatment of the poor (Gauld 1992: 89).[13] In his study of Jung's relationship to Pierre Janet, John Haule suggests that the main foci of interest in late nineteenth-century psychology – hypnosis, hysteria and spiritualism – 'are all variants of somnambulism', which refers to '*any* complex act performed while asleep, in trance, or in some other "altered state of consciousness"' (Haule 1984: 245). The price of Freud's molar opposition between consciousness and the unconscious was the loss of demarcations between different kinds of *states of consciousness*. The role of dissociation in the fragmentation of personal identity, as well the spatio-temporal distortions of both schizophrenia and neurosis, were scotomized by Freudian theories of the unconscious.[14]

In France Janet had attempted to synthesize the popular tradition of thought about somnambulism with academic psychology. Continuing the emphasis on apperception and synthesis in the tradition of Kantian psychology represented by Wundt, Janet had gone on to differentiate apperceptive or synthetic consciousness from other non-representational states of consciousness found in cases of dissociation. For Janet, the hysteric *is conscious* during her state of dissociation; the problem is that she cannot recall it afterwards, and therefore cannot integrate it with her ego-functions. For Bergson too, one is even *conscious* while one dreams; it is just that this kind of consciousness is quite different to the contracted, narrowed-down consciousness one has when one is paying 'attention to life'. The somnambulist is fully aware of what is happening, *while* it is happening; the problem is that they remember nothing of it afterwards (until, perhaps, the next somnambulistic episode). For Jung, in turn, the encounter with an archetype will involve a kind of 'intuition' which occurs outside of representational consciousness, but still possesses a kind of consciousness. In each of these cases, there is no 'molar' opposition between consciousness and the Unconscious. If a dissociative state is subsequently denied or forgotten by the ego, that does not mean that it had not been fully conscious while it was happening. Dissociated, somnambulistic consciousness is trancelike, *single-minded* consciousness, and hence of a different nature to ordinary, representational consciousness, which involves cognitive synthesis. Orgasm and frenzy are central sites of single-minded instinctual consciousness in human culture, and states of dissociation have the same form as them.

But if somnambulists are conscious, then of what are they unconscious? Janet agreed with Charcot that somnambulism and hysteria share a lack of awareness of the purpose of the action, a dissociation from the rest of the mental field (so that the patient cannot remember the state clearly), and the trait that subconscious fixed ideas overwhelm or take over the patient's consciousness during a crisis. Freud, another student of Charcot, decided to discount the last aspect of the phenomenon. Janet and other French psychologists insisted that the patient cannot integrate this somnambulistic state with the rest of their consciousness *because it is too single-minded*, and therefore not available for synthesis under general concepts.[15]

Schopenhauer and Bergson attempted to apply the somnambulistic model of the unconscious to the problem of instinct. Sixty years before Bergson, Schopenhauer had argued at length that it is not just psychopathology that furnishes cases of somnambulism, but that one must attribute it more fundamentally to instinct itself. Instinct is important for Schopenhauer as it is the exact analogue of *blind will*, insofar as it is both uncontrolled by the ego, and yet conscious (just as Milton was both blind and conscious).[16] In the chapter of *The World as Will and Representation* devoted to instinct, Schopenhauer wrote that 'insects are to a certain extent natural somnambulists', since 'the sympathetic nerve has taken over the direction of the external actions as well' (II, 344). However, for Schopenhauer, the *unconsciousness* of instinct specifically concerns the unconsciousness of *ends* or purposes. When 'the spider feels as if it has to spin its web, although it neither knows nor understands its purpose' (II, 344), this is analogous to the somnambulist who carries out actions dictated by a mesmerist without knowing why. Just because the spider is unconscious of the end of its actions does not mean that it cannot be conscious of the stimuli which trigger the instinct, or, in the form of an alertness or adaptability, of a means to the aim. The somnambulist is conscious of the 'subjective representations which stimulate the desire' (II, 541), but not of the end of the desire. In a certain sense, that makes instinctual behaviour more 'subjective' – in the sense of 'interior' or hermetically enclosed – than intelligent consciousness. 'We find in the case of those animals that are largely governed by instinct, especially of insects, a preponderance of the ganglionic system, i.e. the *subjective* nervous system, over the *objective* or cerebral system' (ibid.).[17] The consciousness involved in instinct is 'subjective' because of its partiality. Animals therefore possess a highly 'subjective' consciousness, insofar as their attention is *entirely motivated* by their instincts; all intelligence and habit is subordinated to the consummation of instinct.

In one sense, though, Bergson's view is the opposite to Schopenhauer's, as he says not only that instinctual consciousness must *suppress* intelligent consciousness, but that instinct possesses a kind of *adequacy* of act to idea. With this notion of instinctual 'adequacy' Bergson is consciously harking back to the model of 'intellectual intuition' outlined in seventeenth-century rationalism. Instinct suddenly starts to appear as something monstrous, as possessing a kind of 'knowledge' that dwarfs intelligent consciousness. We come now to the centre of Bergson's theory of instinct.

The Wasp's Sympathy for the Caterpillar

The argument proceeds, perhaps already fatally, via an analogy with memory. 'Is it not plain that life goes to work here exactly like consciousness, exactly like memory' (Bergson 1907: 167)? Consider human memory: 'we trail behind us, unawares, the whole of our past; but our memory pours into the present only the odd recollection or two that in some way complete our present situation' (ibid.). With instinctive knowledge, it is the same: 'It is impossible to consider some of the special instincts of the animal and of the plant, evidently arisen in extraordinary circumstances, *without relating them to those recollections, seemingly forgotten, which spring up suddenly under the pressure of an urgent need*' (ibid.; italic added). There is thus an 'inner history' of nature, a perspective of 'nature from within', which parallels the instinctual patterns of behaviour. The hymenopteran seems to have some sort of 'organic memory' (19), whereby it can reactivate, in the form of an image, another related phyletic line. Under a 'pressure of urgent need', instinct can regress to a common arthropodic form, shared with its potential victim, and intuit the anatomical location of the latter's motor ganglia. If the *Ammophila* knows how to isolate the appropriate ganglia in its victim, that is because it can somehow 'identify' with its victim. Admittedly, it 'discerns but a very little of that force, just what concerns itself; but at least it discerns it from within, quite otherwise than by a process of knowledge – by an intuition (*lived* rather than *represented*), which is probably like what we call divining sympathy' (ibid.: 175). We must 'suppose a *sympathy* (in the etymological sense of the word) between the *Ammophila* and its victim, which teaches it from within, so to say, concerning the vulnerability of the caterpillar. This feeling of vulnerability might owe nothing to outward perception, but result from the mere presence together of the *Ammophila* and the caterpillar, considered no longer as two organisms, but as two activities. It would express, in a concrete form, the *relation* of the one to the other' (Bergson 1907: 173–4).

Thus it is not just that a pure intuitive consciousness is attributable to all of life. With Bergson's theory of instinct, we enter into an alternative (or, more precisely, parallel) universe. It is ruled by the order of the Hymenoptera. Like human beings, some species of hymenoptera are social, but some are also solitary. These latter have developed a strange form of communication, not with others of their own species, but with other species in the arthropod kingdom. Creatures like the *Ammophila* are able to discern the élan vital 'from within . . . by an intuition (*lived* rather than *represented*)' (175). They communicate by recollecting, in the moment of 'urgent need', appealing to their extremely powerful intuition, their phylogenetic community with their prey. This event is not governed by the laws of physics, but depends on an 'organic memory' of the phylogenetic past. We seem to be in a universe utterly unlike our own, which recognizes no known physical or moral laws, where the wasp and the caterpillar stage a weird and cruel spectacle, in which one enters into 'sympathy' with the other and then proceeds to torture them. Bergson talks of instinct as a 'musical theme', but it is obviously difficult to envisage the actuality of this musical theatre, because it takes place within the current of pure duration, without any spatial backdrop. On Bergson's theory, this alternative order of the Insect does not inhabit a different world altogether from the Human order – it inhabits the same world *seen from within.*

Whatever the gothic beauty of Bergson's nightmarish and florid vision of universal sympathy, the arguments in its favour would appear to be easily dispelled. Bergson is arguing that this frenzied regression (in the face of 'the pressure of urgent need') involves a divinatory intuition of a recollected, common past. And the less intelligent such an effort, the better. This summons up Aleister Crowley's remark that 'all divination resembles an attempt by a man born blind to obtain sight by getting blind drunk' (Crowley 1912: 1). The idea of a universal sympathy 'within the virtual' itself is an occult idea. Lorenz's and Tinbergen's idea certainly requires fewer assumptions: instinct is an evolved mechanism for selecting certain patterns in the environment, which will serve as a trigger for the release of a mechanical pattern of behaviour.

Ruyer's Defence of Bergson's Theory of Instinct

But perhaps there are other ways of explaining Bergson's theory. One of Raymond Ruyer's aims in his article on Bergson's theory of instinct ('Bergson et le Sphex Ammophile', 1959) is to show that Bergsonian theory is compatible with ethology. Ruyer ingeniously avoids the full implications of Bergson's theory when he claims that Bergson has made another error in choosing the wrong example – the paralysing instincts of wasps – to get across his point. He should not have referred to the wasp and the caterpillar, but to *the sexual instinct* in human beings. Invoking Fabre's description of the wasp and the caterpillar, Ruyer writes that in the young human male's first experience of sex, 'everything happens as if he had known – before having consulted any Treatise – the anatomy, or the physiology, the reproductive organs of the man and the woman'. Everything happens as if the human who initiates sex knew in advance what to do, without having learned it (Ruyer 1959: 166). The actualization of the sexual instinct, therefore, is a perfect example of a kind of consciousness which is different in kind to intelligent consciousness, and in which 'representation is stopped up by action'. Sexual consciousness involves the 'suppression' of representational consciousness, and can thus be described as somnambulistic.[18]

Ruyer claims that the 'decisive argument' against a purely mechanical view of instinct is furnished, 'as Bergson had seen perfectly' by 'the equivalence between instinct and organisation' (172). Why should this be? Bergson's suggestion that instinct is a continuation of organization seems, of itself, quite neutral about what kind of phenomenon instinct is. Instinct can be said to continue the work of organization in just the same sense as anatomical structure continues the work of the genes. But this is an abstract view. In fact, what is it to say that instinct is the continuation of organization other than to say that instincts come into being through the process of *development*? In other words, if we are to understand instinct, then we must understand it as a form of ontogenesis. The key to the 'competence' or 'virtual power' exhibited in instinct lies in embryogenesis. Ruyer notes that embryologists appeal to the notions of 'capacity', 'competence', 'virtual power' and 'potentiality'. Whether one likes it or not, he says, these terms do not mean anything if they do not imply some sort of knowledge, and that, further, implies some sort of consciousness. Thus not only is instinct conscious, but so is the embryo. The embryo has a *formative* power. 'The unicellular entity has neither hands nor eyes. It nevertheless forms pseudopods, a mouth, a stomach, and it excretes. An egg, an embryo in its initial stage, acts like a unicellular entity. It deforms itself with regard to its overall form' (Ruyer 1988: 25). Ruyer makes much – perhaps too much – of the self-organizing properties of the embryo.

Even before Bergson's *Creative Evolution*, the focus of vitalistic biology had shifted to embryology with Hans Driesch's experiments in the 1890s, which suggested that the embryo had astonishing self-organizing properties. It was discovered that it is possible to transplant parts of an embryo and graft it onto a similar embryo, where it will be incorporated into its development. The embryonic eye can undergo drastic surgical interference and yet still recover fully. Driesch showed that if one separated out the first two segmentation cells of the egg of a sea urchin, each would develop into complete larvae, albeit in dwarfed form. This suggested that there were no pre-determined special regions in the egg that give rise to special organs. 'The relative position of a blastomere in the whole determines in general what develops from it; if its position be changed, it gives rise to something different. In other words, its prospective value is a function of its position' (quoted in Wilson 1925: 1056). Driesch's emphasis on the primacy of spatiotemporal relations in embryogenesis, as well as his observations of the embryo's apparent ability to 'improvise' under the conditions of transplantation are both fundamental for Ruyer. The self-organizing powers of the embryo make it impossible not to attribute some form of subjectivity to it. It is a fundamental mistake, he says, to reduce development to the unfolding of a genetic programme. Observe the embryo when it is displaced to another setting by transplantation. When it continues imperturbably the work it has begun, do not think that this indicates it is a mere robot:

> It seems unconscious or 'distracted' in a task become absurd precisely because it is intensely conscious of this task. It 'finalises' with such ardour that it appears to be a robot. A prodigious calculator, it resembles an electronic calculator . . . Nevertheless, it has moved itself toward the right answer, where an adding machine simply functions . . . It seems 'distracted' because it cannot be distracted. It seems unconscious because it is conscious of what it does and of nothing else. (Ruyer 1988: 27)

The embryo has a consciousness, but it is like the consciousness of an artist absorbed in his work. If it appears to have the efficiency of a machine, which can be lifted up and taken somewhere else while still continuing its performance, that is not because it really is a machine, but because it is so very *busy*. 'It does not see us and it does not speak to us – and for a good reason. But neither does a very busy craftsman, a painter or a mathematician who is quite absorbed, communicate with children who watch him or even with his own wife and children' (ibid.: 25). Ruyer says that such an artist is lost in his work, but then corrects himself: 'not lost, but he identifies himself intensely with the very form of this work being transformed by his hands and before his eyes' (ibid.). We are reminded of Bergson's analogy of instinctual knowledge with the capacity of the artist to identify with his object (Bergson 1907: 177, see next section). The embryo and the artist share the same intense consciousness, in which there is no space for reflective consciousness (if such is possible, that is) because of the very adequacy of act to idea. United in their clairvoyance, the embryo and the artist seem to be the two poles of pure consciousness, the alpha and omega of consciousness.

Deleuze agrees with Ruyer that developmental movements are '*lived* by the embryo' and that it '*experiences* and *undergoes states* and *undertakes* movements' (DR 249; italic added). Embryogenesis is the primary wave of actualization for living beings, and in that respect if no other, 'the world is an egg' (DR 216).[19] Unlike Freud and his followers, he rejects Haeckel's recapitulationism and affirms the more strongly epigenetic theory put forward by Von Baer, who, Deleuze says, 'showed that an embryo does not reproduce ancestral adult forms belonging to other species, but rather experiences or undergoes states and undertakes movements which are not viable for the species but go beyond the limits of the species, genus, order or class, and can be sustained only by the embryo itself, under the conditions of embryonic life' (DR 249). Nevertheless Deleuze does not explicitly affirm Ruyer's embryological model of *instinctual* behaviour. The fact is that he tilts more towards Bergson's position, which proposes the existence of a virtual species consciousness. In *Difference and Rep-*

etition itself, he appeals to embryology for resources to help clarify the spatiotemporal variation which consciousness is capable of undergoing. 'Embryology already displays the truth that there are systematic vital movements, torsions and drifts, that only the embryo can sustain: an adult would be torn apart by them. There are movements for which one can only be a patient, but the patient in turn can only be a larva' (DR 118). The embryological model of consciousness is being used to demonstrate the spatiotemporal constraints on consciousness. The correlative in an adult of embryological 'experience' is the nightmare: 'A nightmare is perhaps a psychic dynamism that could be sustained neither awake *nor even in dreams*, but only in profound sleep, in a dreamless sleep' (DR 118).

Instinctual Consciousness

Is it possible to explain Bergson's theory of instinct more minimally as a characterization of a mode of consciousness with specific spatiotemporal conditions? Perhaps this would allow us to turn around the question about the heritability of instinct. Why not take Bergson's starting point to be, as in the *Essay on the Immediate Data of Consciousness*, the internal relation of consciousness to duration? Let us start with an epistemological point: duration cannot be articulated by the intelligence, and yet is conscious. There thus exists another cognitive faculty, intuition, alongside intelligence. Intuition, Bergson claims, is the kind of cognition we use in non-intellectual acts of consciousness, such as sympathy, or aesthetic appreciation and creation. For instance, a fundamental feature of artistic creativity is its effort to 'get inside' the object that it depicts (Bergson 1907: 177). There is an 'animism' which can be found in most art forms (although a Bergsonian would have to look hard to find it in contemporary visual art). The artist attempts to grasp 'the intention of life, the simple movement that runs through the lines, that binds them together and gives them significance' – in other words, to *animate* the descriptions, paints and forms that render the shape of the thing depicted. He or she develops this power by 'placing himself back within the object by a kind of sympathy' (ibid.). Perhaps, then, it is possible to read Bergson as inferring *from* intuition *to* instinct in animals. In this case, he would be arguing something different. He would be claiming, at most, that if there *were* a consciousness in animals, then it would not look like intelligent consciousness, but intuitional consciousness. If one adds in support the argument, in the 'Introduction to Metaphysics' of 1903, to the effect that the *reality* of duration 'allows one to pass beyond idealism as well as realism, to affirm the existence of objects inferior and superior to us, though nevertheless in a certain sense interior to us, to make them coexistent without difficulty' (Bergson 1903: 184; trans. modified), then Bergson's line of thought does not seem quite so improbable.

Bergson's definition of intuition as 'instinct that has become disinterested, self-conscious, capable of reflecting upon its object' (176) must therefore be reversed to reveal its true meaning: instinct is intuition become overwhelmed with interest. We do not even know what pure instinctual consciousness is like. Aesthetic consciousness is not really 'instinctual', precisely because it can apply the intuitional mode of apprehension to *any* object. The animistic power of sympathy can take anything as its object. Bergson must thus be arguing from the *universality* in the case of human intuition, back to an intuitional specificity that would be proper to instinct in non-intellectual living beings. If one is prepared to make that inference, then one may further infer that in aesthetic or emotional intuition 'we experience in ourselves – though under a much vaguer form, and one too much penetrated with intelligence – something of what must happen in the consciousness of an insect acting by instinct' (175).

This approach has the benefit of a conception of instinctual consciousness that leads us out of the domain of occult biology. With the somnambulist model of dissociation in mind, a species-specific instinctual consciousness can be hypothesized, in which each species would 'fulfil itself' by realizing a pre-existing schema in an external image. The biological origins of the instinct and its associated triggering stimuli could be accounted for in the mechanical way described by Lorenz. What would be added would be an irreducible, 'transcendental' synthesis of time.[20] When it is not occupied with rudimentary forms of intelligent adaptation, animal consciousness would be the 'single-minded' consciousness that necessarily attends instinct. The animal is a temporal being, with a sense of duration, but its temporal experience is moulded by the primordial form of reminiscence. When a signal (an Innate Releasing Mechanism (IRM)) lights up in the environment, the animal knows what it has to do. It is *that* signal which must be followed up and engaged with, and no other. The animal who responds to courtship displays by pairing off monogamously and the child who attaches to *that* face are both captured by a contingent feature in the environment which nevertheless appears *as if it has already been waiting* for them. The bearer of instincts is enchanted, transfixed, fascinated by the signals which they contemplate and which activate their behaviour. The separation of intelligent consciousness from instinctual consciousness involves the modification of an original temporal structure of consciousness: the more intelligent consciousness prevails, the more instinctual consciousness would be experienced as a 'rupture' in the succession of time, resulting in a primary dissociation. This general ('transcendental') field of instinctual consciousness can never be empirically proven; but there is no reason why it should be ruled out.

In this way we can also make sense of Bergson's quasi-theosophical suggestion that the brain should be viewed as a 'valve' for consciousness, which can be rendered more intelligible by distinguishing between empirical and transcendental levels of analysis. Instinct is the most 'involuted' form of intuition in the sense that it is the most 'single-minded' form of possible consciousness. Nevertheless, intuition is the most 'evolved' form of instinct, insofar as its liberation is only made possible by the evolution, over millions of years, of the brain as valve.

The rationalists too had their 'third kind of knowledge' beyond the understanding, their obscure methods of *mathesis*, which already indicate that the intuition they have in mind is not exactly 'intellectual'. Moreover, these types of cognition did not disappear in post-Kantian modernity, it is rather their spaces were mapped more rigorously. Kant, for instance, isolated the specific power of rational Ideas (problematic concepts without sensible intuitions) and aesthetic Ideas (intuitions without empirical concepts), while Schelling reintroduced mythical thinking and even 'clairvoyance'. Perhaps instinctual consciousness is the basis for a higher type of consciousness, without which intelligent consciousness remains empty?[21]

How to Love the Marvellous

It may be that Bergson's text licenses each of these interpretations of the theory of instinct. It might appear that lovers of the marvellous would be best advised to rely on the last interpretation, but it is more than possible that Deleuze would have disagreed. Certain key passages in *Bergsonism* seem to rely heavily on Bergson's theory of instinct as a 'divining sympathy' – albeit circumspectly. During Deleuze's discussion of Bergson's evolutionism, while he is expounding the abstract notion that evolution involves the actualization of 'levels' that coexist in virtuality, many of the footnotes refer back to Bergson's texts on instinct (B 100–4). Although instinct is only mentioned once in the main text of these pages (ibid.: 103), it is doubtful that these pages make a lot of sense without some reference to Bergson's instinct theory. Citing the passage where Bergson says that 'life goes to work like consciousness and memory', cut off from its latent memories, 'save at one or two points that are of vital concern to the species just arisen', Deleuze adds a footnote suggesting that 'these *points* correspond to the outstanding points that became detached at each level of [organic memory]. Each line of differentiation or actualisation thus constitutes a 'plane [*plan*] of nature' that takes up again in its own way a virtual section or level' (ibid.: 133). How this analogy with memory (with its 'dominant recollections') is supposed to work, given that the 'memory' of evolution is located in the gene, is mysterious.

If Deleuze's biological application of the notion of virtuality rests quietly on an affirmation of Bergson's theory of instinct, then this throws some of today's appropriations of Deleuze's 'biology of the virtual' into question. Can one defend the biological significance of the virtual without appealing to this notion of instinct? It remains the case, though, that Deleuze did not explicitly defend the strong interpretation of Bergson's instinct theory in all its glory. In *Bergsonism* itself, the references to instinct are relegated to the footnotes. In *Instincts and Institutions*, where the theory of divining sympathy is harder to ignore, it is presented without a defence from Deleuze himself.

Perhaps not even the love of the marvellous could save the strong version of Bergson's theory. In 1961, at the end of the somnambulistic 'eight-year hole' in his life, Deleuze published what was to be his final reflection on the notion of instinct, outside of the theory of the 'death instinct' in *Difference and Repetition*: his Jungian fantasia 'From Sacher-Masoch to Masochism'. Deleuze's reflections on instinct lead to another lover of the marvellous, C. G. Jung. This article contains an affirmation of Jung's modification of Bergson's notion of instinct, the theory of archetypes. Bergson is not explicitly mentioned, but it seems that Deleuze is appealing to the Jungian theory of archetypes in order to elaborate the biological component of the Bergsonian unconscious.

Chapter 3

Deleuze and the Jungian Unconscious

At the end of his 'somnambulistic' period (1953–61), Deleuze published his article 'From Sacher-Masoch to Masochism', which contains a description and an endorsement of a new theory of instinct, this time borrowed directly from C. G. Jung: 'Instincts are simply internal perceptions of original Images, apprehended in their own place [*appréhendées là où elles sont*] in layers of variable depth in the unconscious [*les diverses épaisseurs de l'inconscient*]' (SM 131). This statement is a paraphrase of a passage in Jung's lecture 'Instinct and the Unconscious', delivered in London in 1919. In this lecture Jung is to be found explicitly elaborating Bergson's theory of instinct. Indeed, Jung's first use of the concept of the *archetype* emerges out of an interpretation of this Bergsonian theory. We alight upon one of a number of natural routes from Bergsonism towards Jungianism, helping to give intelligibility to Deleuze's affirmation of Jungianism in the 1961 article.[1] Once it is seen that Deleuze was, at least at one point in his philosophical career, a Jungian, his problems with Freud become clearer, as does his whole theory of the unconscious.[2] Deleuze turns to Jung partly in order to develop further Bergson's weird somnambulistic notion of instinct. But Jung's notion of archetype will also provide him with a support for a development of the new theory of consciousness and cognition, derived from Kant, that is presented in *Difference and Repetition.* But in addition it should be remembered that Deleuze began his career with one foot in the esoteric tradition, and had already inherited symbolist tendencies from there. Underground crossovers between Jungianism and occultism went on throughout the twentieth century (cf. Regardie 1964; LaDage 1978); but it was unusual for a philosopher to pursue them.

In what follows we will try to understand in more detail why Deleuze was attracted to Jung's theory of the unconscious. Although Deleuze only explicitly affirms Jung's theory of the archetypal unconscious in one relatively obscure text from 1961, Jungianism continues to shape his theory of the unconscious right up to *Difference and Repetition.* If Deleuze's work on masochism began as Jungian and was explicitly 'depth psychological', this approach was carried over to *Difference and Repetition.* In a 'Note for the Italian Edition of *Logic of Sense*' (1976), Deleuze says:

> my book *Difference and Repetition* . . . aspired to a classical elevation at the same time as to an archaic depth. The sketch I made of a theory of intensity

> was marked by a depth, whether it was true or false: intensity was presented as rising from the depths . . . In *Logic of Sense*, however, the novelty for me consisted in taking things from the surface. The notions remained the same: 'multiplicity', 'singularity', 'intensity', 'event', 'infinite', 'problems', 'paradoxes' and 'proportions' – but reorganised according to this dimension. (TRM 65)

Anyone who has seriously tried to accommodate Deleuze's statements about the unconscious in *Difference and Repetition* with Freudianism will have realized that the two just don't fit. Put Jungianism, in all its 'archaic depth', into the equation, and some illumination finally occurs. However, it also seems clear that Deleuze's path to a theory of the unconscious was fairly tortuous; we will see in this chapter how he brings about a Kantian–Jungian synthesis, based around the notion of 'unconscious Ideas'; in the following chapter, we move from Jung's notion of the symbol through to Kant's account of symbolism and beyond.

After 1961 a flood of publications emerges from Deleuze's hand on numerous subjects: the somnambulistic years are over. Deleuze will go on to excise all explicit reference to Jung in his later studies of masochism, and when he talks about archetypes and primordial images in *Proust and Signs* (1964), he will omit Jung's name. It is inappropriate, however, to talk of these influences as if they were 'skeletons in the cupboard'. In his 1993 valediction 'To Have Done with the Judgment of God', Deleuze remarks that all the writers who carry on in the twentieth century Spinoza's attempt to criticize all notions of 'judgement' (i.e. Nietzsche, Artaud, Lawrence and Kafka) 'could be called symbolists' (CC 134). Deleuze remains a symbolist philosopher, and, as we will see in chapter 4, he even develops a symbolist conception of the unconscious. His popularity as a philosopher arguably still rests on his adept manipulations of symbols. Deterritorialization, nomadism, desiring-machines, smooth space, bodies without organs, rhizomes: these concepts are also symbols, and they can often just function as symbols.

Jung, Psychosis and the Transformation of Libido

Keeping in mind the points where the fracture between Freudian 'psychoanalysis' and Jungian 'analytical psychology' first occurred will help orientate us in what follows. As we have seen Deleuze was not coming from a Freudian background at all. Deleuze will write about Jung after having explored Hume, Bergson, Malinowski and the theory of instincts, along with esotericism; there are no traces of interest in Freud, despite – or, why not, perhaps because of – the overwhelming interest in sexual love in his earliest writings (cf. 'Description of Woman' from 1945; see Faulkner 2002 for context). Other traditions of thought about sexuality and the unconscious appear to have been more alive in 1950s France than they were elsewhere and are today. Paradoxically, therefore, it is Deleuze's embrace of Jungianism that gives us the clues to the origins of Deleuze's ideas about Freud and psychoanalysis.

For a number of years before meeting Freud Jung had been working at the largest mental hospital in Switzerland, where his patients were mostly working-class psychotics. In 1907 he cemented his friendship and collaboration with Freud by presenting him with his *Psychology of Dementia Praecox* (1906), in which he applied Freud's concepts of repression, substitution and displacement, and compensatory wish-fulfilment to the flight of ideas in schizophrenia. Jung refused to follow Freud the whole way regarding the sexual aetiology of psychopathology. Following a period of intense collaboration with Freud over the next few years, Jung became deeply immersed in the study of mythology and began to become convinced that some of his psychotic patients' fantasies and deliria contained mythological motifs which could not be explained in terms of 'cryptomnesia'.[3] In the meantime, his dissatisfaction with Freud's conception of libido began to increase. The initial disagreement between Freud and Jung blew up when these issues converged at one point, i.e., the sexuality of psychotics.

In 1911, Freud had attempted to further extend the reach of psychoanalysis by applying it to a case of paranoid psychosis, in his famous analysis of Judge Schreber's *Memoirs of My Nervous Illness.* This was to be a crucial test case for psychoanalysis: could a serious psychotic illness be explained, as neuroses had been by Freud, strictly in terms of sexual aetiology? In his *Three Essays on the Theory of Sexuality,* Freud had argued that psychoneuroses invariably involved a 'regression' of libido back into earlier, infantile organizations of the libido. Libido had become 'dammed-up', initially due to present lack of success in finding a suitable love-object. Dammed up libido has no choice but to flow back along older, earlier channels 'upstream'.[4] In the face of a current lack of outlet, it returns to any strong fixations it had developed at an earlier infantile libidinal stage. Sexuality has a peculiar status in the process of organic development in higher animals, because its organic function is kept 'in reserve' until puberty, unlike the ego-drives, which develop continuously from birth; it is thus left to its own devices, as it were, and occupies itself with autoerotic satisfaction, based around fantasy-activity (SE 12: 222). Therefore strong fixations at early sexual stages are possible, thus providing established channels for any libido that is repressed when the organic function of sexuality is set in motion in puberty. Fixations at oral and anal stages can become reactivated in this way, initiating a variety of compensating neurotic behaviours (neurosis as the 'negative of perversion'). Freud's hypothesis about libido permits him to excavate, identify and articulate early sexual stages in the child on the basis of observations of neurotics. He admits that no amount of observation of children can tell us about what goes on in the postulated oral and anal stages of sexuality. We can really only read the psychic character of these stages back from their manifestations in adult neurotics.

In his analysis of Schreber, Freud attempts to extend this model to psychosi by developing further his account of the earliest sexual stages. He postulate further stage, on the threshold of the transformation of autoerotism to ob choice:

> There comes a time in the development of the individual at which he unifies his sexual drives (which have hitherto been engaged in auto-erotic activities) in order to obtain a love-object; and he begins by taking himself as his own love-object, and only subsequently proceeds from this to the choice of some person other than himself as his object. (SE 12: 60–1)

Freud calls this stage 'narcissism', although he does not develop his views on this subject until he is forced into doing so by Jung's critique. What Freud is concerned with here is the presence of a stage after narcissism, in which the individual moves to 'the choice of an external object with similar genitals'. In order to move from homosexual to heterosexual object-choice, a 'deflection' of sexual object and aim must occur. As far as the aim is concerned, homosexual libido can become attached to the ego-drives and thus channel itself into 'social drives, thus contributing an erotic factor to friendship and comradeship . . . and to the love of mankind in general'. This is an essential component of the move to heterosexual object-choice. In paranoid psychosis, Freud suggests, the failure of heterosexual object-choice precipitates an immediate regression back to the previous homosexual stage (to which the patient must also already be disposed, due to constitution or early fixation), thus sexualizing the social drives. In order to protect himself from this influx of homosexual libido, the individual 'detaches himself' from 'the people in his environment and the external world generally', which precipitates a further regression back to the immediately preceding stage of narcissism; 'the liberated libido becomes attached to the ego, and is used for the aggrandizement of the ego' or megalomania (SE 12: 71, 70, 72). Paranoiac delusions are explained by Freud as a distorted attempt to return to the external world after the period of narcissistic introversion, or, in Schreberian terms, after the 'end of the world'. After having explained paranoia, Freud goes on to suggest that in schizophrenia, 'the regression extends not merely to narcissism . . . but to a complete abandonment of the object-love and a return to infantile auto-erotism' (SE 12: 77). Hallucinations and deliria in schizophrenia are likewise products of the attempt at a 'reconstruction' of reality.

Freud straight away confessed doubt about his own hypothesis that a withdrawal of libido was sufficient to effect a psychotic 'end of the world'. He saw that if psychosis, which involves a radical breakdown of the patient's relation to reality, was to be explained in this way, that would imply that the ego, the self-preserving agent responsible for a relation to reality, itself already depended on the presence of libido in order to function. And this would mean the collapse of Freud's distinction in kind between ego- and libidinal processes, the reality and pleasure principles. There were two ways out: one, to venture that 'what we call possession of the libido (interest from erotic sources) coincides with interest in general' (SE 12: 74; cited in CW B: 126); this outcome would signify failure for Freud, as the idea that psychosis might have specifically sexual aetiology would be refuted. The alternative was to boldly claim that the constitution of reality by the ego was indeed effected by some transformation of libido in its fully sexual sense.[5] Freud proceeded to take the latter path in his 1914 paper on narcissism, where he argued for the existence of an original 'ego-libido', which puts out its cathexes onto 'object-libido'.[6] Jung embraced the other alternative we mentioned: the concept of libido itself must be expanded to include non-sexual energy.

Transformations and Symbols of the Libido was published in two parts in 1911 and 1912 and marked Jung's secession from Freudian psychoanalysis.[7] In it Jung contended against the latter alternative that 'reality is not understood to be a sexual function' (CW B: 128). He recoiled from the idea that the 'sense of reality' was generated from within a purely sexual dialectic. For one thing, 'if that were so, the introversion of libido in the strict sense must have as a result the loss of reality in the neuroses, and, indeed, a loss which could be compared with that of dementia praecox'. Neurotics, despite their inhibitions, symptoms and anxieties, still have a firm, perhaps only intersubjective, criterion of 'reality'.

Jung begins his presentation of his theory of libido with an attack on Freud's concept of infantile sexuality, and an argument for a distinct 'nutritive' or 'vegetative' phase of libido, prior to its transformation into sexuality (CW B: 129; CW 4: 102–11). He had rejected Freud's theory of infantile sexuality from the beginning (CW 3: 4). While he recognized the importance of sexuality for adolescence and maturity, and their corresponding disorders, he rejected the way Freud characterized the desires and pleasures of the infant in terms of anal, oral and genital sexuality. It is indeed evident that the infant gets pleasure from the whole array of expressions of pre-genital sexuality, including the oral drive in thumb-sucking for instance. It is also evident that the infant gets pleasure from sucking at the breast. But just because the infant has many ways of obtaining pleasure from the deployment of its sexual libido does not mean that the pleasure the infant gets from sucking the breast is also sexual. It is a pure hypothesis to state that sexual libido is already at work in the sucking of the breast. But if this cannot be proven, then one should not attempt to force the issue by simply redefining pleasure as sexual pleasure. We should thus draw back from assuming that the sexual drive is present from the first for the child. It could be that the pleasure of sucking at the breast really is just nutritive; there might be an enjoyment specific to eating and drinking (cf. CW B: 129; CW 4: 102–11).

Jung points out that in classical times the Latin word *libido* had the more general sense of 'passionate desire' (CW 4: 111), or simply 'desire' (CW 4: 125; CW B 123). He cites Cicero, who defines 'libido' as desire 'divorced from reason and too violently aroused . . . unbridled desire, which is found in all fools' (*Tusculan Disputations*, IV, vi. 12); and Sallust, who discusses youths who invested more libido 'in handsome arms and war horses than in harlots and revelry' (*The War with Catiline*, VII). Before being sexual, libido is passion, and usually passion for something extravagant. It is desire or *interest*, psychic absorption in something beyond the call of practicality; although it may manifest itself as sexual, even within sexual libido there may be something that points beyond the excitatory aim and the stimulating object or fantasy. The whole body can be host to this 'psychic energy'; in a Bergsonian vein, Jung in turn opts to 'enlarge the narrower concept of psychic energy to a broader one of life-energy, which includes "psychic energy" as a specific part' (CW 8: 17, 30; CW 4: 248).[8]

Deleuze's and Guattari's theory that desire must be articulated in terms of intensities is not so far from the Jungian theory of psychic energy. On the one hand, they condemn Jung for his 'idealist deviation' (AO 128) from the truth that Freud did uncover: the primacy of sexuality in the unconscious. But on the other hand, they are generally happier using the term 'desire' (as Jung had first suggested), and many of the examples of intensive desire they use completely repel being interpreted in terms of sexuality. 'The satisfaction the handyman experiences when he plugs something into an electric socket or diverts a stream of water can scarcely be explained in terms of "playing mommy and daddy", or by the pleasure of violating the taboo' (AO 7), and it would be obviously pushing it to explain it in terms of sexuality as well. Given that *Anti-Oedipus* rejects the Lacanian proposal that desire is sexual in the specific sense that it is essentially constructed around a primordial loss, Deleuze's and Guattari's use of the term 'sexuality' is open to the charge (again already made by Jung against Freud) that it rests on a mere semantic manipulation. After reviewing the construction of Malone's 'stone-sucking machine' in Beckett's *Trilogy*, Deleuze and Guattari themselves ask 'where in this entire circuit do we find the production of sexual pleasure' (AO 3)? In *Dialogues* (1977) Deleuze returns to his previous position: 'We do not believe in general that sexuality has the role of an infrastructure in the assemblages of desire, not that it constitutes an energy capable of transformation or of neutralisation and sublimation. Sexuality can only be thought of as one flux among others, entering into conjunction with other fluxes' (D 101). It is not clear that Deleuze ever really left behind the most fundamental Jungian principles.

One would be forgiven for assuming that Jung would therefore go on to conclude that there is no relation between psychotic libido and the constitution of reality. Since Jung had contended that 'reality is not a sexual function', one might have expected him to maintain the difference in kind between libidinal and reality functions; the 'loss of reality' would have nothing to do with a withdrawal of libido. But such an assumption would involve a premature intrusion of common sense. Instead Jung goes in the opposite direction: the constitution of reality *can* be explained in terms of a transformation of libidinal processes, *because* libido itself is not purely sexual. Libido is vegetative, sexual, and can become desexualized in psychosis. The individual is first of all a biological reality, and any 'sense of reality' that emerges for itself is a result of events in its ontogenesis. 'Reality' is not even necessarily constituted for the developing human being all at once, and may be built up by a set of transformations of neutral libidinal energy. Jung's explanation of how this happens takes the psychoanalytic theory of reality in an entirely different direction to the trajectories produced by Freud's turn to the primacy of narcissism. Jung posits an original, biologically endogenous movement from nutritive self-preservation (building-up and reproduction of the individual body) to the instinct for the preservation of the species (sexual reproduction).[9] These are biological phases of a general formative instinct for 'reproduction', of which the subjective side is felt as 'desire' (CW B: 130). 'With the development of the body there are successively opened new spheres of application for the libido' (CW B: 132). Jung's reconstruction is fairly obscure and *Naturphilosophische* at this point, and he is vague about the levels at which this process is situated: is he presenting evolutionary arguments about functions, or descriptions of endogenous individual development, or metaphysical arguments about the nature of desire?[10]

Jung sometimes writes as if the third phase, in which a 'function of reality' is first born, corresponds to a 'desexualization' which is itself merely a still further stage in the endogenous development of libido.[11] However, Jung remains, on the surface, strictly Freudian about which aspect of sexuality is responsible for this turn. It is the appearance, within the domain of sexual libido, of a particular portion of *incestuous* libido, that triggers the need for transformation. The emergence of a reality-function thus occurs due to a limit that is discovered *within* the field of sexuality. It is ironic, in fact, that Jung is known for his criticisms of Freud's 'pansexualism' and for his insistence on 'spirituality' as opposed to sexuality, when he spends most of the text of *Transformations and Symbols* showing how everything that constitutes humanity is the result of an original repression of the sexual desire for incest with the mother. Far from being a retreat from the Freudian project of relating human culture in its entirety to sexuality, we should see that Jung's text goes further than Freud in attributing the emergence of the reality-function itself to the transformation of incestuous desire. However, where Freud in *Totem and Taboo* relates historical manifestations of the incest taboo to a universal infantile *desire* for incest with the mother, Jung comes to argue against inferring the nature of a desire from the historical existence of a law that represses it.[12] What the child desires from the mother, what the law forbids, and the mother's own intentions, conscious or unconscious, are all quite distinct and neither can be inferred from the others. Further, even if the repression of incestuous libido were the *trigger* of the emergence of the reality-function, it is the mechanism of regression onto pre-sexual terrain that explains that function. Against Freud's insistence on one general line of (sexual) libidinal development, Jung postulates *two* initial endogenous phases of the libido, the pre-sexual nutritive and sexual, with different aims and objects. Once such a duality is in place, the possibility arises of a 'primary' regression. Jung's proposal, therefore, is that the third phase of the libido, desexualization, *is originally constituted by a regression from the sexual phase back onto the pre-sexual, as a result of a resistance to some aspect of sexuality*. It is 'by a regression to the pre-sexual material [that] the libido becomes quasi-desexualised' (CW B: 151).

Jung's argument here also has the advantage of filling a gap in Freud's theory. For Freud, the encounter with the barrier against incest is immediately followed by a 'latency period' of sexuality, in which the process of sublimation and adaptation to social reality is allowed to continue relatively unperturbed until puberty. Only then does libido really encounter the risk of regressing back onto older paths, when a damming-up of sexual libido causes a regression onto forbidden incestuous desires, which in turn push the libido back into older (oral and anal) libidinal formations. Jung sees a missed opportunity here: why not use regression from incestuous libido to explain the shift to the reality-principle itself? The function of reality would be produced by an original transformation of the energy of incestuous desire so that it can be released in the contemplation of an object that is now virtual: the vegetal, nutritive mother. In Jung, there is no mysterious libidinal latency stage: rather there is an initial birth of the reality-function, quite peculiar to itself, in which reality appears in a first 'animistic' guise, charged by the repressed symbol of the mother: the world as symbol.

The transformation of libido produces a corresponding transformation in the way the world appears to the primal human being. Perhaps the reason why it is so hard to remember one's childhood is because one's libidinal map is plotted completely differently at the various stages of childhood, and the move to new libidinal investments is equivalent for the child to stepping into a new world. The repression of incestuous desire for the mother is the most important of these transformations, because the repression of sexual libido is this time not aided by any endogenous, self-preservative tendencies. In the beginning, says Jung, symbols do not yet appear in abstract form, but appear as the rites and ceremonies themselves, conducted under the rule of 'magical thinking', or omnipotence of thoughts (CW B: 48). 'A ceremony is magical so long as it does not result in effective work but preserves the state of expectancy. In that case the energy is canalized into a new object and produces a new dynamism, which in turn remains magical so long as it does not create effective work' (CW B: 46). Whereas in Freud, omnipotence of thoughts occurs in the child when 'they satisfy their wishes in a hallucinatory manner' (SE 13: 83–4), for Jung ritual activities specifically involve the redirection of libidinal activities onto new objects. Jung describes the desexualization of libido by means of the investment of images and symbols as producing a novel state of *expectancy*, in which 'the mind is fascinated and possessed by . . . the newly invested object' (CW 8: 46).

Rather than being a hallucinatory wish-fulfilment, magical thinking is an essential component in the transformation of the *Umwelt* into a world of symbols. It is the first step in the *animation* of a 'reality' beyond the reproductive circuit of nature. Symbolic thinking, it turns out, is precisely the means by which a 'canalization', 'transition', or 'bridge' (CW B: 137) is made out of the domain of immediately sexual libido (or in Freudian terms, the pleasure principle) into a 'beyond' of nature, a transcendent space or ontological clearing within which something called 'reality' can be constituted. Jung's prime examples concern the historical genesis of the reality-function rather than its genesis in the psychic life of the child. His claim is that the ancient material elements, such as earth and fire, first become isolated for the human mind by serving as conduits for repressed sexual libido. Might not the origin of fire lie in the redirection of repressed incestuous libido into the rhythmic boring of holes into wood, or rubbing together of sticks, giving rise to the generation of fire as a by-product? The material element, fire, is thus an actual indirect product of displaced sexual energy.[13] The discovery of the powers of material reality, the transition to the threshold of reality, thus coincides with the emergence of the symbol. If reality originally appears as 'animistic', endowed with mythical powers, this is because it comes into being through the repression of the mother-image. Reality is thus immediately symbolic, and is a by-product of repressed incestuous libido. *Nature itself* (that is, nurturing nature) now emerges as the vast, new symbolic object of a desexualized libido: no longer just nature as nutritive *Umwelt*, but nature as numinous symbol of the mother (*Mater natura*).

Jung is concerned to depict a shift from the symbolic approach to reality to the emergence of a 'directed' kind of thought, which 'adjusts itself to actual conditions, where we . . . imitate the succession of objectively real things'. This directed thinking is now opposed to a 'non-directed', or 'merely associative thinking . . . *a dream or phantasy thinking*' (CW B: 18–20).[14] The shift corresponds to a sort of progressive *de-animation* of reality, an attenuation of its vital symbolic substrate: the symbolic origins of reality now appear as the object of *mere* 'phantasy-thinking'. This capacity for directed thinking intensifies with historical development: 'directed thinking was not always as developed as it is at present . . . The directed thinking of our time is a more or less modern acquisition, which was lacking in earlier times' (ibid.).[15]

Jung develops an epochal account of history derived from sources such as Bachofen and Creuzer. Deleuze concurs that it is impossible to understand a perversion such as masochism 'without taking up some strange historical perspectives' (SM 127); incredibly, he seems to endorse a Jungian, epochal view of history, with Anima and Animus as the main protagonists. In Bachofen's epochal narrative, a primeval 'Mother-right' is eventually replaced by a phallic Law that gained ascendancy in Greece and Rome.[16] Masoch was an avid reader of Bachofen, often making allusions to 'an epoch of beautiful Nature, to an archaic world presided over by Venus–Aphrodite, where the fleeting relationship between woman and man has pleasure between equal partners as its only law'. Why was the primitive, hetaeric and incestuous mode of existence repressed? As we have said, Jung himself was ambivalent about this, and only gained a consistent, if complex position later, after *Transformations and Symbols.* So at this point, we can lend an ear to Masoch's interpretation of the repression of incest. Incestuous existence was not repressed at all, he says; rather, 'beautiful nature was thrown out of equilibrium by a climatic catastrophe or a glacial upheaval' (SM 127). Only 'the catastrophe of a glacial epoch' can account for 'both the repression of sensuality and the triumphant rise of severity' (M 53).[17] On Deleuze's and Masoch's fanciful account, matriarchal law was replaced by a brief, vanishing interregnum which is immortalized by masochists for centuries afterwards: 'the Demetrian era dawned among the Amazons and established a strict gynocratic and agricultural order; the swamps were drained; the father or husband now acquired a certain status but he still remained under the domination of the woman' (M 53). But this epoch of 'precarious splendour and perfection' could not last and the Amazonian order was overcome by force, with patriarchal law, which from now on prohibits incest with the mother, under the threat of castration. Deleuze concludes his epoch history ominously: 'He who unearths the Anima enters on this regression: all the more terrible for being repressed, the Anima will know how to turn patriarchal structures to its own advantage and rediscover the power of the devouring Mother' (SM 127).

Psychosis therefore is above all an anachronism. What happens in psychosis is a regression to the first phase of the function of reality. In psychosis, Jung claims, '*a dropping away of the last acquisition of the function of reality (or adaptation) must of necessity be replaced by an earlier mode of adaptation*' (CW B: 136). It cannot be a regression from a moment of sexual repression back to an earlier sexual stage of omnipotent, self-enclosed fantasy-thinking. It involves a regression which leads back from a secondary, historical function of reality to an *original*, 'mythical' function of reality, in which the energy of sexual libido was redeployed by magical means. For Freud, the psychotic is taking radical measures against sexual anxiety, and in particular against anxiety about homosexuality. If there is sexuality in psychosis, counters Jung, it is not like normal or neurotic sexuality, but is rather a component of a *libido* distinguished by its extravagance, which can become unchecked by intelligent, reflective consciousness. From the latter point of view, psychosis is an anachronistic recollection of a nature imbedded with symbols. It is as if psychosis involves the appearance of individual symbolic systems, cast adrift from any collective value that the symbolic framing of reality might have had in earlier, archaic historical epochs.

But conversely is it possible to foresee a complete de-animation of nature, when the remnants of the symbolic origins of reality are entirely forced underground into fantasy thinking? The first level of reality would have vanished from the human being's objective relationships to the world, and would be completely internalized in the unconscious. In that case, the normal human being would not be an inverted pervert, as Freud thought, but a secret psychotic. Both Jung and Deleuze consider (albeit for different reasons) modernity itself as necessarily pathogenic, as an ever-expanding factory for the production of psychotics. A new historical epoch is dawning. As capitalism leaves us defenceless against our inner schizophrenia, ever more prone to delirium, a new libidinal progression can only come about through a new regression (cf. CW 8: 32–40). There is no longer anything anachronistic about schizophrenia; its motley garb and strange speech are signs of a being from the future, a messenger from distant lunar societies. In the language of *A Thousand Plateaus*, the Earth itself is deterritorialized, becoming a satellite for the reception of cosmic forces. The schizophrenic has been forced against their will to become a sorcerer, a conjuror of forces; and conversely it is possible to learn again from schizophrenics how to be sorcerers. According to *Anti-Oedipus*, the schizophrenic is 'as close as possible to matter, to a burning, living centre of matter' (AO 19); they have entered, without knowing how, an unbearable state of 'celibate misery and glory experienced to the fullest, like a cry suspended between life and death, an intense feeling of transition, states of pure naked intensity stripped of all shape and form' (AO 18).

Neurosis and Psychosis

The neurotic too cannot help falling back into the first, childhood plane of reality, but in a way that is completely different from the Freudian concept of regression. Jung argues that Freud is correct to say that neuroses are triggered in adolescence and young adulthood by failures to find an actual love object. For Freud this failure results in the *reactivation* of the unconscious traces left over from the Oedipus complex. The actual social repression of adolescent sex is the opportunity for repressed, unconscious incestuous fixations to resurface and feed off suppressed actual libido, causing neurotic symptoms. Jung, however, believed that Freud had misinterpreted the situation. He is sceptical about whether personal traumas in the case-histories of neurotics have any solid causal role. His arguments against Freud on this point are always about whether sexuality is a *sufficient* cause for neurosis. He never denies sexual problems are central in the majority of the neuroses of the young. His problem is that the sexual aspect of the neurosis is mostly likely to have originated in adolescence (when the sexual *instinct* emerges), and therefore that if the cause of sexual neuroses is to be sought in childhood, then it might well be non-sexual.

In his 1912 lectures on 'The Theory of Psychoanalysis' Jung took up Freud's retraction (in 1906 in 'My Views on the Part Played by Sexuality in the Aetiology of the Neuroses') of his earlier view that actual historical traumas were causally productive of neurosis. Freud had stated that in fact 'the patient's phantasies (or imaginary memories) were mostly produced in puberty', using 'memories of the subject's own sexual activity (infantile masturbation)' (SE 7: 274). Jung takes Freud's qualification of his trauma theory as further proof of the tenuousness of the idea of the sexual aetiology of the neuroses. He objected to the trauma theory on the grounds that the incompatibility of sexual ideas with the ego cannot account for all traumas, let alone all neuroses. We have seen that he objects to the infantile sexuality theory because not all pleasure is sexual. But he also takes Freud's abandonment of the seduction theory and his consequent embrace of the notion that fantasies are fixated rather than real events to weaken his argument for the primacy of sexuality. For if Freud had admitted that fantasies are mostly produced in puberty, then one cannot be sure they have anything to do with infancy. Jung claims that the hysteric 'stage-manages' her regressions, in order to inveigle the analyst into minute and intimate preoccupation with the details of her life: she wants the analyst too to enter her fantasy-world (CW 4: 161–2). An adolescent girl might only start to feel uncomfortable around her father when her sexual libido is blocked from fulfilment in the outside world; the result of her frustration is that the father's behaviour begins to be interpreted as sexual.[18] Jung also argued that there are many cases of neurosis in which symptoms are entirely absent until a breakdown comes about. A 'critical attitude' (CW 4: 246) to neurosis was therefore necessary.[19]

If there is no sufficient reason for sexual repression at the infantile level, then we should not necessarily look for other possible traumas at the infantile level, but rather look at the possibility that, in order to be seen as traumatic, certain *retrospective* conditions have to be fulfilled. The symbolism of the earlier event has to be relevant to the current problem. The present has to be a critical moment: 'it is usually the moment when a new psychological adjustment, that is, a new adaptation, is demanded' (ibid.). It could therefore be that it is a failure of adaptation *in the present* that reactivates the dormant memory. Psychopathological regression must always be seen in the first place as a regression *from* an adolescent or adult problem in real life. We are not *determined* by original traumas as Freud says; if a trauma exists in the past, then it can only exert its influence on our present by its resonance with our current problem. From adolescence onwards, we are tempted to find our way back to our past libidinal investments in search of alibis for our present failure to resolve current libidinal problems.

But even in neurosis repressed sexual libido can be channelled back into the fundamental, animistic layer of reality, providing progressive escape routes for the libido. In 'From Sacher-Masoch to Masochism' Deleuze writes that 'Jung can therefore reproach Freud for having left in the dark both the real dangers present in a neurosis and the treasures it can contain. He said that Freud had a *deprecating* outlook on neuroses: "it is nothing but . . ."' (SM 133). Deleuze then cites two passages from Jung: 'Hidden in the neurosis is a bit of still undeveloped personality, a precious fragment of the psyche lacking which a man is condemned to resignation, bitterness [and everything else that is hostile to life]. A psychology of neurosis that sees only the negative elements empties out the baby with the bath-water'; 'in neurosis resides our most relentless enemy *or our best friend*.'[20] Deleuze concludes that 'this is not to rule out that a neurosis might be amenable to a Freudian interpretation up to a certain point, but this interpretation loses its rights as soon as one begins to penetrate into the more profound strata of the unconscious, or equally as the neurotic develops and is transformed or reawakened with age'. A Freudian interpretation of neurosis has no validity in two types of case. First, where individuals are 'alienated' in primordial Images which 'lead a dangerously autonomous life'. Deleuze intends masochism to serve as an example of this, where the libidinal life of the individual is completely absorbed in the production of a ritual sexual theatre; but obsessives and hysterics also have their theatres (cf. DI 108). 'There are adult neurotics who are burdened by "Images" *which transcend every experience*: their problem is to be reconciled with themselves, that is, to reintegrate in their personality those very parts which they have neglected to develop' (SM 133). Although Deleuze will soon cease to use the language of 'reconciliation' of 'reintegration' (which, among other things, sits uneasily with his esoteric theory of the eternal return; DR 241–4), the notion that there are Ideas, images, and symbols which 'transcend [*dépasse*] every experience' remains fundamental for his conception of the process of individuation in *Difference and Repetition* and beyond.

The notion of a 'second birth', rebirth or renaissance is fundamental to Deleuze from the beginning. The notion has an esoteric background, going back to Jakob Böhme's theosophy, and beyond into ancient religious ideas of the transmigration of souls (DR 241–4). In *Anarchy and Hierarchy of Knowledge*, Malfatti suggests that the 'transfigurations' brought about by natural and artificial somnambulism are behind 'the idea of rebirth (*palingenesis*) among the Indians, who, as one knows, describe themselves as twice born' (Malfatti 1845: 5).[21] Large tracts of Jung's *Transformations and Symbols* (the work of Jung's to which Deleuze most frequently refers) are devoted to the exposition of a core myth of rebirth which Jung discovers in the background of the mythologies handed down by history. The myth is of a hero who enters on a 'night sea journey' into the maternal womb in order to be reborn again in a new morning. For Jung, this myth records the very process that we have recounted of an emergence of desexualized libido into human reality. But this myth revolves around an essential fantasy of devoration and rebirth that emerges in proportion to the weight attached to the maternal imago as *image of the past*. Either the hero becomes psychotic and reanimates nature, or the libido 'sinks back into its own depths, into the source from which it has gushed forth, and turns back to that point of cleavage, the umbilicus, through which it once entered into this body . . . then man has become for the world above a phantom, then he practically dead or desperately ill' (CW B: 283–4). 'The world of memories' and fantasy themselves then substitute altogether for the 'upper world', and block the progressive movement of sexual libido. Either way, the hero faces the devouring mother, who is 'not only devouring insofar as her image is repressed, but in and by herself' (SM 130). The unconscious fantasies that emerge on this course all tend to an apocalyptic terminus: 'The wish is that the black water of death might be the water of life; that death, with its cold embrace, might be the mother's womb, just as the sea devours the sun, but brings it forth again out of the maternal womb' (CW B: 213). Deleuze says that 'Jung demonstrated that incest signifies the second birth, that is to say a heroic birth, a parthenogenesis (entering a second time into the maternal breast in order to be born anew or to become a child again)' (SM 129). In Jung, incest has become something quite different to what it is in Freud. Incest is not even *repressed* into the unconscious; rather, it is a *symbol* of rebirth. We are not unconscious of deep incestuous desires because they are repressed; we are unconscious of the *meaning or sense* of the symbol of incest.

The problem of the relation of symbols to libidinal forces cannot be solved in terms of libidinal economy alone. Where Lacanian psychoanalysis attempted to resolve the relation of energetics to symbolism through recourse to structural linguistics and anthropology, Jung and Deleuze mine the older epistemological tradition of Kantian philosophy in order to account for the validity of the autonomous space of symbols. What follows is an introduction to Jung's theory of the unconscious, and a reconstruction of its relations to Kantianism, as indicated by Deleuze. As already suggested, from 1961 onwards, Jungianism shapes Deleuze's theory of the unconscious right up to *Difference and Repetition*, which continues to resonate with a Jungian 'archaic depth' (TRM 65). For most of the 1960s, Deleuze's investigations into the unconscious revolve around a Kantian–Jungian synthesis, based on the notion of 'unconscious Ideas', but also pulling various esoteric themes into its orbit. In the subsequent chapter, we follow how Deleuze proceeds from Jung's notion of the symbol through to Kant's account of symbolism, to a radically novel conception of the psychotic basis of all symbolic reality, which, as we have seen, was the fundamental theme of *Transformations and Symbols of the Libido*.

Jung on the Unconscious

The term 'unconscious' has a series of distinct meanings in Jung. Later on in this chapter we will see that there is an important 'transcendental' component to Jung's theory of the unconscious. However, before we encounter the Jungian transcendental unconscious, we should draw attention to a series of *relations of the ego to the unconscious*. The process of individuation, claims Jung, is structured by a series of phases of the development of consciousness, in which the unconscious is encountered at each point in a different form. The child has a somnambulistic consciousness close to animal instinctual consciousness but mediated by human institutions; as an adolescent the unconscious becomes the 'shadow'; during the love-relationship, the unconscious becomes, as anima or animus, the *end* of activity; finally the unconscious reveals itself as what Jung calls 'Self', as a *superior Other* within the mind itself. The unconscious appears as a paradoxical unknown 'Self': 'the ego is, by definition, subordinate to the Self and is related to it like a part to the whole' (CW 9i: 5).

As a zero pole, Jung posits an 'absolute unconscious' to designate the totality of everything that is unconscious. 'Consciousness is like a surface or a skin on a vast unconscious area of unknown extent' (CW 18: 8). For Jung, the unconscious 'includes not only repressed contents, but all psychic material that lies below the threshold of consciousness' (CW 7: 128). The unconscious is not restricted to repressed mental content (as in Freud). 'I define the unconscious as the totality of all psychic phenomena that lack the quality of consciousness' (CW 8: 133). In *Aion*, Jung simply describes the unconscious as 'the unknown in the inner world', in parallel to the 'unknown in the outer world' (CW 9ii: 3). This unconscious no longer has the 'transcendental' status of the previous two versions. Even if one accepts a strong Kantian position about the self-conscious subject, then one must accept that 'empirically' it always finds its limit 'when it comes up against the *unknown.* This consists of everything we do not know, which, therefore, is not related to the ego as the centre of the field of consciousness' (ibid.). The unknown outer world, however, is of less importance than the unknown inner world, which can also be thought of as the Bergsonian 'virtual' aspect of the mind.

But for Bergson, Janet and Jung, the unconscious was also fundamentally defined in a *negative relation* to the 'species activity' of consciousness, in a way that has no parallel in Freud. Consciousness for these thinkers has a biological function, to attend to the environment for practical purposes. Consciousness is 'attention to life'. Therefore what is unconscious is always unconscious *in relation to an active, future-oriented ego.* What is unconscious at any given moment is what is inessential for the practical purposes of the ego; dreaming must be inhibited simply because it incapacitates the activity of the active ego. The unconscious thus can be taken as strictly 'relative' to the ego. But this immediately gives rise to a paradox: how can one *have a cognitive relation* to what is unconscious? We have just seen that the unconscious is 'the totality of all psychic phenomena that lack the quality of consciousness' (CW 8: 133). If the unconscious is entirely unknown, then we cannot enter into relation with it. Thus 'whatever we have to say about the unconscious is what the conscious mind says about it' (CW 18: 7).[22] The Jungian unconscious contains an extra reflexive level absent from the Freudian unconscious. For Freud, what is unconscious is what is repressed, and one is conscious only of the 'derivatives' of the unconscious idea. For Jung, if one is obviously never conscious of the unconscious, then one nevertheless is conscious *that* one has an unconscious, and that in itself can be important. The unconscious enters into relation with the ego by appearing to the ego *as* the unconscious. Thus Jung says that dream-figures more often than not actually represent 'The Unconscious'. The major Jungian psychic 'agencies' – shadow, anima, animus, Self – are all symbols *of* the unconscious. They are distinguished by the different modes of relationship they present between the ego and the unconscious.

In his 'Tavistock Lectures' (1935), Jung gives an account of the differentiation of consciousness, passing through the various relations of ego to unconscious. Consciousness first arises in an instinctual setting, attached to instinctual adaptability. 'In early childhood we are unconscious; the most important functions of an instinctive nature are unconscious, and consciousness is rather the product of the unconscious. It is a condition which demands a violent effort. You get tired from being conscious . . . It is an almost unnatural effort' (CW 18: 10). Consciousness is derived from 'the intensity of feeling'.[23] Hence there is a primary *affective* consciousness. Because children are still instinctual, it is difficult to say that they have an unconscious: rather their conscious activity is, as Ruyer would say, a manifestation of the competent actualization of their instincts. Up until the end of the first decade of life, the child has a peculiar kind of consciousness, 'a consciousness without any consciousness of the *ego*'. But then, suddenly 'for the first time in their lives they know that they themselves are experiencing, that they are looking back over a past in which they can remember things happening but cannot remember that they were in them' (CW 18: 8). The ego first arises during a sudden, profound experience of division: my previous states belong to me, although I don't remember them *as* mine. The seeds for dissociation are thus set up as soon as I identify myself as 'I'. As Kant saw, the 'I think' will never coincide with the 'ego' or 'self'.

The Other does not first appear as superior. It appears first in the form of a shadow of irrationality over the child's attempt to order its priorities. The form taken is the negative of the form taken by egoic consciousness. The unconscious first appears as what is excluded by the adaptive performances of the ego. If the tasks of the conscious ego are narrow and adaptive, the unconscious appears as an adversary. Thus at a certain crucial stage in life (from adolescence to early adulthood), the repressed contents of the mind are indeed the dominant face of the unconscious. The potential for introversion is present at every stage of life, but Jung accepts that the stage of the sexual instinct is a particularly vulnerable moment. In Jung's view, Freud fails to see that the sexual aetiology of many neuroses is connected to the period of adolescence, when the world of introverted fantasy becomes flooded with the sexual energy that is denied immediate expression in the actual world. The passage from childhood to adolescence has involved the gradual acquisition of skill and competence in practical matters, and the kicking-in of the sexual instinct represents the first real challenge to the ego. Where Freud saw the guilt tied to masturbation as due to the re-emergence of incestuous fantasies, for Jung the more important point is that the ensuing retreat into onanistic introversion is itself productive of dissociation. As far as the organization of the psyche is concerned, the important factor is not the sexual drive itself, but the extent of the dissociation produced by the emergence of the sexual instinct, which opposes the synthetic activities of intelligent consciousness. Moreover, the dissociating power of instinct does not only appear in the form of masturbation: other 'thematic' forms of the sexual instinct (such as rivalry or courtship behaviours) might also manifest exaggerated, dissociated characteristics, that could enter into conflict with the ego.

From adolescence onwards, when the opposition between ego and the unconscious has first been established, the unconscious is the 'shadow'. What Freud called 'incompatible ideas' thus first of all appear as the ideas of an incompatible 'self'. The shadow is another *self*, Jekyll to Hyde: another lives inside me. This is of course made possible by the dissociating, somnambulistic capabilities of consciousness. Because dissociation is attended by a peculiar though narrow state of consciousness (this is what Freud overlooked), the shadow is first conceived as a splinter psyche.[24]

The way to overcome the shadow is not to repress it, but to attempt to bring it to the fullest realisation in the external world. By being incarnated in reality, it loses the features it had accrued through being inhibited, and lights up the world from within. When a subject seeks to realise the sexual instinct in reality, it is guided by a pre-existing image which renders the world the arena for the realisation of the sexual instinct. But it is not so much that love is essentially psychotic, rather that love is terminal realization of the sexual *instinct* in human beings. For Jung, when the subject falls in love, he or she encounters the unconscious in a new form – as anima or animus. They no longer repress the unconscious, but actively follow their irrational attraction to another being through to its conclusion. All others disappear, and the external world is essentially reduced to one other person (the minimum for a world). But the unconscious now takes on a different form: the subject consciously pursues means to an unconscious end. Nobody knows *why* they fall in love with a *particular* person. For Deleuze in *Difference and Repetition*, Eros is the central experience of the unconscious, and even has its own 'synthesis of time'. But the pursuit of love to its end always results in the lover getting more than they bargained for. Love has an 'end', that is, it has a *goal* which is not necessarily an end in the sense of a *termination* of the relationship. At the end of love, a new, final form of the unconscious takes shape. This is the form that Jung calls the Self.

In its final form, the unconscious appears as an inner Other, the meaning of whose utterances, whether given in dreams or through 'active imagination', one has to interpret. But for the unconscious to appear *as* unconscious, it must be symbolized. The dream is always a hieroglyph which contains messages about the dreamer's individuation. A dream is never a disguised symbolic representation of an old wish. It addresses the dreamer *now*; it is a vital communication. Every dream is a report on the current situation of individuation. Hence dreams are intrinsically reflexive in that they present the subject's predicament in the form of a hieroglyphic, interior drama. 'Dreams are nothing but self-representations of the psychic process' (CW 7: 131). 'Self-reflexivity' is thus conceived in a fundamentally different way to the Kantian model of self-consciousness. In dreams, my unconscious Self portrays the current state of my individuation in enigmatic terms. A dream is reflexive in the sense that a play within a play (a double dramatization) is reflexive.[25]

This notion of the unconscious as the 'superior' subject reappears in various places in Deleuze. In *Nietzsche and Philosophy*, Deleuze discusses Nietzsche's claim that we live in the age of the 'modesty of consciousness': 'To remind consciousness of its necessary modesty', Deleuze explains, 'is to take it for what it is: a symptom' (NP 39). This is indeed an allusion to Freud's demand that 'we emancipate ourselves from the importance of the symptom of 'being conscious' (SE 14: 193), but Deleuze's trajectory here is not fundamentally Freudian. Deleuze continues that consciousness is 'nothing but a symptom of a deeper transformation and of the activities of entirely non-spiritual forces'. What is this process of 'transformation', which will be something other than repression and the struggle with the return of the repressed? Deleuze's *Nietzsche and Philosophy* is deeply teleological in conception, depicting a twofold historical and ethical movement through the night of nihilism, and towards individuation. Culture 'produces the individual as its final goal, where species itself is suppressed' (NP 137), while the test of the individual is their capacity to affirm the eternal return of the same. In the decisive passage, Deleuze then says:

> Consciousness is defined less in relation to exteriority (in terms of the real), than in relation to *superiority* (in terms of values). This distinction is essential to a general conception of consciousness and the unconscious. In Nietzsche consciousness is always the consciousness of an inferior in relation to a superior to which he is subordinated or into which he is 'incorporated'. Consciousness is never self-consciousness, but the consciousness of an ego in relation to a self which is not itself conscious. (NP 39)

These words mirror the opening pages of Jung's *Aion*, where the unconscious is defined as an unknown 'self': 'the ego is, by definition, subordinate to the self and is related to it like a part to the whole' (CW 9i: 5). As we will see shortly, there is a 'super-ego' in Deleuze, but it is not conceived in Freudian terms, and is closer to this Jungian superior 'Self'.

The final phase of individuation (in which, according to Jung, the ego and Self are related as earth to sun in the solar system) also implies a final overcoming of the negative relationship to the unconscious. The following passage could easily have been written by Deleuze, with its emphasis on the productivity and positivity, as well as 'superiority', of the unconscious.

> The unconscious is not just a receptacle but is the matrix of the very things that the conscious mind would like to be rid of. We can go a step further and say that the unconscious actually creates *new* contents . . . it seems to me far more important to find out what really constitutes the *positive* activity of the unconscious. The positive function of the unconscious is, in the main, merely disturbed by repressions, and this disturbance of its natural activity is perhaps the most important source of the so-called psychogenic illnesses. (CW 8: 364)

Jung's Theory of Instinct

In *Transformations and Symbols and the Libido,* his breakthrough work of 1911–12, Jung develops a recapitulatory model of unconscious repetition. However, he soon abandoned the recapitulation theory for a theory of 'archetypes' generated in part from Bergson's theory of instinct. Jung's 1919 lecture on 'Instinct and the Unconscious' was delivered at a symposium in London with the same title, jointly organized by the British Psychological Society, the Aristotelian Society and the Mind Association. Some of the major proponents of the theory of instinct, such as W. H. R. Rivers, William McDougall and James Drever were present at the symposium, and Jung's paper is in part a response to an earlier paper by Rivers. This gathering in 1919 coincides with the peak of the instinct-theory of the first decades of the twentieth century, since a year later J. B. Watson published his famous behaviourist attack on the very notion of instinct, causing instinct theory to retreat into the shadows, until its revival at the hands of the ethologists. Unlike the other speakers, Jung was relatively new to the theory of instinct, and he tenaciously held to the theory he adopted at the conference throughout the behaviourist years, and indeed until the end of his career. This lecture is significant for any account of the development of Jung's thought, because the very term *archetype* is introduced for the first time in this lecture.

As an example of instinct, Jung begins with the Yucca moth's 'incredibly refined instinct of propagation' (CW8: 132). In a complex operation happening only once in its life, the moth lays its eggs inside a plant whose flowers open for one night only.[26] How can such an instinct be explained? Jung makes a confused criticism of Darwin's explanation of instinct and then says that 'other ways of explanation, deriving from Bergson's philosophy, have recently been put forward, laying stress on the factor of intuition' (ibid.). Can we hope that Jung will make any further sense of Bergson's theory? Intuition, Jung explains, 'is an unconscious process in that its result is the irruption into consciousness of an unconscious content, a sudden idea, or "hunch"'. Jung also says that it 'resembles a process of perception', but that 'the perception is unconscious'. Intuition, more specifically, is the 'unconscious, purposive apprehension of a highly complicated situation'. The notion of an 'unconscious apprehension' does not make sense, but if we assume that Jung makes the error as a result of the influence of Bergson (who also makes the same error, cf. p. 56 above), then we can also hope that our correction of Bergson's theory in the last chapter might also smoothen our reception of Jung's theory of instinct.

Having established a Bergsonian framework for his theory of instinct, Jung now introduces the possibility that the *images* which accompany the actualization of instinct could be '*a priori*, inborn forms of "intuition"' (CW8: 133).

> Just as we have been compelled to postulate the concept of an instinct determining or regulating our conscious actions, so, in order to account for the uniformity and regularity of our perceptions, we must have recourse to the correlated concept of a factor determining the mode of apprehension. It is this factor which I call the archetype or primordial image. The primordial image might suitably be described as the *instinct's perception of itself*, or as the self-portrait of the instinct, in exactly the same way as consciousness is an inward perception of the objective life-process. (ibid.: 136)

Is this just a haphazard soldering together of Bergsonian and Kantian expressions, without real thought, or is Jung getting at something? What possible connection could there be between Bergsonian intuition (sympathy) and Kantian forms of intuition (space and time)? Before we follow up this possibility, we need to briefly examine the more traditional approaches to the notion of archetype, in order to distinguish the originality of Deleuze's trajectory through these ideas.

Biological Models of Archetypes

The fact that in the late 1920s Jung introduces his notion of archetype within the specific context of a synthesis of the Bergsonian and Kantian notions of intuition has been strangely overlooked by Jungians, who have tended to focus on the relation of the theory of archetypes to the opposition between Darwinism and Lamarckism. The problem of how exactly 'archetypes' might be inherited has dominated the literature. Jung's statements on archetypes are always obscure, and are expressed on a number of levels: biological, phenomenological, metaphysical, transcendental, historical. Deleuze may have come across Jung's notion of archetype while researching the theme of repetition. 'Not only are archetypes, apparently, impressions of ever-repeated typical experiences, but, at the same time, they behave empirically like agents that tend towards the repetition of these same experiences' (CW 7: 69–70).

In the years to come Jung generated a number of different hypotheses about how and why archetypal images (assuming they existed) were repeated across millennia in individual experiences. Jungians have never been certain about how to interpret his theory of archetypes. Some have argued that there is no real theory of archetypes, and to suggest that the term is anything other than metaphorical is to participate in a conspiracy whose time is up (Carrette 1994). Others, such as Anthony Stevens or Jean Knox, have broken down and separated out Jung's various formulations of the nature of archetypes and chosen to defend one of the formulations in the light of contemporary evolutionary theory or psychology (Stevens 2002; Knox 2003).[27]

From his first explorations of the impersonal unconscious, Jung was aware that the easiest way to account for archetypes was to present them as actually inherited phylogenetic residues. After all, Lamarckism was not at all foreign to psychoanalysis – it was becoming increasingly central to it. In *Totem and Taboo* Freud had argued for 'the inheritance of psychical dispositions' (SE 13: 158): the historical event of the killing of the primal father had altered the make-up of the minds of the descendants, even if such dispositions 'need to be given some sort of impetus in the life of the individual before they can be roused into actual operation' (ibid.). In *Transformations and Symbols* Jung affirms the recapitulationist theory that 'ontogenesis corresponds in psychology to phylogenesis' (CW B: 25), which usually goes hand in hand with Lamarckism. When in his 1917 essay 'On the Psychology of the Unconscious' Jung says that 'It seems to me that the origin [of the archetypes] can only be explained by assuming them to be deposits of the constantly repeated experiences of humanity' (CW 7: 69), nothing could be more Lamarckian.

However, in the same text he had already warned off such an interpretation: 'I do not by any means assert the inheritance of ideas, but only of the possibility of such ideas, which is something different' (CW 7: 65). In 1918 he was even more explicit: 'It should on no account be imagined that there are such things as *inherited ideas.* Of that there can be no question' (CW 10: 10). Thus from the beginning it looks as if Jung was attempting to draw a distinction between 'archetypes as such', as genetic dispositions, and 'archetypal images', which *express* these dispositions in imaginary form at the ontogenetic level. In his 1954 essay 'On the Essence of the Psychical', he continued to take this anti-Lamarckian line: 'Archetypes are typical forms of behaviour which, once they become conscious, naturally present themselves *as ideas and images,* like everything else that becomes a content of consciousness' (CW 8: 227). He holds that they are 'organizers' of ideas and images, not themselves ideas and images (ibid.: 231). In this essay Jung goes on to correlate these innate structures with the ethological conception of 'inborn "patterns of behaviour"' and it is this approach that has been taken up by Anthony Stevens, who says that archetypes should be understood as 'phylogenetically acquired, genome-bound units of information which programme the individual to behave in certain specific ways while permitting such behaviour to be adapted appropriately to environmental circumstances' (Stevens 2002: 60). For instance, the instinct for attachment is accompanied by the archetype of the mother. In *Evolutionary Psychiatry* Stevens and Price suggest that what evolutionary psychologists variously refer to as 'evolved psychological mechanisms' (David Buss), or 'psychobiological response patterns' (Paul Gilbert) are ultimately identical to what Jung was isolating with his notion of archetype. 'Archetypes are conceived as neuropsychic units which evolved through natural selection and which are responsible for determining the behavioural characteristics as well as the affective and cognitive experiences typical of human beings' (Stevens and Price 2000: 6).[28]

However, if Jung was already retracting in 1918 his Lamarckian suggestion of the previous year that archetypes are 'deposits of the constantly repeated experiences of humanity', then his turn to Bergson in 1919 indicates that he also was reluctant to go straight down a Darwinian path. Moreover, despite his more ethologically inclined statements later on, as late as 1955 Jung still opted to explain the distinction between archetype and archetypal image in terms consistent with his earlier Bergsonian approach, even referring to the proverbial wasp and caterpillar: 'This term is not meant to denote an inherited idea, but rather an inherited mode of psychic functioning, corresponding to the inborn way in which the chick emerges from the egg, the bird builds its nest, a certain kind of wasp stings the motor ganglion of the caterpillar, and eels find their way to the Bermudas. In other words, it is a "pattern of behaviour"' (CW 18: 518).[29] The echo of Fabre and Bergson's wasp suggests that Jung has not extracted himself entirely from his earlier ideas.

Some contemporary Jungians argue that archetypes are not genetically programmed but are instead spatiotemporal schemata that emerge in the developmental process. In his 1918 paper 'The Role of the Unconscious', it is after suggesting that there can be 'no question' of a Lamarckian theory of archetypes that Jung goes on to say that 'there are, however, innate possibilities of ideas, *a priori* conditions for fantasy-production'. This has been taken to indicate that Jung favours a biologically developmentalist view of archetypes. Before turning to a recent example of this view, it is worth recalling that even Konrad Lorenz, who had major reservations about Jung's work, became receptive to an interpretation of the archetypes which stressed the function of the imagination in the development of instinctual behaviour.[30] He came to grant that Jung's theory could be defended for human beings, on condition that the images were understood as developmental phenomena. The key difference between animal and human being is that 'man has the power of visualisation' (Evans 1975: 59). It is the human cognitive capacity for visual imagination that allows the innate mechanical schema to find symbolic and imaginary expression. '[The] innate releasing mechanism . . . combined with the human faculty of visualising – dreaming about a situation – results in phenomenal reactions which are more or less identical with Jung's concept of archetypes. I think archetypes are innate releasing mechanisms invested in visualisation, in the fantasy of the individual. Man can, in his fantasy, perform experiments with himself which an animal cannot' (ibid.).

In *Archetype, Attachment, Analysis: Jungian Psychology and the Emergent Mind* (2003), Jean Knox generates a developmental theory of archetypes as image-schemas. Relying on collaborative work between cognitive scientists and developmentalists, she argues that the earliest stages in the child's development of its information-processing capabilities are structured by basic 'image schemas' (such as path, up-down, containment, force, part–whole, link; see Mandler 1992: 591), so that although 'there may be no such thing as an archetypal mother', there is instead 'an image schema of containment' (Knox 2003: 67). Thus although attachment is as essential for Knox as it is for Stevens, for the former the specifically archetypal contribution to attachment is mediated by a set of *spatio-temporal* conditions. Insecure attachment, for instance, is 'likely to activate the image schema of "force" or "splitting"' (ibid.: 68). There is much to recommend Knox's emphasis on the non-conceptual spatiotemporal conditions of development, but her conclusion is extreme: she believes that the exclusion of symbolic representations from genetic inheritance requires that all symbolic content of the archetypes be thrown out, leaving just spatiotemporal structures. But whatever Jung's notion of archetype was, it seems to have involved a lot more than mere spatiotemporal gestalts. Knox criticizes Stevens for attributing 'too much representational content' to archetypes, and proposes that '"Mother" is a concept, but the image schema of containment", the bodily experience of being held and the accompanying physiological sensations of warmth, comfort and security, are not initially symbolic' (Knox 2003: 64).

There is an opposition between 'representation' and 'intuition' at work here which can be problematized and transcended by appealing to Kantian philosophy, by which both Jung and Deleuze were heavily influenced. Although Knox and other Jungians frequently acknowledge Jung's debt to Kant, they usually overlook the *tripartite* structure that Kant gives to cognition – not just conceptual representations and intuitions, but also *Ideas*, the problems that stimulate the mind in the first place. For both Jung and Deleuze, the notion of Idea is an essential component of Kant's (and their own) theory of cognition. Under certain circumstances, Ideas even determine the shape of space and time, to the point that the entire world appears to become an egg, an embryological sensorium which serves as the stage of the 'subtle theatres' of individuation (cf. Leibniz 1714: # 75; also DR 221, 244).

Instincts and the Imagination

These '*a priori*, inborn forms of "intuition"', says Jung, are 'the *archetypes* of perception and apprehension, which are the necessary *a priori* determinants of all psychic processes' (ibid.: 133). An archetype thus cannot be an 'image' in the empirical sense, but is rather an *a priori* spatiotemporal structure, a way of living in space and time. The archetypes are spatiotemporal forms which constrain perception and apprehension, allowing instinct to fulfil itself in its own 'intensive' sensorium.

> Just as we have been compelled to postulate the concept of an instinct determining or regulating our conscious actions, so, in order to account for the uniformity and regularity of our perceptions, we must have recourse to the correlated concept of a factor determining the mode of apprehension. It is this factor which I call the archetype or primordial image. The primordial image might suitably be described as the *instinct's perception of itself*, or as the self-portrait of the instinct, in exactly the same way as consciousness is an inward perception of the objective life-process. (Ibid.: 136)

At this point in Jung's work, therefore, the concept of archetype is a specifically spatiotemporal structure of perception. In a 1918 essay, 'The Role of the Unconcious', Jung specifies that archetypes are 'innate possibilities of ideas, *a priori* conditions for fantasy-production . . . Though these innate conditions do not produce any contents of themselves, they give definite form to contents that have already been acquired' (CW 10: 10). The mention of '*a priori* conditions for fantasy-production' can be deciphered as gesturing to a possible connection with Kant's theory of productive imagination.

In *Difference and Repetition* and in his work on Kant, Deleuze spends considerable time showing the role of the productive imagination in determining the shape of space and time for the finite being. Deleuze's aim is to show how the productive imagination is ultimately a receptacle for the harnessing of problematic Ideas, beyond the norms of the conceptual understanding. Could Jung be pointing, however obscurely, to some possible synthesis of Bergsonian instinct and Kantian productive imagination? Even though Jung's theoretical suggestions are obscure, Deleuze would certainly have read them with interest, and the fact that he went on to take up the theory of archetypes (paraphrasing this same lecture of Jung's) indicates that he saw an opportunity for theoretical advance here. Given the problems we encountered in Bergson's theory of instinct, it is possible that Deleuze perceived that a Jungian modification of the second interpretation of Bergsonian instinct might be the way forward.

More acutely, in order for the instinct to consummate itself through somnambulistic consciousness of the image, representational consciousness would have to be *suppressed*. Now this suppression would obviously be more problematic in human beings, whose consciousness is dominated by intelligence and its habits. Like Bergson and Deleuze, Jung also believes that human beings do not have instincts in the same way that animals do. In fact, 'it is just man's turning away from instinct – his opposing himself to instinct – that creates consciousness'.[31] Civilized consciousness emerges with the differentiation of the ego that is the result of an increased reliance on intelligent consciousness. For Jung, the consequence of the differentiation of the ego is the tendential 'de-differentiation' of instinct. He seems to have two main models for conceiving the subsistence of instinct in human beings. On the one hand, he seems to maintain that instincts persist *in opposition* to egoic consciousness, so that instinct is always in a relation of homeostatic 'compensation' with intelligence. But in 'The Relations of the Ego to the Unconscious' (Jung 1935) and 'The Stages of Life' another model supervenes that is perhaps not inconsistent with the former, but has more philosophical sophistication.[32]

It can be argued that Deleuze takes up this model in his theory of problematic Ideas in *Difference and Repetition*. Deleuze's insight is to see how this suggestion can be connected up with Jung's indication elsewhere that archetypes in humans take the form of *problems* which transcend the capabilities of intelligent consciousness. Deleuze shows how Kant's theory of problematic Ideas is the narrow gap through which the instinctual image can return – by right – to haunt human intelligence.[33]

This Jungian conception is consistent with the least florid interpretation of Bergson's theory of instinct presented in the last chapter. When the intelligence encounters a problem, a gap would open up for the return of an 'instinct that has become disinterested, self-conscious, capable of reflecting upon its object' (Bergson 1907: 176). Somnambulistic consciousness, therefore, is not necessarily just produced by traumatic events, but also asserts itself by exploiting the problematic holes in intelligence, responding creatively through the productive imagination. If there are instinctual periodicities and intensities at work in the human being, then they can only be activated under particular ideal and intuitive conditions.

Kant, Jung and Sub-Representative Intuition

Jung indicates in a number of places that he understands himself to be a Kantian in his approach to the mind; he even claimed that nobody could understand his works without having first understood their Kantian basis. Despite his terminological obscurity and carelessness, Jung may have been the only psychologist to set about constructing a 'transcendental' theory of the unconscious. In his 1935 Tavistock Lectures in London, he is keen to stress the conformity of his notion of the unconscious with Kantian epistemology. 'The ego is the subject of all personal acts of consciousness. The relation of a psychic content to the ego forms the criterion of its consciousness, for no content can be conscious unless it is represented to a subject' (CW 9ii: 3). In order to count as representations, all representations must potentially be able to be brought into relation to a conscious ego. Kantian philosophy is often held to be inimical to a theory of the unconscious. For Kant, there is a transcendental subject, an 'I think' that must accompany all my representations (Kant 1782/1787: B131). Wilhelm Wundt, a psychologist influenced by Kant's theory of self-consciousness or apperception, states that the very idea of an 'unconscious representation' (*unbewusste Vorstellung*) is incoherent, as it is impossible to conceive of a representation that nobody *has* (cf. Wundt 1908–11: III, 354–6, 489). There are unconscious physiological states, but these do not involve representations.

Jung and Deleuze are sensitive to this charge, due to their own incorporations of the philosophy of Kant. To the first objection, Jung counters with the parry that the unconscious must in that case be considered to be sub-representative: 'it is not a question of "representations" but of sketches, plans or images' (CW 8: 165). Deleuze too talks of the necessity of 'sub-representational dynamisms' beneath representational thought (DI 98; cf. 264). Deleuze's *Difference and Repetition* is first of all a book against *representation*, and in it Deleuze puts forward the theory that 'spatio-temporal dynamisms' are at the basis of the dynamics of the psyche. The problem of the unconscious would therefore be badly posed as long as it is framed in terms of representation. On the basis of what we have gleaned from Bergson about time, we have a new question: are passive syntheses or spatiotemporal dynamisms *unconscious because they are non-conceptual?* It seems unlikely: as Bergson says, it is perfectly possible to be conscious of duration and in disorders of time such as paramnesia, the subject does not lack consciousness. On the other hand, if these spatiotemporal factors are in themselves non-conceptual, then they also cannot be rendered *objective* for consciousness (mediated by conceptual norms). We can actively manipulate representations in the mind; Deleuze might even admit, with Kant, that in a formal sense we are the *subject* of our conceptual representations. But when it comes to spatiotemporal factors, his point is that we are *subject to them.* Time passes, duration accumulates, memory eludes us, déjà vu immobilizes us, space (distance, rises and falls, vertigo) encloses or threatens us, without our being able to do anything about it. The apocalyptic thought of the end of the world, and the pressure it imposes on the present moment, is an example of a spatiotemporal dynamism in schizoid experiences.

These ways of inhabiting space and time are overlooked in normal experience, as there space and time tend to be successfully subordinated to the *practical* needs of the understanding or intellect. But their pure forms are visible at the limits of normal experience. Deleuze contends that they are as essential for understanding biological development as they are for mental disorders. The embryo lives through intensive movements in the womb which would destroy adult organisms; similarly, the neurotic and psychotic are caught up in spatiotemporal structures that preclude the continuation of a well-ordered, practical existence. 'In effect, a pure spatio-temporal dynamism, with its necessary participation in the forced movement, can be experienced only at the borders of the liveable, under conditions beyond which it would entail the death of any well-constituted subject endowed with independence and activity' (DR 118). Deleuze conceives of these dynamisms as direct 'dramatisations' of Ideas or problems into the medium of space and time. When they are lived through, the consciousness involved is that of a dream. 'If the [spatiotemporal] dynamism is external to concepts, and, as such, a schema – it is internal to Ideas – and as such, a drama or dream' (ibid.). If Deleuze's theory is defensible, then it is of immense importance: not only does it solve an old enigma in Kant's philosophy (thus helping to complete Kant's Copernican revolution), but it can illuminate the spatiotemporal structure of mental disorders. Deleuze gives an impromptu, but all too rare example of what a 'larval subject' is in the discussion after his paper at the French Society for Philosophy in 1967 ('The Method of Dramatisation'):

> Take the case of an obsessive compulsive, where the subject keeps shrinking: handkerchiefs and towels are perpetually cut, first in two, then the halves are cut again; the cord for the bell in the dining room is regularly shortened, and the bell gets closer to the ceiling; everything is gnawed at, miniaturised, put into boxes. This is indeed a drama, in the sense that the patient organises a space, agitates it, while in this space he expresses an Idea of the unconscious. An angry fit is a dramatisation that stages larval subjects. (DI 108)[34]

Obsessional neurosis has a spatiotemporal form: the shrinking and cutting of the bell are a spatiotemporal dynamism, and are 'lived' at a different level than the everyday experience of the patient. 'Everyday life is full of dramatisations. Some psychoanalysts use the word, I believe, to designate the movements by which logical thought is dissolved in pure spatio-temporal determinations, as in falling asleep' (DI 108).

Kant, Jung and Super-Representative Ideas

Wundt also criticizes his teacher Fechner's 'mystical intuition' of superconscious and subconscious mental states, which he says borders on the hypothesis of double consciousness.[35] This latter is impossible because a plurality of consciousnesses 'would have to be simultaneously present in one and the same individual' (ibid.: 302n.). In his 1954 essay 'The Nature of the Psyche', Jung gives a review of the history of the notion of the unconscious in German philosophy and psychology, referring at length to Wundt's late rejection of the concept (CW 8: 162–5). There he responds to Wundt's charge about double consciousness. He criticizes Wundt for not seeing that consciousness can alternate without being *actually* double.

Although Deleuze did not respond to Wundt, his emphasis on the merely formal, empty structure of the transcendental *subject*, as opposed to the empirical *ego* (see DR 58, 87) would have helped him disarm the objection. The synthesizing structure of consciousness deduced by Kant may include a plurality of empirical egos or selves. The attitudes of the ego may change over a lifetime, for instance, or even in a single day; as long as some sort of synthesis between these egos can be made, there is no contradiction to Kantian epistemology. In Karl Ameriks's formulation, 'the persistent representation of an "I" need not be the representation of a permanent "I"' (Ameriks 2000: 135).

However, Deleuze does have an account of the 'super-egoic' destination of cognition. In the 'paradox of inner sense' in the *Critique of Pure Reason*, Kant had claimed that the fact that I must experience everything passively under the form of time indeed strictly precluded any encounter with a spontaneous 'I think'. Deleuze infers from this that 'the subject can . . . represent its own spontaneity only as that of an Other' (DR 58). Deleuze thus suggests that it is the very impossibility of appropriating the 'I think' as one's own that acts as the guarantee of its purity, and it is this that helps us ascend from the stage of recollection to that of 'repetition'. In *Difference and Repetition* Deleuze turns to Ricoeur's account of the relation of psychoanalysis to the transcendental 'I think'. Ricoeur suggests that Freud's account of narcissism shows that any coincidence of the 'I think' with its own being is always open to suspicion that it is a false, narcissistic self. 'As soon as the apodictic truth, *I think, I am* is uttered, it is blocked by a pseudo-evidence: an abortive Cogito has already taken the place of the first truth of reflection, *I think, I am.'* Deleuze and Ricoeur agree that the fundamental message of Kant's, Husserl's and Freud's theories of subjectivity is that there is no *experience* of the 'I think' – it is apodictic yet at the same time always inadequately presented. There is always the possibility that I am deceived about the purity of any act of self-consciousness. Ricoeur states that this perpetual non-coincidence introduces a fracture (*fêlure*) into the relation between the 'I think' and the 'I am' (Ricoeur 1965: 378). Deleuze takes up this notion of a fractured Cogito in Ricoeur and relates it to Kant's theory of the subject. In the section on the Paralogisms in the first Critique, Kant too emphasizes that the disjunction of the formality of the 'I think' from any supposed experience of selfhood, or from any substantial notion of the self.

Deleuze refuses to follow Kant in ascribing any syntheses of representation (i.e. apprehension, reproduction or recognition) to the 'I think'. The truth of the Kantian 'I think', suggests Deleuze, is that it is *too pure* for this kind of activity, which should rather be referred back to the reality-testing syntheses brought about by the ego (cf. DR 98). Most of what we call our 'thoughts' are passive. Some of these are not really thoughts at all, but are associations of the imagination derived from habit and memory. Some of what we call 'thoughts' *are* thoughts, but are not yet active because they are subordinated to a logic of recognition or representation that is itself a tool of the practical need for attention to life. Although Deleuze appears to be taking us in a direction that is very far from usual conceptions of the Kantian subject of synthesis, Kant himself also says that the transcendental subject is not to be confused with the self. What we usually refer to as 'I' is for Kant just the empirical self. As far as the transcendental 'I' is concerned, we only ever meet a mere 'consciousness of synthesis'. That is: the mere awareness that there is a synthetic process going on. By denying an immediate awareness of 'our' identity with the subject of this synthetic process, Kant is thus asking us to *make an identification* with the active spontaneous source of this synthesis as an Other. 'The subject can . . . represent its own spontaneity only as that of an Other' (DR 58). To paraphrase Kant, the subject would thus be the You, He, She or It that thinks: but never the *moi* (self or ego). Moreover, as a transcendental philosopher, Deleuze recognizes that he still needs some possibility of an active, spontaneous subject, in order to ground the ultimate unity of syntheses. But Deleuze states that the ultimate nature ('in and for itself') of this active synthesis is in fact only revealed in the thought of the eternal return. In *Nietzsche and Philosophy*, Deleuze openly presents Nietzsche's notion of eternal return as the 'realisation' of Kantian ethics. He writes that 'the eternal return gives the will a rule as rigorous at the Kantian one . . . As an ethical thought, the eternal return is the new formulation of the practical synthesis: *whatever you will, will it in such a way that you also will its return*' (NP 68; DR 7). Klossowski's modification (discussed on p. 37 above) does not necessarily collapse the super-egoic aspect of the notion of eternal return, but it does place it beyond the reach of law.

In *Difference and Repetition* Deleuze constructs a relationship of super-representational 'problematic Ideas' to sub-representational spatiotemporal intensities, mediated by conceptual representation. The path of individuation necessarily involves a series 'transcendent exercises' of the mind carried out beyond conceptual representation, in which unconscious Ideas emerge to shape and reshape the consciousness of the subject (who is both a thinking and a passive subject). The notion of the problematic Idea is also to be found in Jung, as well as in Kant.

In 'The Stages of Life' Jung writes that while 'the psychic life of civilised man' has become dominated by intelligence at the expense of instinct, intelligence itself has its own limits, which in turn allows instinctual consciousness to return. The problem with intelligence is that it sometimes encounters intractable problems. 'It is the growth of consciousness which we must thank for the existence of problems . . . As long as we are still submerged in nature we are unconscious, and we live in the security of instinct which knows no problems' (CW 8: 388). Jung's advance, for Deleuze, must lie in this identification of a 'problematic' zone of human intelligence, through which the instinctual form of consciousness can return. Deleuze takes up Jung's model in his theory of problematic Ideas in *Difference and Repetition*: 'Was not one of the most important points of Jung's theory already to be found here: the force of "questioning" in the unconscious, the conception of the unconscious as an unconscious of "problems" and "tasks". Drawing out the consequences of this led Jung to the discovery of a process of differenciation more profound than the resulting oppositions (see *[The Relations between] the Ego and the Unconscious*)' (DR: 141). Tucked away in a footnote, this is an important reference, taking us beyond Deleuze's more explicit intellectual references, in his theory of problematic Ideas, to Kantian and Leibnizian conceptions of non-representational thought.

Both Jung and Deleuze appear to suggest that the process of individuation is driven by a series of encounters with problems which are 'unconscious' in the sense that they elude the representational activity of consciousness. 'The unconscious . . . concerns problems and questions which can never be reduced to the great oppositions or the overall effects that are felt in consciousness' (DR 108). A problem can elude consciousness in a very particular way. A real problem is a peculiar kind of cognitive object, in that the thinker is never sure whether they have correctly *posed* the problem. The problem may be expressed in representational terms, but if it really is a problem, then one has to treat one's representational framing of the problem as provisional, and keep returning to the 'underlying' problem, always on the lookout for a fresh perspective. There is thus a sense in which a genuine problem is 'sub-representational', even if it is grasped through conceptual representations. It is a problem *because* it has not found a place within the order of representation. Now, if consciousness is defined through the capacity for apperceptive representation, then it is valid to state that problems are 'unconscious' in the strict sense that *in themselves* they hover outside the order of representations. One cannot be conscious *of* them in the same way as one is conscious of an object of a conceptual representation. The problem breaks through first as a problem *for* conscious representation, and then *as* a problem that points to something neglected in the very conceptual hierarchy itself, the activation of which is bound to spell an ordeal of some sort.

Deleuze does not make it clear how strongly we are to take the notion of 'problem' here. There are perhaps three powers of intractability to a problem. First, something could be empirically problematic, due to a lack of empirical knowledge, for instance. Second, there can be problems or ordeals that are particular to a particular stage of individuation. Leaning on Bergson's theory of duration, Deleuze suggests that individual development is punctuated by a series of intensive thresholds which must be overcome to reach the next plateau of intensity. Third, an Idea can be 'problematic' in the Kantian transcendental sense, just as the Ideas of Self, World and God are intrinsically and eternally 'problematic concepts', because their objects cannot be known or experienced, but nevertheless must be *thought* (Kant 1782/1787: A254/B310). But beyond these levels of intractability – empirical, transcendental and genetic – there is a final approach to the 'problematic' unconscious: some sort of contemporary, atheological *mathesis*, a calculus of the cosmos itself as Problem: there are recurring allusions in Deleuze to the traditions of Neoplatonism, Hermeticism, the Renaissance magic, the occult, but always in the context of the death of the God of monotheism. Here we shall focus briefly on the empirical and transcendental senses of 'problem'. In the following two chapters, we will proceed towards the 'esoteric' dimensions of the problem, and attempt to shed light on Deleuze's suggestion that Jungianism is genealogically related to Leibnizian *mathesis*.

The empiricist interpretation is the most general in scope, and the least determined, so is useful to introduce the basic idea. According to this interpretation we could say that *anything* can be a problem as long as it eludes representational cognition for some period of duration. This is a *relative* conception of unconscious problems. Thus, if a sensation, an affect or an image resisted subsumption by conscious representation, then for Jung and Deleuze, that would initiate the attempt to express it in the non-representational means available to the psyche (image or symbol, dream or symptom, or general distortions of the spatiotemporal field). An archetype 'cannot be perceived or 'represented', in contrast to the perceptible psychic phenomena'; it is 'irrepresentable' (CW 8: 436). Once a rationally insoluble problem is hit upon, however, 'the deeper layers of the unconscious, the primordial images, are activated and the transformation of the personality can get under way' (CW 8: 441). The impersonal, archetypal unconscious is awakened when the subject finds themselves 'in an 'impossible' situation . . . In such situations, if they are serious enough, archetypal dreams are likely to occur which point out a possible line of advance one would never have thought of oneself. It is this kind of situation that constellates the archetype with the greatest regularity' (CW 8: 440).

In 'Instinct and the Unconscious', Jung tends to acknowledge the Platonic origins of the notion of archetype as 'pure form' or Idea, and reports that he has taken the term itself from Hellenistic (the *Corpus Hermeticum*) and early Christian philosophy (St Augustine and Dionysius the Areopagite).[36] However, elsewhere he refers to Kant's theory of Ideas as another influence. Jung's references to Kant's term 'archetype' are inconsistent and misleading, but some of them suggest that he did in fact have an obscure apprehension of what he needed from Kant's philosophy. For after having suggested in the lecture on instinct that Kant reduced the Platonic archetypes to the categories of the understanding, in *Psychological Types* (1921) he goes on to quote the relevant passages in Kant about Ideas, in support of his own notion of archetypes. He cites Kant's definition in his *Logic* of the Idea as a 'rational concept whose object is not to be found in experience' and which contains the 'archetype [*Urbild*] of the use of the understanding' (CW 6: 438, cf. 309; cf. Kant 1974: 97).[37] For Kant, he says, an Idea is 'a transcendental concept which as such exceeds the bounds of the experienceable' (CW 6: 438). Kant suggests that Ideas are 'problematic concepts', because their objects cannot be known or experienced, but nevertheless *must* be thought (Kant 1782/1787: A254/B310). Jung explicitly cites Kant's warning that 'although we must say of the transcendental concepts of reason that *they are only ideas*, this is not by any means to be taken as signifying that they are superfluous and void' (A329/B386). Although Ideas may only be 'regulative' as opposed to 'constitutive' for our experience, in a sense they are constitutive of the internal structure of thought. Ideas are necessary conditions of thought, if not of experience. Kant even suggests that there should be a final Transcendental Deduction of Ideas, beyond the central Deduction of the Categories (A669/B697). Deleuze's contribution here is to notice how much weight Kant is quietly putting on the theory of Ideas. In *Difference and Repetition,* he seizes on Kant's suggestion that Ideas are to be taken as 'problematic concepts', and goes on to suggest that if Ideas are 'problematic' that might be because 'conversely, problems are Ideas' (DR 168). Perhaps there are not just three Ideas – perhaps every genuine *problem* has the structure that Kant attributed to Ideas. Perhaps the activity of conceptual or intellectual knowledge is itself already conditioned by another type of cognition: the posing of problems. After all, didn't Kant say in the Preface to the first *Critique* that 'reason . . . compel[s] nature to answer its questions' (Kant 1787: Bxiv)?

> Kant never ceased to remind us that Ideas are essentially 'problematic'. Conversely, problems are Ideas. Undoubtedly, he shows that Ideas lead us into false problems, but this is not their most profound characteristic: if, according to Kant, reason does pose false problems and therefore itself gives rise to illusion, this is because in the first place it is the faculty of posing problems in general. (DR 168)

This introduces a radical new dimension into Kantian thought, as it means that knowledge and experience are not ultimately to be seen in terms of mere discrete acts of judgement, but always in terms of solutions to problems. Established knowledge, in other words, is really nothing but the realm of established solutions. If Ideas are to be thought primarily as problems, this implies that they must already have their own consistency and form *as problems* that stand structurally outside achieved empirical knowledge, 'feeding' and even conditioning knowledge. 'A proposition conceived as a response is always a particular solution, a case considered for itself, abstractly and apart from the superior synthesis which relates it, along with other cases, to a problem *as* problem' (DR 157). In this sense, Deleuze contends that problems transcend their solutions, and even after they have been solved satisfactorily by science, they still retain their power to provoke thought.

But what accounts for this positive power of problems or Ideas, though? Surely not *every* problem is structured in this way? Although Deleuze has a complex and detailed theory of how problems or Ideas are structured, he is elusive when it comes to giving examples. Sometimes it seems as if every 'domain' of objects has its own single problem, so that there is *a problem* of physics, a problem of biology, society, language, the psyche, etc. (cf. DR 184f.). Each of these domains is the field for a distinct discipline that deals with a distinct, specialized problem. But Deleuze also says, following Jung, that there are problems proper to the unconscious as well, and which drive the path of individuation. 'The unconscious . . . concerns problems and questions in their difference in kind from answers-solutions' (DR 108). It is this line of thought we will follow here. Deleuze's explicit reference to Jung's theory of problems can serve as a guide. Jung is also convinced that an eternal 'transcendence' can be ascribed to problems: 'The serious problems in life . . . are never solved.

If ever they should appear to be so it is a sure sign that something has been lost. The meaning and purpose of a problem seems to lie not in its solution but in our working at it incessantly' (CW 8: 394).[38]

Birth, Death and Sexual Difference

We have surveyed the Jungian and Kantian origins of Deleuze's theory that the unconscious must be taken as the site of 'problems', rather than Freudian drives. But at one point in *Difference and Repetition*, Deleuze goes on to suggest that if we want to find out what the true problems of the unconscious actually are, we nevertheless have to turn to a unique text in the Freudian corpus, his 'Sexual Theories of Children' of 1908. Although he affirms Jung's problematic unconscious over Freud's oppositional conception of unconscious drive vs. conscious ego, Deleuze nevertheless writes that 'birth and death, and the difference between the sexes, are the complex themes of problems before they are the simple terms of an opposition' (DR 107). For a brief moment in this text, Freud had argued that the child's *questioning* activity was a fundamental phase of its psychosexual development, to the point that the child's fantasies about castration and incest can be traced back to its questions and theories about its own birth and its sexual identity. This theory did not last long, perhaps because Freud soon realized its proximity to Jung's more vitalistic approach to the unconscious.[39]

In 'The Sexual Theories of Children' Freud claims that the questioning process in the child is usually instigated by rivalry with siblings, 'the product of a vital exigency, as though thinking were entrusted with the task of preventing the recurrence of such events' as the birth of a rival (SE 9: 213). Nevertheless, 'the child's thinking soon becomes independent of this instigation and henceforward goes on operating as a self-sustained drive for research'. Freud goes on to allot an extremely important role to these adventures in thought, claiming that the 'nuclear complex' of neurosis is brought into being by their repression. The child senses that the parents' explanation of birth through stories about storks and so forth is a cover-up, and is forced to theorize on its own about the circumstances of its own birth. In Jungian terms, Freud describes the emergence of a split between conscious and unconscious in terms of a 'psychical dissociation'. 'The set of views which are bound up with being "good", but also with a cessation of reflection, become the dominant and conscious views; while the other set, for which the child's work of research has meanwhile obtained fresh evidence, but which are not supposed to count, become the suppressed and "unconscious" ones. The nuclear complex of a neurosis is in this way brought into being' (SE 9: 214). At this point, the nuclear complex is not yet identified with the Oedipus complex, this identification finally coming about in the Rat Man case history of 1909. This account of the origins of the nuclear complex is strikingly different to the latter account, in that it suggests that the first object of primal repression is the questioning, theorizing activity of the child, not its incestuous desires. Freud's account of the genesis of the unconscious even implies that the activity of the unconscious somehow continues the questioning and problematizing activity of the child. During the period from 1906 to 1909, Freud had increasingly come under the influence of Jung's views, and had begun to admit that there might be a plurality of 'complexes', some of these being social or even professional, not just sexual (see Freud's 1907 additions to *The Psychopathology of Everyday Life*, SE 6: 22–3). The 'Sexual Theories' essay is probably the high-water mark of Freud's influence by Jung, and indeed points towards the kind of theory we have been extracting from Jung in the preceding pages. Nevertheless, Freud's framework for understanding primary processes is too mechanistic to make much sense of the possibility that the unconscious might itself be problematizing, and nothing further comes of it. Although Freud inserts a section on 'The Drive for Knowledge' in the 1915 version of the *Three Essays on the Theory of Sexuality*, he there reduces to the drive to a combination of the drives for mastery and scopophilia (SE 7: 194).

Thus Deleuze's turn to Freud's notion of 'sexual theories' is not at all an embrace of Freudianism, but amounts to a continuation of his Jungian tendencies. From our current perspective, Freud's suggestion that children only initially come to consciousness through the insistence of certain unanswerable questions (where do I come from? why are boys and girls different?) cannot but remind us of the problematic Ideas that hover outside of representation. Like 'how does a world begin?' or 'are there gods?', these problems incite fundamental thought, but cannot be satisfactorily answered by empirical cognition. The light of intelligent consciousness has been spreading out upon all the practical activities of the child, but now it comes up against a realm of darkness which cannot be further penetrated. The insistent 'why?' of the child bores a hole into its empirical conception of the world, arousing a thirst for knowledge that cannot be satisfied by the answers that are available from social representatives of the world.

'The child is a metaphysical being', say Deleuze and Guattari in *Anti-Oedipus*, but '*the unconscious is an orphan*' (AO 49). One of the profoundly anti-psychoanalytic arguments of *Anti-Oedipus* is that 'parental figures are in no way organisers' of the libidinal processes at work in the child, but 'rather inductors or stimuli of varying, vague import that trigger processes of an entirely different nature, processes that are endowed with what amounts to an indifference with regard to the stimulus' (AO 92). In psychoanalysis, the child is completely preoccupied by the signs emitted by the parents to the child. In *Seminar V*, Lacan presents a dialectic of infantile desire which necessarily leads towards triangulation in an abstract, dialecticized version of the Oedipus complex. But Deleuze and Guattari explain these parental signs in ethological terms as triggering stimuli of autonomous processes. But there are other stimuli, and other processes, and multiple milieus for the performance of these processes. In one of his luminous late opuscules on the theory of the unconscious, 'What Children Say', Deleuze reiterates the point: 'The father and mother are not the coordinates of everything that is invested in the unconscious. There is never a moment when children are not already plunged into an actual milieu in which they are moving about, and in which the parents as persons simply play the roles of openers or closers of doors, guardians of thresholds, connectors or disconnectors of zones' (CC 62). 'Doubtless one can *believe* that, in the beginning (?), the stimulus – the Oedipal inductor – is a real organizer. But believing is an operation of a conscious or preconscious nature, an extrinsic perception rather than an operation of the unconscious upon itself' (AO 92). It is not necessarily that anything has been repressed into the child's unconscious (unless there has been a trauma). Rather, the child is continually problematizing, asking questions of the world and taking the latter's hesitations in answering very seriously. 'What does it mean to be alive? What does it mean to breathe? What am I?' These questions have nothing to do with the libido in Freud's sense.

Chapter 4

The World as Symbol: Kant, Jung and Deleuze

For some occupants of the twentieth-century esoteric underground, Jung's emphasis on symbolism was the key to an understanding of sexuality which surpassed Freud's in range and richness. In his 1916 review of *Transformations and Symbols* in *Vanity Fair*, Aleister Crowley wrote 'let us rejoice that the tedious and stupid attempt to relate every human idea to sex has been relegated to oblivion; or if you prefer to put it that way, that we must now interpret sex in vaster symbols' (Crowley 1916: 79).[1] Sexuality and esotericism had often gone hand in hand in the nineteenth to twentieth century. Johann Malfatti's *The Anarchy and Hierarchy of Knowledge*, for which Deleuze wrote an introduction in 1946, is a perfect example. An extravagant blend of nature-philosophy, numerology and Tantrism, this book (entitled *Mathesis* in French) was held by Réné Guénon to be in part responsible for initiating the French occult revival in the late nineteenth century. This curious work contains disquisitions on the anima and animus, the hermaphrodite, the world-egg and the 'subtle body'; all sexo-cosmic themes that occur in Jung and Deleuze. An altogether different approach to sexuality is going on here than in psychoanalysis. According to this line of thought, Freud's approach overlooks certain fundamental aspects of human sexuality, such as the forms of consciousness involved in sexual desire and its paths to consummation, the relation of sexuality to the supersensible and the symbol. In his memoirs, Jung writes:

> In retrospect I can say that I alone logically pursued the two problems which most interested Freud: the problem of 'archaic vestiges' and that of sexuality. It is a widespread error to imagine that I do not see the value of sexuality. On the contrary, it plays a large part in my psychology as an essential – though not the whole – expression of psychic wholeness. But my main concern has been to investigate, over and above its personal significance and biological function, its spiritual aspect and its numinous meaning, and thus to explain what Freud was so fascinated by but was unable to grasp . . . Sexuality is of the greatest importance as the expression of the chthonic spirit. That spirit is the 'other face of God', the dark side of the God-image. (Jung 1961: 192)

From his earliest work, Deleuze can be found seizing upon and investigating a series of bizarre and idealist ideas about sexuality. As well as Sacher-Masoch's accounts of ritualized sexuality, and Jung's anima and animus, Deleuze develops ideas from Ferenczi's notorious recapitulationist fantasy *Thalassa* (1924), and, after writing on Malfatti's nineteenth-century Tantric *Naturphilosophie* in his earliest phase, continues to develop Malfatti's theme of the esoteric sexual symbolism of the hermaphrodite, through *Proust and Signs* and into *Anti-Oedipus* itself. All these references make use of ideas about sexual consciousness which are quite different to Freud. Here too, sex is interpreted in 'vaster symbols'. For Jung and Deleuze, all sexuality has an occluded supersensible dimension. We cannot be excused from citing Jung's recollection of an encounter with Freud at this point:

> I can still recall vividly how Freud said to me, 'My dear Jung, promise me never to abandon the sexual theory. That is the most essential thing of all. You see, we must make a dogma of it, an unshakeable bulwark.' He said that to me with great emotion, in the tone of a father saying, 'And promise me this one thing, my dear son: that you will go to church every Sunday'. In some astonishment I asked him, 'A bulwark – against what?' To which he replied, 'Against the black tide of mud' – and here he hesitated for a moment, then added – 'of occultism'. (Jung 1961: 173)

In Deleuze's use of Jung in his 1961 'From Sacher-Masoch to Masochism' and afterwards, we find sexuality itself swept up and mingling with these very dark tides. In the later version, *Coldness and Cruelty*, Deleuze writes that 'there is a kind of mysticism in perversion: the greater the renunciation, the greater and more secure the gains; we might compare it to a "black" theology where pleasure ceases to motivate the will and is abjured, disavowed, "renounced", the better to be recovered as a reward or consequence, and as a law' (M 120). This is perhaps especially true of the first, explicitly Jungian version of Deleuze's theory of masochism. In the early article, the central thesis is that male masochism must be conceived as a perverse realization of the fantasy of incest – on condition that incest is taken in its 'more profound' significance as a symbol of rebirth, as Jung claims. Deleuze builds on Jung's reformulation of the psychological import of the incest problem in order to claim that masochism is a symbolic operation by which enjoyment is obtained from the punishment that is received for the violation of the law of the father, through the punishment being undergone for the sake of the mother, whose image guides the son towards a 'second birth', the future world-historical birth of a 'new man' outside the patriarchal order. This self-punishment of the masochist is achieved only by the maintaining of a regressive re-actualization of a primordial *image* of the mother. Deleuze sums his thesis up in a bold formulation: 'It is the image of the Mother, it is the regression to this image, which is constitutive of masochism and forms its unity' (SM 130).

Throughout this text, there is an emphasis on 'primordial' or 'original' images and symbols, with Deleuze going so far as to say that '*in truth, all is symbol in the unconscious*' (SM 131). But at the same time, masochism is a *perversion* and not a neurosis. Masochism is a direct ritualization of sexuality, a living fantasy, whereby the masochist deliberately harnesses his sexual forces in reality, not repressing anything but at the same time transforming his libido in the service of a higher end. Masochism for Deleuze is a dramatization of the Idea of rebirth, where the sexual relationship becomes the vessel for a living, symbolic incarnation of the ideal meaning of incest.

In the last chapter, we saw how Jung claimed that the primary layer of reality is 'symbolic'; in this chapter, we explore the notion of symbolism in more detail. After examining Jung's theory of symbolism, we will turn to Deleuze's attempt to ground his own Jungian notion of the symbol in Kant's aesthetics. Finally, we will be obliged to return to Deleuze's early remarks about the esoteric approach to symbols in his preface to Malfatti, which are shown to underlie and make more intelligible Deleuze's later, 'mature' suggestions about the nature of the symbol.

Jung on Symbolism

The seeds for Jung's decision to make a break from Freud were sown in 1909 on the journey back from the USA, after having spent seven weeks solid with Freud on a lecture tour. Jung's disagreement about the primacy of sexuality had been festering away in the meantime, and Freud's reluctance to submit to dream analysis increased the tension of the voyage. Then Jung had a dream which made a deep impression upon him. There are three accounts of this dream, all conflicting in some respect, but I will give the version to which Deleuze and Guattari refer. Jung was wandering down through the levels of a large, complex rococo house, and reached the cellar; but this led to another cellar, which appeared to be of Roman origin. A hole under a slab led in turn to a tomb filled with prehistoric pottery, bones and skulls. The dust was undisturbed, and he felt that he had made a great discovery.[2] When Jung told Freud the dream during the voyage home, Freud was chiefly interested in the skulls: 'He returned to them repeatedly, and urged me to find a *wish* in connection with them.' Freud says the dream indicates a single death wish, against his (Jung's) wife. 'Jung was surprised and pointed out that there were several skulls, not just one' (Bennet 1966: 64).[3] Deleuze and Guattari cite Bennet's version of the story more than once as an example of Freud's monomaniac strategy of interpretation (cf. ATP 30; D 80). If Freud could claim to have 'deconstructed' the drive, his interpretations nevertheless tended to regroup the drives and their objects around one single psychogenic drama. Dream or symptom elements were always reduced to the *familial* situation of the patient. Deleuze and Guattari argue that it is this stress on the familial which is at the root of Freud's inability to deal with psychotics, whose fantasies and hallucinations tend towards the cosmic and metaphysical. It is much harder to relate the forces which assail the psychotic to the symbolic matrix of the family.

Deleuze and Guattari suggest that when he insists that it is important that there were *several* skulls, not just one or two, Jung has himself already descended to the level of unconscious activity inhabited by schizophrenics. Schizophrenic fantasies and hallucinations, they claim, tend to involve 'multiplicities'.[4] Freud's Wolf Man shows the same trajectory when he dreams of a number of wolves observing him from a tree. Freud reduces the multiplicity of wolves to one wolf, and then says that this is a displacement of the father, but the multiplicity of wolves already indicates that Freud's starting premise is problematic. The indeterminate multiplicity of wolves (or skulls) introduces two further interpretative possibilities, which lead us towards a purer conception of the proper activity of the unconscious. First, it raises the possibility that it is something about wolves or skulls *themselves* that has become an issue in the dreamer's unconscious. In this case, wolves or skulls might have nothing to do with any personal memory. This is significant as it suggests that the unconscious process of dreaming can also be populated by impersonal contents; not everything in the unconscious is related to repressed representations. The wolf no longer appears primarily for representational consciousness but for a special *symbolic* type of cognition. Dreams too are composed of symbols, and therefore must be interpreted in a way that is proper to symbols. The second way of interpreting the multiplicity of wolves involves appeal to the particular ethology of the wolf, and the nature of the 'pack'; we return to this in the final chapter. For the moment, we stay with the notion of the symbol. Deleuze's use of Kant's notion of symbolism is predated by his use of Jung's notion of symbolism. So we should look closer at Jung's definition of a symbol before we press onward to Kant.

Jung's critique of Freud's concept of symbolism is crucial to his critique of Freud and is explicitly taken up by Deleuze in his Jungian phase. Deleuze argues that 'symbols do not allow themselves to be reduced or composed; on the contrary they are the ultimate rule for the composition of desires and their object, they form the only irreducible data of the unconscious . . . The irreducible datum of the unconscious is the symbol itself, and not an ultimate symbolised. *In truth, all is symbol in the unconscious*, sexuality and death no less than anything else' (SM 131). Following Jung, Deleuze identifies symbols with 'primordial' or 'original Images'. 'It was not left to [Freud] to grasp the role of original Images'; this was to be Jung's contribution. In examining this debate, it is important to keep in mind that Jung's prime subject-matter of discussion is the dream-image or the visions or hallucinations of psychotics. At question is how to approach such images and experiences.

The first point in Jung's critique of Freud's conception of symbolism is that Freud has been using the term 'symbol' incorrectly:

> The essential thing in Freud's reductive method is to collect all the clues pointing to the unconscious background, and then, through the analysis and interpretation of this material, to reconstruct the elementary and instinctual processes. Those conscious contents which give us a clue to the unconscious background are incorrectly called *symbols* by Freud. They are not true symbols, however, since according to his theory they have merely

the role of *signs* and *symptoms* of the subliminal processes. The true symbol differs essentially from this, and should be understood as an expression of an intuitive idea that cannot yet be formulated in any other or better way. (CW 15: 70)

In his exposition of Jung's critique, E. A. Bennet cites Roland Dalbiez's *Psychoanalytic Method and the Doctrine of Freud* (1936), which contains a detailed critique of Freud's innovations in the theory of symbolism, influenced by Jung's critique, which he says 'reaches the heart of the question' (Dalbiez 1936: II, 103). Dalbiez's two-volume work was the first substantial evaluation of Freud's work in France, and we will see that there is little doubt that Deleuze himself also read it and was influenced by it. It is worth turning to it first, because it is somewhat clearer than Jung's own account, although more restricted in its range. Dalbiez's bone of contention is that 'Freud has completely modified the usual meaning of the word 'symbol'. Psychoanalytical symbolism constitutes the exact antithesis of ordinary symbolism . . . whereas the ordinary symbol implies no direct causal relation with what it symbolises, the Freudian symbol is essentially and by definition an effect of what it symbolises' (Dalbiez 1936: II, 102, cited in Bennet 1966: 41). Dalbiez argues that by always referring symbols back to actual objects, persons or events from personal history, Freud introduced a confusion between the concept of symbol and that of *index* or *effect-sign*.[5] As Bennet puts it, the way Freud conceived the symbol 'was tantamount to claiming it as a substitute for the real thing' (Bennet 1966: 42). But in bringing about this slippage, Freud occluded an entire set of functions which had up until then been attributed to symbols. Dalbiez writes:

> Common parlance unhesitatingly uses white as the symbol of moral innocence, and black as that of moral evil. We at once observe that the idea of a *direct* causal relation between the symbol and symbolised is not essential to symbolism. Material whiteness is no more an effect of moral innocence than moral innocence is of material whiteness. This is enough to set a gulf between the concepts of symbol and of symptom, or, as we prefer to say, of effect-sign. The symptom proves the existence of its cause; the symbol does not prove that of the symbolised. (Dalbiez 1936: II, 101)

Dalbiez's exposition emphasizes the causal nature of sign, as opposed to the non-causal symbol. However, the Freudian might object that Freud's account of symbolism was only strictly causal while he upheld the seduction theory (the theory that actual infantile sexual traumas caused neuroses). From 1906 onward, Freud argued that neuroses were rooted in infantile fantasies rather than actual historical situations.[6] Jung's version of the critique (which he came up with in the 1920s) might be able to escape this objection.

In *Psychological Types*, Jung presents the distinction as between *semiotic* and *symbolic* modes of interpretation. 'Every view which interprets the symbolic expression as an analogue or an abbreviated designation for a *known* thing is *semiotic*' (CW 6: 474). Jung clarifies this by specifying that interpretation is semiotic when a symptom or dream-image is 'reduced' (ibid.: 479) to a signifier of repressed sexual events in the patient's history; Freud's approach resolves the image 'into its memory components and the underlying instinctual processes' (CW 7: 81). The problem is that Freud takes the semiotic interpretation of symbols to be the only one, overlooking the fact that the notion of the symbol has had an important history in aesthetics.[7] It is possible that the distinction between symbol and allegory is relevant for the psychiatric understanding of symbolism. The distinction between symbol and allegory has a long and complicated history in aesthetics, but it is perhaps its development in Schelling's work on mythology that is most relevant for understanding Jung's and Deleuze's approach. Schelling argued that symbols functioned in a different way to allegorical images or scenes – which required knowledge of an actual esoteric 'key' which relates the elements to a historical or mythical narrative. The power of religious and mythical images did not come from their allegorical function. As Beach puts it, 'the function of myths in religions was not to impart information or to reach an intellectual understanding of the world, but rather had something to do with stimulating a special kind of psychological response within the listener' (Beach 1994: 34). It might be similarly possible to 'listen' to dreams in two different ways. On the one hand, as referring to concrete past events, and on the other hand as addressing the listener in the present. Jung makes an analogy with Kant's distinction between analytic and synthetic judgments (the former clarify, while the latter amplify; Kant 1782/1787: A7/B11); dream-symbols too must be approached 'synthetically' as well as 'analytically' (CW 7: 80–9; cf. SM 133). Although the semiotic interpretation may sometimes be appropriate for certain dream interpretations, dreams and all symptoms frequently contain symbols which *might* well be addressing the subject directly with a problem or enigma to be solved in the present, by an act of synthesis.

If we do treat our unconscious as a superior Other, then we have to listen to its cryptic statements very carefully, just as we listen carefully to a piece of music by Beethoven or Stockhausen. Moreover, since the dream addresses us in the present, addressing our current libidinal state, the symbol might equally be trying to communicate something of which we are not yet conscious. 'We know, from abundant experience as well as for theoretical reasons, that the unconscious also contains all the material that has *not yet* reached the threshold of consciousness' (CW 7: 128). A common but important instance of this can be found in apparently premonitory dreams of miscarriage. More generally, Jung says that symbols are used when 'the chosen expression is the best possible description or formulation of a relatively unknown fact, which is nonetheless known to exist, or postulated as existing' (CW 6: 474). The symbol, taken as symbol, expresses something to which existence might be attributed, but whose nature is indeterminate.[8] It expresses some enigmatic aspect of reality, which cannot be reduced to being the 'sign of a definite and generally known underlying process'. It is not just dreams and psychosis which produce symbols: art, humour and religion all use symbols to communicate messages that cannot be uttered in normal, representational language, but which concern problematic *realities* which directly concern us. These images need to be 'amplified' (CW 7: 81). 'Once embarked on the task of examining the dream-material, you must not shrink from any comparison' (CW 4: 145). Symbolic images are communications, and in dreams often occur intensively in sequences, like a sequence of riddles given by a demonic super-ego, always 'superior' to our ego, which we must use 'all the conscious means at our disposal' to crack.[9]

At another level, symbols also testify to special 'synthetic' processes in the unconscious itself. Jung stresses that the unconscious operates by condensing unconscious material into an enigmatic symbol that 'synthetically' expresses each of the sides at work in the current psychic conflict. Thus although Freud appears to give equal weight to both displacement and condensation in *The Interpretation of Dreams*, his model of the psychic process forces him to give primacy to the former, insofar as dream-distortion in general operates through the displacement of psychic intensities across the derivatives of a repressed representation (cf. SE 4: 177). Jung's emphasis on the role of condensation in symbols suggests that condensation involves a different kind of synthesis, perhaps involving something like the 'condensation of singularities' Deleuze discusses in relation to the determination of the Idea in *Difference and Repetition*: in an initial apprehension of a problem, we discover 'the varieties of the multiplicity in all its dimensions, the fragments of ideal future or past events, which . . . render the problem solvable'; then 'we must condense all the singularities, precipitate all the circumstances, points of fusion, congelation or condensation in a sublime occasion, *Kairos*, which makes the solution explode like something abrupt, brutal and revolutionary' (DR 190). The unconscious is creative and 'amplificatory' in Kant's sense that the positive syntheses of the unconscious produce '*new* contents' (CW 8: 364), which cannot be reduced to their previously existing analytic elements.

It is interesting that in his first seminar Lacan suggests that some of the Wolf Man's symptoms must be classed as psychotic rather than neurotic. He does not just fantasize about castration, but hallucinates a bleeding finger. 'At this point in his childhood, nothing entitles one to classify him as a schizophrenic, but it really is a psychotic phenomenon we are dealing with' (Lacan 1953: 59). Lacan suggests that the Wolf Man is *foreclosing* the Oedipal position, rather than repressing it into the unconscious (ibid.: 43). He acts as if the symbolic order (in Lacan's sense) did not exist and has no claim upon him, and thus surrenders all protection against the deceptions and distortions of the imaginary. In his seminar on the psychoses, Lacan argues at length that what distinguishes the psychotic from the neurotic (which includes the 'normal' person) is the latter's entrance into the intersubjective order of linguistic communication. The phenomena of perception and imagination remain the same in each case – everyone is regularly subject to distortions of perception and internal voices – but the neurotic has intersubjective and symbolic or linguistic criteria for what counts as real. Reality is a shared phenomenon, guaranteed by mutual recognition, so hallucinations can be brushed off if nobody else verifies them. The intersubjective conditions of language are so deeply ingrained that internal voices are simply interpreted as inner dialogue between self and one's 'significant Other', 'I' and 'You' (Lacan 1955: 51). In a nutshell, 'what characterises a normal subject is precisely that he never takes seriously certain realities that he recognises exist' (ibid.: 74). The Wolf Man is psychotic because he takes wolves so seriously.

We will see in chapter 6 that Deleuze and Guattari imply that the Wolf Man was a lycanthrope, and that he was therefore quite right to take his wolves seriously. Eighteenth-century descriptions of epidemics of lycanthropy stress the state of trance or dissociation that occurs in the preliminary stages, followed by the frenzy of the feeling of transformation.[10] In other words, for Deleuze and Guattari, the Wolf Man does not necessarily have a latent psychosis. Instead, he is a manifest lycanthrope. Ultimately, the classification of certain symptoms as neurotic and psychotic obstructs the interpretation of symbols. The question is whether certain symptoms or fantasies that are traditionally classified as psychotic should be defined gnoseologically at all, or whether they in fact bear witness rather to different *levels* of unconscious activity, which may emerge in psychosis *or* neurosis. We have seen that in 'From Sacher-Masoch to Masochism' Deleuze endorses Jung's view that 'Freudian methodologies are appropriate mainly for young neurotics whose disorders are related to personal reminiscences and whose problems are about reconciling themselves with the *real* (loving, making oneself lovable, adapting, etc.), without regard for the role of any interior conflicts' (SM 133). But on the other hand, 'there are neuroses of quite another type which are nearer to psychosis' (ibid.). Conversely, as Deleuze points out in *Difference and Repetition*, schizophrenics can exhibit what appear to be obsessional symptoms: 'Consider the gestural or linguistic repetitions and iterations or stereotypical behaviours associated with dementia or schizophrenia. These no longer seem to manifest a will capable of investing an object within the context of a ceremony; rather they function like reflexes which indicate a general breakdown of investment' (DR 290). For Deleuze, the real line of demarcation will be between different levels of the unconscious. Like Jung, he believes that there is an autonomous, productive activity which is proper to the unconscious itself. This productive unconscious is the motor of the process of individuation. It is this level which is characteristically expressed in psychosis, but which can also appear in neuroses under certain conditions. On the other hand, unconscious activity appears in distorted, inverted form, when consciousness approaches it in a *reactive* attitude. Here the unconscious is not met on its own terms, and consciousness is concerned 'reconciling [itself] with the *real* (loving, making oneself lovable, adapting, etc.)', rather than with individuation. Again, this is characteristic of neurosis, but the psychotic will inevitably be profoundly concerned at various junctures with problems of adaptation.

Kant's Theory of Symbolism

In 1961 Deleuze fully affirms Jung's notion of symbolism, but by 1963 he has nevertheless turned to Kant for a fuller explanation of the nature and implications of the symbol. In the psychotic process, it would appear, there is some sort of liberation of the productive and reproductive imagination from the practical norms of conceptual representation. What needs to be understood is how the mind functions upon this release, independently of the processes of reaction which characterizes neurosis. In Kant's *Critique of Judgment,* Deleuze finds a purely aesthetic account of how the imagination becomes immanently reoriented to the symbol when it breaks free of the normative rules of the understanding. But although Deleuze does not talk here about the *symbols of the unconscious,* the turn to aesthetics is consistent with his insistence that the productions of the unconscious should be examined in art and culture as well as in psychopathology, and that the two might be harder to separate than it appears. Deleuze's turn to Kant for a theory of symbolism in fact gives the Jungian theory of symbolism a firmer epistemological grounding. It also produces an unexpected transformation of the Jungian claim that it is the symbolic layer of reality that is re-activated in psychosis. Kant reveals another, more subterranean *destination* of the imagination, beneath the functions of conceptual representation, in the apprehension of the world as symbol. Nature becomes a book of symbols. At that point, in the last part of this chapter, we shall to plunge back into Deleuze's earliest writings on poetic and occult uses of symbolism. For the mysterious Johann Malfatti in his *Mathesis,* to which Deleuze provided the foreword for its first republication in a hundred years, nature itself is hieroglyphic, an expression of the body of a tripartite, living divine reality.

Deleuze's *Kant's Critical Philosophy* (1963) affords an unusually large place to Kant's notion of symbolism. In the fourth of his 1978 Kant lectures, Deleuze still accords supreme importance to Kant's theory of symbolism, and he suggests that it is behind his own suggestions about the spatiotemporal 'dramatisation of Ideas.' At this point in Kant's work, we find the 'schematism' of the imagination lured away from its function in the process of knowledge and empirical perception, towards another destination: the schematizing imagination 'risks being overwhelmed by something monstrous, which Kant is the first to analyse, to my knowledge. It is symbolism' (Fourth Lecture on Kant, 2).[11] Two important things appear to be happening here. First, Deleuze's turn to Kant to develop the notion of symbol suggests an attempt to ground the Jungian approach to symbolism within a more rigorous theory of cognition. Jung himself does not refer to Kant's aesthetics, although we will see that the latter is consistent with his notion of symbolism, and even, with Deleuze's modifications, powerfully augments it. Secondly, with the notion of symbolism, we are now seeing another front opening up in Deleuze's attempt to unearth the internal hierarchies of cognition, and to the elicit the hidden ends of cognition, beneath conceptual representation. Parallel to Deleuze's attempt to push

Kant's theory of schematism in the direction of a theory of 'spatiotemporal dynamisms', symbolism will be the clue to the narrow set of conditions under which the dimension of 'Ideas' can be 'presented' to the mind, overriding the limits of the conceptual understanding.

We have seen that Deleuze deploys his conception of Ideas in ways that move beyond Kant's theory of cognition towards a theory of the unconscious. He claims that Ideas must be taken to be 'necessarily unconscious' (DR 192). It looks as though Deleuze is synthesizing Kant with Jung's theory that cognition is unconsciously motivated by 'problematical states' (CW 8: 391). If this is even half-right, then it is clear how radically non-Freudian Deleuze's notion of the unconscious is. If Ideas are unconscious, they are so in a very specific and restricted sense. They are not unconscious in the Freudian sense that they lie outside consciousness *tout court* and can only be known by their 'derivatives'. Rather they are 'unconscious' only in the sense that we cannot be *conscious of* them in the way we are conscious of empirical things or representational states of mind, by virtue either of our capacity to have intuitions of them, or even to make judgements and inferences about them. The Idea is both more and less unconscious than Freudian repressed representations. It is more unconscious as we cannot even make secure inferences about it on the basis of displaced 'derivatives'. It is less unconscious in the sense that Kant's expanded theory of cognition allows us to conceive of non-representational types of cognition. Symbolic thought is exactly one such type of cognition; artistic creativity is another. Kant's theory allows one to open up the theory of 'the unconscious' to accommodate highly specific types of cognition that cannot be recognized by the Freudian model. For Deleuze, the Idea is a *destination* of cognition that *motivates* representational thought while being *unconscious to* it. This allows Deleuze to introduce a teleology into the theory of the unconscious which is again foreign to Freud. To say that we are unconsciously motivated by an Idea is also to say that our actions are guided by an *end* which remains only implicit, which can only be explicated or unfolded, as we will see in chapter 6, under certain conditions.[12] The end of cognition only becomes fully conscious in the state of 'repetition', but afterwards it is forgotten immediately, and consciousness once again becomes inadequate to the Idea.

As with Jung, cognition and affection must be situated within a process of individuation, during which we 'learn' (always to the cost of our ego and representation) about the forces which really guide us, and then attempt to take charge of them.

> To what are we dedicated if not to those problems which demand the very transformation of our body and our language? In short, representation and knowledge are modelled entirely upon propositions of consciousness which designate cases of solution, but those propositions themselves give a completely inaccurate notion of the instance which engenders them as cases, and which they resolve or conclude. By contrast, the Idea and 'learning' express that extra-propositional or sub-representative problematic instance:

the presentation of the unconscious, not the representation of consciousness. (DR 192)

Deleuze turns to Kant's aesthetics in particular for an account of the role of the imagination in this process of individuation. 'The imagination discovers the origin and destination of all [the] activities [of cognition]', a 'suprasensible destination, which is also like its transcendental origin' (DI 63). Kant suggests that we are first made aware of this destination through the exceeding of representation in the experience of the sublime in nature, which then opens up the more complex and profound possibility of the 'reflection' of natural symbolism in the imagination. If the Ideas cannot be *represented*, then they can be given a 'presentation' (*Darstellung*) *as* Ideas. 'According to Kant, the Ideas of reason can be presented in sensible nature. In the sublime, the presentation is direct, but negative, and done by projection; in natural symbolism . . . the presentation is positive but indirect, and is achieved by reflection' (KCP 59). If the encounter with the formless sublime enacts the *genesis* of the moral destination of all cognition, beauty itself also carries with it a half-concealed moral dimension: 'beauty is the symbol of morality' (Kant 1790: Ak. 351). However, Deleuze suggests that the ultimate destination of cognition and affection is perhaps less straightforwardly moral than Kant himself realizes. 'Aesthetic judgment finds itself referred to something that is both in the subject himself and outside him, something that is neither nature nor freedom and yet is linked with the basis of freedom, the supersensible, in which the theoretical and the practical power are in an unknown manner combined and joined into a unity' (Kant 1790: Ak. 353). There is a third possible kind of presentation in artistic genius, which gives rise to a specifically artistic symbolism. There the possibility arises of the most 'adequate' kind of presentation of the Idea; the artist is responsible for 'the creation of another nature' (KCP 59). In this other nature, 'invisible beings, the kingdom of the blessed, and hell assume a body; and love and death assume a dimension that makes them adequate to their spiritual meaning' (DI 67/66). How could our interest in the *realization* of the Idea not be intensified and altered in nature by such glimpses into another world? Morality is inevitably contaminated by art and myth; the form taken by the Kantian agent's hopes and desires will be shaped as much by the Bible, Shakespeare and Milton, as by abstract rational principles. Our *interest* in the realization of moral freedom forces us to explore other worlds, where we can contemplate love and hell in purer outline than in our own. And this in turn forces us to elaborate our moral world, the *mundus intelligibilis* which Kant speaks of. Deleuze concludes: 'If we are destined to be moral beings, it is because this destiny develops or explicates a supersensible destination for all our faculties' (DI 69/68).

The affirmation of this third possibility produces an 'aesthetic turn' in Deleuze's work, and allows him to qualify the Kantian emphasis on the moral aspect of the Idea. If he retains a teleological conception of individuation throughout his work of the 1960s, the activity of the artist is always the highest form of individuation, not only because in artistic creation the individual achieves the most elaborate kind of self-differentiation, but also because the work of art gives individuality itself its most elaborate and solicitous expression. We care so deeply about good art because each work brings into existence an aesthetic 'world' whose existence is no less real for being entirely 'spiritual'. Deleuze's book on Proust is the most exquisite expression of this transmutation of Kantian moral finality into aesthetic finality. 'Art is the finality of the world, and the apprentice's unconscious destination' (PS 50).

We must now turn to the details of Kant's theory of symbolism. The theory is situated within a complex argument about the beautiful and sublime in nature and art. It is presented in a section devoted to the 'Deduction' of aesthetic judgements, after Kant has explored the two 'Analytics', of the Beautiful and the Sublime, and it introduces some important modifications to what has gone previously. In the Analytic of the Beautiful, Kant has argued that beauty arises because an object produces a harmonious accord between the faculties of sensibility and understanding, so that a feeling of universality is attained without the understanding having to determine the object conceptually. This not only releases the imagination from its reproductive function, but its productive role too is liberated from conceptual representation. The imagination's absorption in *reflective judgement* upon the object is radical, with the consequence that the empirical world can seem to disappear in aesthetic contemplation. Now, in the Analytic Kant argues that the pleasure produced by the beautiful aesthetic object (whether natural or artificial) is disinterested, because it is the *form* of the object that is reflected upon; we are strangely indifferent to the actual existence of the thing depicted. However, in the Deduction Kant proceeds to point out that we are nevertheless in *some* sense deeply invested in the experience of contemplation. Something *matters* in aesthetic experience, so that it is never enough to accept that the experience is *just* an illusion. It turns out that for Kant this strange *interest* we have in the beautiful is precisely directed towards its symbolic aspects. The beautiful is ultimately *not* just indifferent, 'aestheticizing' pleasure, but is, as we have mentioned, a 'symbol of morality'. Although Kant's emphasis is on symbolism in nature, Deleuze suggests that our interest also extends to the symbols produced by the artist. In *Kant's Critical Philosophy*, and a contemporaneous essay 'The Idea of Genesis in Kant's Aesthetics', he brings out the hidden trajectory that moves through Kant's *Critique of Judgment*, and which relates the dimension of the aesthetic to that of the Idea, via the path of symbolism.

Kant's analysis of the sublime first of all uncovers a moral dimension to aesthetic contemplation. Our sense of awe at the sublime spectacles of formlessness and deformation in nature do not simply arise because our productive imagination is striving to synthesise something too immense to take in all at once. Something else happens when 'the imagination is pushed *to the limit of its power*' (DI 62/63).[13] We realize that it is our capacity for reason which in truth is motivating us to 'unite the infinity of the sensible world into a whole . . . The imagination is forced to admit that all its power is nothing in relation to a rational Idea' (ibid.).[14] Deleuze argues that Kant is here providing a model for the *genesis* of the relations of the faculties.[15] Imagination finds itself newly *oriented* by the violent apprehension of its ultimate relation with reason. Whereas the schematism of the imagination is ordinarily subjected to the categories of the understanding, in the event of the sublime it is reoriented towards the Ideas of reason: 'The accord of the imagination and reason is effectively engendered in this discord.' Unlike the beautiful, the accord of the faculties only emerges from a prior discord between imagination and understanding. The pain or unease caused by this discord of the faculties is in turn resolved by a higher-order pleasure: 'Pleasure is engendered within pain.' In Kant's aesthetic of the sublime we encounter an entirely different model of pleasure and pain to Freud's energetic model. Not only are pleasure and pain derived from an analysis of cognition, rather than vice versa (cognition as an emergent property of the process of libidinal discharge), but they are given a teleological significance which is of course lacking in Freud.

'The imagination surpasses its own limitations, in a negative way it is true, by representing to itself the inaccessibility of the rational Idea and by making this inaccessibility something present in sensible nature.' However, if it is the Idea which is making itself present here, that indicates that the formlessness of the canyons, ravines, and mountains found in nature, the deformed billowing of clouds and fire, are ultimately *occasions* for this presentation. One might expect the falling away of form and order in nature to lead to the opposite of the beautiful – the ugly or monstrous – but in fact the fall into the formless abyss is an occasion for the appearance of something unanticipated. The colossal puncture in the sensible world tears open the heavens and reveals this world as other than we had taken it to be. The sensible world is no longer a realm of limitation and finitude, but the scene for the realization of the Idea, a space for incarnation.

The sublime is less an experience of something 'out there', which is in itself awe-inspiring, than a *projection* of our own destination within the realm of sensible nature. 'It is only in appearance, or by projection, that the sublime is related to sensible nature' (ibid.; cf. KCP 58). This use of the model of projection is important, as it helps emphasize that we are unable to encounter our freedom face-to-face, but can only first accede to it by projecting it onto nature. We must first experience reason as Other, as appearing in the formless abysses of nature. The model of projection is not found in Kant's text, and brings out the idea that there is something *unconscious* in our experience of the sublime. We don't see our own shadow in the abyss. Deleuze's remark recalls Jung's idea that the unconscious is first encountered through a projection onto the other (the shadow): 'Projections change the world into the replica of one's own unknown face' (CW 9ii: 9). Freud also ventures a similar idea in *The Psychopathology of Everyday Life*.

> When human beings began to think, they were, as is well known, forced to explain the external world anthropomorphically by means of a multitude of

> personalities in their own image . . . I believe that a large part of the mythological view of the world, which extends a long way into the most modern religions, *is nothing but psychology projected into the external world.* (SE 6: 259, 258)

However, Freud's later development of the concept occurs mostly within the context of paranoia. Projection involves the *disavowal* of some *particular* piece of reality. Schreber disavows his (supposedly) homosexual desires with the result that 'what was abolished [*aufgehoben*] internally returns from without' (SE 12: 71). Therefore, Jung's use of the term to describe the projection of *the unconscious tout court* is closer to Deleuze's use of it here. The 'unknown inner world' is projected, and first encountered outside, in the shadow.

But this line of thought also raises another important issue which is only implicit in Deleuze's reading due to his concentration on the systematic argumentation, rather than on the process of 'transcendental formation' or 'transcendental culture' itself (DI 61/62). The model of projection usually points towards the overcoming of projection through an incorporation by the subject of their alienated aspect. But in Kant and Deleuze something more complex and interesting occurs. The subject never recuperates their projection; rather the projection is itself transformed into *another* 'alienation': this time, the world as symbol.

Once the Idea has been presented in negative form in the sublime, it does not disappear, or simply wait for the next sublime experience to occur. Nor is the moral sense simply awakened, leaving the aesthetic sense behind. A transcendental formation has occurred, which means that the subject is transformed. Therefore although Kant begins the *Critique of Judgment* with an analysis of the disinterested nature of the contemplation of beauty, it turns out that this analysis is an *abstraction* from the whole story about beauty. Once the subject has undergone the experience of the sublime, their experience of *beauty* will also be altered. Beauty is not the same after the sublime. The imagination has been awakened to its destination in the Idea, and this now adds an undercurrent to all experiences of beauty. What this means is that the unconscious *projection* of the Idea into formless nature is now expanded and changes in nature. Now *all of nature* is potentially animated by the Idea. But because we are not yet 'self-conscious' of our role in the projection of the sublime, when this unconsciousness is transmitted to the rest of nature (formed and beautiful nature, that is), it can no longer be called a projection. We now appear to find ourselves in nature; nature appears to *teach* us through its symbols. In our experience of the beautiful, we are now reading the Book of Nature. If in projection we made ourselves Other, now, rather than reincorporating this Other, we truly *forget* that this Other is ourselves. The model changes from projection to recollection, and only thus does a 'return to self' come about. To read the symbols in the Book of Nature is to *recollect* ourselves, to re-find ourselves *in the object.*

Kant specifies that the indirect presentation involved in symbolism operates through analogy. 'Symbolic presentation uses an analogy . . . in which judgment performs a double function: it applies the concept to the object of a sensible intuition; and then it applies the mere rule by which it reflects on that intuition to an entirely different object, of which the former object is only the symbol' (Kant 1790: Ak. 352). He gives the example of the symbolic presentation of absolute monarchy as a hand mill: 'For though there is no similarity between a despotic state and a hand mill, there certainly is one between the rules by which we reflect on the two and on how they operate.' What the despot is to the people, the miller is to grain; the symbol functions through an analogical correspondence between hand-mill and state. Another example is the white lily as symbol of innocence (Kant 1790: 302). Deleuze writes that 'the white lily is not merely related to the concepts of colour and flower, but also awakens the Idea of pure innocence, whose object is merely a (reflexive) analogue of the white in the lily flower (KCP 54).' Deleuze emphasizes almost the same example as Dalbiez does in his discussion of symbolism in psychoanalysis. The white lily is an example of an analogical symbol: 'What innocence is to the mind corresponds to what whiteness is to the body' (Dalbiez 1936: II, 101).

For Deleuze, Kant's notion of symbolism provides the key to the problem of how the imagination becomes set free from the understanding. If the 'schematism' is the basic non-representational matrix of the unconscious, then it finds its ultimate unconscious 'destination' in symbolism. Kant's distinction between symbol and schema in the *Critique of Judgment* is to be found 'among the most admirable pages in Kant' (Fourth Lecture on Kant, 8). Where schematism sketches out the spatiotemporal correlate of a pure concept, symbolism uses the same type spatiotemporal correlate 'not in relation to the corresponding concept A, but in relation to the quite different concept B for which you have no intuition of a schema. At that moment the schema ceases to be a rule of production in relation to its concept, and becomes a rule of reflection in relation to the other concept. So much so that you have the Kantian sequence: synthesis refers to a rule of recognition, the schema refers to rules of production, the symbol refers to rules of reflection' (ibid; cf. Kant 1790: Ak. 352). The destination of the imagination thus lies in reflection. Kant's concept of reflection here is based on the notion of reflective judgement, which he opposes to determining judgement; it obviously has little to do with reflection in the cognitive sense. But perhaps there is, on the other hand, a connotation of the *mirror* in the notion that imagination finds its destination in 'reflection' upon symbols in nature. The symbol is a mirror, or a frozen image, because it is finally a precipitate of the unconscious activity of the productive imagination. But what happens when the subject finally 'finds itself' in the symbol we have still to see.

Let us now follow in more detail the path taken by Kant, pursued by Deleuze, through the *Critique of Judgment* to the concept of symbolism. If aesthetic contemplation is capable of giving Ideas of reason a sensible presentation (as has been shown by the case of the sublime) then a certain kind of interest can be ascribed to it. For 'reason also has an interest in the objective reality of the Ideas; i.e. an interest that nature should at least show a trace or give a hint that it contains some basis or other for us to assume in its products a lawful harmony with that liking of ours which is *independent of all interest*' (Kant 1790: 300). Once we are captured by the claim of reason, how can our experience of beauty, as well as the sublime, not be accompanied by a deeper interest that goes beyond any sensuous interest in the existence of the particular beautiful object? Aesthetic experience must somehow also be the vehicle for a '*rational interest in the contingent accord of nature's productions with our disinterested pleasure*' (KCP 54). Deleuze stresses that it is important to acknowledge that this special interest does not contradict the disinterestedness that is essential to the aesthetic in general. 'It is a question of an interest that is connected to the judgment [of the beautiful] synthetically. It does not bear on the beautiful as such, but on the aptitude of nature to produce beautiful things' (DI 64/65). It is not a sensuous passion, but a peculiar passion of reason that is borne by aesthetic pleasure. But this is a conceptual distinction; how could they avoid being confused in practice? The only way in which disinterested pleasure in a beautiful object and rational interest in that same object could finally avoid being confused (resulting in one submerging the other and covering over any evidence of its existence) would be if 'the interest connected with the beautiful bears upon determinations to which the sense of the beautiful remained indifferent' (DI 65/65). And it happens that there is a gap in the aesthetic experience of nature, where this interest can make itself felt. In the disinterested sense of the beautiful, the imagination reflects the *form* only. It cannot reflect upon mere colour, mere sound. 'On the contrary, the *interest* connected to the beautiful bears upon sounds and colours, the colour of flowers and the songs of birds' (ibid., italic added). That is, it reflects upon the 'free materials of nature' (KCP 54).

It is just this 'remainder' of the beautiful that serves as the vehicle for symbolism, for the indirect, but now *positive* presentation of the Idea (KCP 58; DI 66/66).

> For example, we do not merely relate colour to a concept of the understanding which would directly apply to it, we also relate it to a *quite different* concept which does not have an object of intuition on its own account, but which resembles the concept of the understanding because it posits its object by analogy with the object of the intuition. (KCP 54)

The basic condition of the significance of the analogy between the white body of the lily and the Idea of pure innocence is that the *whiteness* itself be animated by our interest in Ideas being incarnated. It is 'primary matter' that is at the source of the production of symbols in nature (DI 65/65). The identification of this *materia prima* is a delicate process, as it must fall outside of the 'formal' accords found in the disinterested sense of the beautiful, while not falling into the 'formlessness' found in sublime nature. Can it be done? Deleuze writes that 'Kant even defines the primary matter that intervenes in the natural production of the beautiful: fluid matter, part of which separates or evaporates, while the rest suddenly solidifies (the formation of crystals)'. In # 59 of the *Critique of Judgment* Kant gives an account of the '*free formations* of nature' which indicates that primary matter is something more than mere quality, as the examples of colour and sound might have led us to think. 'Under the described circumstances, formation then take place not be a gradual transition from the fluid to the solid state, but as it were by a leap: a sudden solidification called *shooting*; this transition is also called *crystallization*. The commonest example of this type of formation occurs when water freezes' (Kant 1790: Ak. 348). Kant invokes a process of *formation* and even uses the precise example to which Deleuze so often appeals to illustrate the *intensive* nature of quality. The freezing of water is a properly intensive process, as it is both durational and involves the crossing of a threshold (or singularity).

Kant's reflections on the connection between intensive natural processes and symbol-formation are extremely suggestive. He notes that 'many such mineral crystallisations, e.g., spars, hematite, and aragonite, often result in exceedingly beautiful shapes, such shapes as art might invent; and the halo in the grotto of Antiparos [in the Cyclades in Greece] is merely the product of water seeping through layers of gypsum' (ibid.: 349). Given the traces of religious symbolism left in the grottoes of Lascaux and other sites, Kant's theory suggests a hypothesis that certain natural environments might be rich in symbolic 'potential'. If absorption in reflective judgement tends to liberate the imagination from its subordination under the norms of empirical, determining judgement, the descent into the crystalline world of the grotto may have provided the conditions for a founding moment in 'transcendental culture': the transition to a new *a priori* synthesis between the productive imagination and the symbol. The Hall of the Bulls at Lascaux is filled with concretions of minute calcite needles which produce exceptional optical effects, while the entrance to the Chamber of Felines is encrusted with mondmilch.[16] The Idea might have been concretely incarnated for the first time in stalagmite caverns like these, before the enraptured eyes of shamans and priests lately descended from their sublime mountain sanctuaries. In the opening pages of *Difference and Repetition* Deleuze suggests that 'the meaning of the grove, the grotto and the "sacred" object' (DR 2) can only have emerged through an apprehension of the identity of change and permanence in nature. In the liquid silence of the grotto, then, behind the faces of the formed crystals and stalactites, are the traces of a universal process of intensive transformation.[17] What completes the synthesis of image and symbol is the total impression that one has entered a space of intensive transformation. The grotto itself is a crystal. In pursuing this vein in Kant's later thought, Deleuze is consciously mining the Romantic line of thought that followed on from Kantianism and altered its direction. 'Novalis, with his tourmaline, is closer to the conditions of the sensible than Kant, with space and time' (DR 222). Novalis, as well as being the archetypal Romantic poet, also trained as a mining engineer, and saw in crystallization 'schemata of inner transformations' (Novalis 1977: III: 389) more profound than Kant's schematism, which he thought restricted merely to 'outer sensibility'. Kant's schematism of space and time remained at the level of merely '*visible* rules of the order of manifold space or of extensive objects' (Novalis 1977: II: 390). Crystal formation is intensive in the further sense that it is punctuated by geometrical *singularities*; these singularities are nevertheless precipitated by duration. But if crystallization is the key to the schematism, and if 'every body has its time – [and] every time its body' (Novalis 1997: 136), then crystal formation can also unlock the form of consciousness itself: 'The interior resonance of consciousness – of representation under all its forms – is that of a crystallisation, of a formation and a diversification' (Novalis 1966: 285).[18] Deleuze cites Novalis as one of his two main influences among the post-Kantians (along with Solomon Maimon) (DI 114), but if Novalis's excavations of intensive transformation are closer to the conditions of the sensible than Kant's theory of space and time in the *Critique of Pure Reason*, then perhaps he does not get that much closer than Kant himself, when he descends into the crystal grotto in the *Critique of Judgment*.

Deleuze's interest in Novalis may arise as much from his conception of a 'magical idealism' as from his ideas about time and space. Novalis identified a kind of 'transcendental poetry' from which 'a tropology can be anticipated which comprehends the laws of the *symbolic construction* of the transcendental world' (Novalis 1997: 57). His reflections on the schematism meet up with an appreciation of the power of symbolism, the combination of which ushers in the final, 'magical' form of idealism, after Fichte (ibid.: 107). 'If you cannot make your thoughts indirectly (and accidentally) perceptible, then do the reverse – make external things directly (and arbitrarily) perceptible . . . Make external things into thoughts . . . Both operations are idealistic. Whoever has them both perfectly in his power is the *magical idealist*' (ibid.: 126). Philosophically, Novalis's project is rooted in the attempt to synthesize the productive imagination with symbolism, the positive but indirect presentation of the Idea. To the extent that Deleuze's project (at least up until *Difference and Repetition*) tends towards the same end, it too is a magical idealism. The difference is that Deleuze's post-Jungian theory passes through the theory of the unconscious. The task of producing an *a priori* synthesis of the productive imagination with the symbol and with artistic creation is an attempt to chart the *unconscious* origin and destination of cognition and affection.

Schema and Symbol

Let us probe further into Deleuze's account of the relation between schema and symbol. We know that Deleuze never just interprets Kant for reasons of pure scholarship. His aim is always to transform Kantianism for his own purposes, and in Kant's theory of symbolism he glimpses an opportunity to introduce a very far reaching innovation. We have already seen that Deleuze finds in Kantian schematism a pure, *a priori* and productive use of the imagination which produces forms within what might be termed the 'free materials' of the spatiotemporal manifold itself. Deleuze reminds us that Kant's theory of space and time is rooted in his early theory about incongruent counterparts, which already suggests that space has an inner, intensive form (the division between left and right, above and below). Deleuze suggests that the schematism points towards a 'dramatization' of Ideas in the intensive experience of space and time; he rests his case on instances from psychiatry (e.g. the obsessive who shrinks the bell-rope). However, in his 1963 essay on Kant's aesthetics, Deleuze qualifies his use of the schematism, and suggests that another component is required for this model of the schematism to truly work. 'The imagination does not schematise by itself . . . It does so only insofar as the understanding determines or induces it to do so. It only schematises in the speculative interest, as a function of the determinate concepts of the understanding, when the understanding itself has the legislative role' (DI 58–9/60–1). Although Deleuze attempts to liberate the power of the schematism by emphasizing Kant's remark that it is a product of the pure imagination rather than the understanding, he also acknowledges that other conditions need to be in place for this liberation to proceed. It is not enough to show that the schematism already has some autonomy from the operations of the understanding; some other *positive* task needs to be given to spatiotemporal schematism if it is to reveal another destination. 'It would be wrong to scrutinize the mysteries of the schematism as though they harbour the final word of the imagination in its essence or in its free spontaneity. The schematism is a secret, but not the deepest secret of the imagination'. Left to its own devices, he claims, 'without a concept from the understanding, the imagination does something else than schematizing. In fact, it *reflects*'. In other words, it symbolizes. Symbolic cognition no longer determines objects but permits the reflective contemplation of objects outside merely their conceptual significance.[19]

If we return for a moment to our initial discussion of symbolism in Freud and Jung, we are perhaps now able to glimpse the concrete effects of Deleuze's development of a Kant–Jung synthesis in the theory of symbolism. The cross can be taken as a first example; another important example will be introduced shortly. Contra what Jung called the 'semiotic' approach, the cross cannot be reduced to a sign of the event of the crucifixion, but instead functions for the Christian as a mandala for inexhaustible meditation or 'reflection'. In Kant's own terms in the *Critique of Judgment*, it is not entirely clear how the cross functions as a symbol, as it does not seem to be a free formation of nature. However, we have seen that Kant also gestures towards a theory of intensive formation and transformation, which can be taken up in Deleuzian terms. On the full Deleuzian model, then, the cross is the synthesis of two elementary spatiotemporal, intensive schematisms – on the one hand, vertical ascent and descent and on the other, horizontal tension between opposites. As *synthesis*, the cross is much *more* than the sum of two trajectories. By virtue of its implied potential infinity, it divides space itself into four compartments, as well as producing a fifth point, the centre. The synthesis is thus genuinely amplificatory (as the logical sense of synthesis in Kant requires) insofar as these supervening determinations do not pre-exist the synthesis. The cross is therefore a multiplicity (or a 'manifold') *as well* as being a synthesis. Now, as this multiplicity, it is capable of determining the entirety of space. It can divide up the whole of space. But this in turn takes it *out* of space, as it thereby becomes a pure, *a priori* spatial determination; a schema in other words. In other words, the cross functions as an *ideal multiplicity*. But let us now stop to reflect. What does it mean to say that all space can be determined by the form of the cross? There is nothing that subjects *space itself* to this form, or to any other (the circle, for instance). So where does it find a truly *synthetic a priori* application? In fact, its sphere of application emerges only when it becomes *a symbol* of a non-actual Idea. We will develop the question of the role of the Idea in the next section, but let it suffice to mention the Jungian interpretation of the symbolic nature of the cross here, where its significance finally comes from its capacity to give a symbolic (albeit abstract) form to the goal of the process of individuation (reconciliation of consciousness and the unconscious). As a symbol, therefore, we can perhaps see why the cross both predates and exceeds Christianity.

What is true of the cross is also true of incest, albeit at a higher power, at a more complex level of individuation:

> Incest signifies a personal complication only in the rarest cases. Usually incest has a highly religious aspect, for which reason the incest theme plays a decisive part in almost all cosmogonies and in numerous myths. But Freud clung to the literal interpretation of it and could not grasp the spiritual significance of incest as a symbol. (Jung 1961: 191)

Freud had difficulty dealing with the fact that 'incest is traditionally the prerogative of royalty and divinities' (ibid.: 151).

In these cases, incest reveals another dimension: as a symbol of rebirth. Incest symbolizes the convergence of two tendencies: temporal regression to the site of one's own birth and sexual reproduction. Incest condenses these two tendencies into one synthetic image of rebirth, or giving birth to oneself. Again, it is an image which assumes *a priori* status as a schematism or dramatization insofar as it synthesizes the past and future into one moment. Hence, again, its function lies in ordering the process of individuation. Once it has assumed its *a priori* status as a genuine symbol, it is invoked as a symbol of an ideal *telos*: the hierogamy between consciousness and the unconscious.

But let us now return to our line of argument about the consequences of this synthesis of schema and symbol. Kant specifies that the kind of reflection at work here is not only *a priori* (as the judgement 'This is beautiful' also is) *but concerns objects themselves* (symbolism is absorbed in the free materials of nature). But in that case, the productive imagination we first encounter in the schematism really does find a new, positive and objective determination in the function of symbolism. A genuine transcendental deduction is taking place.[20] It is through symbolism that the schematism is liberated from the tasks imposed by the understanding, becoming the vehicle for the presentation of the ideal. Before turning in detail to the role that Ideas play in symbols, we can already observe that from a systematic point of view, such a reorientation of the cognitive functions is extremely significant. It suggests that, beneath the Transcendental Deduction of the Categories (which shows how an *a priori* synthesis between pure concepts and pure intuitions guarantees the rule of representation), there is another, more subterranean Deduction, between schematism and symbolism, pure imagination and pure Idea, which hollows out a passage beneath the sphere of self-conscious, conceptual representation. There is a passage from the pure productive spatiotemporal matrix of the imagination, taken by itself, through to the intensive transformations presented in the 'free materials of nature', which in turn provide a receptacle for the Idea. Deleuze's excavation of Kant's texts has resulted in the discovery of a secret Transcendental Deduction, running underneath the architectonic of Kant's whole theory of cognition, a vein of gold apparently leading away from the order of representation that rules on the surface.

But in order to truly follow this vein, we must also bring about some modifications in our usual conceptions of Kantian subjectivity. Already the suggestion that there are dual trajectories of cognition at work in the apprehension of symbols shows that Kant is no longer presuming a unified, self-conscious subject. The imagination reflects on the symbol, while reason is simultaneously interested in it. How can these two activities take place at the same time? Why don't they jib against each other? The analogical structure of the symbol is the key. If reason's interest is satisfied by the symbol, the latter nevertheless remains an *indirect* presentation of the Idea. As far as the subject is concerned, they are engaged in reflection on a beautiful symbol; they are not *consciously* aware that the beautiful object is symbolizing an Idea. In the conscious experience of contemplating the white lily, one is simply absorbed in and fascinated by the lily, but one does not know why. Does it not follow that if consciousness is taken up with the reflection by the imagination and understanding of the object, then reason's 'interest' in the object is *unconscious*? Kant's whole line of thought points to a *splitting* of the cognitive subject, with the reflecting subject left unaware of *why* it is interested in the lily, while reason pursues its passion unconsciously. With the move to the symbol, Ideas are no longer just objects of thought, but are indirectly presented in nature. The activity of reason has therefore changed in nature, and that is why we can now talk of an unconscious passion of reason.

We have already seen that something like this follows from our account of the movement from projection to the symbol. The very movement from projection to the animation of the whole of nature through symbolism meant that the subject had now truly alienated itself within nature, and become other to itself. Now, whereas the model of projection had analogies within both Jungian and Freudian psychoanalysis, this new model of the world as illuminated book of symbols has no Freudian correlate. Here it is only the Jungian account of archetypal symbols that finds a potential Kantian explanation. Kant's transcendental theory of symbolism shows the conditions under which symbolism assumes significance for cognition, and thus offers a transcendental grounding for the turn to symbolism in Jung (and Deleuze). Kant shows how the subject necessarily confronts the world in an unconscious search for symbolic meaning. The task of Jungian psychology is to show how the subject advances precisely from a projective relation to the unconscious to a symbolic relation. But Jung also supplies the conclusion to this movement, which is not spelled out in Kant. 'Individuation' finally occurs when the ego is able to affirm the fact that it has been, and will continue to be, merely an actor in a symbolic drama that has long pre-existed it.

This Kantian construction of the 'symbolic order' provides a genesis of the development of the unconscious. But if the model of projection tends towards a paranoiac experience of the unconscious, the symbolic model does appear to tend towards what appears to be a *psychotic* reconstruction of the world. As an unconscious seeker of symbols, the subject must not only experience its life and the world in the mode of recollection, there is an inexorable and isomorphic tendency towards the paramnesiac immobilization of experience. When the subject enters the paramnesiac vortex of psychosis, the world inevitably bursts aflame with meaning. The subject henceforth has a leading role to play in a drama whose significance is both undeniable and obscure. Because the synthesis between schema and symbol is so far-reaching, and can potentially become autonomous of the norms of the understanding, it tends towards a psychotic reconstruction of reality. But just as Freud claims that love is a form of psychosis, on the model developed in this chapter, we must admit that any glimmer of beauty or sublimity only flares up because it brings with it a frisson of this danger. The symbolizing subject cannot help but experience itself as an actor wandering through a drama larger than it; at each encounter with a crystalline image, it cannot completely suppress the question 'what does this mean, what is this thing trying to tell me?'

Symbolism and Esoteric Mathesis

Deleuze's work is littered with references to Symbolist literature (Gérard de Nerval, Mallarmé, Villiers de l'Isle Adam, Rimbaud, Barbey d'Aurevilly, Sacher-Masoch) and he grants symbolist aesthetics more credence than would most of his generation. In 'To Have Done with Judgment' (1993), Deleuze returns to his early interest in symbolism, remarking that Nietzsche, Artaud, Lawrence and Kafka all 'could be called symbolists'. Referring to Lawrence's account of symbols (which incidentally was based on Jung's), Deleuze describes the symbol as 'an intensive compound that vibrates and expands, that has no meaning, but makes us whirl about until we harness the maximum of possible forces in every direction, each of which receives a new meaning by entering into relation with the others' (CC 134).

Deleuze already had an interest in symbolism before his turn to Jung, as is testified by one of his 'repudiated' articles from the 1940s.[21] In 1946, Deleuze wrote a foreword to a new French edition of a work of esoteric philosophy bearing the title *Mathesis: or Studies on the Anarchy and Hierarchy of Knowledge*, by one Dr Johann Malfatti de Montereggio.[22] Deleuze was twenty-one when he wrote 'Mathesis, Science and Philosophy' for the first French edition of Malfatti's *Mathesis* for a hundred years.[23] The original text is entitled *Studien über Anarchie und Hierarchie des Wissens, mit besonderer Beziehung auf die Medicin* [Studies on the Anarchy and Hierarchy of Knowledge, with Special Reference to Medicine], and contains five separate but interconnected studies on esoteric numerology ('Mathesis as Hieroglyph or Symbolism of the Triple Life of the Universe, Or the Mystical Organon of the Ancient Indians'), nature-philosophy ('Only in the Process, Not in the Product'), an application of the nature-philosophical notion of embryogenesis to the whole of human life ('On the Architectonic of the Human Organism, Or the Triple Life in the Egg and the Triple Egg in Life'), periodicity in physiology ('On Rhythm and Type, Consensus and Antagonism in General, and Particularly in Man'), and, finally, on human sexuality from the perspective of the esoteric notion of the hermaphrodite ('On the Double Sex in General and on Human Sex in Particular'). In the first French edition of 1849, the entire book has been given the abbreviated title of the first essay, *La Mathèse*, and the edition to which Deleuze adds his introduction in 1946 is a revised translation of this volume.

At first sight, the problem seems to be the obscurity of Malfatti and his book. Who is this Malfatti and by what strange route did the young Deleuze come upon his work? The name is not familiar from histories of Western philosophy, nor does it appear in histories of German thought in the nineteenth century. In the *ABC* interviews, Deleuze and Parnet discuss Deleuze's unusual predilection for authors so obscure that there are not even cults devoted to them. He admits to having a kind of 'mania' in his youth for obscure authors, especially ones who had written little, and admits that he derived prestige from it (ABC, 'L comme Littérature'). Given that Malfatti's name does not appear ever again in Deleuze's writings, we could be forgiven for thinking that Deleuze's introduction to Malfatti's *Mathesis* is merely a youthful dalliance with the occult. But occult themes run throughout Deleuze's work: not only does the term 'mathesis' appear at crucial points of *Difference and Repetition*, along with a weird emphasis on the esoteric use of the mathematical calculus, but his interest in somnambulism, the notion of the world as an egg, the theory of the second birth and the recurring image of the hermaphrodite all refer back to ideas found in Malfatti's book. We will examine the pages on magic and 'sorcery' in *A Thousand Plateaus* in the final chapter, as these are distinct subjects to mathesis; nevertheless, it will be impossible to overlook the relationship between them. Deleuze really did look everywhere for ideas about how to relate to the unconscious.

Malfatti is indeed obscure, but not completely obscure. He was a Viennese physician in the German Romantic tradition, and an early convert to Schelling's project to synthesize 'Brunonian' medicine with *Naturphilosophie* (Lesky 1965: 10; cf. Tsouypoulos 1982); he was sought after as a physician, and became personal physician to members of Napoleon Bonaparte's family, and to Beethoven (Altman 1999). He was one of the main proponents of mesmerism in Vienna (Gauld 1992: 89; Faivre 1996: 53). *Studies on the Anarchy and Hierarchy of Knowledge* was his second book, published thirty-six years after his first, *Entwurf einer Pathogenie aus der Evolution und Revolution des Lebens* [Sketch of a Pathogenesis out of the Evolution and Revolution of Life] (1809). Although it is true that he is rarely referred to in histories of *Naturphilosophie* and therefore seems a thoroughly marginal figure in intellectual history, his portion of fame does not rest only on his status as a physician to royalty and great artists. His *Anarchy and Hierarchy* acquired a certain degree of renown in another, more subterranean milieu: the occult circles of *fin-de-siècle* France. When René Guénon, the leading esotericist of his time, reviewed the 1946 edition of Malfatti (whose book was 'one of those which is often spoken about, but which few have read'), he acknowledged the historical value of the republication, due to 'the considerable role that this work and others of the same genre played in the constitution of occultism at the end of the 19th century' (Guénon 1947: 88). As David Reggio has shown, Malfatti's influence is found most explicitly in the work of one of the leaders of the movement of Martinism, Gérard Encausse, otherwise known as 'Papus' (Reggio 2004; on Martinism, see Harvey 2005).[24] The *eminence grise* of Martinism, Stanislas de Guaita, possessed a copy of Malfatti's *Mathesis* ('an extremely curious and rare' volume, Philipon 1899: 85), and had planned to complete his three-volume opus *The Serpent of Genesis* with an account of *Mathesis* (but he died of a drug overdose at the age of 36, the book remaining unfinished).

The young Deleuze begins his preface by stating that although it is essential not to forget the concrete practices deployed in Indian civilization, the 'capital interest' of Malfatti's book lies in its general reflections on mathesis, which can be of use even to our occidental mentality, where a dualism between philosophy and science has prevailed.[25] The main applications of *Mathesis* mentioned by Deleuze are in the fields of medicine and poetic creation. Deleuze acknowledges that his account of the relations between mathesis, science and philosophy will inevitably leave him on the 'outside' of mathesis, but he nevertheless thinks that it is a *philosophical* approach that can show how mathesis can continue to remain 'one of the great attitudes of the mind [*l'esprit*]' (Deleuze 1946: ix). He promises to criticize the arguments which philosophers have always been tempted to make against mathesis, and also says that Malfatti's text affords us the chance to reflect anew on the meaning of the word 'initiated', which refers to the individuating encounters with the 'principal human realities, birth, love, language or death' (Deleuze 1946: xiii). 'The key notion of mathesis is nothing mysterious', he insists, 'it is that individuality never separates itself from the universal, and that between the living and life one can find the same relation as between life as species and divinity' (xv).

The esoteric technique of mathesis is also presented as a solution to the 'anarchic' dualism between mind and body which eats into every form of life and knowledge. Mind–body dualism is 'anarchic', because sensible qualities can no longer be correlated with the physical quantities that constitute them. In endeavouring to provide explanations, science had to eliminate sensible qualities to get to the object of thought, which is purely quantifiable. 'When one arrives at H2O, there is no more water' (xvi). Conversely, philosophy analyses cognition and knowledge in such a way that actual facts about the physical world are held to be irrelevant. Philosophy is 'reflexive analysis where the sensible world is described as a representation of the knowing subject'. Deleuze notes that the opposition between science and philosophy goes beyond the simple opposition of 'object of thought – thinking subject'. What really happens is that in both cases the sensible world is being referred to a *thought* beyond it: in the case of science, to thought conceived as purely objective, in the case of philosophy, to thought conceived as an act of the subject. 'The object of thought is not only "thought" like the thinking subject, it is also "object" like the sensible object: this is a new depth of opposition' (ibid.). Colour, for instance may be 'subjective' in that its sensible appearance does not belong to objects themselves, which can be reduced to mere vibrations. Nevertheless, it also has its own objectivity. 'It is given to the individual, without reference to anything but itself. The individual knows well enough that things have not waited for him to exist' (xvi–vii). If a three-dimensional shape has three visible sides, then it will have at least six sides in total. Conversely, the six sides of the cube appear in three dimensions. There are intrinsic determinations of space and colour. We thus have a *new duality within the phenomenon* (of colour, space and time, etc.). The task is then to relate the objectivity of phenomenal colour to its subjective, sensible appearances. This would require that 'the object of thought be led back to the sensible, quantity to quality. Let us remark in general that this reduction is itself what is at work in the *symbol*'.

Deleuze here connects with an esoteric tradition which upholds the specific reality of the symbol, where symbols are even *more* real than passing reality itself. In 1946, Deleuze had dedicated his article 'From Christ to the Bourgeoisie' to the esotericist and medievalist Marie-Madeleine Davy, whose studies in twelfth-century medieval philosophy were centred on the idea that medieval culture involved an initiation into symbolic truths which were only comprehensible to those who had been initiated.[26] She shows how medieval philosophy articulated a series of 'degrees' of the love of God, which would each involve an initiation into the deeper truths implicated in the symbols of the age. There were 'secret' levels to symbols which could only be accessed by monks and kings (Davy 1977: 104).

The symbol has a 'double depth' (xxiv). Not only does it have a phenomenal appearance (dimensions, shape, colour, etc.); further, using techniques of *numerology* one can construct an entire 'system of correspondences' that provides us with exactly what we are looking for: an interiorized doubling of matter and meaning. The symbol satisfies thought and sensibility; once a problematic thought has been expressed in a symbol it has been immortalized, and there is nowhere else to go. Where the qualities of the subject of science are eliminated by explanation, 'the symbol is such that what symbolises is now the sensible object, with which the knowledge that it symbolises is completely identified' (xix). The symbol, properly understood, is therefore double. 'The sensible object is called symbolic, and the object of thought, losing all scientific signification, is hieroglyph or Number (*chiffre*)' (xxi). 'The symbol is the *thought of number become sensible object*' (xxiii). Deleuze gives the example of the flag as symbol of the nation, where a sensible object is posited as an incarnation of an object of thought. This object *is* the knowledge (savoir) that it incarnates. But not everything is a symbol; and only certain special things are true symbols.[27]

Malfatti tells us that the 'mother-idea' of his studies is 'the unity of science' as spelled out in 'the mystical *Organon* of mathesis of the Indians' (ibid., xxvii). In his opening remarks to the first study, on mathesis itself, he asserts that metaphysics and mathematics originally maintained a living unity in ancient India. If we look hard enough, we can find in mathematics the 'mute debris of a spiritual monument' (6). Mathematics did not begin as a formal science, but functioned as an essential part of an integrated system of esoteric knowledge about the body and its forces. Its origins were obscure, as everybody who has ever encountered 'mathesis' has regarded it as something that cannot have been created by human beings (1).

Without saying how it happened, Malfatti straightaway laments the loss of this original knowledge:

> Mathesis, broken into its substantial elements, that is to say, redoubled into metaphysics and mathematics, lost the living milieu of sacred unity. In the first of these sciences, its spirit, deprived of all basis, was absorbed into purely ideal logical forms, and in the latter, it left behind (as its corporeal image) only mute hieroglyphics and uncomprehended symbolic figures [*chiffres*], which only preserved a pure quantitative signification. From there, through this disastrous division, idealism and realism arose, like elements contrary to one another, still searching for their point of union; mathesis had ceased to be the universal science of life. (3)

With the decline of the original unity, a long history of occlusion followed, during which it was only possible to 'undo this dualism . . . by means of a certain exaltation and a unitary act of transfiguration, similar to that of our spiritual and corporeal procreation' (4). Immediately, mathesis is related to the sexual act. It is not at all clear which notion is stranger: the idea that sexual reproduction should have anything to do with some quasi-mathematical type of thought, or the idea of 'spiritual procreation'. In case we were in doubt that we have heard correctly, Malfatti goes on to specify that he is talking of 'an act during which results, at its culminating point, in a double erection [*cette double érection*], on the one hand towards the divine, and on the other hand towards nature' (4).

We need to take a step back. Let us start again by asking what this 'mathesis' is. In his fascinating survey of occultist philosophy, the surrealist Sarane Alexandrian connects Malfatti's account of 'mathesis' with an older occult tradition of 'arithmosophy'. The notion of mathesis, he tells us, is used by theologians and occultists to denote the conjugation of metaphysics and mathematics in a *scientia Dei*, or science of God. For instance, in 1660 the bishop of Vigenavo, Juan Caramuel, wrote a *Mathesis audax*, in which he declared that 'there are numerous questions in the philosophy of the divine which can not be understood without mathesis' (cited in Alexandrian 1983: 112). Frances A. Yates, the scholar of the Hermetic tradition, has brought to light a tradition of 'mathesis' that first fully emerges in European thought in the work of Ramon Lull, but which has influences further back in Arabic alchemy and the Hermetic writings of third-century Alexandria. Yates's aim was to show that Giordano Bruno was burned at the stake not because of his affirmation of Copernicanism, but because of his attempts to initiate a 'new religion of Love, Art, Magic and Mathesis' (Yates 1966: 371; Yates 1964: 354). In his introduction, Deleuze places Malfatti in a more mainstream philosophical tradition, reminding us that, despite his mind-body dualism, Descartes too dreamed of a *mathesis universalis* (as reported by Baillet in his biography). Deleuze could have cited other earlier and later philosophical sources, such as Leibniz or Novalis (both important to his work). Leibniz searched for an *arithmetica universalis* or *scientia generalis*, which would allow one to deal with all possible permutations and combinations in all disciplines. Leibniz's interest in mathematics was subordinated to his desire to find a way to formulate all possible variation and change. Novalis in turn took up the project of an *arithmetica universalis* (Novalis 1966: III, 23-25; Dyck 1959: 22). This universal mathesis was to include 'all mental operations, volitional and aesthetic experiences, and all knowledge' (Dyck 1959: 93). In his account of arithmosophy, Alexandrian also discusses the later revivals of mathesis in the nineteenth century, bearing the imprint of Kant's influence. The most notable figure in that later tradition is Hoëne Wronski, who is one of Deleuze's central references in his avowedly 'esoteric' discussion of the calculus in *Difference and Repetition*. Alexandrian writes that 'Wronski holds, in occult philosophy, the place that Kant holds in classical philosophy' (Alexandrian 1983: 133). After Wronski and Malfatti, philosophical interest in mathesis declines, and the works of Papus and Guaita are notably lacking in philosophical references (apart from to Wronski and Malfatti themselves). But the promises made for mathesis were very great. Deleuze cites Malfatti's claim that 'mathesis shall be for man in his relations with the infinite, what locomotion is for space' (Deleuze 1946: xv).

For a definition of mathesis, Malfatti himself refers us back to Proclus's *Commentary on the First Book of Euclid's Elements*, where the relation between mathesis and mathematics is made explicit. Proclus is one of the most interesting Neoplatonists, and was a towering figure in fifth-century Alexandrian culture. Some have speculated that the Jewish development of the cabbala originates in his thought, and there are similarities between his ideas and those of the Hermetic writings. Proclus' discussion of *mathesis* reminds us that the word itself is Greek for 'learning'. Proclus' book is a commentary on Euclid, but he is particularly concerned to show that while mathematics is of intrinsic interest, more profoundly it is also 'the science concerned with learning' (*mathematike*) (Proclus 1970: 46). Plato's *Meno* and *Phaedo* had shown that the nature of mathematics leads us back to a fundamental philosophical question about the nature of knowledge. The ideal forms of mathematics cannot be derived from the world of appearance – so how does one *discover* or even *learn* the truths of mathematics and geometry? Proclus is explicit about the implication: the mind can receive these forms from nowhere but itself. In the *Meno*, Plato suggests that it follows that what is described as 'learning' in these cases must be a recollection: 'If you take a person to a diagram, then you can show mostly clearly that learning is a recollection' (Plato, *Phaedo* 73b). 'Learning' is really the *recollection* of truths that have been forgotten: a reminiscence, an *anamnesis*, an unforgetting – an overcoming of amnesia. It is necessarily so because one can neither learn what one already knows, nor learn what one does not already know (for how could one recognize its validity, or even know what to look for?). For Proclus too, mathematics is the product of *mathesis*, 'the recollection of the eternal ideas in the soul'. Malfatti cites the Latin text of Proclus, which begins with the statement that '*Mathesis (disciplina) reminiscentia est*': mathesis is the discipline of reminiscence.

> According to the tradition, the Pythagoreans recognised that everything that we call learning is remembering, not something placed in the mind from without, like the images of sense pictured in the imagination, nor transitory like the judgments of opinion. Though wakened by sense-perception, learning has its source within us, in our understanding's attending to itself . . . This, then, is what learning [*mathesis*] is, recollection of the eternal ideas in the soul; and this is why the study that especially brings us the recollection of these ideas is called the science concerned with learning [*mathematike*]. Its name thus makes clear what sort of function this science performs. (Proclus 1970: 46)

Proclus adds that this capacity is achieved with the aid of the god Hermes (Thoth) who 'through our searching turns us back on ourselves', and 'through our birth-pangs perfects us', leading us to the blessed life (47). With his notion of mathesis, Proclus goes further into the esoteric ideas found in Plato's texts about reminiscence. Proclus was a practitioner of theurgy, and developed ideas about 'astral bodies' within the Neoplatonic tradition. But these ideas and practices would possibly not have arisen had not the notion of reminiscence produced a powerful motivation for the development of a theory of the unconscious. *Mathesis* is remembering truths that one has buried in one's mind, but which for some reason have been forgotten. Mathematical and geometrical truths are in the mind, and all a 'teacher' needs to do is to show the student how to remember.

But if this is right, then conversely the mathematical forms discovered can themselves be put to use in the recovery of further eternal forms derived from them. In fact, in the *Timaeus*,

> Plato constructs the soul out of all the mathematical forms, divides her according to numbers, binds her together with proportions and harmonious ratios, deposits in her the primal principles of figures, the straight line and the circle, and sets the circles in her moving in intelligent fashion. All mathematicals are thus present in the soul from the first. (Proclus 1970: 14)

The goal of Proclus' account of *mathesis* is therefore to restore number and geometry to their original metaphysical meaning (Malfatti directly follows him on this). But Proclus draws a further implication which is not yet crystal clear in Plato's writings. If mathematical forms are ultimate realities, they must have their own ontological form, their own kind of reality and even their own 'movement' – insofar as geometry, for instance, has its own geneses (for instance in the determination of conic sections, to which Deleuze refers now and again), or insofar as mathematics can generate its own series. This mathematical reality and movement must be distinguished from the realities and movements found in physical reality. Proclus makes a distinction between at least three kinds of cognition: that based on the senses; that based on the intellect, which is motionless; and that based on intuition, which can discover the special 'movements' that are proper to the forms, but which are not like physical movements. The mind that intuitively contemplates the pure forms 'is not motionless, like that of the intellect, but because its motion is not change of place or quality, as is that of the sense, but a life-giving activity, it unfolds and traverses the immaterial cosmos of ideas, now moving from first principles to conclusions, now proceeding in the opposite direction, now advancing from what it already knows to what it seeks to know' (16). These formal movements, or 'living forms', are different in kind from sensible movements. If there are intervals and series in mathematics, these are not to be modelled on empirical spatiotemporal intervals and series. 'Our sense perceptions engage the mind with divisible things', but 'every divisible thing is an obstacle to our returning upon ourselves' (46). Similarly, the formed things we project in our imagination risk separating us from the formation that is proper to ideas themselves. When we 'remove these hindrances', we can become 'producers of genuine knowledge' (46). The forms are 'living and intelligible paradigms of visible numbers and figures and ratios and motions' (15). 'Before the numbers, the self-moving numbers', says Proclus, just as 'before the visible figures the living figures' (ibid.).

Malfatti remarks that the knowledge and techniques of mathesis were kept secret for two reasons. The first reason was because great truths are wisely protected from profanation (6). The Christian fathers were incapable of restraining themselves from attacking oriental mysticism, and so secrecy has been necessary. But Malfatti gives a more profound reason: the Organon has been kept secret because it positively cannot be communicated in words. The Vedic tradition, Hermetism, NeoPlatonism and Renaissance alchemy all instead communicated their ideas through hieroglyphs and symbolic numerology.

Of these symbols, Malfatti writes: 'It is necessary that the spiritual intuition that one discovers in them to be perceived in the shortest space of time, and also that the physical apparitions obtained through efforts undertaken should also take place in the minimum possible extension' (6). The mind seeks adequate knowledge of eternal truths. The only way to gain adequate knowledge of such an object is by means of an intuition which can be spatiotemporally contracted into a symbol and which can be contemplated in the 'shortest space of time' and in 'the minimum possible extension'. Only in such a case can unity be seized in diversity in a glance, where the 'general life is in the particular life, and vice versa'.

In the introduction to the study on mathesis, Malfatti suggests that the loss of the discipline of mathesis was counteracted by one fundamental tendency in human beings. It remained possible to undo the dualism between quality and quantity, metaphysics and mathematics, through a temporary 'combat' or 'ordeal' that leads in each case beyond the state of individuality. That is, it is possible to overcome the duality 'by means of a certain exaltation and a unitary act of transfiguration, similar to that of our spiritual and corporeal procreation; an act during which, at its culminating point, this double erection [*cette double érection*] is joined in one part to the divine, in the other part to nature, without, however, being able to remain there. To dwell there too long would in effect lead to the exhaustion and death of the individual' (Malfatti 1845: 4). How are we to understand this splendid 'double erection'?[28] Malfatti could be referring to some special kind of sexual technique; perhaps some further physiological and mental excitements of the kind offered by unorthodox medical traditions, such as Brunonianism or alchemy, are involved. But the sexualized ontology, or cosmic sexuality, also refers back, more profoundly, to the ideas of the esoteric wing of Indian religion, Hindu Tantrism.[29]

Given that to dwell in a state of double erection for too long would lead to exhaustion and even death, how did 'the Brahmans' manage to maintain themselves in the perspective of mathesis to such an extent?

> The answer is straightforward. This people consecrated their whole existence to the contemplative life, at the price of the greatest individual sacrifices, of the most complete abnegation, exemplified in the numerous gymnosophers and solitaries who inspired the highest admiration among the Greeks. That is how and why they could attain the highest elevation and maintain their spiritual transfiguration by the reiteration and exaltation of their acts. (Malfatti 1845: 4)

In a footnote Malfatti remarks that the prophets produced their prophecies through this act of transfiguration, as did the saints their divine intuitions. He cites Dionysius the Areopagite, who describes how, once one has been penetrated by the rays of divine oracles, it is necessary to proceed with 'sobriety and sanctity' so that we can 'adapt to these eminent splendours of divine things'. Malfatti then remarks that:

> That which, in the contemplation of life, was attained in principle through the mortification of the senses, by the abasement of the individual, has been subject to renewed research in our times (although rarely with enough purity and elevation) through the means of a sort of artificial anticipation of death (animal magnetism). The same fact has long been observed in the case of fortuitous alterations of health, which have for their particular effect the concentration and momentary elevation of the somatic life of the individual. In the first case it is called artificial somnambulism, in the second case spontaneous somnambulism. (Malfatti 1845: 4–5)

For Malfatti, there is something ecstatic about this process of self-healing through natural somnambulism. Whereas Schopenhauer believed that the prime example of natural somnambulism was in instinct in general, for Malfatti, natural somnambulism too needed to be understood as an ecstatic state. Such 'transfigurations' lie behind 'the idea of rebirth (*palingenesis*) among the Indians, who, as one knows, describe themselves as twice born' (Malfatti 1845: 5). The implication here is that spontaneous somnambulism emerges in a person's psychological life like a rebirth, and demands a technique to mediate the reiteration and exaltation of this change. What sounds very much like madness or a psychotic breakdown for Malfatti becomes a precious opportunity to advance to a higher stage of equilibrium. In the same passage, he cites Hippocrates's dictum that 'something divine is hidden in illnesses'. Natural and artificial somnambulism tap into the same forces at work in the disciplines of the original 'Brahmans'. The Indians discovered 'the admirable mystical Organon of mathesis' as the means of reiterating and exalting their acts following their 'second birth'. Contemporary nature-philosophical medicine should therefore return to Indian tradition in order to make known the secrets of this method of mathesis. 'What an astonishing advantage man has drawn from the night-side of his life: to open up through sleep [*sommeil*], by means of a state of interior vigil (the vigil of sleep [*la veille du sommeil*]), the highest, most hidden astral region: this is what the magnetic development of clairvoyance and ecstasy demonstrates to us, in the same way as the natural life of dreams' (Malfatti 1845: 153).

Malfatti's *Anarchy and Hierarchy of Knowledge* is like a Book of the Dead charged with Tantrism. It suggests that under the appropriate, somnambulistic conditions, the internal symbolic structure of the universe may be divined according to a theosophical conception of the microcosm. In Böhme's theosophy, the course of the world, its development in nature and history, was understood as the manifestation of a drama taking place in God himself. The human being is a microcosm, in that it contains every level of physical, organic and psychic differentiation that exists in the macrocosm. In his later work, Schelling developed a nature-philosophical theory of 'potencies', according to which the increasing accumulation of dialectically interrelated levels of being (physical, organic, telluric, uranic) could be proportionally related to each other in an esoteric calculus. With Malfatti's somnambulistic techniques, the mind becomes a 'spiritual automaton', guided only by the symbolism of numbers and bodies. Whereas conscious thought is determined by self-consciousness, if consciousness is relaxed through natural or artificial somnambulism, then the result of unconscious processes can emerge into the mind and be compared and evaluated mathetically. At the limit, then, unconscious thought is determined sub-representatively or subliminally by the play of the 'potencies' (Beach 1994: 182) or 'living numbers'. The hierarchy of potencies in the body and spirit are free to determine themselves and the microcosm expresses the macrocosm.

In his introduction, Deleuze gives two variant suggestions about what the 'essential symbolic operation' might be. On the one hand, following Malfatti, he says that 'in the double depth of the symbol, [mathesis] fulfils itself as the living art of medicine, continually establishing a system of increasingly intimate correspondences, in which ever more individual realities are to be found enclosed' (xxiv). But what he actually discusses is the 'essential symbolic operation' of the poem, with one of the supreme statements of symbolist poetry, Mallarmé's *Autre Evantail*, as exemplar.

The poem is presented as the product of Mallarmé's fascination by the movements of his wife's fan. An air of twilight creeps over her as she flutters the fan, '*dont le coup prisonnier recule/L'horizon delicatement*'. The lines are not directly translatable, but Deleuze indicates that he is imagining the unfolding and refolding fan, as if the fan were the symbol of an enfolded, implicated world, as if it were 'the sceptre of shores of rose stagnant on evenings of gold'. As if, within the shores of rose, there is an inner, intensive landscape, with rose-lit sceptres of kings and priests. Mallarmé's poem is addressed to his wife as '*rêveuse*' (dreamer). Symbolist aesthetics is sometimes accused of embodying a contradiction between a 'transcendental symbolism' which would express pure Ideas and a symbolism which would express feelings. But what happens in Mallarmé's poems is an expression of the Idea in its intensive, pre-individual form. If the brain is the vessel for the involution of virtuality, the poem is in turn the most evolved form of involution, where the folds of evolution and involution achieve their maximum hermetic interiorization, to the point that the world itself is the merely material guise for Madame Mallarmé's fan.

The Sexual Act of the Divine Hermaphrodite

The last study of *The Anarchy and Hierarchy of Knowledge* takes up another central symbol of Hermetic and alchemical thought: the hermaphrodite, whose scintillating image also permeates Deleuze's work. In the *Critique of Judgment*, Kant says that 'the *ideal* of the beautiful [is] the *human figure*' (Kant

1790: Ak. 235). 'An ideal of beautiful flowers, of beautiful furnishings, or of a beautiful view is unthinkable. But an ideal of a beauty . . . that has the purpose of existence within itself' – an ideal symbol in other words – such an ideal could only be found in *'man'* (ibid.). For Malfatti and Deleuze the supreme *symbol* in the sense just explained is not simply 'man', but the hermaphrodite, no matter how rare such a figure is in the actual world. The rarity of orchids and gold enhances rather than diminishes their symbolic value. But in any case, according to Malfatti, the 'hermaphrodite' is a 'living symbol' in a very special sense.

In *Anarchy and Hierarchy* Malfatti can everywhere be found arguing deliriously that sexual polarity is present in all the forces of the universe. Even more deliriously, he goes on to infer that the separate sexes themselves are not to be spared from this polarity, and that sexual polarity is in turn to be found *within* each sex. '"*Man is duplex, and if man were not duplex, there would be no sensation*", the incomparable Hippocrates once said. In two separated bodies live man and woman, and each one however possesses in itself the body of the other, each one is in itself Androgyne and Gynander at the same time; it is only a prevalence of one over the other which separates them and differentiates them . . . It is for that reason that a sexual separation of the body was necessary, both parts remaining masculine-feminine and feminine-masculine' (Malfatti 1845: 168; cf. 164).

So as in Schelling's later theosophical thought, the world is the body of God, and we are its coming to consciousness. The human being is a microcosm, in that it contains every level of physical, organic and psychic differentiation that exists in the macrocosm, in a more interiorized or virtualized form. But in *Anarchy and Hierarchy* it is as if Schelling's final theosophy comes to completion in a hallucinatory Tantrism, in which the living body of God, in its most complete self-development, itself appears in hermaphroditic form in human sexuality, where the coming-to-divine-consciousness becomes identical to the psychosexual attainment of spiritual 'bisexuality'.

Malfatti generates the relations of polarity and power at the 'telluric', 'magnetic' or somnambulistic and 'astral' [*sideral*] or ideal levels of differentiation. The intestines are the zoo-vegetable envelope of 'telluric' forces; the heart is the animal envelope of the magnetic atmosphere, while the brain is the envelope of the astral soul. Each of these anatomical divisions is conceived as an embryo or egg, developing in parallel with the others. There is the stomach egg, with its satellites of liver and spleen; the breast-egg, with its satellites of lungs and kidney, and the head-egg with its satellites of eye and ear. The triadic egg develops at each level in triple form, but is only fully born with the psychosexual attainment of the state of hermaphrodite, in which a polarized 'double body' with a 'double sex' expresses analogically all macrocosmic relations of power in perfect microcosmic form.

Perhaps all that Malfatti means by this 'hermaphrodite' is the sexual couple itself. In the sexual act, the double body finally achieves a 'momentary reunion' that amounts to a complete self-consciousness, a perfect doubling or reflection. The virtual, opposite-sexed body of each is incarnated in the other. 'Through an effort, an act in which the relativity of the sexes neutralise themselves, the sexual couple can 'approach for a moment the hermaphroditic state' (168). On Malfatti's somnambulist model, the sexual act does involve a peculiar kind of consciousness, in which male and female finally attain a hermaphroditic species consciousness.[30] The deepest level of consciousness, therefore, the most *symbolic* level of consciousness, therefore, is discovered in the act of sexual coupling.

However, he also insists that each person is already a doubled body. The human being is psychically and sexually 'duplex'. 'The double body is a twin and bisexual' (174). If one is already a 'hermaphrodite' insofar as one is (in some sense) both female and male, *anima* and *animus* (166, 181), then in the sexual encounter a hermaphrodite takes another hermaphrodite as its object. In that case, sexual consciousness would be the fulfilment of self-consciousness because one's object is an incarnation of an image that must remain virtual in oneself (due to the actual preponderance of male or female biological attributes).[31]

But as a *symbol* Malfatti's hermaphrodite also suggests an original sexual matrix for all sexual relationships. Heterosexual relationships already implicate within them a duplicity, in that the anima in a man can also be in a love-relationship with the animus of the woman. The full polarity of heterosexuality involves the love of a man-woman for a woman-man. In *Anti-Oedipus*, the 'vegetal theme' of hermaphroditism reappears: 'everyone is bisexual, everyone has two sexes, but partitioned, noncommunicating, the man is merely the one in whom the male part, and the woman the one in whom the female part, dominates statistically. So that at the level of elementary combinations, at least two men and two women must be made to intervene to constitute the multiplicity in which transverse communications are established' (AO 69). This relation is actualized in the couple if one keeps Malfatti's hermaphrodite in mind. Nevertheless, for finite beings, there remain the three possibilities of sexual love: heterosexuality, and male and female homosexuality. Within each sex alone, there can be no essential privilege of heterosexual or homosexual object choice, only a combinatory of possible relationships. In fact, Deleuze says that homosexual relationships even have a privilege.

> We live under Samson's prophecy: 'The two sexes shall die, each in a place apart'. But matters are complicated because the separated, partitioned sexes coexist in the same individual: 'initial Hermaphroditism', as in a plant or a snail, which cannot be fertilized 'except by other hermaphrodites'. Then it happens that the intermediary, instead of effecting the communication of male and female, doubles each sex with itself: symbol of a self-fertilization all the more moving in that it is homosexual, sterile, indirect. And more than an episode, this is the essence of love. The original Hermaphrodite continuously produces the two divergent homosexual series. (PS 80)

Indian religion, Tantrism and esotericism experimented with homosexuality long before it became an issue of the State: it was not just part of the autonomous combinatory of sexes and their relations, but by virtue of its sterility creates the conditions for what Malfatti calls a 'spiritual amnion', the womb of the ideal. However, homosexuality may take many different forms: a heterosexual couple may be homosexual insofar as the male loves the male in the other, while the female in turn loves the female. Alternatively, the physical sameness of the other body in actual male homosexuality, say, may be compensated by the presence of two virtual lesbians – and vice versa. At the other extreme would be the celibate, creative hermaphrodite with his or her 'amniotic effigy' (Malfatti 1845: 186), the creative work. With the liberation of the double-sexed hermaphrodite, in whatever form, the gates are opened for the human being to become a libidinal microcosm, no longer symbol of *mater natura,* but of the cosmic body of God, the 'Tantric egg' (ATP 153), or what Deleuze and Guattari rechristen the 'body without organs'.

Chapter 5

Jung, Leibniz and the Differential Unconscious

'Problems and questions . . . belong to the unconscious, but as a result the unconscious is differential and iterative by nature: it is serial, problematic and questioning' (DR 108). In his 1980 lectures on Leibniz, Deleuze says:

> it is Leibniz who first proposed this great idea, this first great theory of this differential unconscious, and it has never gone away since. There is a very long tradition of this differential conception of the unconscious based on minute perceptions and minute appetitions. It culminates in a very great author, who, strangely, has always been poorly understood in France, a German post-Romantic named Fechner. He is a disciple of Leibniz who developed the conception of the differential unconscious. (Third Lecture on Leibniz, 12)

For Bergson, Fechner was the psychophysicist par excellence, one of the founders of the 'reign of quantity'. But although he is largely remembered in this way today (every psychology textbook has a chapter on Fechner's psychophysics), Fechner is a multifaceted figure, being also the author of numerous works both satirical and esoteric, ranging from a treatise on *The Comparative Anatomy of Angels* (1825), through the *Little Book of Life after Death*, to later works on the psychology of plants.[1] But Deleuze also states that Jung is a third figure in this 'differential' tradition of the unconscious. 'There is a psychology with Leibniz's name on it, which was one of the first theories of the unconscious. I have already said almost enough about it for you to understand the extent to which it is a conception of the unconscious which has absolutely nothing to do with Freud's . . . [However] in the lineage that proceeds from Freud, some very strange phenomena will be found, [which] return to a Leibnizian conception' (Third Lecture on Leibniz, 9). Deleuze says he will talk about this later, but unfortunately he only devotes a short paragraph to following up what happens in 'Freud's posterity' (ibid.: 14). He says: 'For example, in Jung, there is an entire Leibnizian side, and what he reintroduces, to Freud's greatest anger – and it is in this that Freud judges that Jung has absolutely betrayed psychoanalysis – is an unconscious of a differential type. And he owes that to the tradition of German Romanticism which is closely linked also to the unconscious of Leibniz' (ibid.). This is the most problematic of Deleuze's suggestions, as although here and there Jung does mention

Leibniz's theory of *petites perceptions*, as well as Fechner's threshold notion of the unconscious, it is hard to see these discussions as decisive for Jung's theory of the unconscious.

In his overviews of the history of the concept of the unconscious, Jung does mention the important role played by Leibniz. 'There had been talk of the unconscious long before Freud. It was Leibniz who first introduced the idea into philosophy' (CW 8: 102; cf. CW 16: 139). In a lecture of 1914, just after the break with Freud, he says:

> We may define the unconscious as the sum of all those psychic events which are not apperceived, and so are unconscious. The unconscious contains all those psychic events which do not possess sufficient intensity of functioning to cross the threshold dividing the conscious from the unconscious. They remain, in effect, below the surface of consciousness, and flit by in subliminal form. It has been known to psychologists since the time of Leibniz that the elements, that is to say the ideas and feelings, which make up the conscious mind – its so-called conscious content – are of a complex nature, and rest upon far simpler and altogether unconscious elements; it is the combinations of these which produces consciousness. Leibniz had already mentioned the *perceptions insensibles* – those vague perceptions which Kant called 'shadowy representations', which could attain to consciousness only in an indirect manner. (CW 3: 203)

In his lecture 'Instinct and the Unconscious', Jung also introduces a 'threshold' conception of the unconscious familiar from Leibniz (although Leibniz's name is not mentioned):

> I define the unconscious as the totality of all psychic phenomena that lack the quality of consciousness. These psychic contents might fittingly be called 'subliminal', on the assumption that every psychic content must possess a certain energy value in order to become conscious at all. The lower the value of a conscious content falls, the more it disappears below the threshold. (CW 8: 133)

Jung also twice cites a remark of Fechner's about the necessity of an idea of the 'threshold of consciousness' for understanding the unconscious:

> the idea of a psychophysical threshold is of the utmost importance because it gives a firm foundation to that of the unconscious generally. Psychology cannot abstract representations from unconscious perceptions, nor even from the effects of unconscious perceptions . . . Perceptions and representations in the state of unconsciousness have, of course, ceased to exist as real ones . . . but something continues in us, psychophysical activity. (Fechner 1860: II, 438; cited in CW 8: 164, 166)[2]

In an important passage from *Transformations and Symbols of the Libido*, Jung discusses the unconscious in terms very similar to Leibniz. Jung discusses the possibility that the ideal creations (for instance, poems or art) of somebody undergoing a psychotic break might contain 'presentiment[s] of the future'. The patient might be subject to 'one of those thoughts which, to quote Maeterlinck, spring from the 'inconscient supérieur', from the 'prospective potency' of a subliminal synthesis'. In a footnote he expands in the following vein:

> Doubtless the unconscious contains material which does not rise to the threshold of consciousness. Analysis dissolves these combinations into their historical determinants . . . Psychoanalysis works backwards like the science of history . . . History, however, knows nothing of two kinds of things, that which is hidden in the past and that which is hidden in the future . . . Insofar as tomorrow is already contained in today, and all the threads of the future are in place, so a more profound knowledge of the past might render possible a more or less far-reaching and certain knowledge of the future. Let us transfer this reasoning, as Kant has already done, to psychology . . . Just as traces of memory long since fallen below the threshold of consciousness are accessible in the unconscious, so too there are certain very fine subliminal combinations of the future, which are of the greatest significance for future happenings insofar as the future is conditioned by our own psychology . . . From this comes the prophetic significance of the dream long claimed by superstition. (CW 5: 50, 51n.)

This passage seems perfectly acceptable as an amplification of Leibnizian conceptions of the unconscious, particularly of the passage from the *New Essays* on the *sympnoia panta* (Leibniz 1765: 54–5; cf. p. 42 above). However, Jung himself does not put it in such a context, and also says at the beginning of the passage that 'this time I shall hardly escape the charge of mysticism'.[3] Nevertheless, the claim that 'the unconscious also contains all the material that has *not yet* reached the threshold of consciousness (CW 7: 128) is not in itself mystical as long as the 'productivity' or 'positivity' of the unconscious in its relations to the ego is understood in its complexity.

It is possible but not likely that these sort of passages provoked Freud's 'greatest anger', and that he thought they 'absolutely betrayed psychoanalysis'. But Freud does not explicitly express any anger about this aspect of Jung's thought. Freud's greatest anger (if that is the right word) with Jung seems to have been about his resistance to the sexual theory (see, for instance, SE 14: 58–66, 79–80). His main bone of contention against Jung does not seem to have been against his revival of Leibnizianism.

We saw that Deleuze indicates that in the work of Jung, 'some very strange phenomena will be found, [which] return to a Leibnizian conception' (Third Lecture on Leibniz, 9). This is vague, but there is one last clue. In summing up the contributions of the Leibnizian conception of the unconscious to psychology, Deleuze also uses the example of rumour: 'You can grasp the concept of singularity . . . on the level of thought-experiences of a psychological type: what is dizziness, what is a murmur, what is a rumour?' While the example of dizziness refers back to Leibniz, the example of rumour might well refer to Jung, who wrote 'A Contribution to the Psychology of Rumour' (CW 4), and who says, in his essay on UFO hysteria, that rumour is an essential mechanism for the activation of archetypes. Rumours of UFOs might arise from a 'primary fantasy originating in the unconscious', so that 'an archetype creates the corresponding vision' (CW 10: 313). However, he adds there that the relation between archetype and the rumour cannot be understood as causal: 'the meaning of the rumour is not exhausted by its being explained as a causal symptom; rather, it has the value and significance of a living symbol' (CW 10: 387). We have already encountered Jung's subtraction of the dimension of causality from symbolism. But here Jung seems to want to make a more radical claim: the process of activation is not an objective causal mechanism, and, it would seem, is also more than a *triggering* of a latent subjective potential. 'To these two causal relationships we must add a third possibility, namely, that of a 'synchronistic', i. e. acausal, meaningful coincidence – a problem that has occupied men's minds ever since the time of Geulincz, Leibniz and Schopenhauer' (CW 10: 313). Jung claims that the correspondence of archetype and rumour must be understood as a properly *acausal* process. It would seem, then, that in our pursuit of references to make sense of Deleuze's claim that there is a differential unconscious in the work of Jung, all the evidence is pointing us to the phenomena that Jung classed under the term 'synchronicity'. In fact, it turns out that the only substantial references to Leibniz in Jung's work occur in the context of the latter's exposition of synchronicity. Now, Deleuze never explicitly refers to this concept in his work. So it remains moot whether these 'very strange phenomena' refer to manifestations of archetypes in general, or to so-called phenomena of synchronicity. The fact that Jung's investigations into synchronicity are indeed an investigation into 'strange phenomena', and the fact that Jung only really actively uses Leibniz's philosophy in his work on synchronicity suggest that it is the latter. There are other considerations that will also come up when we explore this line of thought.

Synchronicity: Acausal Synthesis

'Synchronicity: An Acausal Connecting Principle' is a late work of Jung's, published in 1952 in a volume entitled *Naturerklärung und Psyche* (translated in 1955 as *The Interpretation of Nature and Psyche*, along with a paper on 'The Influence of Archetypal Ideas on the Scientific Theories of Kepler', by the physicist Wölfgang Pauli, who had won a Nobel Prize in 1945. Despite the credentials of Jung's collaborator, 'Synchronicity' is probably the work which has most contributed to Jung's reputation, in some quarters, as a raving New Age madman. He claims to have discovered an 'acausal' principle which allows us to discover a certain *sense* or meaning in certain coincidental relationships between causally disconnected events. 'Evidence' is supplied from the domains of parapsychology (ESP), astrology and dreams to apparently suggest that these acausal connections are really 'out there', that there is a mysterious dimension of correspondences at work beneath our superficial, everyday experience, and which is perhaps located at the microphysical level only accessible to quantum physics. But Jung's theory of synchronicity is in fact open to another, less 'realist' interpretation.

For most of the essay, Jung is content to reduce parapsychological phenomena to projected expressions of the collective unconscious. In a key passage, he concludes that 'synchronicity is a phenomenon that seems to be primarily connected with psychic conditions, that is to say, with processes in the unconscious' (CW 8: 511). Moreover, his central arguments are built on philosophical texts and arguments, not on direct evidence of parapsychological phenomena, nor on quasi-scientific speculation about quantum indeterminacy. Jung claims that an essay on fate by Schopenhauer 'originally stood godfather to the views I am now developing' (CW 8: 427), and in later pages there is a disquisition on Leibniz's theory of pre-established harmony. Jung's discussion emerges out of the philosophical context of the problem of psychophysical parallelism, and he considers the 'principle of acausal connection' to be a contribution to that problem. His basic definition of synchronicity is a philosophical one: the 'coincidence in time of two or more causally unrelated events which have the same or a similar sense [*Sinngehalt*]' (CW 8: 441; trans. modified).[4] An event occurs in an objective sequence of events which has a 'parallelism of sense' with an event in a subjective series, yet lacks any causal connection with it. There are ample indications that Jung intends his core idea to be interpreted at a 'transcendental' rather than a realist *or* a merely psychological level.

Jung begins the text by questioning the range of the framework of universal causality. Causality is defined as the regular correlation of events under repeatable conditions. On this model, causality becomes a 'statistical truth', incapable in principle with dealing with 'unique or rare events' or 'exceptions' (421):[5]

> The experimental method of inquiry aims at establishing regular events which can be repeated. Consequently, unique or rare events are ruled out of account. Moreover, the experiment imposes limiting conditions on nature, for its aim is to force her to give answers to questions devised by man. (CW 8: 422)[6]

Jung notes that causality is usually put in opposition to 'the world of chance' (423), but he immediately states that, as a rule, it should always be taken as possible to reduce what appear as chance correlations down to universal causality. (In the *Physics* Aristotle had suggested that the perception of 'chance' depends on the expectations of the perceiver.) The appearance of an event as random is not enough to suggest that it is truly unique or singular; regularities might in principle be discovered if one looks widely enough. But if chance events are not 'acausal', then what could possibly fulfil the conditions of being the 'unique or rare event' which exemplifies acausality?[7] Jung states that 'acausal events' may only be assumed to exist 'where a causal connection appears to be *inconceivable*' (ibid.: 424). Jung seems to want to suggest a strong sense of inconceivability here. In his 1951 Eranos lecture on 'Synchronicity', he sets out three types of connection in which causality is inconceivable (CW 8: 526). The first and second types give him the notion of 'synchronicity', but the third is not synchronous at all, and Jung's classification of it as synchronistic is quite intriguing.

The first type of acausal connection gives us the basic form of synchronicity. It is *inconceivable* that two *simultaneous* events have an immediately causal connection. This is obviously true: a simultaneous relation is by definition not successive; so what? Jung goes on to specify that he is concerned with 'the coincidence in time of two or more causally unrelated events *which have the same or a similar sense,* in contrast to 'synchronism', which simply means the simultaneous occurrence of two events' (CW 8: 441). Hence a connection can be synchronous without being synchronistic. With this type, Jung seems to be primarily interested in coincidences between the objective, causal sequence of events on the one hand, and the subjective sequence of internal events (subjective trains of thought and desire) on the other. Thus this type of synchronicity occurs within the experience of one subject. What they see with their senses has an acausal correspondence with what they are thinking. We will qualify this later, but it is probably easiest to start with this model in mind. We should note that, formally, the definition of this first type of synchronicity is identical to the formula invoked in rigorous theories of psychophysical parallelism, such as that found most famously in Spinoza. For Spinoza, to affirm parallelism between mind and body is to treat causal relations as only occurring in *each* heterogeneous series (mind or body), not *between* mind and body. Parallelism is thus a way of getting out of the problem of the mind–body relation that dogs Cartesian dualism (how is the immaterial mind supposed to affect the body, and bodies in general, and how is the body supposed to affect the mind; the problem that led Descartes to his famous postulation of the 'pineal gland'). Thus, in Spinoza's theory, the connection between mind and body at any one given moment is indeed strictly speaking 'acausal'. The difference between Jung and Spinoza is that the former clearly has in mind correspondences between series which are not only different *in kind* (Spinoza's Thought and Extension, or mind and body), but which contain different contents. For Spinoza, ideas are ideas of the body; what one is thinking about parallels one's bodily state. Jung never says this, and his examples show that he is concerned with subjective series which are more or less *divergent* from objective series.

The second main type of acausal connection concerns mental events which occur simultaneously with physical events, and appear to be related (insofar as they have a similar sense), but again can have no direct causal relation, this time because their spatial separation makes such a relation impossible. Jung cites Swedenborg's vision of the great fire of Stockholm, while he was two hundred miles away at a party in Gothenburg. Swedenborg was himself on his way home from England to Stockholm. He told the assembled guests of the progress of the fire as he saw it happening, exclaiming relief when it was over, and that it had not damaged his own house. His description of the course of events was then confirmed over the next few days by messengers returning from Stockholm.[8]

The third category of acausal connections is that of precognition, where a mental event is correlated with a successive physical event, but cannot be caused by it, either because of spatial distance or because of temporal disparity (the physical event in question has not yet happened). Jung gives the example of a student who dreams about walking through a Spanish city which he has never visited. Later he visits the city, and experiences everything which was played out in the dream, down to the last detail.

Does synchronicity *exist* in any form, or is all this just a thought-experiment? Here are two of the main examples given by Jung. The first is from Jung's clinical practice, the like of which he says had not happened to him before, nor had he experienced anything like it since: 'A young woman I was treating had, at a critical moment, a dream in which she was given a golden scarab.' The scarab, Jung had mused, is the Egyptian symbol of rebirth or renewal. In an Egyptian Book of the Dead, the dead sun-god metamorphoses into a scarab, which then, at the last station of the Netherworld, 'mounts the barge which carries the rejuvenated sun-god into the morning sky' (CW 8: 439). The symbolism of the scarab arises because of its practice of rolling bits of dung into small balls inside which the female deposits its eggs (Stevens 1998: 350). This is already enough to make the scarab an unsettling presence in a dream (for a Jungian). But nothing prepares for what happens next in Jung's account though. 'While she was telling me this dream I sat with my back to the closed window. Suddenly I heard a noise behind me, like a gentle tapping. I turned around and saw a flying insect knocking against the window-pane from outside. I opened the window and caught the creature in the air as it flew in. It was the nearest analogy to a golden scarab that one finds in our latitudes, a scarabeid beetle, the common rose-chafer, which contrary to its usual habits had evidently felt an urge to get into a dark room at this particular moment' (CW 8: 438). A patient of Jung's had died of a heart attack and his wife had come to see Jung. She recounted a coincidence that was haunting her: just before the deaths of her mother and grandmother, she had witnessed a crowd of birds assembling outside their respective houses. Just after having completed his treatment with Jung, her husband was returning home after a visit to the doctor for a check-up on his heart. He collapsed in the street and was brought dying back to his home, where his wife was waiting for him in a state of anxiety – because a flock of birds had begun to crowd outside their home, as soon as the husband had left for the appointment.

Both of these examples are of the first type of synchronicity. They involve a 'coincidence in time of two or more causally unrelated events which have the same or a similar sense' (CW 8: 441). Two heterogeneous series of events appear to coincide inexplicably. The patient in the first example sees what she has dreamt (in her subjective series) actualized in the external world (the objective series). The second example is slightly different in that the two series are 'subjective' and 'objective' in a looser way. The patient's wife has a series of deaths in her immediate family (the subjective series), and each death is accompanied by an assemblage of birds in the objective, external world.

In each of these examples, there is an acausal connection between subject and object which gives rise to the impression that such an event is *fated*. It is not only that the patient is experiencing the unfolding of her own fate by dreaming of the scarab, but nature itself seems to be conspiring in her fate, by sending the scarab to knock on the window. Examples such as these are legion in Jung, and he often writes without irony of his own experiences of fatedness. While engaged in painting a picture of a dream image with the horns of a bull and the wings of a kingfisher, Jung was 'thunderstruck' to find a newly dead kingfisher lying in his garden. He takes this as proof of 'psychic objectivity, the reality of the psyche' (Jung 1961: 207–8). As further proof of Jung's occult tendencies, we need only recall the incident of the spookery in the bookcase (see note 3, p. 217). At moments such as these, the distinction between subject and world cannot but break down; the world no longer seems indifferent to the patient, but the patient is part of a drama that is greater than they can comprehend. The chasm between subjectivity and objective, neutral order appears to be somehow bridged, and the subject feels oddly 'at home' in the universe.

In his essay on 'The Uncanny' [*Das Unheimliche*], Freud begins his own disquisition on fatedness and all things weird by remarking on the double meaning of the word *heimlich*. Whereas *heimlich* can mean 'homely' and 'intimate', it can also mean 'concealed, kept from sight, so that others do not get to know of or about it, withheld from others' (SE 17: 223). The word *heimlich* therefore seems to include a meaning which is identical with its opposite, *unheimlich*. Freud cites a passage from Schelling's *Philosophy of Mythology*, which he says 'throws quite a new light on the concept of the *Unheimlich*, for which we were certainly not prepared'. Schelling writes: '*Unheimlich* is the name for everything that ought to have remained . . . secret and hidden but has come to light' (Schelling 1857: 649).[9] For Freud, such 'uncanny' experiences are essentially a return to primary *narcissism*. This is ultimately what should have remained hidden, but has come to light. And indeed, what could be more narcissistic than experiencing a coincidence as fate? Jungian synchronicity at first sight would seem to be nothing more than an excuse to raise narcissistic superstition up to an *a priori* principle. For Jung, the appearance of a dead kingfisher on the lawn after a dream about a kingfisher-man is a momentous 'rupture in time'; for others, such an event by itself would be a cause for mere amusement, but the idea of a psychologist taking it deadly seriously would unleash a wave of hilarity. (Freud himself remarks that the 'unintended repetition' one finds in the uncanny can easily tip over into comedy (SE 17: 237, 246).)

A comparison between Freud's and Jung's ideas about fate and the uncanny will therefore be apposite here. Is synchronicity narcissism? Jung's theory of synchronicity competes with Freud's theory of the uncanny in attempting to explain the same psychological phenomena. There is an added motivation in examining this relationship, as it was in his essay 'The Uncanny' (1919) that Freud first suggested the idea of the death drive as a compulsion to repeat. The death drive thus has origins in Freud's discussion of fate. Freud withdrew from some of the more intriguing suggestions ventured in 'The Uncanny', and ended up affirming a materialistic, thermodynamic conception of the death drive in *Beyond the Pleasure Principle*, published a year later. In effect, Deleuze follows up the relationship between fate and the death instinct by turning to Jung's theory of synchronicity, which takes up where Freud left off.

Jung's investigations into synchronicity were also investigations into the 'paranormal'.[10] Jung appeals to 'the mass of facts' engendered in studies on 'psychical research', along with J. B. Rhine's more recent experiments on ESP, which are held to furnish 'decisive evidence for the existence of acausal combinations of events' (CW 8: 432).[11] But he goes on to deny that these findings directly imply telepathic communication between two individuals. 'It seems more likely that scientific explanation will have to begin with a criticism of our concepts of space and time on the one hand, and with the unconscious on the other' (CW 8: 435). Although he spends some time examining the possibility of acausal connections at the microphysical level, he concludes, as we have seen, that 'synchronicity is a phenomenon that seems to be primarily connected with psychic conditions, that is to say with processes in the unconscious' (CW 8: 511). He takes his task to be to search for the '*tertium comparationis*' of significant coincidences, which he claims 'rests on the psychoid factors I call the archetypes' (CW 8: 515). Before saying any more than has already been said about archetypes, it is worth emphasizing this search for a '*tertium quid*', or 'third thing', which guarantees that the conjunction of two contingent events can bear a distinct, but acausal 'sense'.[12]

Schopenhauer and the Lines of Fate

Jung says that Schopenhauer's essay 'Transcendent Speculation on Apparent Deliberateness in the Fate of the Individual' is 'godfather' to his views, and it does help to explain where he is coming from. There Schopenhauer develops the idea that strict fatalism is confirmed empirically by cases in which future events are predicted in states of 'magnetic somnambulism', second sight and dreams. From such divinations, Schopenhauer contends, 'it follows not merely that events occur with complete necessity, but also that they are in some way determined beforehand and objectively fixed, in that they present themselves to the eye of a seer as something existing' (Schopenhauer 1850: 203–4). This suggests a special kind of fatalism, which he calls 'transcendent fatalism'. This kind of fatalism does not arise from theoretical arguments about determinism, but from experiences. Schopenhauer is also interested in how the sense of fatality can arise through a process of retrospection which conjures the sense that 'the course of an individual's life, however confused it appears to be, is a complete whole, in harmony with itself and having a definite tendency and didactic meaning, as profoundly conceived as is the finest epic' (Schopenhauer 1850: 204). In this retrospection on the course of life, it appears that everything 'had been mapped out and the human beings appearing on the scene seem to him to be performers in a play' (205). Schopenhauer here reflects on the experience of patterns in the course of individuation, which was one of the phenomena which led Freud to link the concept of repetition and the death drive in *Beyond the Pleasure Principle.* Freud writes of his impression that those subject to repetition compulsion are 'pursued by a malignant fate or possessed by some daemonic power' (SE 18: 21). The phenomena Schopenhauer, Freud and Jung have in mind are roughly the same, but whereas all three thinkers agree that the fate of such cases 'is for the most part arranged by themselves' (SE 18: 21), only Freud specifically contends that it is also 'determined by early infantile influences'. Although early infantile experiences are obviously the first act in the drama, the repetitions themselves do not come about *because* of the infantile experiences. The structure of fate and repetition can be examined independently of the specific events of childhood, because *whatever* infantile experiences occur, the unfolding of fatal repetition will take place.

Schopenhauer likens the empirical observation of the separate coincidences and fatalities in our lives to the contemplation of a recurrent anamorphic figure, which requires the use of a special conical mirror in order to be seen distinctly. He correlates this anamorphic figure with Kant's notion of an 'intelligible character', distinct from a person's empirical character. But this intelligible character is held to be outside space and time, merely noumenal. How, then, does Schopenhauer think that this 'secret and inexplicable power' actually effectively appears in the phenomenal world, if this latter world is ruled by strict determinism? If an event occurs in the chain of physical causes, that is all there is to it, and there is no need to postulate some 'intelligible character' behind it. On the other hand, Schopenhauer takes intelligible character to be something noumenally real and freely chosen, and which can thus ground the attribution of responsibility to the empirical character who acts within the phenomenal realm. At this point Schopenhauer ventures two important analogies to get across the idea that a single event may simultaneously belong to two different series, the objective series of representations, and the subjective series of the world taken as will. 'Objective and subjective connection exist simultaneously and yet the same event, as a link in two quite different chains, exactly fits them both' (220).

Schopenhauer then suggests that although every event has a distinct place in a causal chain, because these chains are articulated in *space*, 'there are numberless such chains side by side' (215). On the one hand, these chains are relatively independent, and each event may be said to involve a convergence of a multiplicity of separate chains. But on the other hand, 'many causes now operating simultaneously, each of which produces a different effect, have sprung from a common cause higher up and are, therefore, related one another as great-grandchildren are to their great-grandfather'.

> Accordingly, all those causal chains, that move in the direction of time, now form a large, common, much interwoven net which with its whole breadth likewise moves forward in the direction of time and constitutes the course of the world. Now if we represent these individual causal chains by meridians that would lie in the direction of time, then that which is simultaneous, and for this reason does not stand in direct causal connection, can be everywhere indicated by parallel lines. Now although all thins situated under the same parallel circle do not directly depend on one another, they nevertheless stand indirectly in some connection, though remote, by virtue of the interlacing of the whole net or of the totality of all causes and effects that roll along in the direction of time. Their present co-existence is therefore necessary; and on this rests the accidental coincidence of all the conditions of an event that is necessary in a higher sense, the happening of that which fate has willed. (Ibid.: 215)

Thus 'nothing is *absolutely* accidental' (216), for there are acausal correspondences between series that are grounded in a higher unity. The telling of fortunes by cards or the reading of coffee grounds all arise from the conviction that 'it is possible to know from what is present and clearly before [our] eyes that which is hidden by space and time and thus is remote or in the future' (216).

Schopenhauer also uses the analogy of the dream to further his point. He distinguishes between two types of 'obscene dream', one of which is accompanied by a successful nocturnal emission, while in the other, there seem to be no end of obstacles put in the way of reaching the same attractive women as feature in the first type of dream. As in each case, though, it is our subjective will which is responsible for the dream, the internal obstacles that appear (or not) are products of our own fatal character. 'Just as everyone is the secret theatrical manager of his dreams, so too by analogy that fate that controls the actual course of our lives ultimately comes in some way from the *will*' (218). It is exactly the same in 'the great dream of life'. If space, time and causality are ideal structuring forms, and the matter of our sensations depends on our sense organs, then our experience is not much different in nature from a dream. There is only one subject of the dream, and that is 'the will-to-live'. There is only one difference between life and a dream. 'In the great dream of life', the others one interacts and consorts with are also dreaming subjects, inhabiting their own dream.

It is at this point that Schopenhauer introduces the implicitly Leibnizian framework of pre-established harmony (it is this that presumably inspired Jung to discuss Leibniz in 'Synchronicity'). 'A mutual relation occurs since not only does the one figure in the dream of the other exactly as is necessary, but also that other figures in his dream. Thus by virtue of a real *harmonia praestablita* everyone dreams only what is appropriate to him' (219). Sexual intercourse is thus not fundamentally different from a nocturnal emission. The other, the 'object' is not, however, a complete figment of the dreamer's imagination – but nor is it an autonomous, mutually recognized other either. It is more like an incubus or succubus. If this phantom has some otherness that seems to transcend the dream, that is not because they are a 'real' person, but because we do not know what this other might itself be dreaming. What I desire from the incubus or succubus of my dream must, however, correspond in reverse to what they desire from the image that I project into their dream. But the projection in each case is unknowing and unwilled, so that there is never any mutual recognition, as the two perspectives remain permanently mutually excluded from each other, in a perpetual asymmetry.

Although the subject of the drama is always the will-to-live, Schopenhauer also wants to say that each individual will has different powers. Thus each individual will enters a drama, and plays a particular role, which will only become clear to them at the point of death. As they pass through repetitions of their role, or different performances of the same role, they at last see the pre-determined nature of the great dream.

> All the events in a man's life are connected in two fundamentally different ways; first, in the objective, causal connection of the course of nature; secondly, in a subjective connection that exists only in relation to the individual who experiences them . . . Now those two kinds of connection exist simultaneously and yet the same event, as a link in two quite different chains, exactly fits them both, in consequence whereof one man's fate is always in keeping with another's, and everyone is the hero of his own drama, but at the same time figures also in that of another. All this is of course something that surpasses our powers of comprehension, and can be conceived as possible only by virtue of the most marvellous preestablished harmony. (220, also cited in CW 8: 428)

Thus the subjective and objective series are related by an event, an 'object = x' that appears differently in each series. A person can cause an event that has an impact on another's life, but that other will interpret the meaning of the event in an entirely different way, suitable to his or her own purposes. The event or object that circulates in the two series guarantees a peculiar harmony between them, but each series remains different in kind.

The pattern of fate only becomes fully visible at the hour of death. Schopenhauer writes that we are 'forcibly driven to turn away from life to arrive at a regeneration by a Caesarian operation, so to speak' (223). 'At the hour of death, all the mysterious forces (although really rooted in ourselves) which determine man's eternal fate, crowd together and come into action.' All the repetitions and fatal correspondences which have structured one's life are now played before the dying individual, as they realize exactly who they will always have been. Schopenhauer describes the hour of death as a day of judgement, but also as a moment of 'crisis', and also, intriguingly, of 'palingenesis' (223), or rebirth. For Schopenhauer, as for Kierkegaard and Deleuze, rebirth involves a refolding of temporal experience; the difference is that, as Schopenhauer is a strict Kantian about time, treating it as purely ideal, the reorientation of our temporal experience in rebirth is ultimately an *exit from* worldly time. From a transcendental perspective, 'past and future contain mere concepts and phantasms' (Schopenhauer 1818: 279). If there is any progress in life, it is as the progressive revelation of one's eternal, intelligible character. Hence at the hour of death, to realize who one *will have been* is really to realise who one *always already was*. At that point, the flow of time can fall away as an illusion, and one can finally identify with what one has always already been. But this is where the palingenesis becomes possible, as the closure of the hour of death brings with it the possibility of an exit from phenomenal time. The dying person is finally free to perceive that 'the present is the essential form of the phenomenon of the will . . . That which, empirically apprehended, is the most fleeting of all, manifests itself to the metaphysical glance that sees beyond the forms of empirical perception as that which alone endures, as the *nunc stans* of the scholastics' (ibid.). If will is noumenal reality, and time, space and causality are just the ideal forms of representation, then the will is strictly speaking timeless; but because the will is Act, it can also be conceived more concretely as an eternal Now, *nunc stans*. For Schopenhauer, there is no form of mediation between the eternity of will and the temporality of the phenomenal world; hence the apprehension of the eternity of the will is only fully realised at the hour of death. To 'return' to the phenomenal world would be in any case simply to lapse back into phenomenal time.[13]

Jung criticizes Schopenhauer on one point. 'The idea that the simultaneous points in the causal chains, or meridians, represent meaningful coincidences would only hold water if the first cause really were a unity. But it were a multiplicity, which is just as likely, then Schopenhauer's whole explanation collapses' (CW 8: 428). This is not true, though, as Deleuze tries to show. Jung's own exposition of Leibniz (CW 8: 499–506) fails to take advantage of his philosophical resources. There is a sense in which the world can be composed of a multiplicity of series and still be a site for synchronicity.

Synchronicity, Immanence and Possible Worlds

Towards the end of *Spinoza and the Problem of Immanence* (1968), Deleuze says something that, within the confines of a book about Spinoza, appears as quite mysterious. He is returning to the issue of psychophysical parallelism in Spinoza. As we know, Spinoza has a peculiar stance on the issue of parallelism as, on the one hand, he holds Thought and Extension to be attributes of substance which have a strict parallel and corresponding relation to each other, but on the other hand, he says that there are an 'infinite' amount of attributes.

It is true that in Spinoza, infinity simply means 'non-limitation', so by absolute infinity, Spinoza perhaps only means 'the set of whichever unlimited attributes there are'; in that case, there may in fact only be two after all. Nevertheless, there is something mind-boggling in this parallelism, as formally it suggests that there are a plurality of attributes, all without direct causal relation to each other (which would imply limitation; cf. E1P6), but all expressing the same substance. In *Spinoza and the Problem of Expression*, Deleuze shows that he is interested in precisely this possibility when he suggests that Spinoza's notion of parallelism opens up 'the rich and deep world of *noncausal correspondences*' (SPE 326). Compare the following passage with those we have seen from Schopenhauer and Jung:

> One feels that the soul and body have at once a sort of identity that removes the need for any real causality between them, a heterogeneity, a heteronomy, that renders it impossible. The identity or quasi-identity is an 'invariance', and the heteronomy is that between two varying series, one of which is corporeal, the other spiritual.. Now real causality enters into each of these series on their own account; but the relation between the two series, and their relation to what is invariant between them, depends on noncausal correspondence. If we then ask what concept can account for such a correspondence, that of expression appears to do so. For while the concept of expression adequately applies to real causality, in the sense that an effect expresses its cause, and knowledge of the effect expresses knowledge of its cause, the concept nonetheless goes further than causality, since it brings a correspondence and a resonance into series that are altogether foreign to one another. (SPE 327)

The seventeenth-century rationalist project of constructing a philosophy of 'immanence' was deeply implicated in a specific tradition of pantheism, and had its own specific 'danger' in the latter idea. 'It claims to penetrate into the deepest things [*le plus profound*], the 'arcana', to use a word of which Leibniz was fond. It at once gives back to Nature its own specific depth [*Il redonne à la nature une épaisseur qui lui est proper*] and renders man capable of penetrating into this depth. It makes man commensurate with God, and puts him in possession of a new logic: makes him a spiritual automaton equal to a combinatorial world' (SPE 322).

Deleuze's ensuing argumentation recalls Schopenhauer's two models of parallelism, the dream and the globe. We saw above how Schopenhauer first suggests a parallelism of multiple independent series, and then goes on to restrict himself to a parallelism of subjective will and representation. In Deleuze, the order is reversed. He starts with a discussion of psychophysical parallelism (Thought and Extension), and then moves to a generalized picture of an infinity of attributes each in a relation of *repetition* to each other. Following Jung, it is no longer a globe or a collective totality that is being envisaged, but a plurality of independent series, each resonating with each other, but retaining their individual states of development.

Moreover, at this point in *Spinoza and the Problem of Expression* it is also particularly apparent that Leibnizianism is playing an unusually important role in Deleuze's interpretation of Spinoza. After all, the 'problem of expression' is a Leibnizian problem rather than a Spinozist one; the term hardly appears in Spinoza. In an important letter to Martin Joughin, the English translator of *Spinoza and the Problem of Expression*, Deleuze writes:

> the hope of making substance turn on finite modes, or at least of seeing in substance a *plane of immanence* in which finite modes operate, already appears in this book. What I needed was both (1) the expressive character of particular individuals, and (2) an immanence of being. Leibniz, in a way, goes further than Spinoza on the first point. But on the second, Spinoza stands alone. One finds it only in him. This is why I consider myself a Spinozist, rather than a Leibnizian, although I owe a lot to Leibniz. (SPE 11)

What Deleuze seems to effect in the last chapter of *Spinoza and the Problem of Expression* and in more detail in the philosophy of difference expounded in *Difference and Repetition* is a Spinozist conversion of Leibnizianism, an immanent Leibnizianism.

Leibnizianism after the Speculative Death of God

Leibniz imagines that before the dawn of the world God faces an eternal set of logically possible series, from which he must select a subset of series that are not only possible (non-self-contradictory) but *compossible*. Compossibility is weaker than logical possibility; something is compossible only *with* something else, and is therefore contingent upon *which* other realities might exist. To exist, therefore, something must not only be possible (non-self-contradictory), but compossible. To explain why something exists requires a counterfactual account of how other realities do not exist, *because* they are not compossible with each other; that is, that they *are* prevented from existing, by some other thing(s). But the question demands to be pushed further back, as Leibniz has not only to account for why *a* world might exist, but why this one does. Why is *this set* of compossibilities actualized? Leibniz claims that the criterion for this selection is the 'best' of all possible worlds. When he analyses what 'the best' or 'most perfect' might mean, he states that it is 'that combination of things . . . by which the greatest possible number of things exists' (Russell 1900: 295; cf. Leibniz 1697: 151). If A has the potential to be compatible or combinable with more things than B, then A will exist. It follows that the sufficient reason of an existent reality lies in the 'proportion' or 'degree' of potential complexity producible by it. This calculus of compossibility would be the true *ratio* of the world. The best of all possible worlds can be determined ideally through a reciprocal and complete determination between possible series, according to a differential calculus based on their potential contributions to a world with the maximum complexity and continuity. It is the formulation of this geometrically based combinatory, this calculus of compossibilities, that leads Deleuze to say that Leibniz 'discovers a play in the creation of the world' (DR 51).

In Leibniz, this play in creation is of course subordinated to a theological hypothesis. The infinite array of possibles must all eternally subsist in the mind of a God who reflects upon them, 'selects' the best, and then lets them pass into space and time. Being eternal, God's mind can weigh all possible outcomes, and thus judge the potential complexity of each possible series in conjunction with any of the others. God is not, then, responsible, for instance, for the sinning of Adam; God is at most responsible for selecting for existence the world in which Adam sins, according to the criterion of the best. This world did not *have* to happen. In other possible worlds, Adam does not sin. But is this theological formulation the only way Leibniz's theory can be conceived?

Deleuze sees resources in Leibniz's theory for a reformulation of the realm of Ideas discovered by Kant. As we have seen, Ideas in Deleuze's sense involve the identification of problems for cognition. But Leibniz's theory, because it recognizes a 'play in creation', can show us how these problems can be determined. Leibniz shows us from the outset that it is the wrong way around to seek an original monadic essence of Adam, dictating either that he must sin or that he must resist temptation. Rather, he says, there are 'several Adams' that are logically possible.[14] More profoundly, Leibniz suggests that in the first place one must conceive of a 'vague Adam' in which no decision is yet made about what Adam will actually be and do. Thus we can say that there is an Idea of Adam, a problem of Adam. But what are its basic elements? Should we simply say that the vague Idea of Adam is made up of possible series, which can be treated as individuals or monads? No, there is a more basic level. Vague Adam is rather composed of a number of *singularities* – to be the first man, to live in paradise, to give birth to a woman from himself, to sin, to resist temptation (F 59–61). Prior to the determination of compossibility according to the principle of the best, it is not so much that Leibniz merely presupposes a distribution of logically possible series; rather he must be understood, according to Deleuze, as presupposing first of all a distribution of the 'pre-individual singularities' which make up the deciding points of difference between those series (DR 245–6, 279–80). It is these that make up the Idea and that indeed make it a *problem*, for a constellation of singularities may branch off into a number of possible *divergent, incompossible* series. In this case, whether the Adam that is selected for existence actualizes either the fourth (sin) or fifth singularity (resistance to temptation) will be of immense importance for the world in which he is selected. Two different 'worlds', two divergent series, issue from the result of that disjunction.

In Leibniz's own scheme, God calculates that the world of the sinning Adam must be chosen and Adam's nocturnal twin, 'good Adam', must be banished for ever. However, the model of the 'vague Adam' indicates the perfect conceivability or rational transparency of the divergent or incompossible series that branch off ideally in forking paths from each ideal conjunction of singularities. 'With Leibniz', suggests Deleuze, 'it seems to us that *in the first place* there is a calculus of infinite series ruled by convergences and divergences' (F 61). Such an ideal calculus seems quite autonomous from the doctrine of the best, as well as from the theological hypothesis of the selecting God.

For Leibniz, we live in the best of all possible worlds, and everything that happens in it is selected for its *compossibility* with everything else. Deleuze's final gambit is that the death of God does not destroy Leibniz's metaphysics, but liberates all its possibilities. Deleuze thus attempts to wrest the 'play in the creation of the world' from the hypothesis of divine selection. Leibnizianism after the death of God – and after the fracture of the 'I' – implies *the affirmation of incompossible worlds*. The problems which guide our cognition and affection are problems 'in themselves'. In fact it is as if Leibniz's system not only survives, but even only comes to bloom, after the death of God. For if Leibniz's principle of the best is taken instead as a possible solution (albeit a highly generalized and abstract one) nested within a primary matrix of *Ideas*, taken now more strictly in the Kantian sense as focal horizons for thought, then we are able to step out of metaphysics and into transcendental philosophy. *Without* reliance on a pre-established, designed harmony between thought and world, the world is precisely restored to us *as a matrix of problems*, for which the solutions have not been prepared in advance, but which orient or provide a horizon for the ultimate purposes of our thinking. Problems, vague Ideas, are thus affirmed as the true objects of reason. The 'vague Adam, a vagabond, a nomad, an Adam = x' can indeed be understood as 'common to several worlds' (LS 114) but it attains a powerful determinacy of its own at the moment that it is seen as *a problem that frames multiple solutions*, and serves as a witness to an aboriginal 'play in the creation of the world' (DR 51) – that is, of *this* world taken as the body of the absolute, hierarchically organized in levels of interiorization.

For Deleuze, individuation is first of all a biological process, and then a psychic one (DR 256). In psychic life, individuation occurs when the imagination, faced with problematic Ideas, attempts to invoke the power of intuition. For Jung, dreaming, love, 'active imagination', and esoteric experiences are the media and tools of the individuating person (the *individuant*, we could call them). For Deleuze it is art, love, masochism, intoxication, esoteric experience and revolutionary consciousness.

Synchronicity and Repetition in Jung and Freud

Is synchronicity narcissism? Or is narcissism synchronicity? The first half of Freud's essay on 'The Uncanny' is devoted to a reductive analysis of E. T. A. Hoffman's story about the Sandman to a fantasy about infantile castration anxiety. But after completing this analysis, Freud goes on to produce some fascinating reflections on fantasies of living dolls and doubles, and on experiences of fateful coincidences and repetitions. He alights upon the theme of doubling and repetition as fundamental to experiences of the uncanny. We should briefly recount his line of thought here, as he moves from a reductive analysis of the double in terms of narcissism, to a more ambivalent analysis of repetition, which finally seems to lead him to posit compulsive repetition as a primordial force in the psyche, thus opening the way to the invention of the death drive.

Freud approvingly cites Otto Rank's hypothesis that 'the 'double' was originally an insurance against the destruction of the ego . . . This invention of doubling [is] a preservation against extinction' (SE 17: 235). Ideas of the double 'have sprung from the soil of unbounded self-love, from the primary narcissism which dominates the mind of the child and of primitive man'. Freud elaborates then on Rank's theory of the narcissistic component of the double. The double proceeds to become an object of fear, because of the surmounting of the stage of narcissism, and the construction of the ego. Thus insofar as the return to narcissism is repressed, the double becomes an object of fear, but insofar as a return to narcissism promises the attraction of a return to the omnipotence of thoughts and the surety of an immortal soul, the double is an object of attraction. Hence the feeling of the uncanny expresses ambivalence about a regression to primary narcissism. 'The quality of uncanniness can only come from the fact of the "double" being a creation dating back to a very early mental stage, long since surmounted – a stage, incidentally, at which it wore a more friendly aspect. The "double" has become a thing of terror, just as, after the collapse of their religion, the gods turned into demons' (ibid.: 236).

However, narcissism is invoked not just to explain the double as a rudimentary form of self-preservation through multiplication. For Freud, there are two other aspects of narcissism that are relevant to experiences of the uncanny. First, any uncanny experience involves a blurring of the usual demarcation between reality and imagination. This alteration recalls two other features of Freud's account of primary narcissism, which in fact turn out to be inconsistent. On the one hand, there is the omnipotence of thoughts. In the stage of narcissism, the child has the ability to 'satisfy their wishes in a hallucinatory manner' (SE 13: 83–4). But on the other hand, the collapse of the distinction between ego and external world surely must result in a certain passivity, insofar as there is no formed ego to be omnipotent in the first place. Freud says that he is pursuing the idea that uncanny experiences involve 'a harking-back to particular phases in the evolution of the self-regarding feeling, a regression to a time when the ego had not yet marked itself off sharply from the external world and from other people' (SE 17: 236). But the idea of a collapse in distinction between ego and external world is incompatible with the idea of omnipotence of thoughts.[15]

However, as if unsatisfied by this regressive account of the uncanny, Freud goes on to probe deeper into the origins of the act of doubling, through exploring other instances of the uncanny. In certain experiences of apparent coincidence, the presence of a 'factor of involuntary repetition . . . forces upon us the idea of something fateful and inescapable' (SE 17: 237), which can neither be reduced to a regression to a state of narcissism, nor to factors of chance. Freud recalls an occasion he went walking in a provincial town in Italy, and found himself in its red-light district. He hastened to leave the street at the next turning, and wandered some more, only to find himself led involuntarily back to the same street, where his return was now attracting unwanted attention. He hurried away again, only to arrive by another detour at the same place again. A feeling of the uncanny overtook him at this moment. An uncanny impression can also arise with numerical coincidences. Implicitly recalling the superstitions about the number 61 he had shared with Jung after the latter's embarrassing 'spookery' with Freud's furniture, Freud states that if we come across the number 62 a number of times in one day – 'if two such events, each in itself indifferent, happen close together, or if we come across the number 62 several times in a single day' (ibid.), we do feel this to be uncanny. He remarks that what is common to such experiences of the uncanny is an 'unintended recurrence of [a] situation' resulting in a 'sense of helplessness experienced in some dream-states' (ibid.). The 'involuntary repetition' gives rise to the sense that we are helplessly caught in a fateful and inescapable pattern of events, beyond our control. Freud then states that he is reluctant to trace the uncanny effect of such occurrences back to infantile psychology, and says that he must refer the reader to his new work *Beyond the Pleasure Principle*, which he has just completed.

> For it is possible to recognise the dominance in the unconscious mind of a 'compulsion to repeat' proceeding from the drive impulses and probably inherent in the very nature of the drives – a compulsion powerful enough to overrule the pleasure principle, lending to certain aspects of the mind their daemonic character, and still very clearly expressed in the impulses of small children . . . All these considerations prepare us for the discovery that whatever reminds us of this inner 'compulsion to repeat' is perceived as uncanny. (Ibid.: 238)

Although he admits that the notion of repetition is explored 'in a different connection' in *Beyond the Pleasure Principle*, it is striking that the type of 'unintended recurrence of the same thing' (ibid.: 246) discussed in 'The Uncanny' – the experience of fate – is not really covered in the later work. The discussion in 'The Uncanny' appears to be converging on the thought that the experience of 'involuntary repetition' is not necessarily to be seen as a trigger for a regression to a particular state, but as the bursting-through of a compulsion to repeat that is autonomous of the pleasure principle. The 'sense of helplessness' or passivity that results from the 'unintended recurrence of the same thing' is a result of the yielding to this power of repetition, which is 'probably inherent in the very nature of the drives'. There is also the suggestion in this passage that 'the compulsion to repeat' runs through the whole 'evolution of self-regarding', so that Freud would be looking towards a principle of autonomous doubling, which would connect up with his previous remarks about psychic doubling.

It is true that in *Beyond the Pleasure Principle* Freud does write of his impression that those subject to repetition compulsion are 'pursued by a malignant fate or possessed by some daemonic power' (SE 18: 22). In this passage, he discusses repetition in terms of fate. 'We have come across people all of whose human relationships have the same outcome . . . The man whose friendships all end in betrayal by his friend . . . the lover each of whose love affairs with a woman passes through the same phases and reaches the same conclusion' (ibid.: 21). If we take into account cases like these, says Freud, then 'we shall find courage to assume that there really does exist in the mind a compulsion to repeat which overrides the pleasure principle'. However, Freud goes on to say that *despite* the impression of daemonic fate that accompanies instances of repetition, 'psychoanalysis has always taken the view that their fate is for the most part arranged by themselves and determined by early infantile influences' (ibid.). Moreover, as Deleuze complains, the death drive is reduced to the model of a return to inanimate matter. Finally, in 'The Uncanny' itself Freud withdraws from the path opened up by his suggestions about repetition and retreats to his position that 'an uncanny experience occurs either when infantile complexes which have been repressed are once more revived by some impression, or when primitive beliefs which have been surmounted seem once more to be confirmed' (SE 17: 249).

It was recalled earlier that Freud begins his discussion of the uncanny with a quotation from Schelling's *Philosophy of Mythology*, which he says throws new light on the concept of the uncanny, 'for which we were certainly not prepared'. Schelling's passage says that '*Unheimlich* is the name for everything that ought to have remained . . . secret and hidden but has come to light' (Schelling 1857: 649). If Freud had followed up this reference, he might well have found more than he was prepared to see. The context for Schelling's passage lies in a discussion of how Homeric poetry had first emerged because Greek culture had managed to transcend the hitherto dominant culture of religious mysteries through *interiorizing* them: 'The Homeric Age was first able to conceive of that purely poetic narrative of the gods after the actually religious principle had been hidden in the interior and thus allowed the spirit to turn freely toward the outside' (ibid., cited in Beach 1994: 228). But what was at the core of the mysteries themselves according to Schelling? Nothing other than a dramatization of a spiritual rebirth, whereby the aspirant retraced or recapitulated the developmental process of the history of mythical consciousness itself, culminating in a 'regenerative catharsis' (ibid.: 239). What was internalized in Homeric poetry was already itself a recapitulative internalization. Moreover, Schelling stressed the paradoxical temporal logic involved in this recapitulation. The process of repetition culminates in the realization that what has been repeated only finally exists *for itself* in the internalization of the repetition. The mythical drama of rebirth is the unfolding and then final destruction of rebirth *as* a myth, which gives rise to a properly *interior* rebirth through the internalization of the whole process itself. The Homeric fate that is played out in sunlight and open sky in the *Odyssey*, then, is itself an inverted repetition of a drama of rebirth played out in the darkness of the mysteries. But this drama itself, taking place in the entrails of the past, was already a circle of self-interiorizing repetition. 'Greece has a Homer precisely because it has Mysteries, i.e., because it has succeeded in completely conquering the principle of the past, which in the Oriental systems was still dominant and on the surface. It has succeeded in putting that principle back into the interior, i.e., into secrecy, into the Mystery (out of which, after all, it had emerged in the first place)' (Schelling, ibid.). The 'principle of the past', of the already-there, the fated déjà vu, is interiorized, and revealed as having its *fate* only in repetition. Ultimately, it is fated only to be repeated. So the kernel of what 'should have remained hidden' is not simply narcissism, an abstract concept which falls apart once it is made concrete, but the principle of repetition itself.

We have seen that a *Heimlichkeit* is also generated by Jung's notion of synchronicity, and, as with the Freudian uncanny, it also involves the revelation of a *Geheimnis*, something previously hidden from view. Although it can involve a *de facto* regression to narcissism, it also points towards a species of transcendental immortality, *de jure* even if aborted. The pathology of the psychotic broadcasts the message of the eternal return – that death is not the problem, but the immortality of our actions – in magnified form. The psychotic is immobilized by their encounter with finitude, and, by spatializing temporality, they find themselves thrown into a drama which appears to have already been written, and in which they are a pawn. Deleuze and Jung suggest that there is a psychotic moment in the culmination of every process of individuation. Or more precisely, the neurotic only proceeds along the path of individuation by encountering the same processes that engulf the psychotic. The theatre of fate adjoins the 'theatre of terror' (DR 18) of schizophrenia, in which the unconscious is poised to appear 'in person', unleashing distortions of spatiotemporal reality.

Chapter 6

The Occult Unconscious: Sympathy and the Sorcerer

One of the most powerful passages in Deleuze's oeuvre comes at the end of *Bergsonism*, when he sets forth his version of the Bergsonian vision of the place of the human being in the universe:

> It could be said that in man, and only in man, the actual becomes adequate to the virtual. It could be said that man is capable of rediscovering all the levels, all the degrees of expansion [*détente*] and contraction that coexist in the virtual Whole. As if he were capable of all the frenzies and brought about in himself successively everything that, elsewhere, can only be embodied in different species. Even in his dreams he rediscovers or prepares matter. And durations that are inferior to him are still internal to him. Man therefore creates a differentiation that is valid for the Whole, and he alone traces out an open direction that is able to express a whole that is itself open. Whereas the other directions are closed and go round in circles . . . man is capable of scrambling the planes, of going beyond his own plane as his own condition, in order finally to express naturing Nature. (B 106)[1]

Deleuze firmly situates Bergson in the tradition of Schelling and Hegel, for whom the human being must ultimately be understood as the *coming to consciousness* of the universe itself. Of course, this model is much older than German Idealism, as it is the central schema of the Hermetic philosophies of the Renaissance and theosophy. In his article on Malfatti and in his references to Wronski's esoteric use of the calculus, Deleuze relates himself more or less explicitly to this tradition, but in his work on Bergson, Deleuze tends to restrict himself to relating Bergson to Schelling and German Idealism (DI 36, 50; Deleuze 1960).

Bergson's cosmic tableau of the hierarchy of beings in the universe emerges most clearly in his last work, *The Two Sources of Morality and Religion.* In *Creative Evolution*, he had for the most part rested content with detailing the divergent development of the *élan vital* into two Orders of life. The hymenoptera were in effect equal to human beings, insofar as both represented the furthest point of development of the tendencies of instinct and intelligence. *The Two Sources* may be read as Bergson's belated investigation into the specific development of the human order of life. There is a clear asymmetry between the insect and human realms, if one takes seriously the notion that 'life' is defined by its creativity and open-endedness. For in that case, the instinctual mode of life may be taken as a *lapse* in evolution. Insects have 'lapsed into the somnambulism of instinct' (Bergson 1932: 209), whereas conscious intelligence, in breaking away from instinct, opens up the possibility of unforeseen developments through cultural development. If 'the creative effort progressed successfully only along the line of evolution which ended in man', then the human being in effect gained access to a privileged possibility: to transform its consciousness in such a way that it becomes the form in which the '*élan vital* gains self-consciousness' (B 113). This is not to say that human beings are the one and only biological form which can attain this privilege. Bergson quite carefully says that through 'the act of placing in matter a freely creative energy, it is man, or some other being of like significance – we do not say of like form – which is the purpose of the entire process of evolution' (Bergson 1932: 211).

To criticize Bergson and Deleuze for anthropomorphism (or worse, of 'humanism', an almost completely meaningless term) is to miss the point. Jean Hyppolite (following Hegel) says that 'man' merely expresses the sense of being, and that (following Heidegger) man is therefore the 'place of being', rather than a biological genus *or* a self-conscious subject (Hyppolite 1955: 20). For Deleuze, the human being is simply the site of 'the interiorisation of difference'. In the important final pages of *Difference and Repetition* (before the Conclusion), Deleuze constructs a hierarchy of the domains of actualization, derived in large part from the work of the philosopher Gilbert Simondon. There are three domains: physical, biological and psychic systems. In fact, it is only in psychic systems that we effectively meet with the noumenal nature of intensity, through the interiorization of difference. 'To the extent that the individuating factors form a kind of noumenon of the phenomenon, we claim that the noumenon tends to appear as such in complex systems' (DR 256; cf. DR 261). In physical systems, the process of individualization 'happens all at once, and affects only the boundaries' (DR 255). 'The physical individual creates and prolongs itself to the limit of the body – for example, crystal' (DI 88). In turn, 'a biological system receives successive waves of singularities and involves its whole internal milieu in the operations which take place at the outer limits' (DR 255); these 'successive waves' are progressive and durational. But, Deleuze continues, 'What is the formula for this 'evolution'? The more complex a system, the more the *values peculiar to implication* appear within it' (DR 255). This implication, involution or interiorization of difference is accomplished only in 'psychic systems', which attain a completely virtual body through the preservation of the past in the synthesis of memory. 'Complex systems increasingly tend to interiorise their constitutive differences . . . The more the difference on which the system depends is interiorised in the phenomenon, the more repetition finds itself interior, the less it depends upon external conditions which are supposed to ensure the reproduction of the "same" differences' (DR 256). Deleuze thus finds a new way to defend the Hermetic idea that the microcosm contains the macrocosm.

The passage from *Bergsonism* exalting the powers of humanity is thrilling, but it also becomes more enigmatic the closer one examines it. We might ask how and why the human being (or the being that occupies its place) brings about in itself 'everything that, elsewhere, can only be embodied in different species'? If the power of humanity arises through its intelligence, then what has this re-embodiment of different species got to do with intelligence? Indeed, Deleuze suggests that it is in dreams, rather than intelligence, that the human being 'rediscovers or prepares matter'. And what are these 'frenzies' of which the human being is said to be capable? Deleuze's eulogy to humanity in fact seems to have nothing to do with more traditional accounts of the privilege of humanity over the rest of nature. Where are reason and intelligence here?

In the closing pages of *Bergsonism*, where this passage resides, Deleuze is in effect teasing out the logic of Bergson's theory of the distinction between humans and animals. It turns out that it is not intelligence, after all, which marks out the distinctiveness of human beings, but rather the possibility of a *reintegration* of instinct and intelligence. We should now follow how Deleuze draws certain consequences from Bergson's philosophy of humanity which are not even explicitly affirmed by Bergson himself.

Sorcery and the Difference between Human and Animal

To say that the human being brings about 'everything that, elsewhere, can only be embodied in different species' can only refer, once again, to instinct, as that is what is embodied, in durational cycles, in the different species. Now, we have seen that Bergson believes that intelligence is the dominant tendency in human beings, which leads them away from instinctual activity. In human society, however, there is an 'equivalent of instinct' in the 'fabulating function', a notion, as we saw, that Bergson borrowed from Janet. The fabulating or story-telling function necessarily fills the gaps opened up by intelligence, and provides fictions to fill the question of the *ends* of intelligent actions. Bergson's account of fabulation is pre-dated by Janet's theory of fabulation in his *Evolution of Memory*. For Janet, the fabulating function is a development of the power to narrate or give accounts of what is presently absent. In the first myths and epics, the power of memory is used *for* fabulation, giving rise to a specific enjoyment, which, if unchecked, can be transformed into delirium, and the myth being taken as founding (for a society or individual). For Bergson, however, the notion of fabulation is connected with a residue of instinct within human life. At every point where intelligence comes up against its own limits, there arises a 'compensation' on the part of instinct (B 108). This notion of compensation is clearly espoused by Bergson in *The Two Sources*, but is also reminiscent of the Jungian version of the opposition between instinct (or archetype) and intelligence. But it has a more specific function in Bergson's thought. Deleuze gives two examples of how a 'virtual instinct' can arise and enter the problematic gaps of the intelligence: social obligation and religion:

> Take, for example, obligation: It has no rational ground. Each particular obligation is conventional and can border on the absurd; the only thing that is grounded is the obligation to have obligations . . . and it is not grounded in reason, but in a requirement of nature, in a kind of 'virtual instinct', that is, on a counterpart that nature produces *in* the reasonable being in order to compensate for the partiality of his intelligence. (B 108)

In this case, it is no longer a particular instinctual exigency which guides the obligation, but rather the instinctual need to have obligations in general. In other words, it is an 'instinct that has become disinterested, self-conscious, capable of reflecting upon its object' (Bergson 1907: 176): only the *form* of instinct remains. A virtual instinct is a 'counterpart that nature produces *in* the reasonable being in order to compensate for the partiality of his intelligence' (B 108). Deleuze does not say any more about obligation, but that there is more to be said about it emerges when we look at the second example, religion, which reveals the foundation of obligation. Virtual instinct is in fact the 'creator of gods, inventor of religions, that is of fictitious representations . . . As in the case of obligation, each god is contingent, but what is natural, necessary and grounded is *having* gods; it is the pantheon of gods' (B 108). Again, Deleuze's remarks are brief, but we can connect up here with Janet's argument about the potential delirium of the fabulating function, which exploits the impossibility of verifying certain narratives of past events. On the Bergsonian model, memory is preserved as a whole and is not *in itself* ordered chronologically. Janet suggests that fabulation can run riot through the past, scrambling chronology, and returning with a completely mythicized past. What would plug this delirium, on Bergson's account? In the end, it must be reflected instinct. Epic and myth are closely linked with *genealogical* claims in ancient history. The delirium of myth is controlled by stabilizing it to serve genealogy as a reflected biological form of the virtual: lineages, races, blood. The form of instinct would thus allow the mythical narrative to assume a 'biological' form, albeit a reflected one. Instinctual consciousness is therefore still possible at a collective level. Just as the wasp has a peculiar kind of 'species-consciousness', the consciousness of the early Greek would be structured by the dramas of Olympus as racial myths.

Social obligation is referred back to mythical fabulation, which forms the foundation of human society through the reactivation of instinct. Deleuze's argument does not stop there, however, although it could have done so. In a move that proves the decisive role of dialectical thinking in his thought, Deleuze claims that the preservation of 'virtual instinct' in this manner does not yet demonstrate any fundamental difference in kind between human beings and animals. For 'the societies that he forms are no less closed than animal species; they form part of a plane of nature, as much as animal species and societies; and man goes round in circles in his society just as much as the species do in theirs or ants in their domain'. The difference between ants and men is not so great, especially if we are prepared to assume some sort of consciousness in lower organisms. Although the human worker is different from a worker ant insofar as it is blessed with intelligence, when it encounters the limits of intelligence, it reveals itself as resting on instinct after all. If an individual resists social pressure, then this is by virtue of his intelligence, while if an individual conforms to society, then he does so likewise through acquiescing in the stories and fables he is told. There is still no possibility of escaping the plane or circle of nature, and we remain caught in an endless oscillation between individual and social pressure.

Deleuze is quite clear that the requisite 'third thing' is not intuition, as 'in fact, we must on the contrary carry out a genesis of intuition, that is determine the way in which intelligence itself was converted or is converted into intuition' (B 109–10). This is a bit of an obscure formulation, as we have seen that instinct itself must be already taken to be intuitive, so there is no need for a 'genesis' of intuition in that respect. However, Deleuze's claim is more specific: it is to determine how *intelligence* can be converted into intuition. That is, not only must instinct itself be affected by intelligence, thus becoming 'disinterested, self-conscious, capable of reflecting upon its object', but intelligence too must have the possibility of being internally altered by instinct. This is a pure speculative-dialectical formulation: not just intelligence in instinct, but instinct in intelligence.

Again, as with Hegelian phenomenology, we have to scan the horizon to see if there is a suitable object to serve as locus for this dialectical identity. Deleuze says abruptly that there is only one candidate. 'Only *emotion* differs in nature from both intelligence and instinct, from both intelligent individual egoism and quasi-instinctive social pressure' (B 110). But it is not any sort of emotion which differs in nature, as Deleuze suggests. Egoistic passions and the aesthetic pleasures of fabulation both involve emotions which are 'always connected to a representation on which it is supposed to depend' (ibid.). Nevertheless, emotion can in principle be separated from these representations. 'It precedes all representation, itself generating new ideas. It does not have, strictly speaking, an object, but merely an *essence* that spreads itself over various objects, animals, plants and the whole of nature'. This is an odd conception, but we can already see that the notion of *sympathy* must be lurking in the background here. Emotion is being related to the capacity for sympathy; it appears as a kind of *universal sympathy*, made possible by the reflection of instinct out of its particularity. In *Creative Evolution* Bergson had already hinted that instinct could become 'disinterested' in human beings. Emotion then appears to be some sort of process of 'identification' with instinctual attitudes, which nevertheless does not extend to fully incarnating them. In *The Two Sources*, Bergson uses aesthetic 'identification' to get across what he means here. A piece of music which expresses love does not express love for a particular person, but a love that is 'ideal', insofar as it does not belong to the person who has it, but the person who has it participates in an essence. Music 'does not introduce these feelings in us; it introduces us into them, as passers-by are forced into a street dance' (Bergson 1932: 40, cited in B 110). 'To each member of a closed society, if he opens himself to it, it communicates a kind of reminiscence, an excitement that allows him to follow' (B 111).

Universal sympathy is the intuitive basis which allows for the identification with others. Consciousness has been universalized, so that it no longer belongs to one ego, but due to the ability to adjust the 'level' of consciousness (between contraction and relaxation) now assumes a power of dissociation that allows us to enter the conscious perspectives of other beings.

Furthermore, this universalization of consciousness extends all the way to the animal world, and to life itself. Without an object, emotion is 'an *essence* that spreads itself over various objects, animals, plants and the whole of nature' (110). Deleuze often describes the peculiar feeling of sympathy with animals. Which child has not looked into the eyes of a dog or horse and felt overcome with a flood of melancholy? Deleuze frequently alludes to a passage from the novel *Anton Reiser* by the German pre-Romantic writer Karl Philipp Moritz, who 'feels responsible not for the calves that die but before the calves that die and give him the incredible feeling of an unknown Nature – *affect*' (ATP 240). (Deleuze uses the term 'affect' here to denote emotion, rather than affect in the strictly Bergsonian sense.) If emotion is a 'spiritual' (or even daemonic) event rather than the firing of neurons, it is because it is necessarily referred to an *unknown Nature.* The emotions of love and art are not like affects that belong to 'known' or empirically sensed nature (such as the intensities attached to ordinary sensations). Love rather refers to the unknown Nature of the other (in Jungian terms, the anima or animus). Fear is only ever an 'affect' in the proper sense of the word when it refers to an unknown nature. Love, fear and art all participate in a flow of emotion which emanates from our relation to the unknown in nature. The Jungian terms we developed in chapter 3 allow us to specify that the most profound unknown nature is unknown inner nature – the unconscious, the mind beyond ego. Unknown nature is only powerful to us when it refers to an unknown inner nature: 'nature from within'. Affect or emotion is therefore the intensive movement of this unknown nature, and is 'the unconscious' in its pure, intensive form. We know that Deleuze always begins on the principle that the highest serves as the clue to the most fundamental ('the noumenon tends to appear as such in complex systems'), so it is art which reveals the essence of this feeling most clearly. Music is the privileged example of universal sympathy. Here, universal sympathy is at its most 'active'. But art and music are refined forms of universal sympathy. Everything that has been said so far leads Deleuze to suggest that it is this universal sympathy which can claim the special ontological status of lifting us out of the closed cycles of nature. Because emotion in itself is pure intensive quantity, it is the *élan vital in person* (the noumenon appearing within the interior). In a sense, emotion is the substance or subject (in Hegelian terms) of the Absolute. The goal of the occult tradition is to assign a *mathesis* to the microcosmic currents of intensive quantity, allowing for a potential mastery of the domain of pure virtuality. Bergson himself claims that it is the *mystic* who is the final subject of pure emotion. 'At the limit, it is the mystic who plays with the whole of creation, who invents an expression of it whose adequacy increases with its dynamism. Servant of an open and finite God (such are the characteristics of the *élan vital*), the mystical soul actively plays the whole of the universe, and reproduces the opening of a Whole in which there is nothing to see or contemplate' (B 112).

If the passage from *Bergsonism* has been kept in mind, perhaps we are not so unprepared for this conclusion. In *The Two Sources,* Bergson identifies mysticism with 'frenzy'. However, his theory of frenzy is quite specific and needs to be briefly recounted (see Lawlor 2003: 85–111 for a general overview). For Bergson, frenzy is a fundamental possibility of human cognitive and affective life. We have seen enough of Bergson's philosophy to know that he identifies two fundamental 'tendencies' in life – duration and matter. 'In the general evolution of life, the tendencies thus created by a process of dichotomy are to be found in species different from each other', so that evolutionary lineages which develop intelligence do so at the expense of instinct, for instance. The kingdom of the hymenoptera is opposed to the kingdom of humanity. Nevertheless, even if one line – intelligence or instinct – wins out evolutionarily, a tension between the two tendencies still exists when it comes to 'the evolution of psychical and social life' because 'here the tendencies, born of the process of splitting, develop in the same individual . . . can be developed only in succession' (Bergson 1932: 295). Human psychological development, therefore, proceeds through an *alternation* of instinct and intelligence. Whereas the development of the human infant proceeds through formations shaped by instinct, the period of early adulthood is devoted to the cultivation of intelligence, while the development of instinct (for instance, the sexual instinct), conversely, is frozen at a certain stage. Now Bergson suggests that if one of these tendencies gains an unmoderated power over the other, and assumes a development autonomous of the other, then frenzy is the result. 'The mere fact of taking up all the room imparts to each of them such an impetus that it bolts ahead as the barriers collapse one by one; there is something frenzied about it' (296). Intelligence completely uprooted from instinct is frenzied, while instinct without any sort of power of modification through intelligence (or at least habituation) is also frenzied. There is no longer an internal barrier in the counteraction of the opposing tendency, and so a careering freefall comes into being. This duality of tendencies appears to be permanent, and the best one can do is oscillate between them, avoiding the frenzies that come about when one becomes dominant.

Mysticism is nevertheless something more than the mental disequilibrium one might expect if it dwells at the 'dream-pole' of human cognition and emotion. It is not idle dreaming, but taps into the source of life. The mystic's visions are 'a systematic rearrangement aiming at a superior equilibrium'. It is superior, Bergson says, because there is the possibility of action, of realization. Bergson makes clear later that mysticism is a type of frenzy (298). So the conclusion is clear: if there is a correlate to the Hegelian 'substance = subject' in Bergson, a coming-to-consciousness where the noumenal is expressed in pure states of interiority, then it is embodied by the mystic. Mysticism, which is identification with the *Natura naturans*, points towards a superior equilibrium, and the mystic is not at all bothered if people accuse him or her of being mad.

But the very extremity of the mystic's existence forces Bergson to downplay its normativity. A society of mystics is not possible, and Bergson's discussion turns to a novel account of the general conditions for society. But Deleuze insists that it is this interval of emotion – apparently apprehensible in its pure form only in mysticism – which itself 'defines a variability appropriate to human societies' (B 111). Contra Freudian expectations, the Deleuzean individuant is no longer caught within the conflict between instinct and intelligence, but has gone beyond this dualism towards the articulation of an intensive map that makes possible the *alternation* of impersonal powers of intuition in mathetical relationship with each other. The variability in human societies, in other words, must ultimately be traced back to the vicissitudes of deployment of this creative emotion. The condition of any hierarchically ordered society is therefore the management or distribution of frenzy.

But mystical frenzy is just one form of frenzy. More specifically, society is conditioned by an oscillation between two types of frenzy. Writing in 1932, Bergson suggests that 'comfort and luxury [have] apparently become the main preoccupation of humanity . . . We have seen the race for comfort proceeding faster and faster . . . Today it is a stampede' (298). The pendulum has swung in the opposite direction to 'the Middle Ages, [when] an ascetic ideal had predominated . . . Here already you had frenzy' (ibid.). These two frenzies recall Jung's two poles of extraversion and introversion. On the one side, the frenzied extraversion of consumer society, with solitude banished to outer darkness. This is a kind of frenzy of intelligence, in that intelligence itself becomes separated altogether from its instinctual ballast. On the other side, the frenzied introversion of monks and shamans, who have gone beyond all earthly need for human contact. Any society will veer towards one of the frenzies. Bergson concludes: 'We propose to designate *law of twofold frenzy* the imperative demand, forthcoming from each of the two tendencies as soon as it is materialised by the splitting, to be pursued to the very end, as if there was an end!' (296).

Despite the fact that he sees no end to this oscillation, Bergson does accord value to the return to the 'simple life', which led to the dismissal of his late philosophy as quietistic. But in the terms of his argument, things are less straightforward. If mystical life is being identified with frenzy and with the disequilibrium of the senses, it seems somewhat humorous to call it a 'simple life'. Moreover, despite the ontological expressivity of the mystic, he or she cannot in the end be described as an empty vessel through which light pours. In the footnote to the crucial passage with which we started this chapter, Deleuze even refers us to 'the man who tricks nature, extending 'beyond' the plane and returning to a naturing Nature' (B 135). Once again, Bergsonism in Deleuze's hands is revealed to be a superior Neoplatonism: for the ability of the mystic to become *Natura naturans* is achieved only by going *against Natura naturata*. There is a 'life' of nature which is prior to nature itself. 'Nature . . . is the name we give to the totality of compliances and resistances which life encounters in raw matter' (Bergson 1932: 311). The coming to consciousness that Deleuze describes in the passage only occurs through the tricking of nature as it *actually* exists. There is a higher Nature, beyond actual nature. Bergson himself already admits that there is something 'unnatural' about universal sympathy. 'Man outwits nature when he extends social solidarity into the brotherhood of man . . . he is deceiving her', because the maintaining of intergroup hostility is essential to evolutionary development (Bergson 1932: 57). It is as true today that the figure of the mystic still drives Darwinists into a fury. He or she is an unnatural figure, who no longer conforms to the established laws of nature (that is, the laws of established nature). Now, when Deleuze ventures that frenzy involves 'scrambling the planes of nature', he is in effect exacerbating this aspect of Bergson's argument. But in doing so, the mystic's true identity is revealed. What Deleuze shows is that in any case, Bergson is not ultimately talking about mystics, but about sorcerers.

In the mystic's exaltation, says Bergson, things are seen on a vast scale, but through the lens of a simplicity that allows the mystic to act decisively. The mystical soul has access to 'an innate science, or rather an acquired ignorance', which 'suggests to it straightaway the step to be taken, the decisive act, the unanswerable word' (232; trans. modified). But Bergson himself denies that mysticism is equivalent to or comparable to magic, which he instead presents as a kind of deluded belief in the omnipotence of thoughts (as Freud had done in *Totem and Taboo*) (Bergson 1932: 167). Although he recognizes the role of heightened emotion in magic, his main focus is on its lamentable inability to bring about change in nature. The sorcerer is the one who curses his rival rather than attempting to challenge him physically. He turns impotence (the inability to control weather, for instance) to his advantage, gaining personal power through exploiting gaps in human knowledge and technical capacity. He takes associative rules (such as the substitution of part for whole, or the association of like with like) and applies them, with the help of the intrinsic delirium of the fabulating function, to events over which he has no power. The sorcerer is a mere shadow of the mystic, who is on the contrary a 'genius of the will' (58). But the problem is that all the attributes he ascribes to the mystic can also be attributed with even more justification to the magician. First, the 'unnatural' participation of the mystic in life seems only to come into its own in magic and sorcery. The sorcerer takes the short cut to wisdom, over the saint who subordinates his meditations to theological principle. Second, Bergson's statement that mysticism involves a frenzy recalls the statements of sorcerers rather than those of saints. The active cultivation of frenzy is central to the practice of magic, on any account. In his *Magick in Theory and Practice*, Crowley writes that the secret of magical invocation is to '*enflame thyself in praying*' . . . 'Just as the poet, the lover, the artist, is carried out of himself in creative frenzy, so must it be for the Magician' (Crowley 1973: 251). Third, Bergson's claims about the frenzy that is proper to duration and creative force of the *élan vital* lead, as Deleuze suggests, to the idea of unnatural participations in other forms of life (the 'scrambling of the planes of nature'). For if the frenzy proper to capitalism is a frenzy of the intelligence, then conversely medieval frenzy is a frenzy of *instinct*. We know that intelligence is opposed to instinct, and that the latter involves the power of sympathy. So everything points to the conclusion that the frenzy of mysticism proceeds via a revival of the power of instinctual sympathy in universal form. It therefore involves the scrambling of the planes of nature from the beginning. If there is no doubt that the history of magic is filled with tales of charlatans who exploit impotence in order to gain power, legions of charlatans, at the same time it is also host to a tradition of *sorcery* which precisely involves an affective transformation into animals, and an acquisition of their powers. Mystics do not actively identify with animals, but sorcerers do. Thus, by his own lights, Bergson is unjustified in distinguishing mysticism from sorcery.

Deleuze's insight here is to suggest that the connection between Bergson's theories of frenzy and instinct allow in turn for a philosophical defence of sorcery, rather than mysticism. There is no other choice but to descend further into this weird underworld that is opening up beneath our feet. For if emotion is what distinguishes the human being from the animal, this power is the precipitate of a subtraction of interest from instinct. Bergson is gesturing towards an 'innate science' that would be proper to 'sorcery': a science which could manipulate the flows of emotion through frenzy. If emotion is the sublimation or *Aufhebung* of instinct and intelligence, then it is no wonder that man is capable of such frenzies. The instincts (and, if we follow Jung, their archetypes) retain their independence, but now there exists a being that can bring about in itself successively 'everything that, elsewhere, can only be embodied in different species'. Deleuze is drawing the consequences of Bergson's and Jung's suggestion that some sort of reintegration between each half – instinct and intelligence – is possible, and that to achieve that would be to finally earn the right to claim that the human being is a distinctive being in the order of life. Deleuze insists that this is the privilege of the human being, and this alone.

> And what is this creative emotion, if not precisely a cosmic Memory, that actualises all the levels at the same time, that liberates man from plane or the level that is proper to him, in order to make him a creator, adequate to the whole movement of creation? This liberation, this embodiment of cosmic memory in creative emotions, undoubtedly only takes place in privileged souls. It leaps from one soul to another, 'every now and then', crossing closed deserts. But to each member of a closed society, if he opens himself to it, it communicates a kind of reminiscence, an excitement that allows him to follow. (B 111)

Man is therefore not primarily the rational animal, nor even *homo aestheticus*, but is before and above all else, the magical animal. In the substantial section on sorcery in *A Thousand Plateaus*, Deleuze at last fully draws the consequence of his earlier tentative suggestions about the participation in the frenzies of nature. The paradigm shift that is under way here is most starkly exposed in the 'Conclusion' to the book, under the heading 'Rhizome'. After summing up, in a highly condensed passage, their theory of multiplicities – a concept that was fundamental to Deleuze in *Difference and Repetition* – Deleuze and Guattari conclude by quickly listing the three ways in which multiplicities can be *expressed*. One never encounters a multiplicity 'in person' except under the following conditions. The division is as follows: multiplicities can be expressed passively, actively, or in theory. We have already been using this distinction between passive and active relationships to the unconscious. On the one hand, the *passive* relationship to the unconscious is the path of individuation, which is articulated around a psychotic moment, at the heart of every neurosis. Deleuze thinks that normality rests on a hidden psychosis or delirium, which is encountered at one point of the individuation process. But this crisis in individuation in turn is only resolved by taking an *active* approach to the unconscious. Deleuze and Guattari – who refer to themselves in the plateau on 'Becoming-Animal' as 'we sorcerers' – are able to conclude that 'at the level of *pathos* . . . multiplicities are expressed by psychosis and especially schizophrenia. At the level of pragmatics, they are utilized by sorcery' (ATP 506).

Given Deleuze's and Guattari's astonishing conclusion, it is perfectly possible to read their ideas about drugs and secret societies in the plateau on 'Becoming-Animal' as coming from within that general tradition. 'Becoming-Intense, Becoming-Animal, Becoming-Imperceptible' is, among other things, a late modern occult treatise.[2] The human being, in its most active essence, alien and anomalous even to itself, is therefore most purely expressed in the sorcerer, the only successful madman – so successful in fact that he is the universal object of horror, and excluded from history. But the very act of exposing this primal, mad conjuror of forces, at the edge of society and history, as the figure behind the veil of repression is itself an act of historiography. Our historical perspectives our inverted. The witch-hunts did not occur in 'the middle ages', as is commonly thought, but began in earnest with the publication of the *Malleus Maleficarum* in 1484, and ended in the late seventeenth century. They occurred in the Renaissance. One of the witnesses of the death at the stake of Giordano Bruno in 1600 recounts some of the eight heretical propositions which Bruno refused to recant: 'that there are innumerable worlds; that magic is a good and licit thing; that the Holy Spirit is the *anima mundi*; that Moses did his miracles by magic in which he was more proficient than the Egyptians; that Christ was a Magus' (Yates 1964: 354). A contemporary list of censured propositions in Bruno's work includes the claims that the infinity of God implies the infinity of the universe, and that the stars are angels, among others concerned with the creation of the human soul and the motion of the earth. It was Bruno's hermeticism that was repressed before all else, and which resurfaces again, in shifting baroque disguises, in Leibniz, Spinoza, Schelling, Jung and Deleuze.

Becoming-Animal

The themes of sympathy, becoming-animal and sorcery are interlinked, and all come together in the famous chapter on 'Becoming-Animal' in *A Thousand Plateaus*. Deleuze and Guattari introduce their strange theme of 'becoming-animal' with a reference to an obscure American film from the 1970s, *Willard*, which portrays the descent of a man into a society of rats. 'Who has not known the violence of these animal sequences, which uproot one from humanity, if only for an instant, making one scrape at one's bread like a rodent or giving one the yellow eyes of a feline?' (ATP 240).

The relationship between man and animal 'has been constantly misunderstood by psychoanalysis, because psychoanalysis is unable to see in it anything but all-too-human Oedipal figures' (CC 54; cf. ATP 259). Freud's patient, Sergei, had a dream of 'six or seven' wolves observing him from a tree. In his interpretation, Freud reduces the multiplicity of wolves to one wolf, adding that this is a displacement of the father. But the multiplicity of wolves already indicates that Freud's starting premise is problematic. We have already seen that wolves may first of all function as symbols. But the indeterminate multiplicity of wolves, say Deleuze and Guattari also has potency for other reasons. Although the wolf tends to be a lone animal, it also assembles in *packs*. This pack-form of sociality is scarcely a social *organization* of the form taken by, say, primates. A pack of wolves is a strange society of lone animals. The French word (*la meute*) Deleuze uses signifies more than 'pack' (which would more appropriately translate the word *bande*). *Meute* is a term from hunting, rather than ethology. It may be a natural organisation or a domesticated organization, as in a pack of foxhounds. Second, *meute* can also be used to described a crowd or mob of people in pursuit. Third, the etymological root of *meute* is *mouvoir*. Deleuze classes *les meutes* among *les classes, les peoples, les races, les masses* (DI 275) which provoke delirium. This gives the impression of a swarming presence around one, as if being chased by spirits or demons. When the Wolf Man faces a *meute* of wolves, he is *addressed* in peculiar way; it is as if a group is singling him out personally, turning to him and saying: *Hello Sergei, we've been waiting for you. It's time to come with us now.*

The discussion of 'becoming-animal' begins with a comparison between Jung's and Lévi-Strauss's approaches to cases of apparent 'identifications' with animals, whether it be in dreams, fantasies, or in hallucinatory episodes. Deleuze and Guattari state that there are two types of 'analogy' that are involved in the Jungian and structuralist approaches to animal symbolism. Jung's use of animals is restricted insofar as he relies on merely external resemblances between images, and is regulated by the linear logic of individuation (certain symbols only appear at certain stages of life, like the whale and rebirth). Also, Jung's approach only seems to concern 'animals as they are treated in the great divine myths, in such a way as to extract from them series or structures, archetypes or models', and overlooks the 'more demonic animals'. The relation of analogy is falsified by these restrictions. Lévi-Strauss abolishes analogies of resemblance and focuses on structural analogies only. 'A man can never say: 'I am a bull, a wolf . . .', but he can say 'I am to a woman what a bull is to a cow, I am to another man what the wolf is to the sheep" (ATP 236). However, both Jungianism and structuralism leave one particular phenomenon unexplained: 'alongside the two models . . . there is still room for something else, something more secret, more subterranean: *the sorcerer* and becomings, expressed in tales [*récits*] instead of myths or rites' (ATP 237). So what is not being explained by Jungianism or structuralism is a specific set of transformations found most distinctly not in psychopathology or tribal custom, but in magic or sorcery. 'We believe in the existence of very special becomings-animal traversing human beings and sweeping them away, affecting the animal no less than the human.' The first example, to set the scene for the rest of this chapter, is the becoming-bat of the vampire. "From 1730 to 1735, all we hear about are vampires" (ATP 237); next up is the lycanthrope, another creature not often seen in clinic today. Such *transformations* provide the material for the notion of 'becoming' [*devenir*]: 'Structuralism does not account for these becomings . . . A correspondence of relations does not add up to a becoming' (ATP 237).

'We do not become animal without a fascination for the pack' (ATP 239). *Fascination* itself is a magical term, again connected with animal transformation. Crowley refers to 'the arts of 'fascination' in its proper sense – the word comes from the Latin *fascinum*', i.e. enchantment or witchcraft (Crowley 1917: 32). Traditionally, the art of fascination was said to involve the working of magical effects by means of visual 'emissions'. One alchemical text from the fifteenth century by Alonso Tostado links the hypnotic gaze of the basilisk to the visual power of wolves and menstruating women (Newman 2004: 203). But this somniacal gaze is imbued with virtuality rather than actuality. Crowley goes on to compare the *blind* fascination of love with the magical arts of fascination: 'You transform yourself, like Zeus into swan or bull, like Lucius into an ass, like the Egyptian *magi* into an hawk, swallow or ibis, or like the Syrian into a dove, and by this means compel the desired object to your arms.' This blindness of magical fascination defines magical divination itself, the attainment of visions through programmed, ritual intoxication.

Deleuze and Guattari insist that these becomings-animal are not imitations or identifications, because 'they are perfectly real' (ATP 238). They qualify: 'But which reality is at issue here?' Their subsequent explanations are obscure, but some light emerges when they explicitly relate 'the principle according to which there is a reality specific to becoming' to 'the Bergsonian idea of a coexistence of very different 'durations', superior or inferior to 'ours', all of them in communication' (ATP 238). In his 'Introduction to Metaphysics', Bergson suggests that his method also allows one to pass beyond the opposition between realism and idealism, and 'to affirm the existence of objects both inferior and superior to us, though nevertheless in a certain sense interior to us' (Bergson 1903: 184; cf. B 77). If our conscious duration can include simpler instinctive durations, which are in turn components of periodic cycles (for instance, respiration, sleeping and waking, menstrual cycles), then it might be that consciousness itself can be altered so as to be able to select various durations and their associated spatiotemporal dynamisms. Because its being is in time as well as space, the human being has the ability to alter its 'speed', and participate in a vast range of 'fluxes'. In principle, it has the power to isolate the rate of deterritorialization for any entity, to assess how much energy it is not just using but generating. The human being, by being capable of scrambling the planes, in principle possesses the eyes of the world. On the one hand, its body is composed of 'inferior' durations, but on the other hand, its very capacity to divide its consciousness points to the possibility if not necessity of a 'superior' synthesis, beyond the partial integrations of the ego. In their remarks on becoming here, Deleuze and Guattari are effectively redeploying Bergson's theories about duration and cosmic time within a renewed theosophical and pantheistic esotericism.[3] Deleuze's turn to a discussion of sorcery in *A Thousand Plateaus* marks a return to his early interest in esoteric thought. In *The Anarchy and Hierarchy of Knowledge* Malfatti generates the relations of polarity and power between the various human organs, and then goes on to relate them to a 'double body' with a 'double sex', a spiritual hermaphrodite, with its organs each in relation with an aspect of the cosmos. As in Schelling's later theosophical thought, the world is the body of God, and we are its coming to consciousness. Deleuze iterates that '*ecstasy* is precisely the act through which the individual raises itself to the level of the species' (Deleuze 1946: xxii). But this ecstasy will not be our own species consciousness, but our possible participation in other species consciousnesses. 'Before the fall, Adam existed as humanitas' (xxii). But Malfatti rejects the residual traces of Christianity in the theosophical tradition, and returns to the sexual-ecstatic aspects of Indian mysticism, laying out a vast sexualized ontology, culminating in the 'hermaphroditic' consciousness of the human sexual act.

What is remarkable is that all of these ideas resurface in disguise in one of Deleuze's valedictory texts, 'To Have Done with Judgment', published in 1993. There the 'body without organs' (which is a phrase from Artaud, another occult-intoxicated artist) is illuminated by its esoteric roots: 'The body without organs is an affective, intensive, anarchist body that consists solely of poles, zones, thresholds, and gradients. It is traversed by a powerful, nonorganic vitality. Lawrence paints the picture of such a body, with the sun and moon as its poles, with its planes, its sections, and its plexuses' (CC 131). Lawrence's *Fantasia of the Unconscious* contains a chapter entitled 'Plexuses, Planes and so on', which is based on an esoteric account of the 'subtle body', made up of a 'vital magnetism' organized in dynamic polarities.[4]

The sorcerer is the ideal microcosmic being, exposed for better or worse to 'the very forces of the universe' (Lowry 1947: 189), exposed to all the waves and spasms that pass through the body of God. At the close of his case study of President Schreber, Freud remarks that Schreber's 'rays of God' are 'nothing else than a concrete representation and projection outwards of libidinal cathexes' (SE 12: 78); they are 'endopsychic perceptions of the processes whose existence I have assumed . . . as the basis of our explanation of paranoia'. In his seminar on the psychoses, Lacan adds that in Schreber's theory of the divine rays the reader may 'vaguely see something that isn't totally different from what I teach about the way one has to describe the functioning of the unconscious' (Lacan 1955–6: 27). Both psychoanalysts allow, amazingly, that a psychotic can have 'endopsychic perception' of their unconscious forces. In *Anti-Oedipus*, Schreber is one of a gallery of schizophrenics who are said in language that reminds us of the Bergsonian magician to be able to 'scramble all the codes' (AO 15). The schizophrenic is '*homo natura*' (AO 5), the 'celibate machine' who 'gives birth to a new humanity or a glorious organism' (17). 'The being who is in intimate contact with the profound life of all forms or all types of beings, who is responsible for even the tars and organ-machine into an energy-machine, a tree into his body, a breast into his mouth, the sun into his asshole: the eternal custodian of the machines of the universe' (AO 4). Beyond the polarity between schizophrenia and paranoia, therefore, there is a dynamic oscillation between schizophrenia and sorcery, as passive and active expressions of intensive multiplicity. One of the most famous books of medieval magic was Al-Kindi's *On Rays or A Theory of Magical Arts*. 'Each star possesses its proper place in the machine of the world, which is different all the others . . . The rays of stars vary, just as the aspects and properties of stars vary . . . The rays of all the stars operate diversely upon the things of the world according to the diverse properties of things themselves, seeing as everything is born and subsists thanks to the rays' (Al-Kindi 1977: 82, 84). The language of invisible rays runs through both magical and psychotic writings. Deleuze's appeal to the language of 'flows', 'intensities', 'force' and 'power' is rooted in that curious convergence; Deleuze uses philosophy (specifically rationalist philosophers such as Spinoza or Leibniz) to subordinate the hideous couple, psychosis and sorcery, to reason.

Sorcery of Capitalism

In a recent essay entitled 'Deleuze's Last Message' Stengers has cast illumination on Deleuze's last text with Guattari, *What is Philosophy?*, a text that many find both obscure and 'conservative', because of its defence of a strict demarcation between the three disciplines of philosophy, science and art. Stengers emphasizes that the authors' real answer to the question 'what is philosophy?' lies in the following paragraph of the book:

> Thinking provokes general indifference. It is a dangerous exercise nevertheless. Indeed, it is only when the dangers become obvious that indifference ceases, but they often remain hidden and barely perceptible, inherent in the enterprise. Precisely because the plane of immanence is prephilosophical and does not immediately take effect with concepts, it implies a sort of groping experimentation and its layout resorts to measures that are not very respectable, rational, or reasonable. These measures belong to the order of

> dreams, of pathological processes, esoteric experiences, drunkenness, and excess. We head for the horizon, on the plane of immanence, and we return with bloodshot eyes, yet they are the eyes of the mind. Even Descartes had his dream. To think is always to follow the witch's flight. (WP 41)

Stengers is of course aware that taking up this 'answer' to the question 'what is philosophy?' 'may well mean facing such accusations as irrationality, superstition, and regression' (Stengers 2006), but that it is necessary nonetheless, as she proceeds to demonstrate. Stengers is a philosopher and historian of science (among other things, she co-authored the groundbreaking philosophical book on non-linear thermodynamics, *La Nouvelle Alliance* [translated as *Order out of Chaos*], with Ilya Prigogine in 1979), and has recently flown in the face of the increasing dominance of scientific naturalism by translating into French the works of the American neo-pagan witch and political activist Starhawk. Her interest in 'sorcery' appears to arise in part from an increasing interest in the work of Deleuze and Guattari, and not directly from her work on hypnosis and somnambulism (Chertok and Stengers 1992). In a recent work, *La Sorcellerie Capitaliste* (*Capitalist Sorcery*), co-written with Philippe Pignarre, Stengers channels these aspects of Deleuze and Guattari's project towards a future 'counter-sorcery' against the necromantic techniques of contemporary capitalism. They claim that capitalism itself can be thought of as a 'system of sorcery without sorcerers' (Pignarre and Stengers 2005: 59), ceaselessly presenting us with 'infernal alternatives'. They argue that there is a real sense in which contemporary capitalism does not just want your body, but your soul. Instead of calling for a practice of 'demystification' (as in traditional critical theory), they call for a practice of counter-sorcery.

There is of course a tradition within Marxism which compares the experience of the commodity to a bewitchment by a fetish. In *Capital*, Marx had argued that there is a fetishism that is proper to commodities in general, insofar as they possess the power to fascinate the observer, and make them forget that their *value* is intrinsic to them, rather than being produced by labour. The desirability of commodities arises from their power to fascinate, to suspend empirical reality and embody the quality of transcendence. The structure of fetishism is 'We know what it really is, but all the same', and Žižek argues that the 'postmodern' subject is fundamentally cynical, obeying the law in order to have the pleasure of enjoyment of the commodity. In order to counteract this tendency, Žižek invokes a psychoanalytic discourse of trauma: we must recognize that the enjoyment involved is itself a response to a traumatic and contingent encounter. The approach of Pignarre and Stengers is quite different. If commodities have the power to fascinate us, then that is because we ourselves have the power to fascinate and be fascinated, and capitalism has seized upon this power.[5] For capitalism, the unconscious exists first of all as a force to be manipulated. By restricting discussion of the unconscious to the discourse of psychopathology, psychoanalysis has been unwittingly complicit with capitalism. When a salesman or manager (or an academic or writer, for that matter) becomes devoted to advancing their career at any cost, their soul has been stolen or captured. When one is forced to take place in workplace 'bonding' exercises, a level of humiliation is involved which in some ways surpasses physical oppression. 'It no longer concerns a pseudo-contract – your labour time against a salary – but a capture, "soul and body"' (Pignarre and Stengers 2005: 182). When a consumer is targeted through stimulating their sexual desires, they are being manipulated by sorcery, and made to act like somnambulists. Sorcery happens and is happening. The notion of sorcery is therefore defensible, not least because one is forced to defend oneself. Practitioners of sorcery have a simple advantage: they can defend themselves against fascination. If we are bewitched by capitalism, then perhaps we have something to learn from the witches. The modern hermetician has to break into the arsenal of the sorcerer in order to defend their theosophical vision.[6]

Vampires, Intoxication and Night-Consciousness

In Hungary, Czechoslovakia and Serbia in the early eighteenth century there was indeed something of a vampire epidemic. There were many tales of the undead crawling out of their graves, terrorizing the local population and having to be publically executed and laid to rest. Numerous learned studies on vampirism appeared in Latin and German between 1728 and 1735.[7] The reasons for this collective panic are still not clear. Even at the time, sceptics maintained that the 'undead' were really victims of premature burial, who had either been struck down by cholera or the plague, or had ingested some unknown poison. Another sceptic claimed that vampire hunters were under the influence of opium (Introvigne 2001: 603). But theological and esoteric explanations were also proffered, thus heightening the controversy. Some theologians claimed that vampire phenomena, alongside lycanthropy and sorcery, were real, and that vampires were corpses animated by demons or the Devil himself. Michael Ranft, on the other hand, explained the teeth marks on the insides of coffins as due to the failed attempt of the astral body to depart from the corpse. In a 1732 article entitled 'The Dead Eat and Drink', J. C. Dippel appealed to 'the prevailing esoteric wisdom of the time, [that] humans had three souls (vegetative or astral, sensitive and rational)'. This view had been kept alive in Renaissance Germany by the Paracelsian tradition of medicine. Ranft and Dippel advanced the idea that the astral soul remained for a while in the body of the deceased, and could – under particular circumstances – be seen by others and be mistaken for a vampire' (Introvigne 2001: 604). With his *Dissertations sur les apparitions* (1746), however, Dom Augustin Calmet intervened to absolutely deny the existence of vampires, a position that was gladly taken up by the Church. Although the Roman Catholic Church accepted the existence of ghosts (souls confined in Purgatory, and the damned in Hell), they denied that such souls could return to earth, whether in the bodies of the dead or living. To affirm otherwise was to tilt towards esoteric theories of the astral body.

Disappointingly, Deleuze and Guattari do not offer an explanation of the vampire phenomenon. But the wave of vampire terror coming from Eastern Europe at this point perhaps can be related to baroque developments in ideas about the soul happening at the same time. It is perhaps significant that most of the tomes written on vampires during the 1730–5 period were published in Germany. The phenomena of somnambulism were just beginning to emerge into public consciousness. The scholarly treatises on vampirism seem haunted by the idea that the soul could be entrapped in the body at death. One vampire investigator cites the case of the scholastic philosopher Duns Scotus, who, it is reported, was taken for dead and buried, after having fallen into a trance-like swoon (cited in Summers 1929: 180). The question of the survival of the soul after death had been undergoing baroque development in Leibniz's philosophy at this point. Leibniz complains that even the Cartesians have 'accommodated themselves too much to the prejudice of the masses by confusing a *long stupor*, which arises from a great confusion of perceptions, with *death strictly speaking*, in which all perception ceases' (Leibniz 1714: 208; cf. 1714b, #14). But if the experience of dying is akin to swooning, might not death itself, by extension, be a prolonged swoon. 'Death can only be a sleep, and not a lasting one at that: the perceptions merely cease to be sufficiently distinct' (Leibniz 1765: 55).

Dizziness, swooning, dying. In dizziness, and as I swoon, my consciousness 'relaxes', and I am 'invaded by minute perceptions that do not become for all that conscious perceptions'. 'Every time Leibniz speaks of Ideas, he presents them as virtual multiplicities made of differential relations and singular points, which thought apprehends in a state close to sleep, stupor, swooning, death, amnesia, murmuring or intoxication' (DR 213). In his 'Monadology', Leibniz says that 'What we call *generations* are developments [*developpemens*] and growths, as what we call deaths are envelopments [*Enveloppmens*] and diminutions' (Leibniz 1714b: 222, # 73, trans. modified).[8] For Fechner in the *Little Book of Life after Death*, death marks the end of physical development, but the beginning of an envelopment to varying degrees in other, future lives. After presenting Leibniz's philosophical arguments for the existence of unconscious perceptions Deleuze describes how Leibniz might have gone about finding the experience which confirms the concept:

> When the very beautiful coincidence of principles and experience occurs, philosophy knows its moment of happiness, even if it is personally the misfortune of the philosopher . . . So it is necessary for experience to show me that under certain conditions of disorganization in my consciousness, minute perceptions force open the door of my consciousness and invade me. (Third Lecture on Leibniz, 9)

The roaring sea is not enough to reveal the nature of unconscious perceptions, as we can remain stoically on the shore, buttressing the wind, but our souls are still closed to any further repercussions of the din. Hence it is necessary to seek out these unconscious perceptions, by 'slackening the tension' of consciousness. Leibniz's *eureka* might have first occurred after being clubbed in the head, perhaps by some impatient empiricist. Perhaps he found what he was looking for: at such moments, Deleuze ventures, 'the philosopher says: everything is fine, it is as it should be'. Philosophy, at last, can begin. With another blow to the head, or another bite from the vampire, the philosopher's double begins to stir.

This detached, somnambulistic soul passes through the 'weird tales' of the nineteenth and early twentieth century. Deleuze refers at this juncture to Poe's famous 'The Facts in the Case of M. Valdemar', which tells the story of a man who willingly undergoes the experiment of being mesmerized at the point of death.[9] Poe later published the story in England as a hoax, first as 'The Last Conversation of a Somnambule', and then again in a pamphlet entitled *Mesmerism in Articulo Mortis* [in the state of dying], which presented the 'astonishing and horrifying narrative' as a 'plain recital of facts'.[10] The story encapsulates the transition in the attitude towards death that had come about since the emergence of somnambulism. If Leibniz was the first philosopher of the unconscious, it took the emergence of somnambulism into the common culture of the nineteenth century to give concrete shape to the basic idea he had articulated. Poe's story crystallizes a newfound terror that is waiting to be thought in this period. As we have seen, many thinkers increasingly related the function of consciousness to practical adaptation to the environment. But the reality of somnambulistic phenomena pointed in another direction entirely; the somnambulistic unconscious was one step removed from the body and its tasks of adaptation. Could it be that somnambulism was the key to the immortal soul, whose very existence had begun recently to be put in doubt by pragmatic and materialist explanations of consciousness? Poe's story draws the unfortunate consequences of this train of thought: if there is a soul, then it is not in itself conscious in the way that we know from our practical experience. In the eighteenth century, the soul is rediscovered in somnambulism, but it is disoriented, no longer attached to the 'function of reality' (in Janet's terms), lacking the ballast of the present (in Bergson's). It has a 'life' of some sort; it is *lived* in a certain way. Without the constraints of the empirical body it is something horrific and demonic, perpetually in flight.

Vampires are lucid somnambulists, dreaming while awake, refusing to shut their eyes when they dream. In one of his last texts, 'To Have Done with Judgment' (1993), which can be treated as a final summation of his most original ideas, Deleuze contends that the power of dreaming can be harnessed and 'surpassed' by artificial means. He claims that Nietzsche, Lawrence, Kafka and Artaud 'denounce in the dream . . . a state that is still too immobile, and too directed, too governed'. Perhaps the basic reference here is Bergson's theory of dreams, which is expounded in some detail in *Cinema 2*. If the liberation of virtuality is triggered by the dream, the dream always remains tethered to actuality. It is only a partial liberation of the mind, as its freedom is always limited by its ballast, the body paralysed in the bedroom, its consciousness remaining always at the mercy of the stimuli that filter through the disengaged senses (the flickering curtains, the banging coming from the flat above, the television murmuring downstairs). From the perspective of Bergson's later theories about mysticism (and even more so from the perspective of Deleuze's diagnosis that Bergsonian mysticism is really sorcery), dreaming has to be seen as a passive apprehension of the virtual, and hence an inadequate approach to it. Dreaming taps into a power of virtuality, but does not attempt to harness it. Deleuze goes on to turn vehemently on those who model their explorations of the unconscious on the dream: 'Groups that are deeply interested in dreams, like psychoanalysts or surrealists, are also quick to form tribunals that judge and punish in reality: a disgusting mania, frequent in dreamers.' It is no accident, insinuates Deleuze, that 'the question of judgment is first of all knowing whether one is dreaming or not'. Guattari too is to be found saying 'dreams are fundamentally reterritorialization activities' in a fascinating journal from 1972.[11] Our subjective attitude to the dream necessarily occurs in two stages: first, we are passive spectators of the unfolding of the dream, while it is happening; but then, by virtue of our immediate dissociation from the dream upon awaking, we are necessarily always separated from it, and thrown back on the position of decoding it. Our hopeless desire to find the meaning of the dream commits us to a futile chase after its 'shadows' and doubtful appearances.[12]

In the sequel to his *Confessions of an Opium-Eater*, De Quincey claims that 'the object of that work was to reveal something of the grandeur which belongs *potentially* to human dreams' (De Quincey 1845: 132).[13] Dreams are indeed a gateway to another world; the problem, therefore, is how to get through that gateway. If one has got to the point where one has discovered art and creation to be the only acts of perfection possible for human beings, then the framework has changed: we no longer seek to judge life or to get past its illusions to a single truth, but rather to commit ourselves to the task of creation. Dreams bear with them hints of secret powers – divination, complete recall, resurrection of the dead. The 'big dreams' of which Jung speaks, leave the dreamer shaken, sometimes for days. And as we have seen, there is more to nocturnal consciousness than dreams, as the night is filled with other phenomena; nightmares, nocturnal emissions produced without physical stimulation, sleep-talking, sleep-walking. Is it possible for consciousness to 'become adequate to the night'? Deleuze goes on to say that 'once we leave the shores of judgment, we also repudiate the dream in favour of an 'intoxication', like a high tide sweeping over us. What we seek in states of intoxication – drink, drugs, ecstasies – is an antidote to both the dream and judgment. Whenever we turn away from judgment towards justice, we enter into a dreamless sleep' (CC 130).

At first sight, the reference to 'sleep without dream' [*sommeil sans rêve*] might seem to indicate deep sleep, undisturbed by dreams; in other words, profound unconsciousness. To have done with dreams in this case would be to get a refreshing, untroubled sleep. But we know that from a Bergsonian perspective, there are no dreamless sleeps, only sleeps in which dreams are not recalled. Deleuze goes on to draw a distinction (invisible in English, which uses 'sleep' indiscriminately) between *sommeil* and *dormer.* 'We are not asleep [*dormons*] during this sleep without dream [*sommeil sans rêve*]'. The two words have different Latin etymologies: *dormio* refers to the state of physical sleep, whereas *somnio* is translated 'I am dreaming'. It is true that the ambiguity is there even in Latin: *somnium* is a dream or vision, whereas *somnus* can simply mean 'sleep'. But the latter can also refer to death, as well as dream and sleep alike. *Somnio* and *dormio* can therefore be taken to refer to distinct concepts. *Somnio* of course survives in English through the addition of *ambulare* in 'somnambulism', but the words *somnolency,* or *somnolent* do not capture the visionary aspects of the Latin and French terms. Perhaps an obsolete English term, *somniation,* comes closest to Deleuze's meaning here, in that it inserts a current of activity into visionary states.

In the nineteenth century, when drug use was legal, it was nevertheless veiled in polite company by the use of euphemisms, of which 'sleep' was favoured among those of a Romantic disposition. Coleridge tells us that he composed 'Kubla Khan' 'in a profound sleep' (Lefebure 1975: 253). In his notebooks, he writes of the 'somniacal magic . . . superinduced in the active powers of the mind' (Coleridge 1838: III, 397). Mordecai Cooke's classic work *The Seven Sisters of Sleep* (1860) classes opium, hashish and other drugs under the rubric of 'sleep'. In literature, there is often more to the word 'sleep' than mere dozing. But it would be foolish to look for direct 'translations' between terms when we are dealing with esoteric discourse. It could be not so much that sleep, reverie or *sommeil* serve as euphemisms for succumbing to narcosis, but rather that they are the supreme conditions of the visions of successful narcosis. 'Even the Buddha had to sit' (Huston Smith, cited in Regardie 1968: 26). De Quincey says that the opium-eater 'naturally seeks solitude and silence, as indispensable conditions of those trances, or profoundest reveries, which are the crown and consummation of what opium can do for human nature' (De Quincey 1821: 81–2). Is drug experience the privileged state of somniation, then, different in kind to dreaming?

In a 1978 intervention on the theme of drugs, Deleuze argues that the psychoanalytic model cannot capture the most basic feature of the drug experience. 'The failure of psychoanalysis in the face of drug phenomena is enough to show that drugs have an entirely different causality . . . My question is: Can we conceive of a specific causality of drugs and in what sense?' (TRM 152). The causal model of psychoanalysis was premised on the idea that 'desire invests a system of mnemic traces and affects'. Neuroses, dreams, psychosocial formations (for instance, myths) were all treated on this causal model, which dated from Freud's earliest work. The advantage of this model was that through it psychoanalysis managed to escape the established models of social or psychological causation. Deleuze further clarifies this point in *A Thousand Plateaus,* where the discussion of drugs is further expanded. For psychoanalysis, the libidinal investments at work in the unconscious are always *inferred* from their supposed symbolic derivatives. Freud's 'schema still relies on a plane of organization that can never be apprehended in itself, that is always concluded from something else, that is always inferred, concealed from the system of perception: it is called the Unconscious' (ATP 284). The unconscious 'stands in molar opposition to the perception-consciousness system'. Insofar as they are unconscious, the primary libidinal processes (desire) are by definition not themselves perceived. The unconscious is 'transcendent' to the plane of perception. Now as it stands, this point is not yet a critique of Freud, since Freud has perfectly good reasons for stating that the contents of the unconscious can only be inferred, and Deleuze and Guattari do not attempt to engage with these reasons here. The problem, they say, is that 'with drugs, there is something very unique, where desire *directly invests the system of perception*' (TRM 152). They go on to say, in a concluding passage that is finely calibrated to cause maximum howls of outrage, that 'drugs give the unconscious the immanence and plane that psychoanalysis has consistently botched', adding in parentheses that 'perhaps Freud's famous cocaine episode marked a turning point that forced Freud to renounce a direct approach to the unconscious' (ATP 284).

There are at least three heresies jostling in this one splendid sentence. First, there is said to be a '*direct* approach to the unconscious'. To those schooled in psychoanalysis, such a claim would be a simple oxymoron of a particularly idiotic kind. Second, drugs are said to give access to the unconscious in a more profound and 'immanent' way than psychoanalysis. For the same people, reading the discussion of drugs in *A Thousand Plateaus* in English, where '*se droguer*' is translated as 'to get high', this claim will appear risible. Third, Freud is said to have had more insight into the unconscious during his early period of personal and professional experimentation with cocaine. It is often said that the decisive turning point in the development of psychoanalysis is Freud's renunciation of hypnosis and affirmation of free association. But Deleuze and Guattari clearly say that the real, original, 'turning point' in psychoanalysis is Freud's renunciation of cocaine. If we take this passage seriously – that is, if we take it as more than an attempt to gratuitously wind up Freudians – we get a pure measure of how far from the Freudian universe Deleuze and Guattari are. Drugs allow one to *explore one's own unconscious* – without an analyst, and without compromise. Even though it is true that Freud crossed the Acheron in exactly the same fashion in his 'cocaine episode', it is hard to imagine any view more opposed to psychoanalysis, both theoretically and institutionally.

Keeping in mind Deleuze's roots in the 'somnambulist' theory of the unconscious (Bergson, Janet and Jung) helps to make some sense of the idea of a 'direct relationship with the unconscious'. The psychoanalytic model of the mind does indeed involve a strict, 'molar' opposition between the unconscious and the perception-consciousness system. This entails that there is no dynamic space left for the possibility of altered *states of consciousness.* In psychoanalysis, one is either conscious of something or one is not, and it is beside the point whether there are different kinds of consciousness. For the other tradition, though, which emphasizes the model of dissociation rather than a basic dynamic opposition between consciousness and the unconscious, the possibility of different kinds of consciousness is the key to understanding the structure of the mind. If we bear this in mind, then the drug experience presents itself as simply the starkest illustration of the potential for alternation between different kinds of consciousness, and is particularly potent as an example because its sole condition is the ingestion of an external, physical substance. No complex pathogenesis is necessary.

It is true that the psychoanalyst, who is supposed to be the expert on the non-rational motivations that flow through individual and collective life, does have a blindspot with regard to drug use. Psychoanalysts themselves report that there has been an overwhelming failure in the attempt to treat drug addicts with psychoanalysis (Brickman 1988). It is true also that the problem of Freud's involvement with cocaine remains unresolved within the psychoanalytic tradition. But whether drug experience can in any significant way provide a direct encounter with the unconscious is another question. 'It is our belief', announce Deleuze and Guattari, 'that the issue of drugs can be understood only at the level where desire directly invests perception, and perception becomes molecular at the same time as the imperceptible is perceived. *Drugs then appear as the agent of this becoming.* This is where pharmacoanalysis would come in, which must be both compared and contrasted to psychoanalysis. For psychoanalysis must be taken simultaneously as a model, a contrasting approach, and a betrayal' (ATP 283, italic added). Psychoanalysis is a betrayal of the direct approach to the unconscious, through 'vital' drug-experimentation – that is the claim.

But what was betrayed? Surely not the potential of cocaine for mental self-exploration? In fact, the remark about Freud and cocaine is somewhat problematic, as it rests on Deleuze's and Guattari's claim that distinctions between hallucinatory and non-hallucinatory drugs are 'secondary': '*Change perception*: the problem has been formulated correctly because it presents "drugs" as a pregnant whole free of secondary distinctions (hallucinatory or non-hallucinatory, hard or soft, etc.). All drugs fundamentally concern speeds, and modifications of speed' (ATP 282). Leaving aside the notion of 'speeds' of perception for now, it is hard to see how one could claim that non-hallucinatory drugs such as cocaine afford a 'direct approach to the unconscious' at all. In the *Clinical Handbook of Psychotropic Drugs*, 'Drugs of Abuse' are divided between 'hallucinatory' (LSD, psilocybin, cannabis, mescaline), 'stimulant' (cocaine, amphetamines) and 'sedative' drugs (opium, heroin). It is hard to understand how a drug whose main action is as a stimulant could allow one to 'approach' the unconscious, unless Deleuze and Guattari mean that cocaine permits the taker to approach a certain condition of 'unconsciousness of self', of lack of critical reflexivity about one's own or others' utterances. But that would not appear to be the kind of unconsciousness they have in mind. They do not (I think) mean that drugs give one the chance to approach an apotheosis of narcissistic obliviousness. The truth is that what Deleuze and Guattari say about drugs in these pages only plausibly applies to hallucinogens. If Freud's theory of the unconscious was significantly influenced by his intensive use of cocaine during the 1890s, then it is likely, as Peter Swales (Swales 1983) has suggested, that it was by providing Freud with insight into the quantitative aspects of the rising and falling of sexual libido, as well as of general vital energy. Freud used cocaine both as a sexual stimulant and a medication for depression.

But there were other examples of drug use and experimentation in the late nineteenth century which could conceivably have been 'betrayed' by the dominance of psychoanalysis in the twentieth century. An entirely different approach to drugs, based on experience of hallucinogens, was a feature of the landscape of French psychiatry at the *fin de siècle*. Whereas in Britain, studies on cannabis were restricted to the pages of medical and pharmacological journals, in France they appeared in respectable journals of philosophy and in periodicals devoted to hypnosis and psychotherapy. Bergson's work emerges from this atmosphere, and he discusses drug experience several times, first in the context of his theory about the 'dream-pole' of consciousness, and later in the context of a discussion of the transcendence of empirical consciousness towards impersonal consciousness. When Bergson talks of the 'expansion of consciousness', drug-experience is providing him with one of the models for what this is like. In the USA, philosophical enthusiasts of the 'anaesthetic revelation' (in the words of Benjamin Paul Blood, an early psychedelic transcendentalist in the Emersonian tradition) tended to relate drug-experience to religious experience, or specifically to a revival of pantheism. William James's famous remarks about his experience on nitrous oxide (including his climactic realisation, 'at last I understand Hegel') are related to this tradition; James underwent a conversion from empirical psychologist to metaphysical pantheist around the time of his drug experiences. Deleuze can be understood as the latest avatar of this line of thinking.

But Deleuze and Guattari's contention about the role of drug experience in securing 'immanence' is also more fundamentally endebted to Henri Michaux (1899–1984), the Belgian poet, writer and painter. Michaux is a unique figure in French letters, and in *A Thousand Plateaus* he is cited as the pre-eminent European explorer of altered states of consciousness, 'more willing' than the Americans 'to free himself of rites and civilizations, establishing admirable and minute protocols of experience' (ATP 283).[14] Michaux, however, only turned to writing about drug experience in the mid-fifties, over thirty years after his first publications, and eight years after the death of his wife. He had experimented with and written in passing about drugs since the 1920s, but it was only in 1956 that he published his book on mescaline, *Miserable Miracle*, which was followed by a series of other drug-related writings, including *Infinite Turbulence* (1957), *Knowledge through the Abyss* (1961) and *The Major Ordeals of the Mind and Countless Minor Ones* (1966). Michaux's grief in the aftermath of his wife's death (from injuries suffered after her nightgown had accidentally caught fire) may have been a condition for his later urge to plunge headlong into experiments with mescaline, which he believed to mimic the effects of schizophrenia. At the time (LSD had only just been synthesized) mescaline was thought by a number of psychologists to be the drug that most effectively simulated schizophrenia.[15] According to Jean-Pierre Martin, the author of a recent biography of Michaux, 'Michaux was looking for a psychotropic which would not immobilise him and which would permit him to approach madness' (Martin 2003: 517). On his fourth experiment with mescaline, a 'calculating error' with the dosage led him to consume six times the normal dosage, leading to the experiences which are recounted in a chapter of *Miserable Miracle* called 'Experience of Madness'. Martin draws the conclusion: 'Wasn't it precisely this risk that he was looking for? Without having planned it, the error of dosage was a necessary station, even if he had to pass through 'horror' and 'atrocity' (these are his words)' (Martin 2003: 519). In his drug experiments, Michaux apparently did not think of himself as fleeing from harsh reality, even in the aftermath of grief. He refused the sedative attractions of heroin or morphine, and although he regularly used hashish, his most valued drug was mescaline, whose euphoric effects seem to be frequently accompanied by terror.[16] It is mostly the drug writings to which Deleuze and Guattari refer, but the singularity of Michaux's experience begs for caution in any interpretation of the results of his experiments.

The epigraph to Michaux's third drug-themed collection reads: 'Drugs bore us with their paradises. Let them give us a little knowledge instead. This is not a century for paradise.' In their discussion of Michaux in *A Thousand Plateaus*, Deleuze and Guattari suggest that Michaux successfully distinguished drug visions from hallucinations or delirium by isolating a properly 'molecular' type of perception, different in kind from the 'molar' type of perception (in which apperception synthesises a totality, under conceptual norms of recognition).[17] Molecular perception, suggests Michaux, occurs on condition that the 'speed' of cognition and affection is modified. In what sense, one may ask, does thought have a 'speed'? And in what sense, further, do chemical and vegetable substances affect this 'speed'? In a scribbled fragment, Coleridge had already noted this capacity of drugs to alter the 'speed' of consciousness: '*the marvellous velocity of Thought & Image in certain full Trances*' (Coleridge 1957: 4.108). According to Deleuze and Guattari, *The Major Ordeals of the Mind and the Countless Minor Ones* is the book in which Michaux takes furthest his 'analysis of speeds, molecular perceptions, and 'microphenomena' or 'micro-operations'' (ATP 543, n. 70).[18] In *The Fold*, Deleuze makes clear that he sees Michaux as a follower of Leibniz, exploring the movement 'from waking to dream, and from conscious perception to minute perceptions . . . Reminiscences of Leibniz are frequent in Michaux: fog and giddiness, Lilliputian hallucinations, minute perceptions speeding over a tiny surface, spontaneity' (F 155, n. 20).[19] In all these obscurings of thought, Deleuze conceives the object of apperception as imploding into partial durations and repetitions, the whole object thrown into shadow. For Deleuze, Michaux's great Leibnizian *sympnoia panta* is also host to the interior, 'inferior' and 'superior' durations uncovered by Bergson. He seems to believe that at some fundamental level, Leibnizianism and Bergsonism are compatible, and he presents Michaux as the psychic explorer of this uncharted region, in pursuit of an ideal integration or a 'mastery of speeds' (Michaux 1956: 153).[20] If thinking cannot 'grasp itself' (Michaux 1966: 4), according to Michaux, that is not just because of the hermeneutic circle, or because it cannot grasp its own conditions, but also because it is conditioned by minute operations of thought which are *too minute, too slow or too quick* for it to be able to apperceive. While our practical consciousness is attuned to a particular *speed*, with fixed thresholds, the world of lower microphenomena can be opened up under certain exceptional perceptual conditions, 'under the microscope of a desperate attention, when the mind – monstrously excited, for example, from the effect of large doses of mescaline, its field of vision altered – sees its thought as particles appearing and disappearing at stupendous speeds'. The acceleration of single lines of thought, moreover, appears to be paradoxically experienced at another level as a slowing down or suspension, insofar as the movement becomes 'absolute'. So, in a first moment, thought alters its relative speed, *catching up* with movements which previously surpassed it, and of which it has been unconscious.[21] The experience of the nightmarish speeds of mescaline provokes Michaux to conclude that 'man is a slow being, who is possible only a result of fantastic speeds' (Michaux 1966: 23). But in a second moment, this speed of thought can conversely be described as a 'slowing down', in the sense that hours, days, or even centuries appear to be lived in the space of a quarter of an hour. Coleridge and De Quincey both talked of passing *centuries* in obscure regions, before returning back to the demands of empirical reality.[22]

But are Deleuze and Guattari right to give the impression that Michaux detaches himself decisively from the traditions of ritual and religious drug use? He says that, in the West, we have 'forgotten the names' (i.e. the divine names), and that for those who lack gods there is only 'Pullulation and Time'.[23] But Michaux nevertheless often himself explicitly submits his pharmacological voyage to esoteric ends.[24] Deleuze's repeated returns to the image of the 'witch's flight' to describe Michaux's trajectory can – why not? – be given a literal interpretation: 'To think is to follow the witch's flight. Take Michaux's plane of immanence, for example, with its infinite, wild movements and speeds' (WP 41). In one writing, Michaux ingenuously replicates the actual conditions for a witch's alpine voyage.[25] Perhaps Michaux's work, therefore, is not itself the fundamental reference for Deleuze and Guattari's analysis of drugs and the unconscious. Throughout this book, the esoteric theories of Leibniz, Schelling, Wronski, Malfatti and Fechner (not to mention those of Bergson and Jung) have been shown to be behind some of Deleuze's more obscure formulations about the unconscious and individuation. It is in his theories about the unconscious that Deleuze shows himself to be allied to the occult, hermetic tradition of pantheistic thought. As it happens, one also finds explicit reference to a 'direct approach to the Unconscious' through the use of drugs in the French occult tradition. For instance, in the central work of late French occultism, Stanislas de Guaita's *The Temple of Satan*, we hear that 'hashish . . . allows the Unconscious to manifest itself to an astonished consciousness – and the soul, contemplating itself in its own mirror, reveals itself positively to itself' (Guaita 1891: 370). Guaita, who considered himself a 'magician' rather than a 'sorcerer', considered that the magician had to learn the techniques of the sorcerer for his own knowledge and protection. Drugs, Guaita reported, were one of the main weapons in the sorcerer's arsenal. (As mentioned in Chapter 4, he died of a morphine overdose at the age of thirty-six). Other prominent Western occultists offer variations on the same theme (Crowley 1908; Regardie 1968; Grant 1972). Drugs and sorcery have gone hand in hand throughout history; the ethnobotanist Christian Rätsch informs us that 'many magicians consider plants the primary instruments of magic' (Rätsch 1992: 17). The persistence and even growth of occultism in the period of modernity suggests that there is something wrong with the idea that drugs are a contemporary pathology only insofar as we lack a 'set and setting' for their use (as the participants in the rites of Eleusis had, for instance, according to Wasson's thesis). There have been a surfeit of secret societies (both within the capitalist and working classes) at work even throughout the twentieth century (the Nazis saw fit to assassinate the leader of the Martinists in France). The secret society, founded in a complicity between members, provides the social form for the extension of the somnambulist unconscious beyond the asymmetrical relationship involved in therapy, through the adoption of theurgic ritual.[26]

Deleuze follows Kierkegaard in understanding humour as the pursuit of a questionable idea to its consequences, regardless of opprobrium.[27] The idea of a 'pharmacoanalytic' approach to the unconscious will strike many as at least dubious, if not directly laughable. But one can equally take succour from the fact that there is evidence that not just Freud, but Jung as well, had more than a casual involvement with this very line of research. Jung's first reflections on the meaning of 'alchemy' in his commentary on *The Secret of the Golden Flower* were possibly premised on introspective imaginative techniques conditioned by drug-use (cf. CW 18: 751). It would be a mistake to treat this as a marginal, or slightly grubby, aspect of the modern theory of the unconscious. Deleuze and Guattari state that drugs give us immanent access to the unconscious, so if both Freud and Jung used drugs for similar purposes, then we would be looking at a complete upheaval of our established ways of understanding the unconscious. Pursuing this line of enquiry might also shed new light on the great paradox of how the founders of psychoanalysis and analytical psychology constructed their theories. A reflexive paradox has often been noted in the founding of psychoanalysis. Transference is supposed to be intrinsic to psychoanalysis, and yet Freud somehow managed to analyse himself. Jung was the first to advocate that every analyst themselves be analysed, but his own development of his theories only came through a period of withdrawal and a 'confrontation with the unconscious'. In his writings on alchemy, Jung became more and more implicit about the role of drugs in exploring the process of individuation. It would appear that he was advised by his closest collaborators that his explorations of alchemy would bring the status of 'analytical psychology' into disrepute. Instead, it has been left to the occult tradition to discuss this aspect of Jungianism more or less openly.

The Somniacal Imagination

In 'To Have Done with Judgement' itself, Deleuze gives two examples of *sommeil*: intoxication and insomnia. On the face of it, these are two very different states. The tortures of the insomniac seem to be far removed from the ecstasies of the intoxicated person; moreover, *in*somnia is surely a negative term, and really means the inability to physically sleep (hence *indormia* would be a more appropriate term). What could there possibly be in common between intoxication and insomnia? Things become more mysterious when we turn back to *Difference and Repetition*, and recall Deleuze's powerful and haunting remark about nightmares. 'A nightmare is perhaps a psychic dynamism that could be sustained neither awake *nor even in dreams*, but only in profound sleep, in a dreamless sleep' (DR 118). In *Difference and Repetition*, sleep without dream seems to be equivalent to the sleep of nightmares. In the nightmare, Deleuze explains, the sleeping subject is comparable to the embryo in the egg, being twisted and turned about, always on the verge of being torn apart. The nightmare takes us beyond the dream-image, as nightmare-images carry an intense visceral affect. No longer seen through the glass of the dream, they threaten the mind physically from within. The subject of the nightmare feels that they will be destroyed unless they wake up immediately and return to the actual body. But the body is paralysed, and the doorway into the present is locked, and so, in flight from the nightmare, the subject has to struggle to get back into the body.

But this makes the reference to insomnia more perplexing, not less. For surely the state of insomnia is the exact mirror image of the state of nightmare. The insomniac wants to escape from actuality and plunge insensate into virtuality, but the virtual body refuses him entry. The insomniac and the subject of a nightmare are both banging in a frenzy on the same door, from opposite sides. The somniacal nightmare is thus opposed to the in-somniac incapacity to sleep. Deleuze makes some strange literary references here, though. Maurice Blanchot says that only insomnia is 'adequate to the night'. But Kafka writes of sending his 'clothed body' across space to the country, while he remains insomniac in bed. Kafka's night journey almost sounds like a witch's flight. 'The insomniac can remain motionless, whereas the dream has taken the real movement upon itself' (CC 130). Insomnia therefore is not just *indormia*, but can itself take up dream-consciousness and deploy it in a new way. Insomnia, rather than a sleep without dream, would seem to be a dream without sleep. '*The . . . dream has become the guardian of insomnia*' (130). Insomnia is an *insleep*, or an *ensomnia* (in the sense of 'enjoyment'), in that it, like the nightmare, liberates somniacal visionings from their encasement in the dream. *Sommeil* traverses the night and inhabits it with a frightening clarity which is no longer day, but the Lightning-Flash [*l'Eclair*], says Deleuze.

Insomnia lacks the raw visionary power of the nightmare, while the nightmare lacks the vigilance, the ghostly agency, retained by insomnia. But perhaps there is a state in which somniation appears in a pure form, with its visions finally divested of passivity and lability. Here Deleuze returns to intoxication, which appeared at first to be his main topic, before the detour into the phenomena of nightmare and insomnia. He now says that the peyote rites described by Artaud and the songs of the Mexican forest described by Lawrence 'are not dreams, but states of intoxication [*ivresse*] or *sommeil*'. We have to go to Mexico to discover the meaning of *sommeil*, where the dream now really does 'take the real movement upon itself'. It is the peyote rite, and Michaux's Western rendering of it, which takes the dream out of sleep and into somniation. 'The dreamless somniation in which one nonetheless does not fall asleep, this insomnia nonetheless sweeps the dream along as far as the insomnia extends – such is the state of Dionysian intoxication, its way of escaping judgment' (130).

Although Deleuze refers to Blanchot's text on the night, Lawrence's chapter on 'Sleep and Dreams' seems more relevant. 'We have to be *very* wary of giving way to dreams', because the dream is an *automatic* process and is therefore imposed to the spontaneous forces of mental life: 'that which is lovely to the automatic process is hateful to the spontaneous soul' (Lawrence 1923: 170, 169). If one dreams of incest, that is because incest is a pure formula of repetition: the repetition of the child's love for the mother on the 'upper plane' in a sexual love on the 'lower plane'. 'The dream-process *loves* its own automatism' and has a tendency to 'force everything to an automatic-logical conclusion in the psyche'. This is consistent with the Bergsonian model of dream as repetition, but brings out the *sterility* of the repetition to which the dream tends. Lawrence even suggests that the mind changes its activity at night-time, ceding its attention to life and submerging itself in a consciousness of the past. At night, the mind 'collects the results of the spent day into consciousness, lays down the honey of quiet thought, or the bitter-sweet honey of the gathered flower. It is the consciousness of that which is past. Evening is our time to read history and tragedy and romance – all of which are the utterance of that which is past, that which is finished, is concluded: either sweetly concluded, or bitterly' (Lawrence 1923: 172). However, dream, reverie, history and romance are still not, in Deleuze's words, 'adequate to the night'. There are nocturnal *activities* different in kind from nocturnal passivity or diurnal activity:

> Evening is the time also for revelry, for drink, for passion. Alcohol enters the blood and acts as the sun's rays act. It inflames into life, it liberates into energy and consciousness . . . That life of the day which we have not lived, by means of sun-born alcohol we can now flare into sensation, consciousness, energy and passion, and live it out. It is a liberation from the laws of idealism, a release from the restriction of control and fear. It is the blood bursting into consciousness. [Thus the] active mind-consciousness of the night is a form of retrospection, or else it is a form of impulsive exclamation,

> direct from the blood, and unbalanced. Because the active physical consciousness of the night is the blood-consciousness, the most elemental form of consciousness. (173)

Dream-consciousness is either dominated by empirical retrospection (the combing of the day's residues) or else yields to a sterile repetition of the past. How impoverished the dream looks when compared to the consciousness that actively becomes 'adequate' to the night, through intoxication or sex. How astonishing it seems that psychoanalysis, with its molar opposition of consciousness versus the unconscious, cut off conceptual access to the kinds of non-egoic *consciousness* that grant the mind an *activity* that is no more ruled by the reality principle than by the economics of the pleasure principle. 'Sex is our deepest form of consciousness. It is utterly non-ideal, non-mental. It is pure blood-consciousness. It is the basic consciousness of the blood, the nearest thing in us to pure material consciousness. It is the consciousness of the night, when the soul is *almost* asleep' (Lawrence 1923: 173). The *sommeil* of sex, whether heightened by intoxication or not, is the liberation of the virtual body, the subjugation of the actual body by the virtual body, a spatiotemporal 'dramatization' where it is not the body that rules the mind, but where the somnambulistic mind rules the body.

Notes on Sources

Introduction

1 By the time Deleuze finally comes around to affirming a Freudian concept (the notion of the death instinct in *Coldness and Cruelty*, a 1967 interpretation of masochism), it is impossible not to detect the Deleuzian 'humour' with which it is treated. Freud's death instinct, we are told, is a transcendental concept, a condition of temporal synthesis (M 113–15). 'There is always a "one dies" more profound than "I die", and it is not only the gods who die endlessly and in a variety of ways; as though there appeared worlds in which the individual was no longer imprisoned within the personal form of the I and the ego, nor the singular imprisoned within the limits of the individual' (DR 113). Whatever this means, it has nothing to do with Freud or psychoanalysis. The use of the Lacanian concept of the 'phallus' in *Difference and Repetition* is the same: citing a famous passage about the phallus from Lacan's *Seminar on the Purloined Letter*, Deleuze then says 'the passing present which bears itself away has never been better opposed to the pure past which perpetually differs from itself and whose universal mobility and universal ubiquity cause the present to pass' (DR 102). Behind the Lacanian veiled form is Bergsonian paramnesia. When their doctrines are affirmed by Deleuze, Freud and Lacan always serve as masks for other forces.

2 Deleuze's approach to the problem will involve attention to special kinds of consciousness which are 'unconscious' only in the restricted sense that they are unconscious *to* representational thought. Instinct is held to involve a peculiar type of consciousness, as does masochism or psychosis. Deleuze stresses that these tendencies involve *lived experiences.* He is opposed to the view of many contemporary theorists (from the Frankfurt School to Hardt and Negri) that *all* subjective experience is always already penetrated by either representation or the biopolitical imprint of late capitalism (or, at worst, by both of these). Much of Deleuze's most creative thought is focused on articulating a positive account of the autonomous processes of the unconscious. Instincts and intuitions, experiences of love, intoxication, esoteric experiences, breakdowns, dreams and nightmares all involve 'dramatizations' which are relatively independent of our everyday representational activity, and involve what Deleuze and Jung both call 'individuation'. The lurking political claim here is that to act as if processes of individuation do not exist (as the aforementioned thinkers often do) is self-defeating, and robs the agent of the strength to throw the dice in other domains. To recapture for theory and practice the positivity common to processes of individuation might even require making some strange alliances with more 'esoteric' traditions of thought (which were not always associated with the right, especially in France). Deleuze certainly does not appear to have been afraid to make this move.

3 Cf. M 16. In an interview just after the publication of *Anti-Oedipus*, Deleuze explained that 'we didn't think for a minute of writing a madman's book, but we did write a book in which you no longer know who is speaking: there is no basis for knowing whether it's a doctor, a patient, or some present, past, or future madman speaking' (DI 219). With that book, Deleuze and Guattari probably achieved their dubious aim. On 'humour' in Deleuze, see 'Humour, Irony and the Law' in M 81–90.

Chapter 1: The Pathologies of Time

1 French psychology was highly active at this time; other noted psychologists cited by Bergson include Théodule Ribot (1839–1916) and Alfred Binet (1857–1911).

2 In 1935 Jung wrote that 'My own course of development was influenced primarily by the French school and later by Wundt's psychology. Later, in 1906, I made contact with Freud, only to part company with him in 1913, after seven years of collaboration, owing to differences of scientific opinion. It was chiefly considerations of principle that brought about the separation, above all the recognition that psychopathology can never be based exclusively on the psychology of psychic disease, which would restrict it to the pathological, but must include normal psychology and the full range of the psyche' (CW 18: 773–4). In his article 'From Somnambulism to the Archetypes: The French Roots of Jung's Split with Freud', John Haule notes that Jung's 'French heritage is almost suppressed as some kind of secret' (Haule 1984: 242).

3 The explicit objection was that Bergson had omitted the most fundamental aspect of human temporality: our consciousness that we will die, at some indeterminate date in the future. It was held that Bergsonism was unable to recognize the phenomena of *anxiety* that arises from one's relationship with one's death, and that colours, through dread or anticipation, the whole of our experience of time. Heidegger takes Bergson to be no more than the latest heir to a very traditional concept of time, which was inaugurated by Aristotle. For Aristotle, time is 'the number of movement': it provides the quantitative backdrop by which the successive movements of physical bodies are measured; Bergson does not deviate from that model (Heidegger 1927: 501). If Aristotle treats the *human* experience of time as a special case, then it is only within a framework that is appropriate for all living bodies. The internal changes of organic bodies (as distinct from their external, spatial movements) involve a development from potentiality to a state of fulfilled actuality. Heidegger argues that both of these conceptions of time (physical and developmental) are inappropriate for analysing human temporality. At its core, human temporality is related to death: my experience of past, present and future is ultimately articulated in relation to my death (which will happen at some indeterminate future date), and I can either flee from that fact, or consciously take it on. For Heidegger, Bergson covers over the relation of time to finitude, and thus ends up affirming a notion of time as an abstract Heraclitean flux of duration.The existentialist critique of Bergson was echoed by the Marxist tradition. For Lukács, Bergsonism was nothing but a 'recourse to the subjective immediacy of apprehension, grow[n] into a philosophy based on radically irrationalist intuition' (Lukács 1962: 26). The accusation that Bergsonism is just a philosophy of 'immediate intuition' still lingers today; it is false, as Deleuze shows. Walter Benjamin, on the other hand, appeared to have read Bergson in detail, in conjunction with his studies of Proust. Like Heidegger, Benjamin also points out the apparent suppression of death in Bergson, although Benjamin's problem with this is not that Bergson covers over a fundamental existential truth about the individual's relation to death, but that he leaves himself without any way of understanding the importance of tradition, whose precariousness is due to the ever-present possibility of destruction and forgetting. 'The fact that death is eliminated from Bergson's *durée* isolates it effectively from a historical (as well as prehistorical order) order . . . The *durée* from which death has been eliminated has the miserable endlessness of a scroll' (Benjamin 1939: 185). Thus, the objection that Bergson failed to acknowledge the role of finitude in human temporality is common to both Benjamin and Heidegger.

4 Deleuze's use of the concept of intensity plays on each of the following three registers: (1) the intension of a concept, its essential meaning; (2) intensive magnitudes, such as temperatures and tonal relations; and (3) sensible excitation (intense feelings). For Deleuze's most extended discussion of intensity, see chapter 5 of *Difference and Repetition.*

5 As Bergson says of evolutionary change, 'each new piece really requires . . . a complete

recasting of the whole' (Bergson 1896: 169).

6 Bergson contends that clock-time does not really measure time, but rather imposes a type of measurement that is more suited to space, to extension, onto time. We can measure the data of our experience 'extensively', so that we divide things into their separate positions, and then measure their distance from each other in centimetres, metres, miles from each other. If we divide one of these extensive quantities, the units that have been divided still remain the same. If we divide a football pitch in half, it doesn't *change the nature* of the two halves. If we increase a space, we simply add more space to it. Spatial extension is thus homogenous, and change in spatial extension can be termed mere 'difference of degree', in that the nature of the space divided or added never changes. But duration does involve changes in nature, or 'differences in kind' (see B 37–43).

7 Even though Bergson says that 'every sensation is altered by repetition' and that 'the same feeling, by the mere fact of being repeated, is a new feeling' (Bergson 1889: 131, 200), this would seem to only really hold for first repetitions, not *every* subsequent repetition of a sensation. The threshold nature of duration would come out more clearly in the case of sensations that had been repeated a number of times.

8 In fact, the account in *Cinema 2* is probably Deleuze's most accessible and complete, and it helps clarify obscure points in his earlier interpretations in *Bergsonism* and *Difference and Repetition.*

9 These two forms of memory should not be confused (Bergson, 79). First, take the learning of a lesson: When I learn a poem, I attempt to learn it by heart. When it is learnt, I can repeat it as a whole, without thinking of the discrete times during which I learnt it. But now isn't this more like a habit than a memory? The 'memory' of the poem is not linked with any past event, and is more truly 'a part of my present, exactly like my habit of walking or of writing. It is lived and acted, rather than represented' (81). Habits are nothing more than a 'series of mechanisms, wound up and ready, with reactions to external stimuli ever more numerous and more varied and answers ready prepared to an ever growing number of possible solicitations'. But there is another type of memory. The memory of *each* successive reading, on the contrary 'has *none* of the marks of a habit' (80). Each reading of the poem is a definite, separate event. My English teacher was wearing a cordoruy suit one day, and the next week she read the poem with a cold. 'It is like an event in my life; its essence is to bear a date, and consequently, to be unable to occur again . . . Though my effort to recall this image becomes more and more easy as I repeat it, the image, regarded in itself, was necessarily at the outset what it always will be' (80). This kind of memory involves us 'remounting the slope of our past'. In other words, this is true memory, or memory proper, rather than 'habit-memory', which is ultimately analysable into habit. Habitual consciousness 'no longer *represents* the past to us, it *acts* it; and if it still deserves the name of memory, it is not because it conserves bygone images, but because it prolongs their useful effect into the present moment' (82). But these are two totally different processes. The first process, learning a lesson, as a habitual action, can be classed as a species of adaptation. A being which did nothing but fulfil its biological instincts would require nothing more than 'habit-memory' in order to fine-tune its instinctual responses.

10 The 'reality of the past' can be explained by appealing to a 'causal' or 'direct' theory of memory, such as that advanced by C. B. Martin and Max Deutscher in their influential 1966 paper 'Remembering'. In a renewed effort to undermine the notion that memories are simply weak representations, the authors attempt to present the necessary conditions of a proper case of remembering. Without acknowledging Bergson's analysis, they confirm his distinction between habit-memory and memory proper, but they point to a third problematic case, 'remembering *that*'. 'He remembers how to swim' is different from 'He remembers going swimming', which is different in turn from 'He remembers that he went swimming'. They argue that remembering in the

second sense must be taken as causal: 'a person can be said to remember something happening or, in general, remember something directly, only if he has observed or experienced it' (Martin and Deutscher 1966: 163). But surely the problem of the reliability of memory, as psychoanalysis shows, arises out of our inability to distinguish between what are real memories and what are fantasies, or on the other hand, what merely appropriations of other's reports into my own narrative of my life. An analysis of the third case, 'remembering *that*', helps to bring out the notion that the causal criterion is a necessary condition for memory proper. 'Remembering that' can be used in two senses: one may remember that Julius Caesar invaded Britain without having been present at the event itself; alternatively one may remember that one had an English lesson, even though one remembers nothing about it. The former type of 'remembering that' involves no causal reference, but the latter type, even though it lacks detail, conforms to the criteria for remembering in the second sense (or memory proper) in that it involves some fragment of *direct* memory. Thus Martin's and Deutscher's point is that if memory proper exists, it occurs through the operative effect of a past experience. A condition of memory proper is that *traces* of past events continue to have effects in the mind. In 'Persons and their Pasts', Sydney Shoemaker takes up Martin's and Deutscher's initial proposition that memory has a 'previous awareness condition': he says that 'a claim to remember a past event implies, not merely that the rememberer' experienced such an event, but that his present is in some way *due to*, that it came about *because of*, a cognitive and sensory state the rememberer had at the time he experienced the event . . . . It is part of the previous awareness condition for memory that a veridical memory must not only correspond to, but must also stand in an appropriate *causal* relationship to, a past cognitive and sensory state of the rememberer (Shoemaker 1970: 272). There is perhaps a sense in which Bergson and Deleuze share something with proponents of a causal theory of memory. But it is quite hard to isolate this sense. The fact that previous events *have actually happened* certainly may be said to give them a 'reality', insofar as in principle they now permanently have potential to exert influence over subsequent events (even though, in themselves, their reality is now virtual). However, Martin and Deutscher conclude their discussion by suggesting that this causal power of memory-traces must be neurological, which is obviously not the conclusion that Bergson would want to draw. Furthermore, for both Bergson and Deleuze, the operative effect of the past is not 'causal' in any linear sense. As has been suggested, their model is not causal at all, but is close to the Leibnizian model of actualization. The primacy Deleuze gives to the notion of temporal synthesis is also relevant to this problem.

11 In a footnote to the passage where Deleuze claims that 'pure memory has only an ontological significance', Deleuze refers to two texts by Jean Hyppolite which are said to attack 'psychologistic' interpretations of *Matter and Memory*. But in these texts, Hyppolite does not defend a substantially ontological view of pure memory, but in fact what can only be called a transcendental interpretation (or at least a 'post-Kantian' interpretation, as Hyppolite is obviously ultimately a Hegelian rather than a Kantian). Hyppolite says 'Memory is not merely the mechanical reproduction of the past, but *sense*' (Hyppolite 1949b: 117). If pure memory is ontological, then, it is so in a very specific, post-Kantian sense. In Deleuze's important review of Hyppolite from 1954, he notes that 'Being, according to Hyppolite, is not *essence*, but *sense*' (Deleuze 1954: 193); Deleuze goes on to say that 'Following Hyppolite, we recognise that philosophy, if it has a meaning, can only be an ontology and an ontology of sense'. What, then, is 'sense'? The simplest definition is to be found in Deleuze's 1978 own Kant lectures, where he says that for Kant, 'there is no longer an essence behind appearance, there is rather a sense or non-sense of what appears (First seminar, p. 5). This signifies 'a radically new atmosphere of thought, to the point where I can say that in this respect we are all Kantians'. After Kant, we no longer look for a substantial essence behind appearances,

but take a different approach: we say 'something appears, tell me what it signifies or, and this amounts to the same thing, tell me what its condition is' (ibid.). Thus if Hyppolite attacks psychologistic interpretations of Bergson, he does so from a post-Kantian idealist perspective, rather than a substantial-ontological one. For Hyppolite, Hegel is the only philosopher who arrives at a consistent, post-Kantian 'ontology of sense' and thus eliminates all anthropological, merely empirical coordinates from philosophy. In the other essay to which Deleuze refers 'Du Bergsonisme à l'existentialisme', Hyppolite implies that the fact that 'Bergson defines philosophy in this formula: "philosophy must be an effort to transcend the human condition"' (Hyppolite 1949a: 458) makes him closer to this Hegelian ideal than his existentialist heirs, who remain caught in merely anthropological claims. All this is to say that Deleuze's reference to Hyppolite supports the transcendental interpretation of Deleuze's Bergsonism. For further evidence of Deleuze's fundamental Kantianism, see my 'The Vertigo of Philosophy: Deleuze and the Problem of Immanence' (Kerslake 2002).

12 The idea of the integral preservation of the past is clearly bound up with the pervasive spiritualism that gripped Paris during this period. Janet, whose father was a spiritualist philosopher, wrote that 'everything that has existed still exists and endures in a place which we do not understand, to which we cannot go' (cited in Ellenberger 1970: 353). He confessed: 'I am not absolutely certain that the past is dead and gone, and I have a weak spot for Wells' novel *The Time Machine*. A day will come when man will know how to walk in the past in the same way as he now travels through the air. One day he will be able to make voyages in the past and will search in the past for events which have disappeared and for people who have died, in order to bring them back into the present' (Janet 1923: 17). With the invention of a 'paleoscope', marvellous adventures in time will be possible which exceed the tales of Jules Verne, not to mention the impoverished imaginations of the *romanciers* of the day (cf. Janet 1928: 491; on the paleoscope, see the other references in Ellenberger 1970: 353). Janet concluded a series of lectures at the University of London with the expectation that one day, man might make the same kind of progress in time as he has done in space through the conquest of the natural world (Janet 1920: 164).

13 'Human reality by which lack appears in the world must itself be a lack. For lack can come into being only through lack; the in-itself cannot be the occasion of lack in the in-itself. In other words, in order for being to be lacking or lacked, it is necessary that a being make itself its own lack; only a being which lacks can surpass toward the lack' (Sartre 1943: 87).

14 There are neuroscientific hypotheses that can be interpreted in the light of Bergson's governing theory. Bergson's theory of the two 'jets' of time might be taken to be incarnated in two separate sets of neurons, evolving in tension with each other. The cerebral mechanisms that instantiate the preservation of the past for the future would have to be relatively insulated from the attentional and perceptual processes. The neuroscientist Jonathan Winson suggests that information essential to the survival of a species is gathered during the day is later reprocessed into memory during REM sleep (Winson 1990: 42). Dreams, as Stevens and Price put it, 'could be the means by which animals update their strategies for survival by reevaluating current experience in the light of strategies formed and tested in the past. This is done when the animal is asleep as it is only during sleep that the brain is free of its outer preoccupations and able to perform this vital activity' (Stevens and Price 2000: 221). There is a common electro-encephalic rhythm (theta) to dreams and to behaviour related to the survival of mammals, so dreams might be responsible for preserving memories relevant to the latter. Thus there could be a diurnal cycle of mnemonic preservation which is proceessed independently of present-oriented adaptive behaviour. Winson concludes that

> there is an unconscious, and dreams are indeed the 'royal road' to its understanding. However, the characteristics of the unconscious and associated processes of

functioning are very different than Freud thought. Rather than being a cauldron of untamed passions and destructive wishes, I propose that the unconscious is a cohesive, continually active mental structure that takes note of life's experiences and reacts accordingly to its own scheme of interpretation. Dreams are not disguised as a consequence of repression. Their unusual character is a result of the complex associations that are culled from memory. (48)

15 Deleuze writes that pure memories are 'like Leibnizian possibles . . . try[ing] to become embodied, exert[ing] pressure to be admitted, so that a full scale repression [*refoulement*] originating in the present and an "attention to life" are necessary to ward off useless or dangerous recollections' (B 72); although at first sight this looks like a *dynamic* account of repression, this impression is misleading. Leibniz does sometimes say such things as 'everything possible demands that it should exist' (cited in Russell 1900: 296; *Philosophische Schriften*, ed. Gerhardt VII. 194). But his argument is ontological. First, it is based on the claim that existence is not a 'perfection' or 'attribute', as that would 'add something new to things'. So there must be an '*essentiae exigentia*', a demand *of* essence *within* essence to exist. But this claim, by itself, can only hold up within pre-Kantian rationalism. In effect, Kant pushes Leibniz's point further in his critique of the Ontological Argument: if existence would add something new to essence, that means that existence cannot be attributed to essence *at all*, whether as property or as 'tendency'. Hence existence is something else altogether; you can only say something exists if you can have a possible intuition of it. But Leibniz also says that 'the possible demands existence . . . in proportion to its possibility or according to the degree of its essence' (ibid.).

16 Deleuze's reference to *mens momentanea* is to Leibniz, who also claimed that 'body lacks memory', and makes a further step towards the revolutionary, modern idea that the function of the mind is to synthesize elements across time. In an early discussion, he writes:

> No conatus without motion lasts longer than a moment except in minds. For what is conatus in a moment is the motion of a body in time. This opens the door to the true distinction between body and mind, which no one has explained heretofore. For every body is a momentary mind, or one lacking recollection, because it does not retain its own conatus and the other contrary one together for longer than a moment . . . Hence body lacks memory; it lacks the perception of its own actions and passions; it lacks thought. (Loemker 141; G IV, 230)

As the reference to *conatus* indicates, Leibniz is concerned with desire here. In the ellipsis, he writes 'for two things are necessary for *sensing pleasure* or pain – action and reaction, opposition and then *harmony* – and there is no sensation without them'.

17 Deleuze presents this argument a number of times across the whole range of his early writings, but that in most of them he gives somewhat different accounts of it. In *Nietzsche and Philosophy*, for instance, he does not even mention that it is an argument from Bergson, silently passing it off as Nietzsche's; we will see in a moment that he also adds two other important premises to the argument which cast the Bergsonian argument in a different light. The nearest Deleuze gets to Bergson's actual argument is his citation of the previous passage in a footnote to *Bergsonism*, and the accompanying claim that 'if [the past] were not constituted immediately, neither could it be reconstituted on the basis of an ulterior present' (B 59). However, even there he neglects to mention the specific Bergsonian arguments quoted above for the impossibility of fixing the past after it has passed. Deleuze's first 1956 article on Bergson ('Bergson, 1859–1941') also has the same formulation: cf. DI 29. But strangely, Deleuze's second 1956 article ('Bergson's Concept of Difference') omits the explanation altogether, as it opts for a different argumentative strategy for defending Bergson's theory. Instead of starting with duration, heterogeneity and memory, and then proceeding to Bergson's biology (as *Bergsonism* does), it starts with a quasi-biological account of 'the virtual' and moves

from there to memory. So when we get to the part on memory, instead we get this: 'Pure memory is virtual because it would be absurd to seek the mark of the past in something actual and already realised; a memory is not a representation of something, it represents nothing, it *is*', and then 'It does not have to wait for perception to disappear, it is not subsequent to perception' (DI 44/55). Deleuze's strategy in this latter article puts an inordinate amount of weight on Bergson's theory of instinct. The versions in *Proust and Signs* (PS 57–8) and *Difference and Repetition* itself are also weak as they do not make the point about *re*constitution. There, Deleuze's version of Bergson's argument instead looks as if it is relying on the claim that 'if a new present were required for the past to be constituted as past, then the former present would never pass and the new one never arrive' (DR 81). We get a similar sort of claim in *Proust and Signs*: 'If the same moment did not coexist with itself as present *and* past, it would never pass, a new present would never come to replace this one' (PS 58). I am afraid I cannot find any meaning in these claims as explanations. As explanations, they seem to appeal to a crude 'physics' of time which it is impossible to evaluate. At best they seem to function as assertions; which means that the explanation must be found elsewhere. The central explanation seems to me to be this: the past must be contemporaneous with the present *because* the content of each past cannot be delimited immediately after it has passed, and must both remain open to reinterpretation as well as continuing to be *that* past. But the consequence of taking this interpretation is that it would seem that Bergson's model of the constitution of the past really involves the constitution of the past as what *will have been*: the past as future anterior. There are some indications that Deleuze thinks that this is where the main weight of the argument lies. In his second article on Bergson from 1956 ('Bergson and the Concept of Difference') he remarks that 'in a different way than Freud, though just as profound, Bergson saw that memory was a function of the future, that memory and will were the same function, that only a being capable of memory could turn away from its past, free itself from the past, not repeat it, and do something new' (DI 45/56). When Deleuze concludes in *Bergsonism* that 'in other words, each present goes back to itself as past'(B 59), this indicates that he has a complex temporality in mind.

18 In the theoretical section of *Studies in Hysteria* (1893), the functional rationale for the need to distinguish perception from memory was first given by Breuer: 'The perceptual apparatus, including the sensory areas of the cortex, must be different from the organ which stores up and reproduces sense-impressions in the form of mnemic images. For the basic essential of the function of the perceptual apparatus is that its *status quo ante* should be capable of being restored with the greatest possible rapidity; otherwise no proper further perception could take place. The essential of memory, on the other hand, is that no such restoration should occur but that every perception should create changes that are permanent. It is impossible for one and the same organ to fulfil these two contradictory conditions' (SE 2: 188, 189n.) However, whereas for Bergson the preservation of the past requires something more than a neuroscientific explanation, Freud's early theory of memory is a theory of how physical events are *recorded* in nervous tissue. 'A main characteristic of nervous tissue is memory: that is, quite generally, a capacity for being permanently altered by single occurrences' (SE 1 299).

19 The Bergsonian temporality that structures the introversion/extraversion distinction is already visible in Jung's breakthrough work, *Transformations and Symbols of the Libido*, where he makes a division between 'two kinds of thinking'. 'Directed' thought, which 'adjusts itself to actual conditions, where we . . . imitate the succession of objectively real things' is opposed to a 'non-directed', or 'merely associative thinking . . . *a dream or phantasy thinking*' (CW B 18–20). Directed thinking serves the practical orientation to the future: it 'creates innovations, adaptations, imitates reality and seeks to act upon it.', while phantasy thinking, on the contrary, turns away from this tendency, 'sets free subjective wishes, and is, in regard to adaptation, wholly unproductive'. Jung adds that

whereas the material of the first kind of thinking comes from movements presently occurring in the actual world, 'the material of these thoughts [in the second kind of thinking] which turns away from reality, can naturally be only the past with its thousand memory-images' (ibid.). The schema is thus highly reminiscent of Bergson's dualism between perception and memory in *Matter and Memory*.

20 The late Kant was preoccupied with this problem of rebirth in his *Religion within the Limits of Reason Alone*.

21 In its early formulation in *Nietzsche and Philosophy*, what Lacan called 'the Perspective of the Last Judgment' is still at work. Eternal return only manages to invest *this* moment to the fullest on condition that it is on the rebound from the furthest limit of the future. Nietzsche's idea of eternal return is an unstable mix of atheism and theology (one might be tempted to argue that it is the point at which atheism and theology dialectically collapse into each other). Theology is not absent from a concept whose intended effect is to establish how the great drifting wastes of a material universe deprived of any teleological fulfilment, any moment of redemption, might forever recombine in the same way in the infinite passageway of time, thus opening them to 'vertical' totalization – or, contemplation *sub specie aeternitatis*. On the 'Stoic' view of the eternal return, the moment attains a kind of eternity by virtue of its absolute, identical singularity: in the great cosmological circle revolving in infinite time, each particular combination is repeated infinitely many times. What this interpretation misses out are 'the two themes most profoundly linked to eternal return, that of qualitative metamorphosis and that of quantitative inequality' (DR 242). The willing agent of the eternal return wills it only on condition of 'becoming an other'. The perspective of the Last Judgement must therefore be problematized by the thought that I will inevitably look back on my resolution or act of will as partial, because I will have been ignorant of the future consequences of that resolution. The goal of being able to say 'I willed it thus' about any past action implies that the content of the 'thus' will never at any future point budge retrospectively. 'It will always have meant this': what I will today I will also continue to will tomorrow – *thus* will I have done with half-willing and will integrally. But this is exactly what is excluded by Deleuze's Bergsonian theory of the past. The point of that was that on principle we never know until later what the content or implications of any present are. Hence integral willing is an illusion.

22 Leibniz's relationship with Hermetic and mystical philosophy has been discussed in Allison Coudert, *Leibniz and the Kabbalah* (1995).

23 Completed in 1705, but Leibniz withdrew it from publication following Locke's death in 1704; it was first published in 1765.

24 Take Thomas Reid's Brave Officer Paradox. As a boy, a brave officer had once been flogged for robbing an orchard. Later in life, he commits a brave deed as an officer, and at that point, remembers his juvenile crime and punishment. In advanced life, he is made a general, and remembers the brave deed, but has now forgotten the flogging. On Locke's account, the boy is the same person as the brave officer, and the general is the same person as the brave officer, but the general is not the same person as the boy who was flogged (Reid 1785: 114).

25 Jolley's concluding sentence also suggests a confusion, for whereas Locke's criterion is that the ability to *consciously* remember past events guarantees personal identity, Leibniz claims that *unconscious* memories should also be included as markers of identity. As Jolley himself says, for Leibniz, 'at every moment in his history a person is *unconsciously* 'remembering' every previous state'. But this actual unconscious identity, if such exists, could not secured by means of personal, conscious identity and would depend on some future 'improvement' which would allow that we can integrate all previously unconscious states.

26 Fechner, another of the great disciples of Leibniz, and the founder of a psychophysics inseparable from the spiritual mechanisms of the monadic soul, does not

hesitate to develop classifications endlessly, from vertigo or dizziness to luminous life. In them he envisions the three ages of man, with all their possibilities of regression and damnation, through which Fechner himself passes as a monad, reduced to his dark room or his sombre depths, delivered up to the digestive swarming of little perceptions, but also, expanding towards the power of a resurrection, of an ascent towards an intensive light. Few monads fail to believe themselves damned at certain moments of their existence. When their clear perceptions are gradually distinguished, when they recede into a night, compared with which the life of the tick seems singularly rich. But with freedom there comes a moment where a soul reconquers itself, and can say to itself with the astonishment of a convalescent: my God, what did I do in all these years? (F 93; trans. modified)

27 Goethe, Napoleon, Luther 'still live among us, thinking and acting in us, as awakened creative individuals, more highly developed than at their death – each no longer restrained by the limitations of the body, but poured forth upon the world which in their lifetime they moulded' (Fechner 1836: 31). However, Fechner does not stop with this cultural immortality, but rather deduces another kind of spiritual *existence* that he says is proper to the third age of man. What might be left over at the end of the second age of human existence, when sensible intuitions cease to be possible?

> Even now, the more thoroughly all my senses are closed to external things, the more I withdraw into the gloaming of the outer world, the more aware and bright will be my memory life, and things long forgotten will come back to me. Death, on the other hand, does nothing but extinguish the senses entirely and for all time, so that all possibility of reviving them is also extinguished. No closing of the eyes during our lifetime can be so profound, no awakening of memories so luminous as in death . . . All the force which is divided between the life of intuition [*Anschauungsleben*] and the life of memory [*Erinnerungsleben*] in this world, becomes, in the next, the property of the life of memory only, and our present life of memory owes its weakness to the very fact that the life of intuition here below claims the greater part of the strength that is bestowed upon us by the higher spirit. Complete remembrance of the former life will begin only when that life lies entirely behind us, and all remembrance during that lifetime is but a brief preview of what lies ahead. (Fechner 1851: III, 16; trans. modified)

In the *Little Book*, Fechner writes that any strivings of the human being to perform good actions which will never be rewarded in this life can only be made intelligible in the light of a 'presentiment' that every action will somehow be recorded:

> The repentance that arouses in us an unfathomable distress for bad actions, even though they bring us no disadvantage here, rise from haunting presentiments [*ahnenden Vorgefühlen*] of what all this will bring to us in that world in which the fruit of our slightest and most hidden activity becomes a part of our true self. This is the great justice of creation, that every one makes for himself the conditions of his future life. Deeds will not be requited to the man through exterior rewards or punishments; there is no heaven and no hell in the usual sense of the Christian, the Jew, the heathen, into which the soul may enter after death . . . But after [the soul] has passed through the great transition, death, it unfolds [*entwickelt*] itself according to the great unalterable law of nature upon earth. (Fechner 1836: 33)

28 In a chapter on 'The Grand Arcanum of Death' in his *Key to the Mysteries*, Éliphas Lévi writes:

> During embryonic life it seemed to [the embryo] that the placenta was its body, and it was in fact its special embryonic body, a body useless for another life, a body which had to be thrown off as an unclean thing at the moment of birth. The body of our human life is like a second envelope, useless for the third life, and for that reason we throw its aside at the moment of our second birth. Human life compared to Heavenly life is veritably an embryo. When our evil passions kill us, Nature miscar-

ries, and we are born before our time for eternity, which exposes us to that terrible dissolution which St John calls the second death.

Lévi then says that 'according to the constant tradition of ecstatics', the 'abortions of human life', which have a human form, but always lopped and imperfect, are prevented from rising to heaven by a 'moral wound' which they have contracted in the course of their life. 'These wounded souls are the larvae of the second formation of the embryo . . . Frequently they attach themselves to vicious men and live upon their lives, as the embryo lives in its mother's womb. In these circumstances, they are able to take the most horrible forms to represent the frenzied desires of those who nourish them, and it is these which appear under the figures of demons to the wretched operators of the nameless works of black magic. These larvae fear the light, above all the light of the mind' (Lévi 1861: 202). We come back to Deleuze's relation to occultism in chapter 6.

29 I have not been able to trace the term 'metaschematism' in Leibniz; in the passage cited above, Leibniz uses the French word '*metamorphose*'. Deleuze may be referring to the 'schematic' imitations of God mentioned in 'The Monadology', # 83.

Chapter 2: The Wasp's Sympathy for the Caterpillar

1 An English-language bibliography (Murphy 1996) preserves the details of Deleuze's first phase of publication, which include a preface to Johann Montereggio de Malfatti's *Mathesis, or the Anarchy and Hierarchy of Knowledge*, an important book in the late nineteenth-century French occult revival, discussed in chapters 4 and 6 below.

2 Deleuze only makes a few references to Janet in his work, but they are important ones (cf. DR: 144; and C2: 51).

3 It was the second of a series entitled *Textes et Documents Philosophiques*, published by Hachette under the general editorship of Georges Canguilhem. The latter had himself edited the first volume, *Besoins et Tendances* (1952). I do not know whether Deleuze himself chose the exact combination of the concepts of instinct and institution for his volume, but the former was already of interest to him in his Bergson and Hume studies, while the concept of institution had also played an important role in the latter.

4 However, Deleuze's assertion in the introduction to the volume that animals inhabit 'specific worlds' or 'milieus' probably contains an implicit reference to von Uexküll. The only author in *Instincts and Institutions* who is in any way attached to the discipline of ethology is F. J. J. Buytendijk, who contributes two extracts. The first selection is entitled 'Instinct and Organisation', on the relationship between anatomical structure, organization and instinctive action (I & I: # 24, *Psychologie des Animaux*, 1920), and the second is on 'Instinctive Life and Beauty', where Buytendijk suggests that beauty is a 'luxury' of organic nature, extending beyond the principle of sexual selection (# 46 from *Les differences essentielles des functions psychiques de l'homme et des animaux*, 1930). In an early article, Lorenz criticises Buytendijk for entertaining a 'vitalist fantasy' about animal behaviour on a par with Jung's speculations (Lorenz 1939: 31). Buytendijk was also heavily influenced by phenomenology. For a stimulating discussion of Deleuze's relation to Uexküll and ethology, see Ansell-Pearson 1999: 139–208.

5 See Fletcher 1968 for a sympathetic survey of this group of thinkers.

6 The one passage from *Instincts and Institutions* on the topic of 'Instinct and Reflex' is from Kurt Goldstein's *The Organism*, and it is a critique rather than an endorsement of the notion that reflexes can be isolated as independent entities, without regard for the wholeness of the organism (I & I: 31). Again, Deleuze's editorial policy shows itself to be profoundly out of line with mainstream developments in the theory of instinct.

7 In an informative interview, he says about this period, 'I know what I was doing, where and how I lived during those years, but I know it only abstractly, rather as if someone else were relating memories that I believe but don't really have. It's like a hole in my life, an eight-year hole . . . There are catalepsies, or types of somnambulism [*des espèces de somnambulisme*] over several years, in most lives. Maybe it's in these holes that

movement takes place' (Deleuze 1990: 189). The mention of somnambulism is intriguing, as (on the evidence of *Instincts and Institutions*) it suggests that Deleuze was not just researching the concept of somnambulism during this period, but also *living* it as a problem. The eight-year gap begins after the publication in 1953 of *Empiricism and Subjectivity* (Deleuze's study of Hume) and *Instincts and Institutions*. At the end of the eight years, in 1961, Deleuze published two very different articles, 'Lucretius and Naturalism' and the first piece on masochism. The anomaly in Deleuze's account of his somnambulistic phase is his publication in 1959 of 'Sense and Value', an extract from his forthcoming *Nietzsche and Philosophy*, reprinted more or less complete as part of the book in 1962. Deleuze's first work on Nietzsche thus emerges in the sixth year in the eight-year gap, three years *prior* to his affirmation of Jung. The two 1961 texts appear to be so opposed that one would think they had different authors. The first text argues for a philosophical naturalism that overcomes the religious appeal to myth and fate, and the second is a Jungian depth-psychological voyage into mythical history! However, it should be noted that the Lucretius essay contains references to the Jungian concepts of anima and animus. The fact that Deleuze's eight-year hole was brought to an end by the publication of two texts in such tension with each other is extremely interesting from both philosophical and biographical points of view.

8 Making an implicit allusion to Kant's distinction between two types of zero in his essay on 'Negative Magnitudes', Bergson writes that 'both are equal to zero, but in the one case the zero expresses the fact that there is nothing, in the other that we have two equal quantities of opposite sign which compensate and neutralise each other'.

9 Deleuze also appeals to this notion of consciousness in 'Bergson and the Concept of Difference' (Deleuze 1956b: 57), and it lurks under the surface in *Difference and Repetition* (DR 284).

10 Following Bergson, Ruyer claims that this *knowledge* is a non-intellectual knowledge, or more exactly, says Ruyer, a non-perceptual knowledge, in that its knowledge does not rely on sensory information coming from outside. He suggests that we should first turn to semantics for help with regard to the issue of knowledge. In European languages, there are some uses of the term 'knowledge' which are closer to the meaning of 'power' (*pouvoir*). Ruyer notes that the English and German say 'I can swim' (*je peux nager*), whereas the French say 'I know how to swim' (*je sais nager*). 'Know-how' is indeed a borderline case between knowledge and power. When I say I *know* how to swim, I don't mean that I can articulate its rules intellectually or conceptually. Alternately, when I say that I *can* swim, I don't mean that my ability to swim is a purely physical power. We understand by this notion of power 'a psycho-physiological "competence", an "effective knowledge"' (Ruyer 1959: 167). It is neither intelligent learning nor purely physical behaviour. This is the sense we need to have in mind when we are dealing with instinctual knowledge. Bergson claims the wasp 'knows' how to paralyse the caterpillar. 'No, reply the positivist biologists, it is quite simply that it can do it mechanically. Given the structure of the organism with the sting, and the structure of its victim's organism, 'it jabs where it can'. The Peckhams make it seem as if the Sphex blindly rummages, scoring a hit by accident, but then learns precision through habituation. But why, then, does the Sphex use its sting when faced with the caterpillar or the cricket in the first place? There is no 'knowledge' here, the positivist biologist retorts, it is simply that a sensory stimulus releases a series of 'micro-powers' located in the nervous system (powers in the strictly physiological sense, that is).

11 A. R. Lacey criticizes Bergson for incoherence in even attempting to defend the notion of unconscious instinctual knowledge. 'Knowledge, we might say, has two features in particular: it is associated with consciousness, and it requires a certain connexion, of an admittedly controversial kind, between knower and known' (Lacey 1989: 145). But instinct is (mostly) unconscious, and although Bergson argues that instinct embodies a special kind of direct knowledge which is focused on matter rather than relation, it is

hard to imagine what knowledge *without* relations, formal discriminations and concepts would be. A knowledge without distance (the application of universal concepts to *this* thing implies some awareness of the gap between knower and known) is no knowledge at all. Bergson likens the enactment of an instinct to the somnambulist who 'acts his dream'. But if 'unconsciousness may be absolute' in the somnambulist, how could they really enact a dream in the external world? 'Does the somnambulist avoid obstacles because his eyes are open and he has some sort of 'subliminal' perception of them, or not?' (Lacey 1989: 146). Bergson is asking us to imagine some miraculous harmony between the mindscape of the sleepwalker and the environment in which he is walking. Lacey's problems can perhaps be resolved if a precise distinction is made between the structure of instinctual consciousness and that of intelligent consciousness.

12 At the beginning of his career, Wundt had argued that the lower cognitive processes exhibited a hierarchy of unconscious *inferences*, thus synthesizing data for the higher activity of judgement at the level of consciousness (Diamond 1980: 31–3; Hatfield 2003: 100). For instance, at the most basic level, perceptions were synthesized out of sensations through unconscious inferences. However, his defence of unconscious inferences was qualified: 'this process is unconscious, and we can infer it only from those elements which enter into consciousness. But when we translate it into conscious terms, it takes the form of an *inference*. The *unconscious inference* is the process that joins itself to sensation, giving rise to perception' (Wundt 1862: 65; cited in Diamond 1980: 32). But later he denied that unconscious processes were carriers of logical syntheses, and he explicitly denied the existence of unconscious mental states which he reduced to physiological states.

13 In 1834, there is record of a visit by Malfatti to the theosophist Franz von Baader, with whom he discussed the decadence of medicine due to materialism. Both von Baader and Malfatti saw in animal magnetism the proof of the incorrectness of materialism, and agreed that Mesmer himself had been an 'arch-materialist' whose therapy could only be understood properly within Schellingian pantheism (Faivre 1996: 53).

14 Lucie, a patient of Janet's, had periods of 'somnambulism' in which she was completely absorbed in her activity (whether it be eating or bookkeeping), but was oblivious to everything else. These somnambulic activities were dissociated from the rest of her consciousness. But the dissociation of her mental faculties went further than this, as Janet found separate 'personalities' encharged with different mental faculties. Lucie 1 depended on visual information, while Lucie 2 depended on tactility. It was in this state that Lucie regularly adopted a posture of terror, which repeated her precipitating trauma, in which she had been frightened by two men hiding behind a curtain. 'To have one's body in the posture of terror is to feel the emotion of terror; and if this posture is determined by a subconscious idea, the patient will have the emotion alone in his consciousness without knowing why he feels this way. "I'm afraid and I don't know why", Lucie can say at the beginning of her crisis when her eyes take on a wild look and her arms make gestures of terror. The unconscious is having its dream; it sees the men behind the curtain and puts the body in a posture of terror' (Janet 1889: 409; cited in Haule 247). Freud had criticized the notion of 'subconsciousness' as it implied that there was another consciousness somehow beneath the surface, but Janet's conception of the subconscious here shows itself rooted in the somnambulist model. *The unconscious is having its dream*: there *is* a state of consciousness going on, but it is trancelike and dissociated from all other psychological interests.

15 Alfred Binet was working concurrently with Janet on this approach to mental pathology. In his *Alterations of the Personality* (1892) he wrote of the division of consciousness:

> It is not an alteration of sensibility, but it is rather a peculiar attitude of the mind – the concentration of attention on a single thing. The result of this state of concentration is that the mind is absorbed to the exclusion of other things, and to such a degree insensible that the way is opened for automatic actions; and these actions,

becoming more complicated, as in the preceding case, may assume a psychic character and constitute intelligences of a parasitic kind, existing side by side with the normal personality which is not aware of them. (Binet 1892: 93)

16 Although Schopenhauer is sometimes seen as materialist or nihilist, his theory of will makes him a peculiar sort of vitalist, for when he talks about the will, he always refers to an 'inner force': 'At the very lowest grade, the will manifest[s] itself as a blind impulse, an obscure, dull urge, remote from all direct knowableness' (I, 149)

17 Oddly, in his citation of this passage in *Instincts and Institutions*, Deleuze deletes the reference to insects (I & I 27–8).

18 One of the unwanted consequences of Ruyer's theory, however, is that it appears to make the existence of homosexual love impossible to explain. Nevertheless, Ruyer implicitly makes available a potential interpretation of homosexuality through his recourse to the biology and myth of the hermaphrodite; in chapter 4 we will see that Deleuze himself opts to take up this possibility.

19 Deleuze takes up Bergson's attempt to define life in predominantly *developmental* terms (against the grain of neo-Darwinian definitions of life as the self-replication of genetic material). It is a Platonizing mistake to treat life as if it were the result of purely genetic determinants, outside of the spatiotemporal constraints that are imposed on the genes during the process of development. In *Bergsonism*, Deleuze contends that evolution 'does not move from one actual term to another actual term in a homogeneous unilinear series, but from a virtual term to the heterogeneous terms that actualise it along a ramified series' (B 99–100). Just because genes are 'ideal' entities does not mean that they coexist in an ideal realm akin to logical possibility, from which actual series are simply selected for existence. The movement from the virtual to the actual requires a transcendental account of the 'spatio-temporal dynamisms' that allow for the actualization of ideal genetic combinations. The relation between genes and environment more profoundly determine discrete *anatomical and morphological thresholds* at which change in function comes about. Deleuze cites the debate between Geoffroy Saint-Hilaire and Cuvier over the classification of anatomical elements. Against Cuvier's empirical approach to the problem, Geoffroy argues that the basic unit of biology should be abstract, purely anatomical and atomic elements, independent of both form and function (DR 184). These atomic elements 'are linked by ideal relations of reciprocal determination: they thereby constitute an 'essence' which is the Animal in itself' (DR 185). Here the elements of the Idea are not genes, but pure anatomical parts. The relation between an Idea and its actualization mirrors the relation between anatomical elements and the actualization in embryonic development. However, Deleuze thinks that Geoffroy's method can be transferred directly to genetics. Insofar as genes act 'only in relation to other genes . . . the whole constitutes a virtuality, a potentiality' (ibid.). In evolutionary theory, the combination of genetic effects is determined by assessment of adaptive function. Deleuze seems to accept such a view when he writes 'the genesis of development in organisms must therefore be understood as the actualisation of an essence, in accordance with various speeds and reasons determined by the milieu, with accelerations and interruptions' (DR 185/241). In accordance with evolutionary theory, then, the differential relations between elements are guided by the exigencies of adaptation (the 'speeds and reasons determined by the milieu'). However, Deleuze makes the anti-Darwinist point that all this happens 'independently of any transformist passage from one actual term to another' (ibid.). The constraints on anatomical change allow for the determination of ideal, fixed invariants at a virtual level. Contrary to traditional 'fixism', it is not species themselves which are 'fixed', but rather the threshold points that constrain morphological change, and which can be determined autonomously at a virtual level (the universal Animal) prior to their actualization. 'Fixism and evolutionism tend to be reconciled to the extent that movement does not go from one actual term to another, nor from general to particular, but – by the inter-

mediary of a determinant individuation – from the virtual to its actualisation' (DR 251).

20 In the preface to *Instincts and Institutions* Deleuze says that that problem of instinct is: 'How does the synthesis of tendencies and the object that satisfies them come about? The water I drink does not resemble at all the hydrates my organism lacks. The more perfect an instinct in its domain, the more it belongs to the species, and the more it seems to constitute an irreducible power of synthesis' (DI 21).

21 The paralysing instinct of the wasp would thus be an example of intellectual intuition. Perhaps we can finally understand the real reason for Spinoza's hobby of observing spiders fighting – they are exemplars of the blessed life.

Chapter 3: Deleuze and the Jungian Unconscious

1 This relationship between Bergson and Jung has been noted before, but still remains relatively unstudied. See Pete Gunter's informative article 'Bergson and Jung' (1982), which is a more general overview of the connections.

2 It is worth pointing out that Deleuze's Jungian essay was not published quietly in a particularly obscure place, but in *Arguments*, one of the most innovative French journals of the time. Deleuze clearly has a higher view of Jung's work than is common among philosophers.

3 A term used by Theodore Flournoy in *From India to the Planet Mars* (1899) to explain how mediums and spiritualists could apparently recall in detail ancient mythological and religious motifs to which they had had no access. The process of cryptomnesia occurs when 'certain forgotten memories reappear in the subject to see in them something new' (quoted in Shamdasani, 2003: 128).

4

> The process of regression is beautifully illustrated in an image used by Freud. The libido can be compared with a river which, when it meets with an obstruction, gets dammed up and causes an inundation. If this river has previously, in its upper reaches, dug out other channels, these channels will be filled up again by reason of the damming below . . . The river has not permanently flowed back into the old channels, but only for as long as the obstruction lasts in the main stream . . . [These channels] were once stages or stations in development of the main river-bed, passing possibilities, traces of which still exist and can therefore be used again in times of flood (Jung, *Theory of Psychoanalysis*, in CW 4: 163)

5 In the Schreber case history itself, Freud leaves the alternative open, although he re-emphasizes his commitment to seeking sexual aetiology by suggesting that since the paranoiac still 'perceives the external world and takes into account any alterations that may happen in it', it is more probable that psychosis can be explained by a loss of libidinal interest (75). But who would deny that the psychotic has the capacity for perception or registration of change in the external world? The function of reality must involve something more than that. Moreover, Freud himself appeared to accept at the beginning of the argument that psychosis involved a loss of 'reality'. Clearly this point only problematizes further what is required by a psychoanalytic account of the relation to the external world or to reality.

6 Freud developed his account of the emergence of reality in two main directions. The first trajectory lends itself readily to the kind of elaboration produced by Ferenczi in his 'Stages of the Development of the Sense of Reality', in which the 'sense of reality' is gradually built up through the mechanisms of introjection of libidinally invested objects into the psyche, and projection of such objects outside the ego if they are productive of unpleasure. (Ferenczi, 1913: 226f; and 'Introjection and Transference', ibid.: 47f.). In his 1925 paper 'Negation', for instance, Freud writes 'What is bad, what is alien to the ego, and what is external are, to begin with, identical'. The second trajectory is taken up by Lacan, who insists that we first of all must remember that the human child is 'born prematurely', and so any lack of satisfaction is always already understood as a lack of care, related to the enigmatic desire of the other who has duty of care. There is

no self-enclosed state of 'primary narcissism'; rather, narcissism concerns the identification with the image of another that one would like to be. If 'reality' means anything in this context, it must refer less to some putatively 'external world', than to 'other people', that is, to the coherence of the symbolic order, as ideally underwritten by an intersubjective pact of mutual recognition.

7 *Transformations and Symbols of the Libido* was 'written at top speed . . . without regard to time or method . . . The whole thing came upon me like a landslide that cannot be stopped: it was the explosion of all those psychic contents which could find no room, no breathing-space, in the constricting atmosphere of Freudian psychology and its narrow outlook' (CW 5: xxiii). The book is indeed bizarrely structured, with passages of theory continually being interrupted and unbalanced by lengthy outbreaks of mythological and etymological excavation, the reader being left to draw his own conclusions about where the book is going and how it might all hang together. It is perhaps best read as the description on two levels of a process of psychic regression, one particular and the other universal. It announces itself as an analysis of a text written and published by a young American woman, Frank Miller, who Jung claims later went on to develop schizophrenia. Psychosis is characterized by Jung (initially following Freud) as involving a process of regression to an earlier psychic stage. Psychosis demonstrates a particular kind of regression – loss of the 'function of reality' – and, according to a psychoanalytic logic we will examine in a moment, it thus promises in turn to hold the key to the very *genesis* of this reality-function. The guiding method and purpose of the book is thus to retrace the genesis of the higher cognitive processes through the mirror of a complex process of regression of libido: the book is subtitled 'A Contribution to the History of the Evolution of Thought'. The particular fantasies of Miss Miller are thus the door through which Jung travels back in time to recover the traces of the universal genesis of the human psyche. *Wandlungen und Symbole der Libido* was originally translated by Beatrice Hinkle in 1916 as *Psychology of the Unconscious*. In 1952 Jung revised the book substantially and reissued it as *Symbole der Wandlung*; this was first translated in 1956 as *Symbols of Transformation* (trans. R. F. C. Hull, Princeton: Princeton University Press, 1967, 2nd edn). Unless otherwise stated, I refer here to the reprinted translation of the first edition (Princeton: Princeton University Press, 1991), which makes up Appendix B to the *Collected Works* of Jung. However, in order to preserve the sense of the original German title, I refer to it in the main text as *Transformations and Symbols of the Libido*, but in the footnotes it is referred to by its English title, *Psychology of the Unconscious*.

8 Lacan suggests that with Jung 'we come upon a very traditional mode of thought clearly distinct from orthodox analytic thought. Psychic interest [or libido in Jung's general sense] is here nothing other than an alternating spotlight, which can come and go, be projected, be withdrawn from reality, at the whim of the pulsation of the psyche of the subject' (Lacan 1953–4: 115). Lacan proceeds to criticize this conception for 'illuminat[ing] nothing in the way of mechanisms'. His criticism on this point is unjust, as we will see. He overlooks the mechanism that is really at the heart of Jung's essential insight in *Transformations and Symbols of the Libido*, and which is the 'transformation' that reveals the true interest of Jung's genetic conception as a whole: the case of the third phase of the libido, that of 'desexualisation'.

9 'In nature', he asserts, 'this artificial distinction [between nutritive and sexual phases] does not exist.'

10 Sometimes it can seem that Jung genuinely understands this primal, self-differentiating libido to be an objective, biological process. However, Jung also adopts Kantian, Schopenhauerian and Bergsonian positions on the nature of this primal libido. So, in Kantian mode he will call the libido 'a complete X, a pure hypothesis, a model or counter, [which] is no more concretely conceivable than the energy known to the world of modern physics' (CW 4: 124). But then he will allow himself a quasi-Schopenhauer-

ian conception of a 'continuous life-urge, a will to live' (CW 4: 123), according to which we are permitted to think the thing-in-itself in general through an analogy with our own non-phenomenal aspect, the will. Jung admits that this conception of libido is 'a bit of psychological "voluntarism"', 'a throwing of psychological perceptions into material reality' (CW B: 130). Jung's appeal to Bergson's *élan vital* adds a certain amount of further confusion. For a survey of the influences on Jung's speculative endeavours, chapter 3 of Sonu Shamdasani's *Jung and the Making of Modern Psychology* is indispensable.

11 For instance, the transition from the sexual to the de-sexualized stage is explained in these terms: 'part of the energy required in the production of eggs and sperma has been transposed into the creation of mechanisms for allurement and protection of the young . . . The differentiated libido is henceforth desexualised . . . This now presupposes a very different and very complicated relation to reality, a true function of reality, which, functionally inseparable, is bound up with the needs of procreation' (CW B: 129, 133). Jung's account indeed suggests a more ethological approach to the libido than is to be found in Freud, for whom the drives have a blind, repetitive character. So if nutritive and sexual libido in some sense guide the organism in its navigation of the *Umwelt*, then what need is there for a separate 'function of reality'?

12 One of Jung's most powerful critiques of Freud is his argument that it is fallacious to infer the nature of a desire from the historical existence of a law that represses it. It is in a letter to Freud that Jung most clearly draws the conclusion:

> The large amount of free-floating anxiety in primitive man, which led to the creation of taboo ceremonies in the widest sense (totem, etc.) produced among other things the *incest taboo* as well . . . Incest is forbidden *not because it is desired* but because the free-floating anxiety regressively reactivates infantile material and turns it into a ceremony of atonement (as though incest had been, or might have been desired). (Freud/Jung 1975: # 315J)

This will be exactly Deleuze's and Guattari's argument in *Anti-Oedipus*. 'The law tells us: You shall not marry your mother, and you shall not kill your father. And we docile subjects say to ourselves: so that's what I wanted! . . . One acts as if it were possible to conclude directly from psychic repression the nature of the repressed, and from the prohibition the nature of what is prohibited' (AO 114). Deleuze and Guattari don't refer to this letter (which was not published until 1975), but make oblique reference to other passages in Jung where the same point is made, albeit in a caricatural form, with somewhat less logical force. In *Transformations and Symbols of the Libido*, Jung writes that

> incest probably never possessed particularly great significance as such, because cohabitation with an old woman for all possible motives could hardly be preferred to mating with a young woman. It seems that the mother acquired incestuous significance only retrospectively . . . Incest prohibition can be understood, therefore, as a result of regression and as the result of a libidinal anxiety, which regressively attacks the mother. Naturally it is difficult or impossible to say from whence this anxiety may have come'. (CW B: 396)

Deleuze and Guattari write that 'Freud couldn't abide a simple humorous remark by Jung, to the effect that Oedipus must not really exist, since even the primitive prefers a pretty young woman to his mother or his grandmother. If Jung betrayed everything, it was nevertheless not by way of this remark' (A-O 114).

13 In his central chapter on 'The Transformation of the Libido', Jung highlights the example of fire, inviting the conclusion that in the last instance reality as such, transcendence pure and simple, is constituted as the accidental by-product of an illicit, displaced act of masturbation.

14 This distinction is made in 'On the Two Kinds of Thinking', the opening chapter of the book. Directed thinking 'creates innovations, adaptations, imitates reality and seeks to act upon it', while fantasy thinking, on the contrary, turns away from this tendency, 'sets

free subjective wishes, and is, in regard to adaptation, wholly unproductive'. Jung adds that whereas the material of the first kind of thinking comes from movements presently occurring in the actual world, 'the material of these thoughts [in the second kind of thinking] which turns away from reality, can naturally be only the past with its thousand memory-images' (ibid.). The schema recalls Bergson's dualism between perception and memory in *Matter and Memory.*

15 The de-animation of reality would thus correspond to a tendency to complete de-sexualisation at the level of directed thinking (and not just the 'quasi' desexualization of animistic reality).

16 Deleuze also refers to Pierre Gordon's *Sex and Religion,* which recounts an equally speculative primal history populated with Hyperboreans and Amazons. For Deleuze's comments on Bachofen in *Coldness and Cruelty,* see M 52–3. Deleuze also continues to refer to Gordon's book right up to *A Thousand Plateaus.*

17 Thus, says Deleuze in *Coldness and Cruelty,* at the origin of civilization lies the effect of the Cold on the sexual instinct. Both the sexes are impoverished by the advent of the Ice Age. The males became physically coarsened, less sensitive, seeking to rediscover their dignity in the development of thought. This had an effect on the females, who could not but become 'sentimental' at seeing such brutes try to think. The sentimental Amazon is a new figure in history, and exerts a fascination upon the subordinate male. This fascination is intensified by the Amazon's sudden displays of 'severity' at the sight of coarseness. A transformation in consciousness comes about, in which the sexes interact in an entirely new way. Deleuze refers to hypotheses about the glacial period elsewhere in his work, thus his insistence that 'the glacial period was wholly responsible for the transformation' of sexuality and consciousness (M 54). He even identifies a 'freezing point, the point of dialectical transmutation, a divine latency corresponding to the catastrophe of the Ice Age' (M 52).

18 On this reading, Freud's insistence on sexual aetiology finds its application in patients who experience sexual problems in their current life, because they cannot help but interpret their past in terms of their sexual frustrations. In other words, Freud's method tallies first of all with the 'neuroses of the young', who are indeed both obsessed with sex *and* subject to restrictions on their access to it.

19 At first, in *Transformations and Symbols of the Libido* Jung argues that the transition from nutritive to sexual libido results in the mother being taken as the first sexual object. But in the same work he ends up denying that incestuous sexual desires have pre-eminent importance in psychosexual development (CW B: 396–7).

20 The passage in square brackets is omitted by Deleuze. Deleuze cites these passages as coming from a correspondence between Jung and R. Löy ('Some Crucial Points in Psychoanalysis: A Correspondence between Dr. Jung and Dr Löy', CW 4). However, the passages actually come from Jung's notorious 1934 essay 'The State of Psychotherapy Today' (cf. CW 10: 167–9). Deleuze's article also contains reference to a 'deeper unconscious which encircles us in a tie of blood' (SM 128). On Jung's relations with the Nazis, see the remarks of Andrew Samuels in *The Political Psyche* (Samuels 1993: 287–316); also Grossman 1979, and the collection *Lingering Shadows: Jungians, Freudians and Anti-Semitism* (Maidenbaum & Martin 1991). Aside from mentioning the important passage in *Nietzsche and Philosophy,* I leave aside here the question of Deleuze's possible views about Jung's relationship with Nazism, but this question should be dealt with. One of the complaints about Jung's comments in the 1934 essay concerns his claims about racial differences in Jewish and 'Aryan' psychology:

> The Jewish race as a whole – at least this is my experience – possesses an unconscious which can be compared with the 'Aryan' only with reserve. Creative individuals apart, the average Jew is far too conscious and differentiated to go about pregnant with the tensions of unborn futures. The 'Aryan' unconscious has a higher potential than the Jewish: that is both the advantage and the disadvantage of a youthful-

ness not yet fully weaned from barbarism. In my opinion it has been a grave error in medical psychology up till now to apply Jewish categories – which care not even binding on all Jews – indiscriminately to Germanic and Slavic Christendom. Because of this the most precious secret of the Germanic peoples – their creative and intuitive depth of soul – has been explained as a morass of banal infantilism, while my own warning voice has for decades been suspected of anti-Semitism. This suspicion emanated from Freud. He did not understand the Germanic psyche any more than did his Germanic followers. Has the formidable phenomenon of National Socialism, on which the whole world gazes with astonished eyes, taught them better? Where was that unparalleled tension and energy while as yet no National Socialism existed? Deep in the Germanic psyche, in a pit that is anything but a garbage-bin of unrealizable infantile wishes and unresolved family resentments. A movement that grips a whole nation must have matured in every individual as well. That is why I say that the Germanic unconscious contains tensions and potentialities which medical psychology must consider in its evaluation of the unconscious. (CW 10: 166)

One of the many reasons this passage is so horrible is that it sounds like an invocation rather than a description of libidinal forces. In the section on the Judaic priest in *Nietzsche and Philosophy*, Deleuze can be found taking up the issue of racial 'types'. In Nietzsche, he claims, 'race only ever intervenes as an element in a *cross-breeding*, as a factor in a *complex* which is physiological but also psychological, political, historical and social. Such a complex is exactly what Nietzsche calls a type' (NP 125). Deleuze's motto for dealing with race is Rimbaud's 'I am a beast, a Negro of an inferior race for all eternity'. In the orphanic unconscious, '*bastard* no longer designates a familial state, but the process or drift of the races'. Just as a conscious bastard's unconscious fantasies will tend towards identification with other lineages than their adopted family, so there are bastard lines within 'molar' races. Deleuze's politics is profoundly influenced by Arnold Toynbee's focus on 'creative minorities', which usurp decadent civilizations.

21 Deleuze's piece on the theme of islands concerns a collective and individual 'second birth' (DI 13).

22 Jung proposes the same solution to this paradox of the unknown as was to be later taken up by Lévi-Strauss with regard to the Melanesian term *mana*. Referring to Hubert's and Mauss's claim that *mana* should be taken as a 'category' in a quasi-Kantian sense, Jung went on to interpret *mana* as the primitive form taken by the concept of 'psychic energy' (or libido in its expanded sense) (CW 8: 61–6; cf. CW 9i: 89, 153). Lévi-Strauss objected to the predominant conception of *mana* as an essentially 'primitive' category, which also happened to be Jung's conception. 'Far from characterising certain civilisations, or archaic or semi-archaic so-called "stages" in the evolution of the human mind, might be a function of a certain way that the mind situates itself in the presence of things', in particular things that 'do not yet have a common name' (Lévi-Strauss 1950: 54). In fact, *mana*, insofar as it qualifies an unknown object, has the same function as a term like 'thingumajig'. *Mana* should therefore be treated as a 'floating signifier' which *gives a name to the class of unknown and as yet unarticulated entities*. Lévi-Strauss argues in explicitly Kantian terms that the floating signifier (or 'zero-symbol') is the condition of possibility for social organization. Mauss was right to 'invoke the notion of *mana* as grounding certain *a priori* synthetic judgments' (56), and Lévi-Strauss sets himself the task of purifying this fundamental category down to a basic 'object = x' which grounds the relation of mind to world. 'The sole function' of *mana* 'is to fill a gap between the signifier and the signified, or, more exactly, to signal the fact that . . . a relationship of non-equivalence becomes established between signifier and signified' (56). Lévi-Strauss, in fact, criticizes Jung in the same essay for inadequately purifying his conception of the symbolic character of the unconscious. In both Mauss and Jung, 'the unconscious is conceived as a symbolic system; but for Jung, the unconscious is not reduced to the system; it is filled full of symbols, and even filled with symbolized things

which form a kind of substratum to it'. He then briefly criticizes the notion of archetype on the grounds that it is impossible to see how it could be innate or acquired. 'If it is innate, one must object that, without a theological hypothesis, it is inconceivable that the content coming from experience should precede it; if it is acquired, the problem of the hereditary character of an acquired unconscious would be no less awesome than that of acquired biological features' (Lévi-Strauss 1950: 36–7). The former objection is weak, as it does not even address the biological aspects of the archetype. Despite these criticisms of Jung by Lévi-Strauss, Jung makes the same basic move in his conception of the unconscious (although Lacan is the first to explicitly take up this theory within psychoanalysis) (Lacan 1966: 690). His notion of the 'unconscious' functions exactly like *mana*: we have a relation to the unconscious only insofar as some fluid entity stands in for the unknown.

23 Jung's argument is vitiated by the analogy he draws between the minds of children and 'primitives' such as the Pueblo Indians. Even if the two are proved to share similar traits, the differences between the two would undermine the analogy.

24 Because of the dominance of the ego at this stage, the shadow is often projected onto an other. The unconscious thus first tends to appear in projected form. Lacan's early work on paranoiac identification also goes in this direction.

25 In an important passage in *Cinema 2*, Deleuze rethinks the nature of cinematic reflexivity (the film within a film) in a way that can be extended to all images, including dream images. To have a reflexive component in a film or image can often seem like a quick way for the artist to escape from the inadequacy of their work (it's bad, but he *knows* that it's bad). Reflexivity is therefore no guarantee of superior intelligence or intuition, and in contemporary 'visual culture' it could be said to have become its opposite: an unthinking reflex. Deleuze says that if reflexivity is successful in film, then it is always grounded in a 'higher justification': 'It will be observed that, in all the arts, the work within the work has often been linked to the consideration of a surveillance, an investigation, a revenge, a conspiracy or plot' (C2 77). Deleuze's subsequent reference to the play within the play in *Hamlet* is probably the key example here. The play within the play is reflexive in a specific sense. Rather than putting the whole play in question marks, so that the spectator stands *outside* the whole play, the play within the play thrusts the spectator deeper into the play, so that they are now installed *in* the whole play (as spectators in the play itself). The play within the play tells the truth about the spectators, and about the whole play, but it does so by depicting the truth of the dramatic events from a more distant, yet more interiorised perspective.

26 'The flowers of the yucca plant open for one night only. The moth takes the pollen from one of the flowers and kneads it into a little pellet. Then it visits a second flower, cuts open the pistil, lays its eggs between the ovules and then stuffs the pellet into the funnel-shaped opening of the pistil. Only once in its life does the moth carry out this complicated operation' (Jung 1919: 132).

27 Following a survey of secondary literature on the archetypes, Jean Knox has recently proposed that there exist four fundamental models for making sense of the notion of archetype, all of which can claim support from Jung's writings (Knox 2003: 30–6):

1. As 'biological entities in the form of information which is hard-wired in the genes, providing a set of instructions to the mind as well as to the body'.
2. As 'organising mental frameworks of an abstract nature, a set of rules or instructions but with no symbolic or representational content, so that they are never directly experienced'.
3. As 'core meanings which do not contain representational content and which therefore provide a central symbolic significance to our experience.'
4. As 'metaphysical entities which are eternal and are therefore independent of the body'.

It seems that there is considerable overlap between the last two models. The examples for the third model are Plato's and Kant's Ideas, which both have a transcendent and eternal status; moreover these species of Idea are not really 'representational', as Knox seems to think. Our representational concepts participate in and are guided by Ideas, but Platonic or Kantian Ideas themselves do not function like conceptual representations. We can therefore reduce these two models to one essential one, that of archetype as Idea. As none of these models is necessarily inconsistent with each other, it may be that all can be defended, and organized into a systematic theory; on the other hand it may be that only one or two, or none, of the models is defensible. I will suggest that Deleuze's philosophy can help to make sense of each of each of these three models.

28 Knox claims that Stevens does not consistently maintain the distinction between archetype as such and archetypal image, as he 'suggests that the former can be located in the limbic system of the brain and illustrates this with the mother-child archetypal system, a concept which suggests that the archetype-as-such contains specific representational content rather than being purely an "innate neuropsychic potential"' (Knox 2003: 32). It may be that if one clarifies the notion of instinct, this confusion (if such there is) will evaporate.

29 For Stevens, a passage such as this indicates the complementarity of Jungianism with ethology. He suggests that the ethological account of the sign stimulus that triggers the release of an instinctual motor pattern is practically identical to Jung's theory of archetypes. 'Having been neglected for the greater part of this century, the archetypal hypothesis is being rediscovered and rehabilitated by those psychologists and psychiatrists who have adopted the ethological orientation to their subject matter and allowed an evolutionary perspective to illuminate their thinking' (Stevens and Price 2000: 8).

30 In ethology, there are only instinctual gestalts in a restricted sense. In his early essay 'The Comparative Study of Behaviour', Lorenz complained that when Jung refers to innate behaviour patterns, he 'proceeds from the assumption of innate gestalt images, rather like pictures perceived, and indeed assumes that a 'projection' of such pictures into the motor system can take place!' (Lorenz 1939: 29). But there are only instinctual gestalts in a restricted sense. When attempting to understand how a fledgling's instinctive potential to fly is triggered by seeing the patterns of plumage under the mother's wing, the ethologists insisted that the triggering power of the image should be distinguished from the instinctual motor activity that follows it. The two aspects of the instinct do not resemble each other. When Lorenz showed how easy it was to trigger a gosling's instinctive feeding mechanisms by presenting his own face rather than its mother's, his conclusion was that the triggering image needed only to conform to the vaguest schema (two eyes and a mouth). The turkey's 'bird of prey' schema is composed of discrete geometrical elements (with, for instance, quantitative constraints on relative head size) In themselves, the various features characterizing a stimulus situation or an object had neither wholeness or gestalt. They could be analysed into discrete stimuli, whose eliciting effect was strictly summative. It was also important that the schema was presented at the appropriate time in the animal's neurological development, which underlined the rudimentary character of the image schemas. Strictly speaking, therefore, there is no need for 'images' at the animal level. 'In an animal you can demonstrate very clearly that innate responses are a combination of single responses to small, simple stimulus combinations, each of which has an eliciting effect in itself' (Evans 1975: 59). Lorenz did come to grant that Jung's theory could be defended for human beings, but only on condition that the images were understood as developmental phenomena.

31 One of the major problems with Jung's work is the frustrating lack of terminological precision. We have already seen that instinct presupposes a sort of consciousness, so Jung must here be talking about egoic, reflexive consciousness in particular. But as we have seen Bergson and Deleuze are also prey to this ambiguity.

32 After all, why should the psyche be conceived as a compensatory, negative feedback

mechanism, when Jung seems in general to be opposed to purely mechanical conceptions of the mind? Moreover, in *Transformations and Symbols of the Libido*, Jung had ascribed the emergence of human thought to the *opposite* of a homeostatic process: if anything, the process of desexualization is a positive feedback process, which increases the difference between sexual libido and thought. See my 'Rebirth through Incest', cited above, for more on desexualization. It is not clear on the compensatory model exactly *why* a homeostatic process should eventually intervene.

33 The opening words of the *Critique of Pure Reason* lay out the vision: 'Human reason has the peculiar fate in one species of its cognitions that it is burdened with questions which it cannot dismiss, since they are given to it as problems by the nature of reason itself, but which it also cannot answer, since they transcend every capacity of human reason' (Kant 1782/1787: Avii).

34 The example recalls the phenomenological psychiatry of Eugène Minkowski and Ludwig Binswanger.

35 In the 1911 edition of *Principles of Physiological Psychology*, Wundt expands the section on anomalous mental states to discuss Freud's *Interpretation of Dreams*, but Freud is taken to be the latest advocate of the tendency, already present in the Schelling school, to look to dreams and hypnotism for a 'liberation of the soul': 'It is a remarkable sign of the times that this mystical dream-psychology should find its most enthusiastic followers in neuropathology' (ibid.: 636).

36 In Plato, the pure forms are what are most real, in the sense that they are eternal and self-sufficient; the world of appearance is defined by impermanence. There are many forms, to the point that Plato has to ask whether everything (not just justice, but dirt) has its own eternal idea. In the Hellenic age, the multiplicity of Platonic forms is given order through drawing up a hierarchy of reality; the term 'archetype' now refers to one of the *primordial* forms (for instance, the original form of fire in the *Corpus Hermeticum*). As with Plato, the archetype remains the object of a special *vision*. Jung wants to retain the Platonic notion that the archetypes are what have most *reality*, but he recognizes that the history of modern Western philosophy is the story of the descent of the Ideas, the collapse of the objectivity of Ideas into subjectivity. 'From Descartes and Malebranche onward, the metaphysical value of the "idea" steadily deteriorated. It became a "thought", an internal condition of cognition' (CW 8: 136). The sense that archetypes are realities starts to fade, and they become the products of cognition. Jung goes on to say that this shift is 'clearly formulated by Spinoza: "By 'idea' I understand a conception of the mind which the mind forms by reason of its being a thinking thing"' (*Ethics* II Def. 3). He then adds that Kant in turn 'reduced the archetypes to a limited number of categories of the understanding'. From Deleuze's perspective, with these last two remarks Jung begins marching off in exactly the wrong direction. If Jung's aim is to preserve the 'reality' of Ideas, in this passage he overlooks two possible allies, Spinoza and Kant. Deleuze's work on these two thinkers puts right Jung's mistake here, and in fact helps to strengthen the possible philosophical basis for Jungian archetypes.

37 Oddly, the translation of *Psychological Types* has it that the archetype is of 'the practical employment of reason'. However, this conception is in any case not exactly wrong, as the archetype does ultimately have a practical status, as Kant makes clear in the *Critique of Pure Reason* (A569/B597). If Jung had cited other uses of the term *Urbild* in the *Critique of Pure Reason* (cf. A317/B374; A569/B597), he could have pinned it down to being another term for the Idea of God. The archetype of the understanding seems to refer to the ultimate horizon that encompasses and totalizes all our partial claims to knowledge. It is the image of absolute totality. One can see why Jung did not play up this aspect of Kant's theory, as it means that there is only one archetype. Kant himself could have stretched to three possible archetypes, inasmuch as there are three basic Ideas: those of Self, World and God. Each of these is 'primordial' with regard to its own kind of cognition, and nothing is to be gained from reducing the first two to the latter,

even if they are subordinate to it. The Self represents the thought of an ultimate ground for thinking in general; the World represents the thought of an ultimate ground for empirical representation; and God represents the whole of reality or the *ens realissimum* (cf. A397). Each corner of this ideal triangle is necessary for a full mapping of the absolute. These three Ideas are each distinguished from other universal concepts by virtue of their radically unconditioned nature, which makes them unavailable to experience, yet necessary as *regulative* Ideas which guide and constrain our cognitive conduct. The Self, for instance, is an Idea rather than a concept or an empirical intuition, because reason demands the representation of an absolute subject to which all thoughts can ultimately be attributed, even though it is not possible to prove the existence of such a subject. Kant's Idea of God, on the other hand, does not so much represent the necessity for a transcendent creator, but rather 'is a transcendental ideal which is the ground of the thoroughgoing determination that is necessarily encountered in everything existing, and which constitutes the supreme and complete material condition of its possibility' (A576/B604). This 'material condition of possibility' is a necessary thought if we are to integrate the piecemeal knowledge we have of the world, but it is not possible to argue from the concept of the supreme being to the existence of such a being (as the Ontological Argument claims to do), as we can only say that something exists when we possess the evidence of empirical intuition.

38 Kant's conception of problematic Ideas can in fact be taken in a strong sense, so that at the highest point, it concerns Ideas which are not just beyond experience yet somehow transparently available for thought, but whose very enunciation is problematic for thought as well, because they cannot be affirmed by an identical subject. Take the Idea of God. On the one hand, the existence of God cannot be deduced from the concept of God, which leaves it a merely regulative idea. But on the other hand, as soon as we surrender God to the status of a regulative fiction, then we are no longer really thinking about God, but about the coherence of our own knowledge. Hence God is an 'impossible', problematic concept in a strong sense. In order to think the Idea of God adequately – i.e. in a way that does not reduce God to an object of knowledge – one must already 'know' him or it.

39 The article in which this theory is expounded, 'The Sexual Theories of Children', is written during the period of collaboration with Jung. Freud writes that 'It is one of the most valuable results of our psychoanalytic investigations to have discovered that the neuroses . . . have no special mental content that is peculiar to them, but that, as Jung has expressed it, they fall ill of the same complexes against which we healthy people struggle as well' (SE 9: 210).

Chapter 4: The World as Symbol

1 'We ought not to be surprised to learn that Dr Jung of Zurich balked at some of Freud's conclusions. Instead of relating will to sex, he related sex to will. Thus all unconsciously, he has paved the way for a revival of the old magical idea of the will as the dynamic aspect of the self' (ibid.: 78).

2 In his 1925 Cornwall Seminar, Jung simply talks of 'skulls' and describes two cellars on top of each other (cf. Jung 1925: 23). In his 1961 autobiography he writes that there were two human skulls, but does not mention there being two cellars (Jung 1961: 183). E. A. Bennet's *What Jung Really Said* (1966) contains another account again of the story, and it is Bennet's version to which Deleuze and Guattari refer. Jung told Bennet the story in 1951 and asked Bennet to report that the dream was about *his own* house.

3 All versions also have a slightly different account of what happened when Jung told Freud the dream during the voyage home. In the earliest account, Freud says that the dream meant that there were two people that Jung wanted dead and buried (hence the two cellars). In 1961 Freud is chiefly interested in the two skulls, and Jung had a strong sense that Freud was pushing him to suggest a death wish concerning two people. Jung

objects to Freud on different grounds in each of the accounts: in the first version, he protests that in any case there is a level below the two cellars, and in the second he objects that he is newly married and really doesn't have any death wishes at present.

4 Deleuze and Guattari do not mention that Jung has a multiplicity of different versions of this dream and of the conversation with Freud. But Jung's inability to remember whether Freud suggested that he had a death wish against his wife or against his parents unfortunately does not help prove anything.

5 Deleuze implicitly takes up this distinction in *Difference and Repetition*, but reinterprets it within the context of the theory of intensity. 'The sign is indeed an effect, but an effect with two aspects: in one of these it expresses, *qua* sign, the productive dissymmetry, in the other it tends to cancel it. The sign is of a completely different order to the symbol; nevertheless, it makes way for it by implying an internal difference' (DR 20, translation modified). We will see how intensive signs 'make way' for symbols first when we turn below to Kant's remarks about symbolism in nature.

6 In *Difference and Repetition* Deleuze appears to change his mind about the efficacy of this Jungian critique of Freud. He writes that 'a decisive moment in psychoanalysis occurred when Freud gave up, in certain respects, the hypothesis of real childhood events, which would have played the part of ultimate disguised terms, in order to substitute the power of fantasy which is immersed in the death instinct, where everything is already masked and disguised' (DR 17). But there is more to this statement than meets the eye. First, Freud changed his mind about the role of real childhood events long before he adopted the theory of the death drive (in 1920). Why, then, is Deleuze correlating this change with the introduction of the death drive? As we will see, it turns out that after criticizing Freud's notion of the death drive from a Jungian point of view, Deleuze later changes his attitude towards it. The theory of the death drive, argues Deleuze, is what allows Freud to move to a purely symbolic theory of repetition: 'Repetition is in essence symbolic; symbols or simulacra are the letter of repetition itself. Difference is included in repetition by way of disguise and by the order of the symbol' (ibid.). Thus the death drive allows Freud to move to a theory in which sign is transcended by symbols, and fantasy is never reduced to real situations. In other words, Freud overcomes Jung's objection and is ultimately in agreement with him with regard to the notion of the symbol. However, Deleuze's reading is tendentious. We will see that what Deleuze finds in Freud's death drive is almost entirely what he has himself put there, and in fact he remains much more Jungian than Freudian; hence it is no surprise that he returns to his critique of Freud from *Anti-Oedipus* onwards. Deleuze's enthusiasm for Freud is shortlived, lasting from 1967 (*Coldness and Cruelty*) to 1972 (*Anti-Oedipus*) at the latest.

7 'The analysis which the literary historian makes of the poet's material is exactly comparable with the method of psychoanalysis' (CW 4: 146). This is said in 1912, when Jung still classed himself as a 'psychoanalyst'.

8 This is reminiscent of Kant's qualification of the Cartesian *cogito*, which he says really refers to 'an indeterminate empirical intuition' that I exist as a thinking being, rather than pointing to an immediate connection between thinking and existence (which would allow one to infer that everything that thinks exists) (Kant 1787: B422). Just as the Self is an Idea for Kant, rather than a concept, the symbol is image of something that exists, but whose nature is indeterminate.

9 Certain kinds of psychic material mean next to nothing if simply broken down, but display a wealth of meaning if, instead of being broken down, that meaning is reinforced and extended by all the conscious means at our disposal – by the so-called method of amplification. The images or symbols of the collective unconscious yield their distinctive values only when subjected to a synthetic mode of treatment (CW 7: 81).

10 See Charlotte Otten's *Lycanthropy Reader* (Otten 1987), which contains extracts from the major medieval texts on lycanthropy. The *were-* prefix of the term 'werewolf' originally

indicates the Old English term 'man', so that werewolf simply means 'wolfman'. Wolves were the most common beast of prey in medieval Europe.

11 In the same way that the sublime threatens at each instant to overwhelm the imagination's act of synthesis, the operation of symbolism and symbolisation threatens at each instant to overwhelm this other act of imagination which is the schema. So much so that between symbolism and the sublime, there will obviously be all sorts of echoes, as if they brought about the emergence of a sort of ground [*fond*] which is irreducible to knowledge, and which will testify to something else in us besides a simple faculty of knowing. Feel how beautiful it is. (Ibid.)

12 Of course, Hegel's *Phenomenology of Spirit* is perhaps the best-known philosophical example of such a teleological conception of unconscious activity. At the end of each phenomenological movement on the winding path to full self-consciousness, a new object 'presents itself to consciousness without its understanding how this happens' so that the dialectic always proceeds 'behind the back of consciousness' (Hegel 1807: 56).

13 Citations are from D. W. Smith's translation of this essay in *Angelaki* 5: 3, 2000; the second reference is to this translation.

14 'Our imagination strives to progress toward infinity, while our reason demands absolute totality as a real idea' (Kant 1790: Ak. 250).

15 Deleuze's aim (particularly in the 'Idea of Genesis' essay) is to show that in the *Critique of Judgment* Kant changes his transcendental method from an analysis of the conditions of cognition to a proper genesis of the relations of the faculties. Deleuze claims that Kant had thus already answered the calls of Maimon and Fichte for a genetic account of cognition which would avoid the factual, quasi-empirical premises required by the analyses of the conditions of knowledge and practical reason. 'The critique in general ceases to be a simple *conditioning* in order to become a transcendental formation, a transcendental culture, a transcendental genesis' (DI 61/62). Deleuze's argument is restricted to following the chain of deductions and geneses in the third *Critique*, but here I focus on the phenomenological (in Hegel's sense) aspect of the geneses; that is, the transitions as they take place in the subject (the 'formation' or the movement of 'culture' in the sense of *Bildung*, rather than the genesis as such). Deleuze's suggestion of a 'transcendental culture' already implies this phenomenological moment (although only in Hegel's sense that a 'for-the-subject' can be distinguished from 'for-us' the philosophers).

16 See Norbert Aujoulat's *Lascaux: Movement, Space and Time* for an account, with photographs, of the crystal formations at Lascaux (Aujoulat 2005: 42–7). He writes that 'the conjunction of these calcite deposits and the aurochs head theme, which is found as many times as this concretion exists in Lascaux (i.e. seven), is quite remarkable' (46). Hearths and lamps were used to illuminate the caverns.

17 Eliade suggests that streams, galleries of mines and caves served initially as symbols of the Earth-Mother (he alerts us to the etymology of the oracle at Delphi – 'delph' is uterus in Greek). If that is true, then 'everything that lies in the belly of the earth is alive, albeit in a state of gestation. In other words, the ores extracted from the mines are in some way *embryos*: they grow slowly as though in obedience to some temporal rhythm other than that of vegetable and animal organisms. They nevertheless do grow – they "grow ripe" in their telluric darkness' (Eliade 1956: 42). In these terms, the alchemist can be called an accelerator of embryonic development. He accelerated the speed of development, precipitated the crossing of thresholds, and discovered intensive matter.

18 In Novalis's description of the ascent of the miners into 'earth's dark womb' in *Heinrich von Ofterdingen* (Novalis 1802: 79), a hermit tells Heinrich that 'You miners are almost astrologers in reverse . . . To them the sky is the book of the future, while to you the earth reveals monuments of the primeval world' (ibid.: 86). The suspended time of the crystalline cavern would no doubt provoke the explorer to wonder if he has found himself back inside the womb of the earth.

19 Schelling went on to develop the distinction between schema and symbol. A genuine symbol is a 'representation of the absolute with absolute indifference of the universal and the particular'. In other words, clarifies Beach, 'it simultaneously represents a particular object or image as standing for some universal idea, while it also represents the universal idea, in turn, as being concretely active in some particular object or event' (Beach 1994: 35).

20 Deleuze points out that this why the discussion of symbolism occurs within a 'Deduction'.

> 'The problem of a transcendental deduction is always objective . . . But if we consider the judgment of the sublime, we can see that no objective problem of deduction is posed in this regard. The sublime is indeed related to objects, but only through a projection of the state of our soul; and this projection is immediately possible, because it is directed toward what is formless or deformed in the object . . . [T]he great difference between the sublime and the beautiful is that the pleasure of the beautiful results from the form of the object. Kant says that this characteristic is enough to ground the necessity of a "deduction" for the judgment of taste. No matter how indifferent we may be to the existence of the object, there is nonetheless an object *in relation* to which, *on the occasion* of which we experience the free harmony of our understanding and our imagination'. (DI 63/64)

21 In the French bibliography of Deleuze's writings (published at the end of *The Desert Island*, a collection of early articles), all texts published prior to 1953 are omitted, apparently in accordance with wishes expressed by Deleuze prior to his death. An earlier American bibliography contains a list of an initial group of writings, published from 1945 to 1947, when Deleuze was in his early twenties (Murphy 1996). These writings are on quite disparate subjects, but thematically can be grouped under two headings. The first are the somewhat libido-soaked musings on sexuality, centred on a pronounced cult of woman (e.g. 'Description of a Woman'). The second group is composed of two curious articles from 1946 which are hard to categorize, but which have something in common: the article on Malfatti and 'From Christ to the Bourgeoisie' was published in the literary journal *Espace*, and combines esoteric, elitist political ideas with a dialectical account of the relationship of Christian 'interiority' and modern capitalist bourgeois subjectivity.

22 Called 'Jean' in the French translation; sometimes also called 'Giovanni'.

23 It is not *a priori* a mistake to take a philosophical text written by a twenty-one-year-old seriously. There are rare examples of writings by extremely young philosophers studied today in their own right, perhaps the best comparison being Schelling, who produced some extraordinary and powerful writings at the age of nineteen, still studied closely today by august and bearded philosophers and historians. Schelling's case is more extreme than Deleuze's, as he ceased to publish anything after the age of thirty-four, and instead developed his ideas solely in lectures over the next thirty years. Deleuze, of course, remained a prolific writer right up until his suicide in 1995, at the age of seventy. Deleuze's motivations in retracting his 'acknowledgement' of these texts, and what in particular he might have wanted to disown, could only be uncovered through a combination of intellectual biography and speculation.

24 Papus appended a detailed analysis of Malfatti's *Mathesis* to his 1894 medical dissertation *L'Anatomie philosophique et ses divisions*, and in his ensuing occult works he continued to refer to Malfatti at crucial points. Reggio notes that another Martinist, Paul Sédir, gave lectures on Malfatti at the turn of the century to the *Amities spirituelles* organization in Paris (Reggio 2004). The new edition of *Anarchy and Hierarchy* for which Deleuze wrote the introduction was issued in a limited edition by a small publishing house, Griffon d'Or, which published books mostly on occult themes in the immediate aftermath of the Second World War. They published a number of books on Martinism. The medievalist Marie-Madeleine Davy edited a series entitled 'Sources and Fires'

(*Sources et feux*) for Griffon d'Or. Deleuze had dedicated his article 'From Christ to the Bourgeoisie' to her, and had attended intellectual soirées hosted by her during and after the war (attended by Pierre Klossowski, Jacques Lacan and Jean Paulhan). In the book series directed by her are listed a book on palmistry (with a preface by Davy herself), Cyrille Wilczkowski's *Man and the Zodiac: Essay on Typological Synthesis*, selections from Paracelsus, Jean Richer's 1947 book on the esoteric significance of the works of Gérard de Nerval, Strindberg's *Inferno* and, rather on its own, Lucien Goldmann's *Man, Community and the World in the Philosophy of Immanuel Kant.*

25 In Réné Guénon's negative review of the Deleuze–Malfatti volume, he criticizes Malfatti's knowledge of the Indian tradition for being based on fragmentary and inaccurate information. As this tradition was 'little known' during the nineteenth century, writers such as Malfatti seem to have been content to invent a spurious symbolism which made up for their lack of knowledge of the 'true symbolism' (Guénon 1947: 88–9). Deleuze's approach can be seen as directed against Guénonism, in that he does not believe that mathesis and esoteric philosophy must necessarily be rooted in original, pure traditions. Mircea Eliade claims that the decline of the occult in France can be partly attributed to the influence of Guénon, so Deleuze's affirmation of Malfatti's work, with his insistence on the relevance of *mathesis* for science and philosophy, can be seen as an attempt to rescue occult philosophy precisely through the affirmation of its most syncretic tendencies. Guénon had been initiated to a number of occult 'orders' in France (he had been initiated into the Martinist 'order' before breaking with Papus and departing in 1909), only to be disappointed with all of them for their syncretism and patchwork of various occult sources, not all of them demonstrably ancient. After coming to the conclusion that the only genuinely alive esoteric tradition of thought and practice was to be found in the East, he became a Muslim in 1912. He published excoriating critiques of contemporary theosophy and spiritualism, and in 1930 moved to Egypt, where he lived until his death. He inaugurated an approach to esoteric history which he called 'Traditionalism' and which was founded on the Tantric view of cosmic-historical cycles. The Western world was irredeemably decadent, and had entered 'Kali Yuga', the end of the cosmic cycle, a period characterized by dissolution, spiritual anarchy and revolt. Nothing could be done to reverse the process, and the best the individual could do was reconnect with properly traditional sources of wisdom or convert to Islam or the Indo-Tibetan tradition. 'Guénon denied not only the authenticity of modern Western so-called occultism but also the ability of any Western individual to contact a valid esoteric organization . . . He pointed out that any endeavour to practise any of the occult arts represents, for contemporary [Western] man, a serious mental and even physical risk' (Eliade 1974: 66). Guénon's influence led to an increasing emphasis on searching for 'pure' traditions, absolved from any charge of syncretism. Guénon is most critical of Malfatti's presentation of the correlation between symbolism and number, which he takes to be arbitrary both in choice and in their ordering: Malfatti has devoted himself to discovering in the symbolism that he happens to have at hand 'things which are certainly not there'. It is this approach, Guénon suggests, which has been unfortunately most influential. Malfatti's work is flawed in exactly the way that the *fin-de-siècle* occultist tradition is flawed. Occultism relies on inadequate information, strives to overcome traditional interpretations of symbolism, and conjures up 'an assemblage of reveries without the least solidity'. The principal interest in the republication of the book, therefore, is that we can now refer these occultist vices back to their source. Guénon is silent about the young philosopher Deleuze's attempt to find philosophical significance in the text in question.

26 The second part of her *Initiation à la symbolique roman* (originally published as *Essai sur la symbolique roman* in 1955) is entitled 'The Royal Road of the Symbol'. She is heavily endebted to Eliade and Jung's conception of the symbol, as well as Husserlian phenomenology. For Eliade, 'the symbol reveals certain aspects of reality – the most

profound – which defy the access of consciousness'. 'The symbol uncovers a new world. All dialectical construction is transcended, and one must return to intuitive nature of the understanding. Symbolism situates itself on the plane of essences [*sur le plan des essences*] . . . As pure science, symbolism is an impersonal science' (Davy 1977: 97).

27 The word for number here is *chiffre*, which can mean 'cipher' as well as 'number'. Malfatti takes this distinction between sensible symbol and numerical hieroglyph once again back to Neoplatonism, this time to Dionysius the Areopagite. He cites a passage from Dionysius's *Ecclesiastical Hierarchies* in order to postulate a distinction between sensible symbol and ideal, numerological content:

> There is in us a double hierarchy, sensible and intelligible, due to the nature of contemplation. To the first correspond human symbols, and to the second, angelic intuitions. Now contemplation is the immediate application of spirit to that which is proposed, bypassing the senses. The symbols of a hierarchy of this kind are therefore mysteries for the profane and those who are strangers to the assembly of the faithful; at all times contemplation, as supreme knowledge, has need of faith and it is called a mystery. However, symbols only remain mysteries for those who are not yet initiated. (Ecc. hierarch. PG III, c. 381–2 C; cited in Malfatti 1845: 9–10)

28 Malfatti's original German is in fact not as weird as the French translation: 'unsrer geistigen und leiblichen Zeugung, wo sie in ihrem Culminationsacte einerseits an das Göttliche, andrerseits an die Natur sich anschliessen'.

29 This identification of Malfatti's theosophy as 'Tantric' may require some justification, at which only a minimal attempt can of course be made here. There are two distinct issues, first of the historical status of Tantrism, and then of whether Malfatti's Hindu mathesis can properly be called 'Tantric', given that he does not use that term. André Padoux, a prominent contemporary scholar of the Tantras, has noted that although the 'Tantras' are an established body of Indian texts dating from the early medieval period, the term 'Tantrism' is a recent Western category (cf. Padoux 1990, 2002). The meaning of the term 'Tantra' itself is unclear (warp, weave, web, development, unfolding, have all been suggested as translations; the root is *tan*, to extend, continue, develop), but the term could simply mean 'treatise' or 'exposition'. But it could be argued that the term 'Tantrism' can be justified if it denotes a distinct set of practices whose existence can be isolated and traced throughout the history of Indian religion. Given that there are many thematic continuities between the medieval Tantras and passages in the ancient *Atharva Veda*, it seems reasonable to give this tendency a distinct name. It is of course one of the traditions of Tantrism that it was a secret doctrine before the arrival of *Kali Yuga*, after which the secrets were made public in the Tantric texts. There is no reason why this might not be historically correct, and aspects of Hugh Urban's recent work on secrecy in Bengali Tantra could even support such a possibility (Urban 2001). Taking such a view would also help to justify the application of the label 'Tantric' to Malfatti's *naturphilosophische* version of Hindu mathesis, which is the second possible point of contention. There are, nevertheless, real questions about how much was known about Tantrism in Europe in the early to mid-eighteenth century. Malfatti does not go into great detail about the sources of his interpretation of Indian ideas about number and the body, mentioning only Schlegel's *Über das Sprache und Weisheit der Indien* [*On the Language and Wisdom of the Indians*] (1808), the work of the idealist mythographer Friedrich Creuzer (whose enormous *Symbolik und Mythologie der alten Völker, besonders der Griechen* [*Symbolism and Mythology of the Ancient Peoples, with especial reference to the Greeks*] (1810–1843) was also very influential on Schelling and Hegel) and Niklas Müller's *Über Glauben, Wissen, und Kunst der alten Hindus* (1822). The work of Schlegel and Creuzer had indeed been instrumental in 'reorienting' idealism towards India; in 1808, Creuzer had departed from eighteenth-century predecessors by tracing the origin of ancient religion to India, rather than to Greece or Egypt (cf. Williamson 2004: 129). Müller's book is the only one to contain detailed discussion of Indian esotericism (Malfatti also

derived the remarkable illustrations in his book from Müller). But still little or nothing was said in these works about the Tantras and their adherents, and it is usually thought that Tantrism entered Western consciousness with the researches of the Calcutta magistrate, John Woodroffe, whose most famous exposition of Tantrism, *The Serpent Power* (1918), was published under the pseudonym 'Arthur Avalon'. The early French phenomenologist of religion, Paul Masson-Oursel, for instance, avers that before Woodroffe, little had been written in Europe on Tantrism: 'a chapter of Burnouf, some remarks of Augustin Barth, various researches of Louis de la Vallée Poussin, constituted before 1913 all that was written on the Tantras, whose encyclopaedic character, ritualistic nature and bizarre mysticism repelled the analysts' (cited in Taylor 2002: 140). On the other hand, Tantrism had been known about in early nineteenth century Europe under various names (Shivaism, Civaism, Shaktism, and also through the names of various Tantric sub-sects). In his *A Sketch of the Religious Sects of the Hindus* (1828), for instance, Horace Hayman Wilson provided a vivid sketch of the excremental practices of an extreme Tantric sect, the Aghoris, whose 'wand and water-pot were a staff set with bones and the upper half of a skull' (Wilson 1828: 233–4). His detached mode of description seems to have been uncommon, as is attested by the presence of other more censorious accounts. In a later account, for instance, *The Buddhism of Tibet* (1895) by L. Augustine Waddell, Tantrism is essentially presented as a demonic religion, populated by malignant 'fiendesses' who bestowed supernatural power, and whose 'mysticism became a silly mummery of unmeaning jargon and "magic circles"' (mandalas) (Waddell 1895: 14–16). Works by Joseph Görres and Joseph von Hammer-Purgstall (the notorious *Mysterium Baphometis revelatum* [*The Mystery of the Baphomet Revealed*], 1818) also discussed and speculated on oriental magic and mysticism. Further research needs to be done into the question of Malfatti's possible sources for his understanding of Hindu mysticism. For the moment it can minimally be said that Malfatti's interest in Hindu mysticism alights on all those aspects which were taken up in Tantrism. As for Deleuze, his references to the 'Tantric egg' are sporadic but insistent, and a number of correspondences suggest themselves, which can only be touched on intermittently in this chapter. Deleuze's conceptions of 'power' in *Nietzsche and Philosophy*, as well as his notion of immanence, may also be endebted to Tantrism. In her study of John Woodroffe, Kathleen Taylor notes Masson-Oursel's claim that Tantra is 'a triumph of the conception of immanence' and 'Man's conquest of himself', by means of which 'man can realise the divine in him and outside him' (Taylor 2002: 140). Taylor suggests that this conception, together with the claim that the body is not an obstacle to liberation, and there is no opposition between nature and spirit, sums up the kernel of Woodroffe's own presentation of the significance of Tantrism. Alongside Woodroffe's own *The World as Power* (1930), the right-wing occultist Julius Evola's *The Yoga of Power* (first published as *L'uomo come potenza* [*Man as Power*] in 1925) also outlines a Tantric metaphysics of power.

30 Manulāl Miśra, an early-twentieth century systematizer of the beliefs of the Kartābhajā sect of Tantrism in Bengal, wrote that one of the goals of Tantrism is a kind of 'inverted' sexual act, in which the male absorbs the female principle, in order to 'become a woman' (Urban 2001: 88). 'First, one must cultivate devotion with a female companion . . . and develop the Body of Ecstasy. Then one must arouse the arrested semen, and prepare it in the Pingalā vein . . . As a result of practice with a female partner, the Female Nature arises within his own body. Once he has attained the female nature, an actual female partner is no longer needed. The *sādhaka* himself experiences the female nature'. Urban notes the unique problems of sexual politics that occur within the Tantric tradition which both glorifies women, while tending to treat them as means for the male to attain his own 'divinised androgynic body' (ibid.).

31 At the outset of this study we discussed Bergson's theory about the wasp's instinctual sympathy for the caterpillar, and mentioned Raymond Ruyer's objections to this theory.

Ruyer went on to suggest that Bergson's theory of instinct nevertheless perfectly describes the actualization of the sexual instinct in human beings. Bergson's argument for the presence of sympathy involved an invocation of the phylogenetic *unity* of the wasp and caterpillar, but Ruyer now claims that this unity is much better situated at the level of the egg, the very first stage of ontogenesis, using the model of embryological consciousness. He appeals to vegetal hermaphroditism in order to get his strange idea afloat. 'The male and the female of a dioecious species are two distinct organisms. The male and female organs of a monoecious species are formed in two regions of the same embryo' (Ruyer 1959: 177). Monoecious (haploid) plants grow unisexual male and female flowers on different parts of their bodies, while hermaphroditic organisms grow their male and female parts in different regions of the egg. With dioecious (diploid) plants and animals, the sexually different organs assume a spatially distinct existence in different vehicles (male and female). Ruyer takes this to indicate that between hermaphroditism and sexual differentiation it is but a small step: the organism divides itself into two relatively autonomous parts now separated in space – each of which, nevertheless, in Bergson's words, 'continues the work of organisation'.

Chapter 5: Jung, Leibniz and the Differential Unconscious

1 One of these early works was *Defensive Measures for Cholera*, written in 1832 at the height of the European cholera epidemic. In it Fechner presents a series of ingenious protective measures *for* the rampant cholera bacterium in its struggle against the human species; the work was the most popular of Fechner's works, running to four editions (Lowrie 1946: 33). The *Little Book of Life after Death* is the only work mentioned by name in Deleuze's discussions of Fechner.

2 However, he qualifies his support of Fechner's position by stating that 'this conclusion [the last sentence in the above citation] is a little incautious, because the psychic process remains more or less the same whether conscious or not. A "representation" exists not only through its 'representedness', but – and this is the main point – it also exists in its own psychic right' (CW 166n.).

3 The fact is that Jung interpreted these 'prospective potencies' in a bizarrely literal manner. He was not averse to attributing premonitory powers to himself either. In *Memories, Dreams and Reflections*, Jung recounts, with remarkable ingenuousness, a story about a demonstration of his psychic powers in front of Freud. On a visit to Vienna in 1909, he had solicited Freud's views on parapsychology, but had been met with a complete rejection of the whole field. As he listened to Freud's objections, he felt a strange sensation in his diaphragm, as if it was becoming a red-hot vault of iron. The next moment there was a loud crack in the bookcase, and Jung triumphantly exclaimed, 'There, that is an example of a so-called catalytic exteriorisation phenomenon'. Come on, Freud retorted, 'that is sheer bosh'. 'You are mistaken, Herr Professor', said Jung, 'and to prove my point I now predict that in a moment there will be another loud report!' And sure enough, says Jung, another detonation went off in Freud's bookcase. Jung comments that he knew beyond all doubt that the noise would come. 'Freud only stared aghast at me', he admits (Jung 1961: 179). In a letter to Freud of 2 April 1909, directly after the bookcase incident, Jung admits to feeling '*sentiments d'incomplétude*' about his 'spookery' with regard to the bookcase. Nevertheless, he is adamant that there is something to it, and proceeds to justify its possibility in the terms he will later used in the passage from *Transformations and Symbols* cited above: 'If there is a 'psychoanalysis' there must also be a 'psychosynthesis' which creates future events according to the same laws' (Freud/Jung 1974: 138J). In his next letter, Freud is certainly none too pleased about 'the poltergeist business' (139F), but responds by presenting his own speculations on numerical coincidences, with relation to his fear of dying between the ages of 61 and 62. He concludes 'Consequently, I shall receive further news of your investigations of the spook complex with the interest one accords

to a charming delusion in which one does not oneself participate' (ibid.).

4 Jung uses *Sinn* or *Sinngehalt* in such passages. In philosophy since Frege and Husserl, this term has often been translated as 'sense', in distinction to *Bedeutung* (translated as 'reference'). The English term 'meaning' has been held to be too overdetermined and ambiguous, while 'sense' is also etymologically closer to the original German. Frege and Husserl clarified this distinction by stating that the *Bedeutung* of an expression is the thing to which it refers, while the *Sinn* is the 'ideal' content which is invoked by the expression, and which cannot be reduced to its reference. 'Sense' allows one to make intelligible how the expressions 'morning star' and 'evening star' can continue to be distinguished, even though we now know that both expressions refer to the same object. There is no indication that Jung was familiar with the work of Frege or Husserl, but I will translate *Sinn* as 'sense' to avoid confusion in what follows, because in the passages where Deleuze alludes to synchronicity, he uses the French term *sens* (sense), which has been translated as 'sense'. Although Deleuze's *Logic of Sense* could theoretically be translated as *Logic of Meaning*, 'sense' has been used because the Frege/Husserl distinction is important to him. Obviously there is more in Deleuze's use of the concept of 'sense' than there is in Jung's, but I will be suggesting that Deleuze's use is at least compatible with Jung's. While not wanting to put any philosophical weight on this, I see no reason not to translate Jung's '*Sinn*' as 'sense' for the purposes of our discussion.

5 In 'Synchronicity' itself, Jung argues that 'natural laws are *statistical* truths, which means that they are completely valid only when we are dealing with macrophysical quantities' (CW 8: 421). It looks like instances of acausality will therefore be primarily instanced at the microphysical level. But in Jung's helpful 'Résume' to the work, included in the English translation of the Jung and Pauli volume, but not published in the *Collected Works*, Jung simply argues that 'since causality is a *statistical* truth, it holds good only on average and thus leaves room for *exceptions* which somehow be experienceable, that is to say, *real*. I try to regard synchronistic events as acausal exceptions of this kind' (Jung and Pauli 1955: 144). First, the claim about the statistical truth of causality is not connected with 'macrophysical quantities', but with 'averages'. While microphysical quantities cannot be experienced, exceptional singular events clearly can. Second, he even states straight out that these exceptions must be experienceable. The reference to quantum indeterminacy gets the essay off to a bad start.

6 This passage has an almost exact correlate in Deleuze's *Difference and Repetition* (DR 3).

7 Presumably 'unique or rare event' really means a unique or rare combination of two or more events.

8 Kant attributed 'the greatest weight' to this incident (which took place in 1756), in a remarkable letter to Charlotte von Knobloch of 10 August 1763 (Kant 1999: Ak. 10: 47). He took care to have the details of the incident confirmed to him by a friend who had questioned those present at the fateful party in Gothenburg seven years before. However, in 1766, Kant published *Dreams of a Spirit Seer*, a satire on Swedenborg's metaphysical speculations, in which he mentioned the same tale again in less elevated tones: 'The reader will probably ask what on earth could have adduced me to engage in such a despicable business as that of spreading fairy-tales abroad, which every rational being would hesitate to listen to with patience – and indeed, not merely disseminating them but actually making them the subject of philosophical investigations. However, since the philosophy, with which we have prefaced the work, was no less a fairy story from the *cloud-cuckoo-land* of metaphysics, I can see nothing improper about having them make their appearance on the stage together' (Kant 1766: Ak. 2: 356). The relations between Swedenborg, Kant and Jung are discussed in detail in Bishop 2000.

9 Freud finds the reference to the passage in Daniel Sanders's *Wörterbuch der Deutschen Sprache*. The passage is from the twenty-eighth lecture of Schelling's late lecture series on mythology, published posthumously.

10 The contemporary selection of 'key readings' on synchronicity is actually entitled *Jung*

on Synchronicity and the Paranormal; it contains an excellent introduction to Jung's writings on synchronicity by Roderick Main (Main 1997).

11 In these experiments, two subjects face each other, while one turns up one-by-one a series of twenty-five cards which the other cannot see. There are five sets of five cards, each set bearing a star, square, circle, wavy lines, or cross. The other subject then has to guess the symbols as the first one looks at them. Rhine found that some subjects scored higher than was probable.

12 The model here echoes the model used by Kant from his earliest writings. The fact that this model of a 'third' which grounds the synthesis of contingent terms was continuous in Kant's writings from his early rationalist period through to his critical period is worth noting here, as any study of Jung and Deleuze will also have to be alert to possible points of intersection between rationalism and Kantianism. Deleuze returns to Leibnizian theory *after* Kant in order to reclaim from Leibniz a theory of the unconscious. Jungian synchronicity similarly mines the pre-Kantian rationalist tradition of Leibniz and Malebranche in the wake of Kant's emphasis on spatio-temporal finitude. Following Leibniz, the early Kant had contended that if there was to be a principle of sufficient reason, it had to function independently of the principle of contradiction; the principle that 'everything must have its reason' must be, in Kant's later critical terms, synthetic rather than analytic. Kant's first metaphysical work, the *New Elucidation of the First Principles of Metaphysical Cognition*, is an attempt to reformulate Leibniz's two principles. What is sought in the principle of sufficient reason is the 'determining reason' for non-necessary (i.e. synthetic) conjunctions between subject and predicate (Kant 1755: 1:392). How does Kant deal with the options left open by Leibniz for providing an ultimate ground for the selection for existence of 'synthetic' or contingent possibilities? Throughout his philosophical career, Kant will often address the situation formally by simply saying that *synthesis requires a third*. 'Where is the third thing', Kant asks in the first *Critique*, 'that is always requisite for a synthetic proposition in order to connect with each other concepts that have no logical (analytical) affinity?' (Kant 1781/1787: A259). Synthesis for Kant is always a contingent connection, as opposed to the analytic connections involved in logical statements of conceptual identity or inclusion. Being sensitive to the problems in accounting for causality (which were already apparent before Hume's criticisms of the concept), Kant refused to state that the answer to what grounds the empirical synthesis of contingent events is simply 'causality'. Before Hume's contention that causality could not be derived from sense impressions, Leibniz had rejected the reduction of the relation of ground and consequent to the real relation of causality because of misgivings about substance-substance interaction; this was one of his reasons for affirming pre-established harmony. Thus the whole problem was that causality itself had to be accounted for, as did the gamut of other non-derivable concepts such as substance, causality, existence, possibility, necessity, etc. Kant's answer as to the ultimate nature of the *tertium quid* would vary throughout his career but the 'triangular' structure of synthetic *a priori* cognition will remain constant. The development of the critical project arises out of Kant's renovation of the 'principle of sufficient reason' (or, as Kant put it, 'determining reason') in the 'pre-critical' writings. Whereas the status of this 'principle' in Kant's early writings remained unclear, by the time of the critique, the *a priori* rules that govern synthesis are taken to be two sets of pure forms, actualized by the subject: the pure forms of space and time, and the pure concepts of the understanding (categories). In the first *Critique* time (A155/B194) and then experience in general (A157/B196) are said to be the 'third things' that guarantee *a priori* synthesis; more complex 'thirds' follow in the ensuing *Critiques*.

13 But at this point a contradiction arises in Schopenhauer's theory of death. For, on the one hand, death is the apotheosis of the will because it brings with it the extinction of personal identity, and identification with the will as ineluctable, *impersonal* force. Hence palingenesis occurs when the ego dissolves, and the subject identifies itself with the

impersonal will. The will is ultimately undifferentiated; there is only One Will. In his reflection 'On Death and its Relation to the Indestructibility of our Inner Nature' in the second volume of the *The World as Will and Representation*, Schopenhauer identifies the subject, taken in itself, with this impersonal will: 'The I . . . is the dark point in consciousness, just as on the retina the precise point of entry of the optic nerve is blind, the brain itself is wholly insensible, the body of the sun is dark, and the eye sees everything except itself' (Schopenhauer 1844: 491). But on the other hand, he also upholds the doctrine of eternal, intelligible character, which implies that there is some form of noumenal differentiation between 'types of will'. In the essay on fate, he speculates that 'at the hour of death, the mysterious forces . . . which determine man's eternal fate, crowd together and come into action'. Judas always will have been Judas because he already was Judas: a space had been made for Judas in the cosmic scheme of things.

14 The classic discussion is in the first letter to Arnauld, May 1686 (Leibniz 1686–7: 72f.).

15 Following Lacan's criticisms, Jean Laplanche argues that Freud's postulation of 'a hypothetical initial state in which the organism would form a closed unit in relation to its surroundings' (Laplanche 1970: 70) is inconsistent with two fundamental Freudian theories: (1) that the first fulfilment is a repetition of an 'experience of satisfaction' in relation to an *object*, and (2) that there is no initial 'identity', only a primary *identification* with others. Lacan and Serge Leclaire teased out two kinds of identification (with the 'ideal-ego' and then the 'ego-ideal'), which were already at work in the paper on narcissism itself (Lacan 1953–4: 129–42). Lacan's theory of the imaginary is an attempt to sort out this unstable oscillation in Freud between 'monadic' and 'identificatory' narcissism, by giving the oscillation dialectical form. So the reduction of doubling and the uncanny to primary narcissism in 'The Uncanny' is problematic.

Chapter 6: The Occult Unconscious

1 Bergson himself refers to Spinoza here in the relevant passage: 'It might be said, by slightly distorting the terms of Spinoza, that it is to get back to *natura naturans* that we break away from *natura naturata*' (Bergson 1932: 58). The difference between Bergson and Spinoza here is that there is no 'breaking away' from 'natured nature' (nature as product) in Spinoza, as *Deus sive Natura* is in itself eternal. Bergson is dealing with finite, temporal existence, so the breaking away from nature as product involves a genuine antagonism with nature: in order to be 'installed in the mobile reality . . . to grasp it intuitively . . . it must do itself violence, reverse the direction of the operation by which it ordinarily thinks' (Bergson 1903: 190). Normally, the mind operates in the service of adaptation. But when using intuition, the mind has to turn back on itself, do violence to its intelligence.

2 Very little has been written on Deleuze and Guattari's unusual ideas about sorcery. See Lee (2003) and Jacques-Chaquin (1982). Their influence is to be found most powerfully hitherto in the incendiary sufi mysticism of Peter Lamborn Wilson (aka Hakim Bey), whose writings can be found at www.hermetic.com. Cf also Bey (2003).

3 Gustav Fechner's pantheism also involves the affirmation of inferior and superior consciousnesses, and this may provide the key to understanding how Deleuze would go about reconciling Bergson and Fechner, who initially appear to be opposed. At the outset of *Elements of Psychophysics*, Fechner says that there are two species of psychophysics: 'inner' and 'outer' psychophysics. Whereas the object of outer psychophysics is to relate external physical stimuli to mental sensations, the object of inner psychophysics is to relate the stimuli of the nervous system to our sensations. His concentration on 'outer psychophysics' arises because he admits that 'it is only this part that is available to immediate experience' (Fechner 1860: I, 9). In 1860, study of the nervous system was in its infancy. But Fechner nevertheless stipulates that 'there can be no development of outer psychophysics without constant regard to inner psychophysics, in view of the fact that the body's external world is functionally related to

the mind only by mediation of the body's internal world' (ibid.). Once the possibility of inner psychophysics is taken into account, it is possible to correlate the relations between external and internal nature in more detail, because one can, so Fechner believes, envisage a hierarchy of 'nervous systems', from the most simple to the most complex, that parallels the development of types of consciousness, to the relatively unconscious to the *superconsciousness* [*Überbewusstsein*] one can postulate in the case of divine beings.

4 Robert Montgomery states that 'if one were forced to described the thought of the later Lawrence in one word, that word would have to be "theosophical". During the period from *Women in Love* to his death, the important new influences on him were theosophical, and his most important writings were based on ideas drawn from theosophical sources' (Montgomery 1994: 168). Lawrence's account of the *chakras* is borrowed from a curious esoteric interpretation of the Book of Revelation, *The Apocalypse Unsealed* (1910) by James Pryse, a member of Madame Blavatsky's group of Theosophists. Pryse reads the Book of Revelation as a veiled account of occult anatomy, derived from ancient Tantric sources (see Tindall 1949). For instance, the 'seven breaths' and 'five winds' of John of Patmos are related to the seven *tattvas* and the five *pranas*. In Tantrism, 'kundalini' denotes vital energy, symbolized as a Serpent, coiled around the spine. While this energy initially appears to be sexual, it is able to move up three pathways (*nâdis*, which Pryse translates as 'pipes' or 'tubes') in the body, changing in nature as it develops. On the one hand, the *sushumna* is the pipe leading from the spinal cord up to the cranium, while *îdâ* and *pingala*, correspond to the left and right vertical pathways of the sympathetic nervous system (Pryse 1910: 19). The gnostic yogi tries to awaken each of the seven *chakras* or 'nerve centres', which are arranged in ascending order up the spine. The central path of 'serpent power', the *sushumna*, can only be activated through the creation of polarities between *îdâ* and *pingala*, which are symbolized as moon and sun. Pryse is happy to call the *chakras* 'nerve centres' or 'ganglia', and even suggests that readers of his work should have a detailed knowledge of 'psycho-physiology' (6, 15). 'The esotericist, refusing to be confined within the narrow limits of the senses and the mental faculties, and recognizing that the gnostic powers of the soul are hopelessly hampered and obscured by its imperfect instrument, the physical body, devotes himself to what may be termed intensive self-evolution, the conquest and utilization of all the forces and faculties which lie latent in that fontal essence within himself' (8).

5 Adam Curtis, in his television series *The Century of the Self*, and Eli Zaretsky in his study *The Secrets of the Soul* (2004) have shown the role played by psychoanalysis in the development of contemporary consumer capitalism. In the hands of Freud's brother-in-law, Edward Bernays, psychoanalysis became a tool for the analysis of motivation and the discovery and manipulation of the vulnerabilities of workers and consumers. Capitalism saw that psychoanalysis could be used for the purposes of sorcery long before the critics of psychoanalysis claimed that it amounted to a 'pseudo-science'.

6 Citing Starhawk, Stengers then admits that 'pronouncing the word "magic" is already an act of magic' (Pignarre and Stengers 2005: 181).

> I choose to take the risk of using the term 'magic' just as witches do take this risk. For them, the very fact of naming what they do as magic is already an act of magic, producing the experience of discomfort which makes perceptible the power over us of the consensual functions of the lived. And if those contemporary witches took upon themselves to call themselves witches, such a shocking name, it was in order to produce the living memory of the Time of Burning, the destruction of the Great Art, which did happen at the very epoch when Man as the majority standard came to impose converging, consensual functions of the lived, explaining away as illusions and superstitions every active divergence but the three surviving ones, philosophy, science and art. (Stengers 2006)

7 Within one year (1732–3), twenty books and articles were published on the subject in Germany. I cite the some of the list from Montague Summers's *The Vampire in Europe*: *De masticatione mortuorum in tumulis liber* (Leipzig, 1728); *Dissertatio de cadaveribus sanguisugis* (Jena, 1732); *Relation von den Vampyren oder Menschensaugern* (Leipzig, 1732), *Besondere Nachricht von denen vampyren oder sogenannten Blut-Saugeren* (1732), *Uisus et repertus über die sogenannten Vampyren* (Nuremburg, 1732), *Dissertatio de hominibus post mortem sanguisugis, vulgo dictis Vampyrea* (Leipzig, 1732). There are several more (Summers 1929: 132). Summers cites several works dating back to the late sixteenth century, and also emphasizes the groundbreaking work of Philip Rohr in his *Dissertatio de masticatione mortuorum* (1679). Michael Ranft, author of *De masticatione mortuorum*, noted in his later 1734 treatise on vampires that 'at the last Easter fair in Leipzig it was impossible to enter a bookstore without seeing something about bloodsuckers' (cited in Introvigne 2001: 601).

8 In Ariew's and Garber's translation of this passage, '*enveloppe*' is translated as 'involve', and in the preceding passage '*Enveloppemens*' is rendered 'enfoldings'. See the *Leibniz Lexicon* (Finster *et al.* 1988) for a selection of further examples of 'development' and 'envelopment'. 'Envelopment' is a term that Leibniz tends to use in logical contexts, for instance when he claims that 'according to me, [a] complete individual notion envelops relations to the whole series of things' (Leibniz 1686–7: 69; trans. modified).

9 As he lies dying and unconscious, the hypnotist asks him questions. 'M. Valdemar, do you still sleep?' 'Yes', he responds, 'still asleep – dying.' The hypnotist asks him the same question a final time, but at that moment his eyes roll upwards and he dies. As the nurses prepare to administer to the body, a hideous vibration begins to emanate from his jaws. The dead M. Valdemar begins to speak, and to make a belated reply to the hypnotist's final question: 'Yes; – no; – I *have been* sleeping – and now – now – *I am dead.*' M. Valdemar is now caught in this position, but further efforts at communication with him fail, as if he seemed no longer to have 'sufficient volition' to speak. 'Death (or what is usually termed death) has been arrested by the mesmeric process.' In the course of the next seven months, the hypnotist continues to visit M. Valdemar daily, and finally resolves that the best course of action is to re-awaken him from his hypnotic state. As M. Valdemar begins to revive, the hideous voice emerges once more: 'For God's sake! – quick! – quick! – put me to sleep – or, quick! – waken me! – quick! – *I say to you that I am dead!*' Just as the hypnotist appears to have succeeded in reviving M. Valdemar, his body instead crumbles and rots away within the space of a minute (Poe 1845: 350–9).

10 It was subtitled 'An Astounding and Horrifying Narrative shewing the extraordinary power of mesmerism in arresting the progress of death'. The advertisement on the first page read: 'The following astonishing narrative first appeared in the *American Magazine*, a work of some standing in the United States, where the case has excited the most intense interest . . . The narrative, though only a plain recital of facts, is of so extraordinary a nature as almost to surpass belief. It is only necessary to add, that credence is given to it in America, where the occurrence took place' (Poe 1846).

11 In his journal of 1971, Guattari writes about his anxieties about being catapulted into fame by *Anti-Oedipus*. He had not published any books before 1972, the year *Anti-Oedipus* appeared, and wrote the following note: 'Impossible to turn back. Fear – because of this diary – that I have been taken too far. Until now I had an exit, always, some kind of accommodation with the local socius. But with *Capitalism and Schizophrenia*, I have become – I have been – toppled over into what is irreversible' (Guattari 2006: 305). This diary is intriguing because it begins in Le Brusc, a town in the South of France in Toulon Bay, where the Deleuze and Guattari families were staying during the summer while *Anti-Oedipus* was being finalized. It appears to be part of some agreement made with Deleuze; Guattari remarks on the reaction of Deleuze's wife Fanny to his diary while she types it up ('I thought she found it to be in poor taste'). Guattari goes on to report that he keeps having dreams about 'Lacan and desks'. It ends with

Lacan 'chasing out some rebels that I had only half followed', and with Guattari concerned that 'I didn't know how to go back to his desk without getting yelled at'. The next day he writes, 'Another dream about Lacan! This is insane'. Guattari doesn't attempt to interpret either dream. In the first, his relation to Lacan is highly ambivalent: on the one hand, he is facing the master behind the desk, but on the other hand he himself is trying to 'go back' to Lacan's desk. Disgusted with his unconscious, Guattari concludes that 'all this confirms me in my idea that dreams are fundamentally reterritorialization activities, conjuration, protection against the most brutal machinic incidence of desire. Fundamentally right-wing Eros activities.' After the second dream about Lacan his reaction is more violent: 'I have oedipal rot sticking to my skin . . . The more I become disengaged – the more I try to become disengaged – from twenty years of Lacano-Labordian comfort, the more this familialist carcass enfolds me secretly. I would rather admit anything else!'

12 Deleuze cites Artaud's writings on cinema as a further instance of the descent into the dream in order to capture something beyond the dream. He expresses his wish to write a film screenplay which would

> ignore knowledge and the logical connection of facts, and would search beyond, in the occult and in the tracks of feeling and thought for the profound motives, the active and obscure impulses of our so-called lucid acts, while always *maintaining* their evolutions in the domain of sources and apparitions. It is to show how far the scenario can resemble and ally itself with the *mechanics of a dream* without really being a dream itself, for example. It is to show how far it restores the pure work of thought. So the mind, left to itself and the images, infinitely sensitised, determined to lose nothing of the inspirations of subtle thought, is all prepared to return to its original functions, its antennae pointed towards the invisible. (Artaud 1928: 63)

In his short piece 'Sorcery and Cinema', Artaud suggests that the ability of film to eternalize movements can be used to promote a new non-representational type of thinking. Its images have 'virtual power' that points us towards the 'depths of the mind': 'essentially the cinema reveals a whole occult life with which it puts us directly into contact' (Artaud 1949: 66). Raw cinema is opposed to narrative cinema, and is suited to expressing a 'turning-point in human thought' that has occurred in late modernity, in which the power of the symbol has been occluded. After this unspecified turning-point, 'language loses its symbolic power and the mind tires of a succession of representations. Clear thought is not enough. It allocates a world which has been utterly consumed' (ibid.). Deleuze's whole *Cinema* project, with its central claim that cinema is the means of discovering 'spiritual life' has its seed in Artaud's reflections on cinema. With the help of cinema, in which actors themselves become symbols and no longer (as on the stage) mediate and obscure the symbolic power of the drama, 'we soon realise that this over-familiar life which has lost all its symbols is not the whole of life. So today is a time for sorcerers and saints, a better time than ever before. An imperceptible substance is taking shape, yearning for light. The cinema is bringing us nearer to this substance' (ibid.). This 'imperceptible substance' seems to be related to the body without organs, an esoteric subtle body which senses acausal sympathies with the world which it inhabits. Artaud's way of using the dream to reach visionary states is profoundly occultist. He concludes that cinema has the potential to present a 'plastic, objective and attentive examination of the inner *self* which has hitherto been the exclusive domain of the "Illuminati"'. Cinema is a democratization of sorcery; it seizes occult powers from the hands of magicians and sorcerers.

13 De Quincey continues: 'The condition of human life, which yokes so vast a majority to a daily experience incompatible with much elevation of thought, oftentimes neutralises the tone of grandeur in the reproductive faculty of dreaming, even for those whose minds are populous with solemn imagery.' According to De Quincey, the reproductive faculty of dreaming is internally restricted by the demands of the present, but to an

almost intolerable degree in industrialized society, the noise and speed of which tends to smother the creative imagination, which requires silence and withdrawal to emerge.

14 We shall see in a moment that this evaluation is slightly misleading, as Michaux was indeed interested in situating drug experience within ritual settings. So Deleuze and Guattari are more likely to be saying that Michaux's approach to the religious significance of drugs was conditioned by a preliminary *freedom* with regard to the texts and practices of the world religions. Deleuze and Guattari cite with approval the conclusion of the literary historian Leslie Fiedler, whose book *The Return of the Vanishing American* (1968) set forth 'the poles of the American Dream: cornered between two nightmares, the genocide of the Indians and the slavery of the blacks, Americans constructed a psychically repressed image of the black as the force of affect, of the multiplication of affects, but a socially repressed image of the Indian as subtlety of perception, perception made increasingly keen and more finely divided, slowed or accelerated' (ATP 283). By being a sophisticated representative of an already established tradition of research into drugs, Michaux was able to avoid these traps and gain access, as it were, to the 'drug in itself', the *Soma* an sich.

15 See the chapter 'Expérience de la folie' in *Miserable Miracle* (translated as 'Experimental Schizophrenia'). In his book on Michaux, Malcolm Bowie cites a number of studies from the 30s to the 50s which worked from the premise that mescaline produced artificial psychoses (Bowie 1973: 193).

16 Mescaline is synthesised from peyote. Many of the drugs associated with shamanism (peyote, ayahuasca, salvia divinorum) are acknowledged to be devoid of attraction from a hedonistic perspective.

17 It appears to be Michaux who coins the idea of a 'molecular' unconscious: 'Everything in thought is somehow molecular. Tiny particles that appear and disappear. Particles in perpetual associations, dissociations, reassociations, swifter than swift, almost instantaneous' (Michaux 1966: 13).

18 The authors specify the first eighty pages of this book, which corresponds to pp. 1–61 of the English translation. These pages end with the single word sentence 'Visions', to which is appended the blank footnote, 'of which no trace remains'.

19 Deleuze's reference to 'Lilliputian' perceptions refers to the work of the French psychiatrist, Gaëtan de Clérambault, who used this concept in his account of toxicomanic delirium. Clérambault specialised in the analysis of delirium, and in the first decades of the twentieth century wrote extensively on the hallucinations associated with use of alcohol, chloral and ether. His aim was to produce a differential analysis of the actions of various intoxicants in order to isolate different cerebral functions. In *The Fold* Deleuze cites his distinction between the types of confusion in alcoholism and chloralism. Whereas the mind of the alcoholic plunges into a profound and general 'obscurity', it is as if the mind of the chloralic is 'surrounded by a veil', in which 'the play of folds produces an unequal transparency' (Clérambault 1942: 204). Clérambault noted that chloral addicts often hallucinated that the walls were decorated with veils of detailed arabesques (composed of spiders, flowers or inscriptions), in flat relief. Also, 'there is a striking tendency towards striping, striations, latticing' (ibid.: 251) in chloralic hallucinations. These 'veils' are the result of the rising to the surface of minute marks or lines, amplified into latticed networks. In fact, it is this surging up of 'microscopic' perceptions which makes chloral hallucinations 'non-global and intermittent', targeting particular zones of perception at particular moments. The judgment of chloral users is not wholly affected (as is that of the alcoholic, whose consciousness is profoundly 'obscured'), but is rather a 'mixture of lucidity and somnolence'. Hallucinations thus tend to be 'microscopic' and even 'pointilliste' (196–7). Insects swarm in and around the skin, phantom odours and tastes rise up and dominate consciousness; one addict becomes paranoiac about the various 'powders' he sees everywhere in his home (170). The framework is indeed Leibnizian: hallucinations emerge through a

'swarming' (*fourmillement*) of microscopic perceptions which threaten to overwhelm the global contours of apperceptive consciousness, and which disappear just as rapidly as they arise. Working with chloral and ether addicts had revealed another kind of microscopic perception beneath global perception of objects, in which the murmuring background of perception came to the surface. Clérambault uses the notion of 'liliputian hallucinations' (derived from Leroy) to describe hallucinations in which the dimensions of objects are altered while conserving their relative proportions (250): insects become enormous while people shrink into tininess. In his private life, Clérambault was obsessed with veils and folds and his pastime of composing photographs of women dressed in Islamic coverings were first seized upon by psychoanalysts as evidence of fetishistic tendencies in their author. Deleuze opposes this reading. 'If Clérambault manifests a delirium, it is because he discovers the tiny hallucinatory perceptions of ether addicts in the folds of clothing' (F 38).

20 In a letter to Ernst Jünger, Albert Hofmann, the discoverer of LSD, writes in a similar vein: 'these magic substances are themselves cracks in the infinite realm of matter, in which the depth of matter, its relationship with the mind, becomes particularly obvious' (Hofmann 1980: 157).

21
> Intensity increases along with speed, an intensity revealing and emphasizing the speed already there, a speed now seen as much more considerable than previously supposed, an intensity which brings to perception the images (and micro-impulses) otherwise imperceptible, vague, and remote. The drug makes the subject conscious of many other transitions and also of desires, which become sudden, violent, lightninglike impulsions. (Ibid.)

22 In his discussion of unconscious perception in *The Fold* (F 155 n. 19–20), Deleuze refers to another literary text, a short piece by Jean Cocteau ostensibly on dreams, but for which the occasion is an 'internal voyage' while on nitrogen protoxyde (*protoxyde d'azote*). Cocteau is administered the drug by a dentist as an anaesthetic. "Doctor, take care, I am not asleep", he mutters; 'but the journey begins. It lasts for centuries. I reach the first tribunal. I am judged. I pass. Another century. I reach the second tribunal. I am judged. I pass and so it continues. At the fourteenth tribunal I understand that multiplicity is the sign of this other world and unity the sign of ours (Cocteau 1957: 55). On returning to unified consciousness, he knows he must forget everything that he has seen: 'I see unity reforming. What a bore! Everything is one'. Cocteau goes on to speculate about the difference in kind between waking and dream consciousness in general. What strikes him is that the dreaming consciousness does not feel astonishment at the remarkable things seen in dreams, or at the speed with which he can come to 'know' things. Freud borrowed Fechner's insight that the dream is another stage or scene (*ein andere Schauplatz*), with entirely different laws to normal consciousness. But Cocteau emphasises the normality or 'naturalness' of dream consciousness ('the dream is the sleeper's normal existence', 56), and the regularity of the alternation between waking and dream ('I take advantage of it to live a double life', 57).

> What is certain is that this enfolding [*pliure*], through the medium of which eternity becomes liveable to us, is not produced in the same way as in life. Something of this fold unfolds [*Quelque chose de cette pliure s'y déplie*]. Thanks to this our limits change, widen. The past, the future no longer exist; the dead rise again; places construct themselves without architect, without journeys, without that tedious oppression that compels us to live minute by minute that which the half-opened fold shows us at a glance. Moreover the atmospheric and profound lightness of the dream favours encounters, surprises, knowledge [*connaissances*], a naturalness, which our enfolded world (I mean projected on to the surface of a fold) can only ascribe to the supernatural. (57; trans. modified)

23 See Octavio Paz's preface to *Miserable Miracle*: 'Battered by the gale of mescaline, sucked up by the abstract whirlwind, the modern Westerner finds absolutely nothing to hold

on to. He has forgotten the names, God is no longer called God. The Aztec or the Tarahumara had only to pronounce the name, and immediately the presence would descend, in all its infinite manifestations. Unity and plurality for the ancients. For us who lack gods: Pullulation and Time. We have lost the names' (Paz 1967: x).

24 Michaux had an intense interest in magic and occultism. See his 1941 collection 'In the Land of Magic' (from which Deleuze cites a prose poem about the 'twenty-two folds' of human life (Michaux 1968: 243; cited in F 93); as well as *The Major Ordeals of the Mind* itself, which ends with disquisitions on Tantrism, inspired by *The Serpent Power* by Arthur Avalon (John Woodroffe). Michaux was the editor of *Hermes*, a journal of religious and esoteric ideas in the late 1930s. The reference to the 'paradises' afforded by drugs may thus refer not only to Baudelaire's essay on *Artificial Paradises*, but also further back to the alchemical use of the symbol of the 'tree of life' (which can allude to its psychotropic properties). In a passage that is like a numbed, a thousand-times repeated, recollection of James's anaesthetic revelations of pantheism, Michaux ingenuously insists that he has indeed seen 'gods in their thousands':

> The incredible, that which I have desperately desired since childhood, that which was apparently excluded and which I thought I would never see, the unparalleled, the inaccessible, the excessively beautiful, the sublime which was forbidden me, the incredible has occurred. I HAVE SEEN THE GODS IN THEIR THOUSANDS. I have received the gift of wonderment. They have appeared to me who was without faith (who did not know the faith of which I was capable). They were there, they were present, more present than anything else I have ever seen. And it was impossible and I knew it was impossible and yet. And yet they were there, lined up in their hundreds next to each other (but behind them were thousands, barely perceptible, and there were many more than thousands, there was an infinite number). They were there, these calm and noble beings, suspended in the air by an apparently natural form of levitation, in gentle movement where they stood. These divine beings and myself were alone together . . . I had not lived in vain. (Michaux 1964: 57)

The poet frequently discusses his work as an exploration of 'magical' or religious states of reality. According to Michaux's gnostic vision, we are all 'prisoners', possessed in flashes by the desire to find means of storming heaven: for 'prison displayed is prison no longer' (cited in Bell 1994). Michaux also thought of writings as 'exorcisms', and even as maledictions or curses, calling his work 'poetry for power'. Something like 'magic' was needed in order to countenance the 'major ordeals of the mind', a genus of magical writing which would 'ward off the surrounding powers of the hostile world', so that 'evil is progressively dissolved, replaced by an airy demonic sphere', which he informs us, is 'a marvellous state!' (Preface to *Ordeals, Exorcisms*; in Michaux 1994, 83–4).

25 In *The Major Ordeals of the Mind*, Michaux describes a long-held interest he had in taking 'cannabis indica at high altitude', where he could contemplate a mountain skyline. He prepares himself over a period of days, and then consumes the substance. However, he miscalculates the time while he is having dinner, and by the time he ventures out into the landscape, it is night, and the mountains have disappeared in the darkness surrounding the remote location. Dismayed, he has no idea what to do. At length, he raises his head up to look up at the night, and he feels himself sinking into the black sky full of stars. 'It was extraordinary. Instantaneously stripped of everything as though of an overcoat, I passed into space. I was projected into it, I was hurled into it, I flowed into it. I was violently seized by it, irresistably . . . An utterly unsuspected marvel . . . Why hadn't I known of it earlier? After the first minute of surprise, it seemed altogether natural to be borne off into space' (Michaux 1966: 92). Whether by design or not, Michaux has replicated the conditions for the witch's flight: hemp, a mountain-top, and a night full of stars. Michaux's experience here is not just similar but perhaps even identical with the witch's flight.

26 The original founder of what became known as Martinism, Martinès de Pasqually, instituted a secret society devoted to theurgic ritual under the influence of the fly agaric mushroom.

27 Deleuze's opposition to masochistic humour and sadistic irony is based on Kierkegaard's distinction between humour and irony, which is in turn endebted to Hegelianism. In the *Philosophy of Right*, Hegel had written that the subject reaches the position of irony 'when it *knows* itself as that power of resolution and decision on [matters of] truth, right, and duty' (Hegel, *Philosophy of Right*, # 140). But when '*subjectivity declares itself to be absolute*', this 'ironic position' becomes dialectically identical with *evil*. 'It is not the thing [*Sache*] which is excellent, it is I who am excellent and master of both law and thing; I *merely play* with them as with my own caprice, and in this ironic consciousness in which I let the highest of things perish, I *merely enjoy myself*.' Kierkegaard initially developed his distinction between irony and humour by reference to a Danish Hegelian, J. L. Heiberg, who characterized humour as 'content overreaching the current form' whereby content is 'enriched . . . by forcing us to see anomalies we hadn't seen before' (Hannay 2001: 59). Rather than the subject extracting himself from the empirical domain through appealing to an always higher, abstract principle of subjectivity, the act of humour involves following the law *to the letter* in order to subvert it. The transgression of law is procured through an exaggerated fidelity to the law. It accepts that there is no other choice but to conform to the constraints of the law, but pursues an idiosyncratic project through legitimate channels, always concealing its clandestine end, in the expectation that any general laws are too universal to have fully accounted for every eventuality. Humour thus seeks *the last laugh*, beyond even the 'superior' laughter of irony. But the last laugh is not at all bitter, because it also signals the triumphant achievement of its clandestine goal.

Bibliography

The dates in the first set of brackets refer to the original date of publication, except for ancient and medieval sources, where the date of the translation used is given.

Alexandrian, Sarane (1983) *Histoire de la philosophie occulte* (Paris: Seghers).

Al-Kindi (1977) 'Des rayons ou théorie des arts magiques', in Sylvain Matton, ed. *La Magie Arabe Traditionelle* (Paris: Bibliotheca Hermetica, 1977).

Allison, Henry (1996) 'On Naturalising Kant's Transcendental Psychology', in *Idealism and Freedom* (Cambridge: Cambridge University Press).

Altman, Gail S. (1999) *Fatal Links: The Curious Deaths of Beethoven and the Two Napoleons* (Florida: Auguste-Schöne).

Ameriks, Karl (2000) *Kant and the Fate of Autonomy* (Cambridge: Cambridge University Press).

Ansell Pearson, Keith (1999) *Germinal Life: The Difference and Repetition of Deleuze* (London: Routledge).

Aron, Max, Courrier, Robert and Wolff, Etienne (1969) *Entretiens sur la sexualité* (Centre Culturel International de Cerisy-la-Salle, 10–17 Juillet 1965) (Paris: Plon).

Artaud, Antonin (1928) 'Witchcraft and Cinema', trans. Alastair Hamilton, in *Antonin Artaud: Collected Works: Volume Three* (London: Calder & Boyars, 1972).

—— (1949) 'The Shell and the Clergyman', trans. Alastair Hamilton, in *Antonin Artaud: Collected Works: Volume Three* (London: Calder & Boyars, 1972).

Atiyeh, George N. (1966) *Al-Kindi: The Philosopher of the Arabs* (Rawalpindi: Islamic Research Institute).

Aujoulat, Norbert (2005) *Lascaux: Movement, Space and Time*, trans. M. Street (New York: Harry N. Abrams).

Avalon, Arthur [Sir John Woodroffe] (1919) *The Serpent Power* (New York: Dover, 1974).

Bachofen, J. J. (1973) *Myth, Religion & Mother Right* (Princeton, NJ: Princeton University Press).

Badcock, Christopher (1994) *PsychoDarwinism: the New Synthesis of Darwin and Freud* (London: HarperCollins).

—— (2000) *Evolutionary Psychology: A Critical Introduction* (Cambridge: Polity Press).

Baldwin, James Mark (1902) ed. *Dictionary of Philosophy and Psychology* (New York: Peter Smith).

Barlet, Frederic-Charles (1888) 'Initiation', trans. A. P. Morton, in Papus, *The Tarot of the Bohemians* (London: George Redway, 1896).

Barron, Frank (1987) 'Bergson and the Modern Psychology of Creativity', in A. Papanicolaou and P. A. Y. Gunter, eds. *Bergson and Modern Thought* (Chur: Harwood).

Barzilai, Shuli (1999) *Lacan and the Matter of Origins* (Stanford: Stanford University Press).

Baugh, Bruce (1993) 'Deleuze and Empiricism', in *Journal of the British Society for Phenomenology* 24: 1, 1993.

Beach, Edward Allen (1994) *The Potencies of God(s): Schelling's Philosophy of Mythology* (Albany: State University of New York Press).

Beck, Lewis White, 'Kant's Letter to Herz', in E. Förster, ed. *Kant's Transcendental Deductions* (Stanford: Stanford University Press, 1989).

Beer, Th., Bethe, A. and Uexküll, J. von (1899) 'Vorschläge zu einer objektivierenden Nomenklature in der Physiologie des Nervensystems', in *Biologisches Zentralblatt* 19.

Bell, David (1994) 'Introduction' to Henri Michaux, *Darkness Moves* (Michaux, 1994).

Benjamin, Walter (1939) 'On Some Motifs in Baudelaire', in *Illuminations*, trans. H. Zohn (New York: Schocken, 1968).

Bennet, E. A. (1966) *What Jung Really Said* (London: Abacus, 2001).

Bensaud-Vincent, Bernadette and Stengers, Isabelle (1993) *A History of Chemistry*, trans. D. van Dam (Cambridge, Mass: Harvard University Press, 1996).

Benz, Ernst (1968) *The Mystical Sources of German Romantic Philosophy*, trans. B. R. Reynolds and E. M. Paul (Pennsylvania: Pickwick, 1983).

Bergson, Henri (1889) *An Essay on the Immediate Data of Consciousness; translation entitled Time and Free Will*, trans. F. L. Pogson (London: Allen & Unwin, 1913).

—— (1896) *Matter and Memory*, trans. N. M. Paul & W. S. Palmer (New York: Zone Books, 1994).

—— (1903) 'Introduction to Metaphysics', in *The Creative Mind*.

—— (1907) *Creative Evolution*, trans. A. Mitchell (London: Macmillan, 1911).

—— (1908) 'Memory of the Present and False Recognition', in *Mind-Energy*, trans. H. Wildon Carr (London: Macmillan, 1920).

—— (1919) *Mind-Energy*, trans. H. Wildon Carr (London: Macmillan, 1920).

—— (1932) *The Two Sources of Morality and Religion*, trans. R. Ashley Audra and C. Brereton (New York: Doubleday, 1935).

—— (1934) *The Creative Mind*, trans. M. L. Andison (London: Philosophical Library, 1946).

Bey, Hakim (2003) TAZ: *The Temporary Autonomous Zone, Ontological Anarchy, Poetic Terrorism* (New York: Autonomedia)

Binet, Alfred (1892) *Alterations of Personality*, trans. H. G. Baldwin (London: 1896).

Binswanger, Ludwig (1952) *Le Cas Suzanne Urban: Étude sure la schizophrénie*, trans. J. Verdeaux (Bruges: Desclée de Brouwer, 1957; reprinted, Paris: Gérard Monfort: 2004).

—— (1956) *Sigmund Freud: Reminiscences of a Friendship*, trans. N. Guterman (New York: Grune & Stratton, 1957).

—— (1957) '*Introduction to Schizophrenie*', trans. J. Needleman, in J. Needleman, ed. *Being-in-the-World: Selected Papers of Ludwig Binswanger* (London: Souvenir Press, 1975).

Bishop, Paul (1999) ed. *Jung in Contexts: A Reader* (London: Routledge).

—— (2000) *Synchronicity and Intellectual Intuition in Kant, Swedenborg and Jung* (Lewiston, NY: Lampeter: E. Mellen Press).

—— (2002) *Jung's Answer to Job* (Hove: Brunner-Routledge).

Boon, Marcus (2002) *The Road of Excess: A History of Writers on Drugs* (Cambridge, Mass. and London: Harvard University Press).

Borch-Jacobsen, Mikkel (1991) *Lacan the Absolute Master*, trans. Douglas Brick (Stanford: Stanford University Press).

Bowie, Malcolm (1973) *Henri Michaux – A Study of his Literary Works* (Oxford: Clarendon Press).

Brickman, Bernard (1988) 'Psychoanalysis and Substance Abuse: Towards a More Effective Approach', reprinted in D. L. Yalisore, ed., *Essential Papers on Addiction* (New York: New York University Press, 1997).

Brown, Robert F. (1977) *The Later Philosophy of Schelling: The Influence of Boehme on the Works of 1809–1815)* (London: Associated University Presses).

Brown, Stuart (1998) 'Some Occult Influences on Leibniz's Monadology', in A. Coudert, R. H. Popkin & G. M. Weiner, eds. *Leibniz, Mysticism and Religion* (Dordrecht: Kluwer).

Budge, E. A. Wallis (1899) *Egyptian Magic* (London: Kegan Paul, Trench, Trübner & Co.).

Buller, David J. (1999) 'DeFreuding Evolutionary Psychology: Adaptation and Human Motivation', in Valerie Gray Hardcastle, ed. *Where Biology Meets Psychology* (Cambridge, Mass.: MIT Press).

Burkhardt, Richard W. Jr. (2005) *Patterns of Behavior: Konrad Lorenz, Niko Tinbergen, and the Founding of Ethology* (Chicago: University of Chicago Press, 2005).

Buytendijk, Frederik (1968) *Woman: A Contemporary View*, trans. Dennis J. Barret (New York: Association Press).

Cahagnet, Louis (1849) *Sanctuaire du spiritualisme* (Paris).

Canguilhem, Georges (1943) *The Normal and the Pathological*, trans. Carolyn R. Fawcett (New York: Zone Books, 1991).

—— (1952) *Besoins et tendances: textes choisis et présentés par G. Canguilhem* (Paris: Hachette).

Capek, Milic (1973) 'Leibniz on Matter and Memory', in I. Leclerc, ed. *The Philosophy of Leibniz and the Modern World* (Nashville: Vanderbilt University Press).

Carl, Wolfgang (1989) 'Kant's First Drafts of the Deduction of the Categories', in E. Förster ed. *Kant's Transcendental Deductions* (Stanford: Stanford University Press).

Cavell, Marcia (1993) *The Psychoanalytic Mind: From Freud to Philosophy* (Cambridge, Mass.: Harvard University Press).

Chacornac, Paul (1926) *Eliphas Lévi: Rénovateur de l'occultisme en France* (Paris: Chacornac).

Chertok, Leon and Stengers, Isabelle (1992) *A Critique of Psychoanalytic Reason: Hypnosis as a Scientific Problem*, trans. M. N. Evans (Stanford: Stanford University Press).

Clérambault, Gaëtan de (1909) *Oeuvre psychiatrique*, ed. Jean Fretet (Paris: Presses Universitaires de France, 1942), Vol. 1.

Cocteau, Jean (1957) *The Difficulty of Being*, trans. E. Sprigge (London: Peter Owen, 1966).

Coleridge, Samuel Taylor (1838) *Literary Remains*, ed. H. N. Coleridge (London: William Pickering).

—— (1957–1962) *The Notebooks of Samuel Taylor Coleridge*, ed. K. Coburn, 2 double vols. (London: Routledge).

Cooke, Mordecai (1860) *Seven Sisters of Sleep: Popular History of the Seven Prevailing Narcotics of the World* (London: James Blackwood).

Copenhaver, Brian P., ed. (1992) *Hermetica* (Cambridge: Cambridge University Press).

Coudert, Allison (1980) *Alchemy: The Philosophers' Stone* (London: Wildwood House).

—— (1987) 'Elixirs', in M. Eliade, ed. *The Encyclopedia of Religion* (New York: Macmillan); reprinted in L. E. Sullivan *Hidden Truths: Magic, Alchemy and the Occult* (New York: Macmillan).

—— (1995) *Leibniz and the Kabbalah* (Dordrecht: Kluwer).

Crowley, Aleister (1908) 'The Psychology of Hashish', in Regardie (1968).

—— (1912) 'A Description of the Cards of the Tarot', in *The Equinox* 1: 8.

—— (1916) 'An Improvement Upon Psychoanalysis', in *The Revival of Magick and other Essays* (Tempe: New Falcon, 1998).

—— (1973) *Magick* (London: Routledge & Kegan Paul)

Dalbiez, Roland (1936) *Psychoanalytical Method and the Doctrine of Freud*, trans. T. F. Lindsay (London: Longmans, Green & Co., 1941).

Dalcq, A. M. (1957) *Introduction to General Embryology*, trans. J. Medawar (Oxford: Oxford University Press).

Danziger, Kurt (1980a) 'The History of Introspection Reconsidered', in *Journal of the History of the Behavioral Sciences* 16.

—— (1980b) 'Wundt and the Two Traditions of Psychology', in R. W. Rieber, ed. *Wilhelm Wundt and the Making of a Scientific Psychology* (New York: Plenum Press).

Darwin, Charles (1859) *The Origin of Species* (London: Penguin Books, 1982).

—— (1958) *The Autobiography of Charles Darwin 1809–1882*, ed. Nora Barlow, (London: Collins).

Davy, Marie-Madeleine (1977) *L'Initiation à la symbolique romane* (Paris: Flammarion, 2nd edn).

De Lancre, Pierre (1607) *Tableau de l'inconstance des mauvaises anges et demons* (Paris: Aubier, 1982).

Deleuze, Gilles (1945) 'Description of Woman', trans. K. Faulkner, *Angelaki* 7:3, 2002.

—— (1946a) 'Mathèse, Science et philosophie', in French edition of Malfatti (1845).

—— (1946b) 'Statement and Profiles', trans. K. Faulkner, *Angelaki* 8:3, 2003.

—— (1953) *Empiricism and Subjectivity: An Essay on Hume's Theory of Human Nature*, trans. Constantin V. Boundas (New York: Columbia University Press, 1991).

—— (1953b) *Instincts et institutions* (Paris: Hachette). Preface in DI.

—— (1955) 'Review of Jean Hyppolite, Logique et Existence', in Jean Hyppolite, *Logic and Existence*, trans. Leonard Lawlor and Amit Sen (Albany: State University of New York Press, 1997).

—— (1956) 'Bergson, 1859–1941', in DI.

—— (1956b) 'Bergson's Concept of Difference', trans. Melissa McMahon, in John Mullarkey ed. *The New Bergson*, (Manchester: Manchester University Press, 1999). Also in DI.

—— (1960) 'Cours inédit de Gilles Deleuze sur la chapitre III de *L'Évolution créatrice*', in F. Worms, ed., *Annales bergsoniennes II: Bergson, Deleuze, la phenomenology* (Paris: PUF, 2004).

—— (1961) 'From Sacher-Masoch to Masochism', trans. C. Kersslake, *Angelaki* 9:1, April 2004.
—— (1961b) 'Lucrèce et le naturalisme', in *Études philosophiques* 1, 1961.
—— (1962) *Nietzsche and Philosophy*, trans. Hugh Tomlinson (London: Athlone, 1983).
—— (1963) 'The Idea of Genesis in Kant's Aesthetics', trans. D. W. Smith, *Angelaki* 5:3, 2000.
—— (1963b) *Kant's Critical Philosophy*, trans. Hugh Tomlinson (London: Athlone, 1983).
—— (1964) *Proust and Signs*, trans. Richard Howard (London: Athlone, 2000).
—— (1966) *Bergsonism*, trans. H. Tomlinson and B. Habberjam (New York: Zone Books, 1988).
—— (1967) *Coldness and Cruelty*, trans. Richard Howard, in *Masochism* (New York: Zone Books, 1989).
—— (1968) *Difference and Repetition*, trans. P. Patton (London: Athlone, 1994).
—— (1968) *Expressionism in Philosophy: Spinoza*, trans. Martin Joughin (New York: Zone Books, 1992).
—— (1969) *The Logic of Sense*, trans. Mark Lester et al. (London: Athlone Press, 1990).
—— (1972) 'How do we Recognise Structuralism?' trans. M. McMahon & C. J. Stivale, in C. J. Stivale ed. *The Two-Fold Thought of Deleuze and Guattari*, (New York: Guilford Press, 1998).
—— (1973) 'Nomad Thought', trans. D. Allison, in David B. Allison ed. *The New Nietzsche* (London: MIT Press, 1985).
—— (1978) 'Four Lessons on Kant', trans. Melissa McMahon, published on 'Deleuze Web', www.webdeleuze.com.
—— (1980) 'Leibniz' Seminar, trans. C. Stivale, www.webdeleuze.com.
—— (1981) *Francis Bacon: Logique de la Sensation* (Paris: Editions de Minuit); trans. D. W. Smith as *Francis Bacon: The Logic of Sensation* (London: Continuum, 2003).
—— (1981) *Spinoza: Practical Philosophy*, trans. Robert Hurley (San Francisco: City Lights,1988).
—— (1983) *Cinema 1: The Movement Image*, trans. Hugh Tomlinson and Barbara Habberjam (London: Athlone Press, 1986).
—— (1985) *Cinema 2: The Time-Image*, trans. Hugh Tomlinson and Barbara Habberjam (London: Athlone Press, 1989).
—— (1988) 'A Philosophical Concept', trans. Julien Deleuze, in E. Cadava, ed. *Who Comes after the Subject?* (London: Routledge, 1991).
—— (1988) *The Fold: Leibniz and the Baroque*, trans. Tom Conley (Minneapolis: University of Minnesota Press, 1993).
—— (1990) *Negotiations [Pourparlers]*, trans. Martin Joughin (New York: Columbia University Press).
—— (1993) *Essays Critical and Clinical*, trans. Daniel W. Smith and Michael A. Greco (Minneapolis: University of Minnesota Press, 1997).
—— (1995) 'Immanence: A Life . . . ', trans. Nick Millett, in *Theory, Culture and Society* 14, 1997.
—— (2002) *Desert Islands and Other Texts, 1953–1974*, ed. D. Lapoujade, trans. M. Taormina (New York: Sesmotext(e), 2004).
—— (2003) *Two Regimes of Madness: Texts and Interviews, 1975–1995*, ed. D. Lapoujade, trans. A. Hodges and M. Taormina (New York: Semiotext(e), 2006).

(With Félix Guattari)
—— (1972) *Anti-Oedipus: Capitalism and Schizophrenia*, trans. Robert Hurley, Mark Seem & Helen R. Lane (London: Athlone Press, 1984).
—— (1975)*Kafka: Toward a Minor Literature*, trans. Dana Polan (Minneapolis: University of Minnesota Press, 1998).
—— (1980) *A Thousand Plateaus: Capitalism and Schizophrenia*, trans. Brian Massumi (Minneapolis: University of Minnesota Press, 1998).
—— (1991) *What is Philosophy?* trans. Graham Burchill & Hugh Tomlinson (London: Verso, 1994).

(With Claire Parnet)
—— (1977) *Dialogues*, trans. Hugh Tomlinson & Barbara Habberjam (New York: Columbia University Press, 1987).
—— (1997) *L'Abécédaire de Gilles Deleuze* (video), dir: P-A. Boutang (Paris: Editions de Montparnasse).

De Quincey, Thomas (1821) *Confessions of an English Opium Eater* (Harmondsworth: Penguin Books, 1987).

—— (1845) 'Suspiria de Profundis', extract in De Quincey (1821).

Descartes, Réné (1644) 'Principles of Philosophy', trans. John Cottingham, Robert Stoothoff and Dugald Murdoch, in *The Philosophical Writings of Descartes, Volume I* (Cambridge: Cambridge University Press, 1985).

Diamond, Solomon (2001) 'Wundt Before Leipzig', in R. W. Rieber *Wilhelm Wundt and the Making of a Scientific Psychology* (New York: Plenum Press, 1980).

Drever, James (1921) *Instinct in Man* (Cambridge: Cambridge University Press).

Dyck, Martin (1959) *Novalis and Mathematics* (North Carolina: Chapel Hill).

Eliade, Mircea (1956) *The Forge and the Crucible*, trans. S. Corrin (New York: Harper, 1971).

—— (1974) 'The Occult and the Modern World', in *Occultism, Witchcraft, and Cultural Fashions* (Chicago: University of Chicago, 1976).

—— (1987) 'What is Alchemy?', in M. Eliade, *Encyclopedia of Religion* (New York, Macmillan), reprinted in L. E. Sullivan, *Hidden Truths: Magic, Alchemy and the Occult* (New York: Macmillan).

Ellenberger, Henri F. (1970) *The Discovery of the Unconscious: The History and Evolution of Dynamic Psychiatry* (London: Penguin Books).

—— (1993) *Beyond the Unconscious: Essays of Henri F. Ellenberger in the History of Psychiatry*, ed. Mark S. Micale (Princeton, NJ: Princeton University Press).

Encausse, Philippe (1949) *Sciences Occultes* (Paris: Ocia).

Escohatodo, Antonio (1996) *A Brief History of Drugs*, trans. Kenneth Z. Symington (Vermont: Park Street Press).

Evans, Richard (1975) *Konrad Lorenz: The Man and His Ideas* (New York: Harcourt Brace Jovanovitch).

Evola, Julius (1968) *The Yoga of Power: Tantra, Shakti, and the Secret Way*, trans. G. Stucco (Rochester, Vermont: Inner Traditions). [First Italian edition, 1925].

—— (1969) *Eros and the Mysteries of Love: the Metaphysics of Sex* (Vermont: Inner Traditions, 1991)

—— (1971) *Introduction to Magic: Rituals and Practical Techniques for the Magus*, trans. Guido Stucco (Rochester, Vermont: Inner Traditions, 2001).

Fabre, Jean-Henri (1918) *The Wonders of Instinct*, trans. A. T. de Mattos and B. Miall (London: T. Fisher Unwin).

—— (1920) *Souvenirs entomologiques* (Paris: Delagrave), Vol. II.

Faivre, Antoine and Hanegraff, Wouter J. (1998) 'Introduction', in *Western Esotericism and the Science of Religion* (Gnostica 2) (Leuven: Peeters).

Faivre, Antoine (1996) *Philosophie de la nature: Physique sacrée et theosophie, XVIIIe–XIX siècle* (Paris: Albin Michel).

—— (1998), 'Questions of Terminology Proper to the Study of Esoteric Currents in Modern and Contemporary Europe', in A. Faivre & W. J. Hanegraff eds. *Western Esotericism and the Science of Religion* (Gnostica 2) (Leuven: Peeters).

Fechner, Gustav Theodore (1836) 'The Little Book of Life after Death', trans. M. Wadsworth, in G. T. Fechner *Life after Death* (New York: Pantheon, 1943).

—— (1851) Zend-Avesta: Über die Dinge des Himmels und des Jensetts (Leipzig: Voss); parts translated in *Fechner, Life After Death*, trans. M. Wadsworth and G. Jolas (New York: Pantheon, 1943).

—— (1860) *Elements of Psychophysics*, Volume I, trans. H. E. Adler (New York: Henry Holt, 1966).

—— (1860b) *Elemente der Psychophysik*, Volume II (Leipzig: Breitkopf & Hartel).

—— (1873) *Einige Ideen zur Schöpfungs- und Entwickelungsgeschichte der Organismen* (Leipzig: Breitkopf & Härtel).

—— (1879) *Die Tagesansicht gegenüber der Nachtansicht* (Leipzig: Breitkopf & Härtel).

—— (1946) *Religion of a Scientist: Selections from Gustav Th. Fechner*, ed. & trans. W. Lowrie (New York: Pantheon) (Includes extracts from *On the Highest Good, Nanna or the Psychic Life of Plants, Zend-Avesta, Concerning Souls, The Three Motives, and the Day-View contra the Night View*).

Ferenczi, Sandor (1913) 'Stages in the Development of the Sense of Reality', in Ferenczi, *First Contributions to Psycho-Analysis*, trans. Ernest Jones (London: Karnac, 2002).

—— (1924) *Thalassa: A Theory of Genitality* (London: Maresfield Library 1989).

Finster, Reinhard; Hunter, Graeme; McRae, Robert; Miles, Murray & Seager, William, eds. (1988) *Leibniz Lexicon* (Hildesheim: Olms–Weidmann).

Fletcher, Ronald (1968) *Instinct in Man* (London: Unwin).

Freud, Sigmund (1923) *Introduction à la Psychanalyse*, trans. S. Jankélévitch (Paris: Payot).

—— (1953–1974) *The Standard Edition of the Complete Psychological Works of Sigmund Freud*, ed. James Strachey in collaboration with Anna Freud assisted by Alix Strachey and Alan Tyson, trans. J. Strachey, 24 vols. (London: Hogarth Press and the Institute of Psychoanalysis).

—— (1987) *A Phylogenetic Fantasy: Overview of the Transference Neuroses*, trans. Ilse Grubrich-Simitis (Cambridge, Mass.: Harvard University Press).

Freud, Sigmund and Jung, Carl Gustav (1975) *The Freud/Jung Letters* trans. Ralph Manheim and R. F. C. Hull, ed. William McGuire (London: Routledge).

Gardner, Sebastian (1991) 'The Unconscious', in Jerome Neu, ed. *The Cambridge Companion to Freud* (Cambridge: Cambridge University Press).

Gauld, Alan (1992) *A History of Hypnotism* (Cambridge: Cambridge University Press).

Glasenapp, Helmuth von (1960) *Image of India [Das Indienbild Deutscher Denker]*, trans. S. Ambike (New Delhi: Indian Council for Cultural Relations, 1973).

Goldstein, Kurt (1939) *The Organism: A Holistic Approach to Biology Derived from Pathological Data in Man* (New York: Zone Books, 1995).

Gordon, Pierre (1949) *Sex and Religion*, trans. Renée and Hilda Spodheim (New York: Social Sciences Publishers).

Gould, Stephen Jay (1977) *Ontogeny and Phylogeny* (Cambridge, Mass. and London: Harvard University Press).

Grant, Kenneth (1972) *The Magical Revival* (London: Muller).

Guaita, Stanislas de (1890) *Au seuil du mystère* (Paris: Carré). First edition 1886.

—— (1891) *Le Serpent de la genèse. I: Le Temple de Satan* (Paris: Durville, 1915).

Guattari, Félix (2006) *The Anti-Oedipus Papers*, trans. Kélina Gotman (New York: Semiotext(e)).

Guénon, René (1947) Review of J. Malfatti de Montereggio, *La Mathèse*, reprinted in *Comptes Rendus* (Paris: Villain et Belhomme, 1973).

Gunter, Pete A. Y. (1982) 'Bergson and Jung', reprinted in P. Bishop, ed. *Jung in Contexts* (1999).

Haage, Bernard D. (2005) 'Alchemy II: Antiquity–12th century', in W. Hanegraaff, ed., *Dictionary of Gnosis and Western Esotericism* (Leiden: Brill).

Haeckel, Ernst (1874) *The Evolution of Man*, trans. J. McCabe (London: Watts, 1905).

Hallward, Peter (2006) *Out of this World: Deleuze and the Philosophy of Creation* (London: Verso).

Hannay, Alastair (2001) *Kierkegaard: A Biography* (Cambridge: Cambridge University Press).

Harvey, David Allen (2005) *Beyond Enlightenment: Occultism and Politics in Modern France* (Dekalb: Northern Illinois University Press).

Hatfield, Gary (2003) 'Psychology Old and New', in T. Baldwin, ed. *The Cambridge History of Modern Philosophy, 1870–1945* (Cambridge: Cambridge University Press).

Haule, John R (1984) 'From Somnambulism to the Archetypes: The French Roots of Jung's Split with Freud', in P. Bishop, ed. *Jung in Contexts* (1999).

Hegel, Georg Wilhelm Friedrich (1805–6) *Hegel and the Human Spirit: A Translation of the Jena Lectures on the Philosophy of Spirit*, trans. L. Rauch (Detroit: Wayne State University Press, 1983).

—— (1807) *The Phenomenology of Spirit*, trans. A.V. Miller (Oxford: Oxford University Press, 1977).

—— (1821) *Elements of the Philosophy of Right*, ed. and trans. A.W. Wood (Cambridge: Cambridge University Press, 1991).

—— (1840) *Lectures on the History of Philosophy*, volume III, trans. E. S. Haldane and F. H. Simson (London: Kegan Paul, 1896).

Heidegger, Martin (1927) *Being and Time*, trans. J. Macquarrie and E. Robinson (Oxford: Blackwell, 1962).

Heidelberger, Michael (2004) *Nature from Within: Gustav Theodor Fechner and his Psychophysical Worldview*, trans. C. Klohr (Pittsburgh: University of Pittsburgh).

Hofmann, Albert (1980) *LSD: My Problem Child* (New York: McGraw-Hill).
Holland, Eugene W. (1999) *Deleuze and Guattari's Anti-Oedipus: Introduction to Schizoanalysis* (London: Routledge).
Hone, Joseph (1971) *W. B. Yeats 1865–1939* (London: Penguin Books).
Hopkins (1982) 'Introduction: Philosophy and Psychoanalysis', in *Philosophical Essays on Freud* (Cambridge: Cambridge University Press).
Horder, T. J. , Witkowski, J. A. and Wylie, C. C. (1985) *A History of Embryology* (Cambridge: Cambridge University Press).
Howe, Ellic (1972) *The Magicians of the Golden Dawn* (London: Routledge).
Hughes, Ted (1997) *Tales from Ovid* (London: Faber & Faber).
Hume, David (1739) *A Treatise of Human Nature* (Oxford: Clarendon Press, 1888).
Hyppolite, Jean (1946) *Genesis and Structure of Hegel's 'Phenomenology of Spirit'*, trans. Samuel Cherniak and John Heckman (Evanston: Northwestern University Press, 1974)
—— (1949a) 'Du Bergsonisme à l'existentialisme', in J. Hyppolite, *Figures de la pensée philosophique* (Paris: PUF/Quadrige, 1991, vol. I).
—— (1949b) 'Various Aspects of Memory in Bergson', trans. A. V. Colman, in Leonard Lawlor *The Challenge of Bergsonism* (London: Continuum, 2003).
—— (1971) *Figures de la pensée philosophique: écrits 1931–1968 (Tome I & II)* (Quadridge: PUF).
Idel, Moshe (1988) *Kabbalah: New Perspectives* (New Haven, Conn.: Yale University Press).
Introvigne, Massimo (2001) 'Antoine Faivre: Father of Contemporary Vampire Studies', in Richard Caron, Joscelyn Godwin, Wouter Hanegraaf and Jean-Louis Vieillard-Baron, eds. *Ésotérisme, Gnoses & imaginaire symbolique* (Leuven: Peeters).
Jacques-Chaquin, Nicole (1982) 'Introduction' to Pierre de Lancre, *Tableau de l'inconstance des mauvaise anges et demons* (Paris: Aubier-Montaigne).
Jahn, Ilse (1994) 'On the Origin of Romantic Biology and its Further Development at the University of Jena between 1790 and 1850', in S. Poggi and M. Bossi, eds. *Romanticism in Science* (Dordrecht: Kluwer).
James, William (1909a) *A Pluralistic Universe* (London: University of Nebraska Press, 1996).
—— (1909b) 'Confidences of a Psychical Researcher' ['Final Impressions of a Psychical Researcher'], *Memories and Studies* (New York: Longmans, Green, 1911).
—— (1911) 'A Pluralistic Mystic', in *Memories and Studies.*
Janet, Pierre (1889) *L'automatisme psychologique* (Paris: Évreaux).
—— (1903) *Les obsessions et la psychasthénie,* 2 vols. (Paris: Alcan).
—— (1920) 'La Tension psychologique, ses degrees, ses oscillations', in *British Journal of Psychology, Medical Section,* Vol. I (1920–1).
—— (1924) 'Les Souvenirs Irréels', *Archives de psychologie,* vol. 19, 1925.
—— (1928) *L'Évolution de la mémoire et de la notion du temps* (Paris: Chahine).
Jankélévitch, Vladimir (1959) *Henri Bergson* (Paris: PUF; orig. edn, 1931).
Jolley, Nicholas (1984) *Leibniz and Locke: A Study of the New Essays on Human Understanding* (Oxford: Clarendon Press).
Jung, Carl Gustav, *The Collected Works of C. G. Jung,* trans. R. F. C. Hull, ed. Herbert Read *et al.* (New York and Princeton, Bollingen Series 20, 1953–83), 21 vols.
—— (1961) *Memories, Dreams, Reflections,* trans. R. and C. Winston, ed. A. Jaffé (London: Fontana, 1967).
—— (1973) *Letters 1: 1906–1950,* trans. R. F. C. Hull, ed. G. Adler (London: Routledge).
Jung, Carl Gustav and Pauli, Wölfgang (1955) *The Interpretation of Nature and the Psyche* [translation of *Naturerklärung und Psyche,* 1952], trans. R. F. C. Hull and P. Silz (London: Routledge & Kegan Paul).
Kant, Immanuel (1763) 'Attempt to Introduce the Concept of Negative Magnitudes into Philosophy', in *Theoretical Philosophy 1755–1770.*
—— (1772) 'Letter to Marcus Herz', in *Correspondence,* trans. A. Zweig (Cambridge: Cambridge University Press, 1999).
—— (1772) *Anthropology from a Pragmatic Point of View,* trans. Victor Lyle Dowdell (Carbondale and Edwardsville: Southern Illinois University Press, 1978).
—— *New Elucidation on the First Principles of Metaphysical Cognition, in Theoretical Philosophy*

1755–1770, trans. D. Walford and R. Meerbote (Cambridge: Cambridge University Press, 1992).

—— (1781/1787) *Critique of Pure Reason*, trans. Paul Guyer and Allen W. Wood (Cambridge: Cambridge University Press, 1997).

—— (1790) *Critique of Judgment* (including First Introduction), trans. Werner S. Pluhar (Cambridge: Hackett, 1987).

Kerr, John (1994) *A Most Dangerous Method: The Story of Jung, Freud, and Sabina Spielrein* (London: Sinclair-Stevenson, 1994).

Kerslake, Christian (2002) 'The Vertigo of Philosophy: Deleuze and the Problem of Immanence', in *Radical Philosophy* 113, May/June.

—— (2004) 'Rebirth through Incest: Deleuze's Early Jungianism', in *Angelaki: Journal of the Theoretical Humanities*, 9: 1.

—— (2005) 'Transcendental Cinema: Deleuze, Time and Modernity', in *Radical Philosophy* 130, March/April 2005.

Kierkegaard, Soren (1843a) *Johannes Climacus*, trans. Howard V. Hong and Edna H. Hong (Princeton, NJ: Princeton University Press, 1985).

—— (1843b) *Repetition: A Venture in Experimenting Psychology*, trans. Howard V. Hong and Edna H. Hong (Princeton, NJ: Princeton University Press, 1983).

—— (1843c) *Either/Or*, trans. Alastair Hannay (London: Penguin Books, 1992).

—— (1844) *The Concept of Anxiety*, trans. Reidar Thomte (Princeton, NJ: Princeton University Press, 1980).

—— (1844) *Philosophical Fragments*, trans. H. V. Hong and E. H. Hong, (Princeton, NJ: Princeton University Press, 1985).

Klossowski, Pierre (1969) *Nietzsche and the Vicious Circle*, trans. Daniel W. Smith (London: Athlone, Press 1997).

Knox, Jean (2003) *Archetype, Attachment, Analysis: Jungian Psychology and the Emergent Mind* (London: Brunner–Routledge).

Kohn, Marek (1987) *Narcomania: On Heroin* (London: Faber & Faber).

Lacan, Jacques (1951) 'Intervention on the Transference', in J. Mitchell and J. Rose, eds, *Feminine Sexuality* (London: Macmillan, 1982).

—— (1953–4) *Seminar I: Freud's Papers on Technique*, trans. John Forrester, ed. Jacques-Alain Miller (London: W. W. Norton & Co., 1991).

—— (1954–5) *Seminar II: The Ego in Freud's Theory and in the Technique of Psychoanalysis*, trans. Sylvana Tomaselli, ed. Jacques-Alain Miller (London: W. W. Norton & Co., 1991).

—— (1955–6) *Seminar III: The Psychoses*, trans. Russell Grigg, ed. Jacques-Alain Miller (London: Routledge, 1993).

—— (1956–7) *Le Séminaire, Livre V: Les formations de l'inconscient* (Paris: Éditions du Seuil, 1998). Unpublished translation by Cormac Gallagher.

—— (1959–1960) *The Ethics of Psychoanalysis: The Seminar of Jacques Lacan, Book VII*, trans. Dennis Porter (London: Routledge, 1999).

—— (1966) *Écrits*, trans. Bruce Fink (London: W. W. Norton & Co., 2004).

—— (2001) *Autres écrits* (Paris: Éditions du Seuil).

Lacey, A. R. (1989) *Bergson* (London: Routledge).

LaDage, Alta J. (1978) *Occult Psychology: A Comparison of Jungian Psychology and the Modern Qabalah* (Minnesota: Llewellyn Publications)

Lalande, André (1960) ed. *Vocabulaire technique et critique de la philosophie*, 8th edn (Paris: PUF, 1960).

Laplanche, Jean (1970) *Life and Death in Psychoanalysis*, trans. J. Mehlmann (Baltimore: Johns Hopkins University, 1976).

—— (1989) *New Foundations for Psychoanalysis*, trans. D. Macey (Oxford: Blackwell).

Laurant, Jean-Pierre (1992) *L'Ésotérisme Chrétien en France au XIXe Siècle* (Paris: L'Age d'homme).

Lawlor, Leonard (2003) *The Challenge of Bergsonism* (London: Continuum).

Lawrence, D. H. (1923) *Fantasia of the Unconscious and Psychoanalysis and the Unconscious* (Harmondsworth: Penguin, 1971).

Lee, Matt (2003) 'Memories of a Sorcerer: Notes on Gilles Deleuze, Félix Guattari, Austin Osman spare and Anomalous Sorceries', in *Journal for the Academic Study of Magic*, 1.

Lefebure, Molly (1974) *Samuel Taylor Coleridge: A Bondage of Opium* (London: Gollancz).
Leibniz, Gottfried Wilhelm (1686) 'Discourse on Metaphysics', in *Philosophical Essays*, trans. and ed. R. Ariew and D. Garber (Indianapolis: Hackett, 1989).
—— (1686b) 'A Specimen of Discoveries about Marvellous Secrets of Nature in General', in *Philosophical Writings*, ed. G. H. R. Parkinson (London: J. M. Dent, 1973).
—— (1686–7) 'Letters to Arnauld', in *Philosophical Writings*.
—— (1697) 'On the Ultimate Origination of Things', in *Philosophical Essays*.
—— (1710) *Theodicy*, trans. E. M. Huggard (La Salle: Open Court, 1985).
—— (1714) 'Principles of Nature and Grace', in *Philosophical Essays*.
—— (1714b) 'The Principles of Philosophy, or, The Monadology', in *Philosophical Essays*.
—— (1765) *New Essays on the Human Understanding*, trans. P. Remnant and J. Bennett (Cambridge: Cambridge University Press, 1996).
—— (1969) *Philosophical Papers and Letters*, trans. Leroy E. Loemker (Dordrecht: D. Reidel Publishing).
Lesky, Erna (1976) *The Vienna Medical School of the 19th Century* (Baltimore: Johns Hopkins University Press).
Le Vay, Simon (1993) *The Sexual Brain* (Cambridge, Mass.: MIT Press).
Lévi, Éliphas (1896) *The Key of the Mysteries*, trans. A. Crowley (London: Rider, 1959).
Lévi-Strauss, Claude (1950) *Introduction to the Work of Marcel Mauss*, trans. Felicity Baker (London: Routledge & Kegan Paul, 1987).
—— (1958) *Structural Anthropology*, trans. Claire Jacobson and Brooke Grundfest Schoepf (London: Penguin Books, 1993).
Lévy, Bernard-Henri (1977) *La Barbarie à Visage Humain* (Paris: Grasset).
Lipowski, Zbigniew J. (1990) *Delirium: Acute Confusional States* (Oxford: Oxford University Press).
Locke, John (1690) *An Essay Concerning Human Understanding*, ed. Roger Woolhouse (London: Penguin Books, 1997).
Logic, trans. R. S. Hartmann and Wolfgang Schwarz (Indianapolis: Hackett).
Long, Charles H. (1987) 'Cosmogony', in M. Eliade ed. *The Encyclopedia of Religion*, 4.
Lorenz, Konrad (1939) 'The Comparative Study of Behavior', in K. Lorenz and P. Leyhausen, *Motivation of Human and Animal Behavior: An Ethological View*, trans. B. Tonkin (New York: Van Nostrand Reinhold, 1973).
—— (1950) 'Part and Parcel in Animal and Human Societies', in *Studies in Animal and Human Behaviour*, 2, trans. R. Martin (London: Methuen, 1971).
Lossky, N. O. (1936) 'Three Chapters from the History of Polish Messianism', in International Philosophical Library (Prague), vol. II, no. 9.
Lowry, Malcolm (1947) *Under the Volcano* (London: Penguin Books, 1962).
—— (1996) *Sursum Corda! Collected Letters of Malcolm Lowry*, ed. S. E. Grace (London: Jonathan Cape), 2 vols.
Lowrie, Walter (1946) ed., *Religion of a Scientist*. Selections from Gustav Th. Fechner (New York: Pantheon Books).
Lucie-Smith, Edward (1972) *Symbolist Art* (London: Thames & Hudson).
Lukács, Georg (1962) *The Destruction of Reason*, trans. P. Palmer (London: Merlin Press, 1980).
McGowan, Todd (2004) *The End of Dissatisfaction? Jacques Lacan and the Emerging Society of Enjoyment* (Albany, NY: State University of New York Press).
McGuire, William and Hull, R. F. C. (eds) (1980) . *C. G. Jung Speaking: Interviews and Encounters* (London: Picador).
McIntosh, Christopher (1972) *Eliphas Lévi and the French Occult Revival* (London: Rider).
McRae, Robert (1976) *Leibniz: Perception, Apperception, and Thought* (Toronto: University of Toronto Press).
Maidenbaum, Aryeh and Martin, Stephen A. (eds) (1991) *Lingering Shadows: Jungians, Freudians, and Anti-Semitism* (London: Shambhala).
Main, Roderick (1997) ed. *Jung on Synchroncity and the Paranormal* (London: Routledge).
Malfatti de Montereggio, Johann (1809) *Entwurf einer Pathologenie aus der Evolution und Revolution des Lebens* (Vienna: Wappler and Beck).
—— (1845) *Studien über Anarchie und Hierarchie des Wissens, mit besonderer Beziehung auf die Medicin*

(Leipzig: Brockhaus). Trans. into French as *Études sur la mathèse ou anarchie et hiérarchie de la science* (Paris: Editions du Griffon D'Or, 1946).

Malinowski, Branislaw (1927) *Sex and Repression in Savage Society* (London: Routledge).

—— (1929) *The Sexual Life of Savages in North-Western Melanesia* (London: Routledge).

Mandler, Jean (1992) 'How to build a baby II: conceptual primitives', in *Psychological Review* 99: 4.

Martin, C. B. & Deutscher, Max (1966) 'Remembering', in *Philosophical Review* 75: 4.

Martin, Jean-Pierre (2003) *Henri Michaux* (Paris: Gallimard).

Masson, Jeffrey (1985) ed. *The Complete Letters of Sigmund Freud to Wilhelm Fliess* (Cambridge, Mass.: Harvard University Press).

Meissner, W. W. (1962) 'The Problem of Psychophysics: Bergson's Critique', in *Journal of General Psychology*, 66.

Merleau-Ponty, Maurice (1945) *The Phenomenology of Perception*, trans. C. Smith (London: Routledge, 1962; rev. 1979).

Michaux, Henri (1956) *Miserable Miracle*, trans. Louise Varèse and Anna Moschovakis (New York: Review Books, 2002).

—— (1964) *Infinite Turbulence*, 2nd edition, trans. M. Fineberg (London: Calder & Boyars, 1975).

—— (1966) *The Major Ordeals of the Mind & the Countless Minor Ones*, trans. Richard Howard (New York: Harcourt Brace, 1974).

—— (1968) *Selected Writings*, trans. R. Ellman (New York: New Directions).

—— (1994) *Darkness Moves: An Henri Michaux Anthology, 1927–1984*, ed. D. Ball (Berkeley: University of California Press).

Miller, Jacques-Alain (1996) 'An Introduction to Seminars I and II', in *Reading Seminars I and II*, eds. R. Feldstein, B. Fink, and M. Jaanus (Albany, NY: State University of New York Press).

Mitton, Jeffry B. (1993) 'Theory and Data Pertinent to the Relationship between Heterozygosity and Fitness', in Thornhill (1993).

Minkowski, Eugène (1932) 'Le problème des hallucinations et le problème de l'espace', in *Évolution Psychiatrique*, IV (2): 3.

—— (1933) *Lived Time: Phenomenological and Psychopathological Studies*, trans. N. Metzel (Evanston: Northwestern University Press, 1970).

Montgomery, Robert E. (1994) *The Visionary D. H. Lawrence: Beyond Philosophy and Art* (Cambridge: Cambridge University Press).

Moore, F. C. T. (1999) 'Magic', in J. Mullarkey, ed., *The New Bergson* (Manchester: Manchester University Press, 1999).

Müller, Niklas (1822) *Glauben, Wissen und Kunst der alten Hindus* (Leipzig; Editions Leipzig; 1968 reprint).

Murphy, Timothy S. (1996) 'Bibliography of the Works of Gilles Deleuze' in Patton (1996).

Nietzsche, Friedrich (1878) *Human all too Human*, trans. R. J. Hollingdale (Cambridge: Cambridge University Press, 1986).

—— (1881) *Daybreak*, trans. R. J. Hollingdale (Cambridge: Cambridge University Press, 1997).

—— (1884; fourth volume 1892) *Thus Spake Zarathustra*, trans. R. J. Hollingdale (London: Penguin Books, 1969).

—— (1887) *On the Genealogy of Morals*, trans. W. Kaufman (New York: Vintage, 1967).

—— (1967) *The Will to Power*, trans. W. Kaufmann and R. J. Hollingdale (New York: Random House).

Novalis (1802) *Heinrich von Ofterdingen*, trans. Palmer Hilty (Illinois: Prospect Heights, 1992).

—— (1966) *Werke*, Gerhard Schulz, ed. (München: Beck, 1969).

—— (1984) *Hymns to the Night*, trans. Dick Higgins (New York: McPherson & Co.).

—— (1997) *Philosophical Writings*, trans. Margaret Mahony Stoljar (Albany: State University of New York Press).

Otten, Charlotte F. (ed.) (1987) *A Lycanthropy Reader: Werewolves in Western Culture* (New York: Syracuse University Press).

Ovid, *Metamorphoses*, trans. M. Innes (London: Penguin Books, 1955).

Padoux, André (1990) *Vāc: The Concept of the Word in Selected Hindu Tantras*, trans. J. Gontier (Albany: SUNY).

—— (2002) 'What do we mean by Tantrism?', in K.A. Harper and R.L. Brown, eds, *The Roots of Tantra* (Albany: SUNY).

Papus (1894) 'La Doctrine d'Éliphas Lévi', Appendix to Éliphas Lévi, *Le Livre des Splendeurs* (Paris: Chamuel, 1894).
—— (1901) *What is Occultism?* trans. F. Rothwell (London: Rider, 1913).
Patton, Paul (ed.) (1996) *Deleuze: A Critical Reader* (Oxford: Blackwell).
Paz, Octavio (1967) 'Introduction' to Michaux, *Miserable Miracle* (NY: New York Review of Books, 2002).
Peckham, George W. and Elizabeth G. (1905) *Wasps Social and Solitary* (Westminster: Archibald Constable & Co.).
Penna, Antonio Gomes (1988) 'Bergson's Critique of Fechner', in J. Brožek and H. Gundlach *G. T. Fechner and Psychology* (Passau: Passavia Universitätsverlag).
Perry, Marvin (1996) *Arnold Toynbee and the Western Tradition* (New York: Peter Lang).
Philipon, René (1899) *Stanislas de Guaita et sa bibliothèque occulte* (Paris: Dorbon).
Pignarre, Philippe & Stengers, Isabelle (2005) *La sorcellerie capitaliste* (Paris: Découverte).
Pippin, Robert B. (1987) 'Kant on the Spontaneity of Mind', in *Canadian Journal of Philosophy* 17: 2, June.
—— (1989) *Hegel's Idealism* (Cambridge: Cambridge University Press).
Plato (1956) *Protagoras and Meno*, traans. W. K. C. Guthrie (London: Penguin Books).
Poe, Edgar Allan (1845) 'The Facts in the Case of M. Valdemar', in E. A. Poe, *The Fall of the House of Usher and Other Writings* (London: Penguin Books, 1986).
—— (1846) *Mesmerism in Articulo Mortis* (London: Short & Co.)
Pradines, Maurice (1943) *Traité de psychologie générale* (Paris).
Price, H. H. (1941) 'Henri Bergson', in *Proceedings of the Society for Psychical Research*, vol. XLVI, 1940–1.
—— (1942) *The Search for Truth: My Life for Psychical Research* (London: Collins).
Proclus (1970) *A Commentary on the First Book of Euclid's Elements*, trans. G. Morrow (Princeton, NJ: Princeton University Press).
Pryse, James Morgan (1910) *The Apocalypse Unsealed* (London: J. M. Watkins).
Rätsch, Christian (1992) *The Dictionary of Sacred and Magical Plants*, trans. John Baker (Dorset: Prism Press).
Regardie, Israel (1964) *The Art and Meaning of Magic* (Cheltenham: Helios, 1971).
—— (1968) *Roll Away the Stone: An Introduction to Aleister Crowley's Essays on the Psychology of Hashish* (Minnesota: Llewellyn Publications).
Reggio, David (2004) 'Jean Malfatti de Montereggio: A Brief Introduction', article published at http://www.goldsmiths.ac.uk/departments/history/news-events/malfatti_intro.php.
Reid, Thomas (1785) 'Of Mr. Locke's Account of our Personal Identity' (from Chapter 4, 'Of Memory', in *Essays on the Intellectual Powers of Man*), reprinted in J. Perry, ed. *Personal Identity* (Berkeley: University of California Press, 1975).
Ricoeur, Paul (1965) *Freud and Philosophy: An Essay on Interpretation*, trans. D. Savage (New Haven, Conn.: Yale University Press, 1970).
Ridley, Matt (1993) *The Red Queen: Sex and the Evolution of Human Nature* (London: Penguin Books).
Roudinesco, Elisabeth (2000) *Jacques Lacan & Co.: A History of Psychoanalysis in France, 1925–1985*, trans. Jeffrey Mehlman (Chicago: University of Chicago Press).
Rowland, Susan (2002) *Jung: A Feminist Revision* (Cambridge: Polity).
Ruse, Michael (2002) 'Evolutionary Biology and Teleological Thinking', in A. Ariew *et al.*, eds. *Functions: New Essays in the Philosophy of Psychology and Biology* (Oxford: Oxford University Press).
Russell, Bertrand (1900) *The Philosophy of Leibniz* (London: Routledge, 1992)
—— (1910) 'The Monistic Theory of Truth', in *Philosophical Essays* (London: Longmans, Green & Co).
—— (1921) *The Analysis of Mind* (London: George Allen & Unwin).
Ruyer, Raymond (1958) *La genèse des formes vivantes* (Paris: Flammarion).
—— (1959) 'Bergson et le Sphex ammophile', in *Revue de Métaphysique et de Morale*, 64: 2.
—— (1988) 'There is no Subconscious: Embryogenesis and Memory', trans. R. Scott Walker, in *Diogenes* 142 (Summer).

Samuels, Andrew (1993) *The Political Psyche* (London: Routledge).

Schelling, F. W. J. (1857) *Sämmtliche Werke, vol. 12: Philosophie der Mythologie* (Stuttgart: J. G. Gottascher).

—— (1994) *Idealism and the Endgame of Theory: Three Essays by F. W. J. Schelling*, trans. Thomas Pfau (Albany: State University of New York Press).

Schopenhauer, Arthur (1850) 'Transcendent Speculation on the Apparent Deliberateness in the Fate of the Individual', in *Parerga and Paralipomena*, vol. I, trans. E. F. J. Payne (Oxford: Clarendon Press, 1974).

—— (1844) *The World as Will and Representation*, 2 Vols, trans. E. F. J. Payne (New York: Dover, 1969).

Sedgwick, Mark (2004) *Against the Modern World: Traditionalism and the Secret Intellectual History of the Twentieth Century* (Oxford: Oxford University Press).

Shamdasani, Sonu (1990) 'A Woman called Frank', in *Spring: A Journal of Archetype and Culture*, vol. 50.

—— (1995) 'Memories, Dreams, Omissions', reprinted in P. Bishop, ed. *Jung in Contexts.*

—— (2003) *Jung and the Making of Modern Psychology* (Cambridge: Cambridge University Press).

Shoemaker, Sydney (1970) 'Persons and their Past', in *American Philosophical Quarterly* 7: 4 (October).

Siorvanes, Lucas (1996) *Proclus: Neo-Platonic Philosophy and Science* (Edinburgh: Edinburgh University Press).

Sjövall, Björn (1967) *Psychology of Tension: An Analysis of Pierre Janet's Concept of 'Tension Psychologique'*, trans. A. Dixon (Norstedts: Scandinavian University Books).

Smith, Jonathan Z. (1987) 'Sleep', in M. Eliade, ed. *The Encylopedia of Religion*, vol. 13 (New York: Macmillan, 1987).

Smith, Daniel W. 'Gilles Deleuze and the Conditions of the New' [unpublished article].

Spriel, Stéphen (1960) 'Le cryptogramme Lowry', in *Les Lettres Nouvelles*, vol. 5, July–August 1960.

Stengers, Isabelle (2006) 'Deleuze's Last Message', available online at Recalcitrance.com.

Stevens, Anthony (1998) *Ariadne's Clue: A Guide to the Symbols of Humankind* (Princeton, NJ: Princeton University Press).

—— (2002) *Archetype Revisited* (London: Routledge); orig. edn 1982.

Stevens, Anthony and Price, John (2000) *Evolutionary Psychiatry* (London: Routledge).

Sulloway, Frank (1992) *Freud: Biologist of the Mind* (Cambridge, Mass.: Harvard University Press, 1992).

Summers, Montague (1929) *The Vampire in Europe* (Wellingborough: Aquarian, 1980).

Swales, Peter J. (1983) *Freud, Cocaine and Sexual Chemistry: The Role of Cocaine in Freud's Conception of the Libido* (privately published by the author).

[Tannery, Jules] (1875) 'La mesure des sensations. Réponses à propos du logarithme des sensations', in *Révue Scientifique*, 2e série, 4e année, No. 43. [Article appeared anonymously.]

Taylor, Eugene (1980) 'William James and C. G. Jung' in *Spring: An Annual of Archetypal Psychology and Jungian Thought*, vol. 20.

—— (1996) *William James on Consciousness beyond the Margin* (Princeton, NJ: Princeton University Press).

Taylor, Kathleen (2001) *Sir John Woodroffe, Tantra and Bengal* (Richmond: Curzon).

Thornhill, Nancy (1989) 'The Evolutionary Significance of Incest Rules', in *Ethology and Sociobiology*, 11.

—— (1993) ed. *The Natural History of Inbreeding and Outbreeding* (Chicago: Chicago University Press).

Thorpe, W. H. (1979) *The Origins and Rise of Ethology* (London: Heinemann Educational Books).

Tinbergen, Niko (1951) *The Study of Instinct* (Oxford: Clarendon Press, 1951).

Tindall, William York (1939) *D. H. Lawrence & Susan his Cow* (New York: Columbia University Press).

Tsouyopoulos, Nelly (1988) 'The Influence of John Brown's Ideas in Germany', in W. F. Bynum & R. Porter *Brunonianism in Britain and Europe* (London: Wellcome Institute for the History of Medicine).

Uexküll, Jakob von (1926) *Theoretical Biology*, trans. D. L. MacKinnon (London: Kegan Paul).

—— (1934) 'A Stroll through the Worlds of Animals and Men: A Picture Book of Invisible Worlds', trans. Claire Schiller, in Schiller, *Instinctive Behaviour* (New York: International Universities Press, 1957).

Ulanov, Ann (1997) 'Jung and Religion: The Opposing Self', in P. Young-Eisendrath & T. Dawson eds. *The Cambridge Companion to Jung* (Cambridge: Cambridge University Press).

Van Haute, Philippe (2002) *Against Adaptation: Lacan's 'Subversion' of the Subject*, trans. Paul Crowe & Miranda Vankerk (New York: Other Press).

Van Haute, Philippe and Geyskens, Tomas (2004) *Confusion of Tongues: The Primacy of Sexuality in Freud, Ferenczi and Laplanche* (New York: Other Press).

Verhaeghe, Paul (2004) *On Being Normal and Other Disorders: A Manual for Clinical Psychodiagnostics*, trans. Sigi Jottkandt (New York: Other Press).

Viatte, Auguste (1928) *Les sources occultes du Romantisme* (Paris: Honoré Champion, 2 vols).

Vickers, Brian (1984) 'Analogy and Identity', in B. Vickers, ed. *Occult and Scientific Mentalities in the Renaissance* (Cambridge: Cambridge University Press).

Waddell, L. Augustine (1895) *The Buddhism of Tibet, or Lamaism* (London: W. H. Allen).

Warrain, Francis (1925) *L'Armature métaphysique établie d'après la Loi de Création de Hoené Wronski* (Paris: Alcan).

Wasserstrom, Steven M. (1999) *Religion after Religion* (Princeton, NJ: Princeton University Press).

Williams, Thomas A. (1975) *Eliphas Lévi: Master of Occultism* (Albama: University of Alabama Press).

Wilson, E. B. (1925) *The Cell in Development and Heredity* (London: Macmillan).

Wilson, Horace Hayman (1828) 'A Sketch of the Religious Sects of the Hindus', reprinted in *Works*, Vol. 1/i, (London: Trübner & Co, 1862–1877).

Willson, A. Leslie (1964) *A Mythical Image: The Ideal of India in German Romanticism* (Durham: Duke).

Winson, Jonathan (1990) 'The Meaning of Dreams', in *Scientific American*, 264: 5, November.

Wolpert, Lewis (1985) 'Gradients, Position, and Pattern: A History', in T. Horder *et al.*

Wronski, Hoëne (1847) *Messianisme ou réforme absolue du savoir humain* (Paris).

—— (1878) *Prospectus de la philosophie absolue et son développement* (Paris: Depot des ouvrages de l'auteur).

Wundt, Wilhelm (1862) *Beiträge zur Theorie der Sinneswahrnehmung* (Leipzig: Winter).

—— (1863) *Vorlesungen über Menschen- und Thierseele* (Leipzig: Voss).

—— (1892) *Lectures on Human and Animal Psychology*, trans. J. E. Creighton and E. B. Titchener (New York: Macmillan, 1894).

—— (1896) *Outlines of Psychology*, trans. C. H. Judd (Leipzig: Engelmann, 1897).

—— (1908–11) *Grundzüge der physiologischer psychologie* (Leipzig: Engelmann).

Yates, Frances (1964) *Giordano Bruno and the Hermetic Tradition* (Chicago: University of Chicago Press).

—— (1966) *The Art of Memory* (London: Routledge).

Zeltner, Hermann (1954) *Schelling* (Stuttgart: Frommanns).

Žižek, Slavoj (1989) *The Sublime Object of Ideology* (London: Verso).

—— (1998) 'The Cartesian Subject versus the Cartesian Theater', in S. Žižek, ed., *Cogito and the Unconscious* (Durham: Duke University Press).

—— (2001) *Enjoy your Symptom! Jacques Lacan in Hollywood and Out*, 2nd edition (London: Routledge).

—— (2004) *Organs without Bodies: Deleuze and Consequences* (London: Routledge).

Index

Absolute, the 37, 159–60
Aesthetics, see Bergson; Kant; Symbolism
Al-Kindi 173
Alexandria 37, 129
Alexandrian, Sarane 129
Ameriks, Karl 95
Ammophila hirsuita, see Hymenoptera
Anatomy, Occult 171–3, 221
Anima/Animus
  in Malfatti 103, 134–7
  in Jung 77–8, 85
Ansell-Pearson, Keith 52, 198
Apperception 21, 40–2, 57, 59, 85, 93, 95
Apuleius 45
Art 3, 64, 65, 113, 115, 126, 129, 154, 164, 167
Artaud, Antonin 70, 124, 172, 177, 223
Attention 19, 22, 27, 55, 59, 83, 95, 187
Aurevilly, Jules Barbey d' 124
Augustine, Saint 98

Baader, Franz von 200, 216
Bachofen, Johann Jakob 77, 204, 205
Baer, Karl von 64
Beach, Edward Allen 108, 134, 137
Beauty, the Beautiful 113–24
Beckett, Samuel 74
Becoming-animal 167, 170–73
Behaviourism 51, 87
Beethoven, Ludwig van 126
Bennet, E. A. 103–7
Benjamin, Walter 190
Bergson, Henri 5–36, 48, 49–57, 50, 59, 61–8, 87–9, 159–68, 177, 183, 187, 189
  Aesthetics 65–6, 163–4
  Duration 8–16, 65, 165, 171, 183–4
  Instinct 49–57, 59, 61–8, 86–7, 159–60, 165, 168
  Intensity 14–16
  Intuition 56, 61–8, 87–8, 90, 163, 168
  Memory 8–9, 16–36, 61, 168, 191, 195, 204–5
Bey, Hakim 220
Binet, Alfred 190, 200
Binswanger, Ludwig 1, 209
Birth 100–1, 126
Bishop, Paul 219
Blood, Benjamin Paul 182
Body without Organs 137, 172
Böhme, Jakob 133
Brain 5, 20–5, 27, 39, 57, 164
Brave Officer Paradox, the 196
Bruno, Giordano 129, 169
Brunonian medicine 125
Buller David 58
Buytendijk, F.J.J. 198
Buss, David 89

Canguilhem, Georges 198
Capitalism 78, 173–5
Caramuel, Juan 129
Castration 78, 100, 109
Caves 119, 212 n. 16–17
Cavell, Marcia 58
Charcot, Jean-Martin 60
Childhood 26, 45, 49, 71, 83, 101–2
Cicero 73
Cinema 7, 177, 207, 223–4
Clérambault, Gaëtan de 224–5

Cocteau, Jean 225–6
Coleridge, Samuel Taylor 179, 183
Cooke, Mordecai 179
Coudert, Allison 196
Consciousness 5–8, 20–5, 29, 43–8, 54–61, 64, 66–7, 83–4, 85, 93, 180–1
  Pure consciousness 55–6, 58, 64, 199–20
Creuzer, Friedrich 77, 216
Crowley, Aleister 62, 103, 167, 171, 185
Crystals 119–20
Curtis, Adam 221
Cuvier, Georges 50, 51, 53, 201

Dalbiez, Roland 107–8
Darwin, Charles 51, 52, 54, 88
Davy, Marie-Madeleine 127, 214
Dead, the 27, 175–8
Death 27–8, 100–1, 149–50, 158, 175–8, 189, 190, 197, 220
Death drive/instinct 146, 156–8, 189, 211
Déjà vu, see Paramnesia
Dennett, Daniel 58
Descartes, René 39–41, 43–4
Desexualization 75, 203, 204, 205, 209
Desire 73, 106
Deutscher, Max 192
Differential thresholds, see Intensive difference
Differential unconscious 38–48, 138–40, 150–54, 224
Dionysius the Areopagite 98, 133, 215
Dissociation 35, 58, 84, 100, 200, 224
Dreams 26, 53, 59, 77, 85, 94, 133, 148–9, 154, 156, 159, 161, 177–9, 189, 223
  and Drugs 177–88
Drever, James 51, 86
Driesch, Hans 63
Drugs 154, 169, 177–88
Duration, see Bergson

Ecstasy 60, 132–3, 172, 178, 186, 216
Egg, World- 48, 64, 91, 137, 215
Eliade, Mircea 212, 214, 215
Embryology 48, 63–5, 93, 125, 135, 186, 201
Emotion 163–4
Esotericism, see Occultism
Eternal Return, see Nietzsche
Ethics 25, 36–7
Ethology 50–3, 87, 89, 101, 208
Evola, Julius 216

Fabre, Jean-Henri 51, 53–7, 62
Fabulation 161–2
Family, see Parental Figures
Fascination 171
Fate 34, 145–50, 154–8, 199
Father 78, 88
Faulkner, Keith 70
Fechner, Gustav 1, 10–16, 47–8, 138, 184, 197, 217, 220–1, 225
Ferenczi, Sándor 104, 202
Fichte, Johann 120
Fiedler, Leslie 224
Fletcher, Ronald 198
Flournoy, Theodore 202
Frankfurt School 189
Frege, Gottlob 218
Frenzy 60, 62, 159, 161, 165–9, 186
Freud, Sigmund 5,7,17, 30–2, 35, 49, 70, 83, 100–1, 145, 154–8, 180–1, 185, 189, 209, 211, 225
  Drive [*Trieb*] 49
  Libido theory 72–3, 75
  Memory 34, 195
  Project for a Scientific Psychology 5, 22
  Repression 5, 18, 22, 27, 50, 71, 83, 100–1
  Sexuality 7, 34, 49
  Trauma 31–2

Gardner, Sebastian 58
Geoffroy Saint-Hilaire, Étienne 201
Gilbert, Paul 89
God 37, 97, 101, 129, 133–5, 137, 151, 154, 210, 226

Gordon, Pierre 205
Guattari, Félix 74, 101, 105, 169, 222 n.11
Guaita, Stanislas de 126, 129, 184–5
Guénon, René 126, 214–5

Habit 19, 191
Haeckel, Ernst 64
Hardt, Michael 189
Haule, John 59, 190
Hallucination 39, 76, 181–84, 224–6
Hartmann, Eduard von 51
Hegel, Georg Wilhelm Friedrich 21, 33, 39, 159, 163, 165, 182, 212
Heiberg, J. L. 227
Heidegger, Martin 6, 25, 160, 190
Heliogabalus 44
Hermeticism, see Occultism
Hermaphrodite 62–3, 103–4, 125, 134–7, 172, 201, 217
Hofmann, Albert 225
Holland, Eugene 3
Hoffmann, E. T. A. 154
Homer 27, 157
Hopkins, Jim 58
Hume, David 8, 28, 50
Humanism 24, 160
Humour 189, 227
Husserl, Edmund 95, 218
Hymenoptera 53–7, 61–2, 159
Hypnosis, see Somnambulism
Hyppolite, Jean 160, 192 n. 12
Hysteria 59, 79–80

'I', Fractured 1, 39, 95–6, 154
Ice Age 205
Ideas 67, 90–2, 94–100, 111–13, 118, 152–4
Immanence 37, 150–2
Incest
in Freud 75
in Jung 75, 81, 122
in Lawrence 187
Royal 122
Indian religion 126, 132–3
Individuation 2–3, 23, 48, 81–2, 85, 91, 96–7, 99, 113, 147, 154, 158, 160, 169, 184, 189, 202
Instinct 49–70, 86–92, 159
Intensive difference 10–16, 33, 48, 69, 74, 79, 91–3, 96–7, 119–20, 225
Interiorization of Difference 21–23, 160
Intuition 51, 56, 60, 61–8, 87–8, 90, 92–4, 154, 163
Irony 227
See Humour

James, William 182
Janet, Pierre 5–8, 18, 20–22, 35–6, 50, 58–60, 83, 161
Jung, C. G. 6–8, 19, 35–6, 42, 69–102, 103–111, 138–46, 150–1, 158, 164, 170, 178, 180, 185–6
Anima-Animus 77–8, 85
Archetypes 68, 69, 79–80, 87–92, 98, 146, 161, 170
Critique of Freud 73–77, 79–80, 100–1, 103–4, 106–8
Individuation 2–3, 81–6, 154, 158, 189
Introversion/Extraversion 35–6, 83
Instinct 69, 75, 86–92
Memory 35, 81, 204–5
Rebirth 81, 104–5, 122, 144, 170
Self 82, 85–6
Shadow 82, 84–5
Symbolism 70, 76, 81, 103–111, 121–24, 215
Synchronicity 141–46, 148, 150, 154, 158
Time 35–6, 91, 93, 141–6

Kafka, Franz 70, 124, 177, 186
Kant, Immanuel 21, 24, 37, 40, 57, 67, 70, 82, 83, 87, 90, 91–100, 106, 129, 147, 194, 196, 199, 203, 209, 218–20
Aesthetics 67, 113–24
Apperception 21, 57, 58, 84, 85, 93, 95–6

Ethics 36–7
Intuitions 90, 92–4, 120
Ideas 67, 90–2, 94–100, 111–13, 118, 152–54
Symbolism 111–24
Kierkegaard, Søren 24–5, 28–30, 34, 42, 185, 227
Klossowski, Pierre 37, 96
Knox, Jean 88, 90, 207–8

Lacan, Jacques 6, 35, 49, 74, 82, 101, 109, 173, 189, 196, 203, 207
Lacey, A. R. 199
Lamarckianism 88–9
Lamborn Wilson, Peter 220
Language 126
Laplanche, Jean 220
Lascaux 119, 212 n. 16–17
Lawrence, D. H. 70, 124, 172
Lee, Matt 220
Leibniz, G. W. 38–48, 97, 129, 138–41, 150–4, 169, 173, 176–7, 183–4, 194
Metempsychosis 38–48, 176–7
Possible worlds 150–4
Unconscious perceptions 38–43, 139, 176, 183–4
Vague Adam 153–4
Virtual 25–6, 41, 46
Lévi, Eliphas 197
Lévi-Strauss, Claude 170–1, 206–7
Libido 71–82
Lloyd Morgan, Conwy 51
Locke, John 39–46
Lorenz, Konrad 52, 62, 66, 89–90, 208
Lowry, Malcolm 173
Love 82, 85, 126, 129, 154, 163–64, 167, 189
Lukács, Gyorgy 190
Lull, Ramon 129
Lycanthropy 110, 212
Lynch, David 43–44

Madness, see Psychosis
Maïmon, Solomon 120
Malfatti de Montereggio, Johann 1, 59, 103, 111, 124–37, 159, 172, 184, 200, 213–16
Malinowski, Bronislaw 8, 70
Mallarmé, Stephane 124, 134
Martin, C. B. 192
Martinism 126
Marxism 174, 190
Masochism 77–8, 103–5
Masson-Oursel, Paul 216
Mathesis 67, 97, 124–37, 164
Mauss, Marcel 205–6
McDougall, William 51, 86
Memory
See Bergson; Freud; Jung
Mesmer, Franz Anton 58–9, 200
Michaux, Henri 182–4, 187
Microcosm 37, 42, 48, 133–8, 160, 164, 172
Minkowski, Eugène 6, 209
Moritz, Karl Philipp 164
Mother 75–6, 81, 90, 137
Mountains 115, 119
Müller, Niklas 216
Music 163–4

Nachträglichkeit 31–2
Narcissism 72, 75, 145–6, 154–7, 220
Negri, Antonio 189
Nerval, Gérard de 124
Neurosis 34–6, 39, 79–82, 110
Nietzsche, Friedrich Wilhelm 23–4, 30, 34–37, 124
Eternal Return 17, 25, 36–7, 196
Night 39, 175, 178, 186–8, 227
Nightmares 65, 186–8, 189
Nocturnal emissions 148, 178
Novalis 119–20, 129, 213 n. 18
Numerology 103, 125, 127–28, 131–2, 134, 156, 218

Oedipus 2
Oedipus complex 75, 79, 100–2

Occultism 69, 97, 103–4, 124–37, 154, 159–86, 221
Alchemy 129, 185, 226
Hermeticism 37, 38, 48, 97, 129, 175, 209
Magic 76, 120, 129, 130, 167, 185, 221–2
Sorcery 79, 167–9, 173–5, 185, 223–4, 226–7
Theosophy 133–35, 175, 221
Witchcraft, see Sorcery

Packs [*meutes*] 170
Paleoscope 20, 25, 192
Papus (Gérard Encausse) 126, 129, 213–4
Paramnesia 28–34, 37, 93, 158
Parapsychology 142–6, 217–19
Past 9, 16–37, 50, 195
Parental figures; 101–2, 105–6
See Mother; Father
Pauli, Wölfgang 141
Personal Identity 43–48
Plato 20, 33, 37, 98, 209
Pignarre, Philippe 174–5
Poe, Edgar Allen 177, 222
Problems, see Ideas
Proclus 129–31
Proust, Marcel 30, 114, 195
Pryse, James M. 221
Psychosis 1–2, 39, 71–82, 110, 115–6, 124, 133, 158, 169, 173
Paranoia 72, 116
Schizophrenia 71–2, 78–9, 158, 173

Quincey, Thomas de 178–9, 224

Race 162, 170, 205–6
Ranft, Michael 171, 222
Rank, Otto 155
Reality 74–9, 137, 158, 172–3, 202
Rebirth (Second Birth, Regeneration) 81, 104–5, 122, 133, 157–8, 170
Recapitulation 64, 86, 88, 104
Recollection (Reminiscence, *Anamnesis*) 20, 28–34, 61–2, 130–1, 137
Reggio, David 126, 214
Repetition 17, 23–5, 27, 34, 36–8, 39, 56, 88, 95, 112, 147, 154–8
Repression 5, 18, 19, 22, 27, 50, 71, 75–80, 84–5, 100
Revolutionary consciousness 154
Ressentiment 34–5
Ricoeur, Paul 95
Rimbaud, Arthur 124, 206
Rivers, W. H. R. 51, 86
Russell, Bertrand 51
Ruyer, Raymond 49, 62–5, 83, 199, 217

Sacher-Masoch, Leopold von 77–8, 103–5, 124
Sallust 73
Sartre, Jean-Paul 6, 21, 57
Schelling, Friedrich Wilhelm Joseph 59, 67, 108, 134, 145, 157–8, 159, 169, 172, 184, 200, 209, 213
Philosophy of Mythology 67
Potencies 134
Symbolism 108, 213
Schematism, see Spatio-Temporal Dynamisms
Schizophrenia, see Psychosis
Schopenhauer, Arthur 49, 55, 59, 60–1, 141, 142, 146–50, 201, 203, 220
Schreber, Daniel Paul 71–2, 116, 172–3
Sense 218
Sex, Sexuality 7–8, 49, 71
Adolescent 79–80, 84, 205
Difference, Sexual 63, 100–1, 134–7
Ecstasy 60, 132, 188
Eros 8, 85
Hermaphroditic 62–3, 103–4, 125, 134–7, 172, 201, 217
Homosexuality 136–7, 201 n. 18
in Freud 7, 31–2
in Jung 74–9, 103–105
in occultism 70, 103-05, 128, 132
Incest 75, 81, 122

Instinct 8, 49, 62–3, 85
Libido 71–82
Masochism 77–8, 103–5, 189
Masturbation 71, 84, 204
Perversion 71, 77, 105
Psychotic 78
Tantric, see Tantrism
and Trauma 31–2
Shamdasani, Sonu 202, 204
Simondon, Gilbert 160
Singularity 13, 120, 153
Sleep 94, 133, 178–9, 186–8
Smith, Huston 179
Somnambulism 49–68, 92, 133–4, 146, 174, 177, 198–9
in Instinct 49–68, 160
Sorcery, see Occultism
Space 13–4, 158–9
Spatiotemporal Dynamisms 89–94, 98, 120–24
Spinoza, Baruch 41, 143, 150–2, 169, 220, 173, 202, 209, 220
Stengers, Isabelle 173–5
Stevens, Anthony 88–9, 208
Structuralism 171, 205–6
Sublime, the 113–15, 119
Sufism 220
Super-ego 86, 95–6, 100
Swales, Peter 182
Swedenborg, Emmanuel 144, 218–9
Symbolism 70, 76, 81, 103–137
Aesthetics 70, 111–124, 127–8, 134, 135
Sympnoia panta 42, 140, 183
Synthesis of Time 5–8, 21, 29, 35–6, 194

Tannery, Jules 12–13
Tantrism 103, 132, 135, 214–17, 221
Time, Temporality 5–8, 20–5, 29, 35–6, 91–3, 132, 150, 157, 177, 184
Tinbergen, Niko 50, 62
Toynbee, Arnold 206
Transcendental philosophy 5, 9, 20–25, 28, 32–4, 48, 88, 113, 116, 119, 120, 122–4
Trauma 31–2, 35, 174

Uexküll, Jakob von 50, 52
Uncanny, the 145–6, 154–8, 220
Unconscious
Bergsonian 5–8, 16–36, 50, 54–7
Freudian 5–8, 18, 24, 41, 42, 57, 112, 123
Hegelian 21, 212
Jungian 19, 42, 81–6
Kantian 92–100, 111–12, 123
Leibnizian 38–48
Occultist/Hermetic 37–8, 171–3, 184–6
Platonic 20, 33, 37, 42, 130, 137
Psychedelic 180–5
Schellingian 134
Schopenhauerian 60–1
Wundt's critique of 57–8

Vampires 171, 175–77, 222
Vegetal, the 77, 132
Verne, Jules 192
Villiers de l'Isle Adam, Auguste 124
Virtual and Actual 16–36, 41, 46, 83, 186–8

Weird tales 177
Wolf-Man 32, 106, 109–110, 170, 212
Woman 70, 77, 213
Becoming-woman in Tantrism 216–7
See Anima/Animus; Sexuality – Sexual Difference
Woodroffe, John 216
Wronski, Hoëne 1, 129, 184
Wundt, Wilhelm 57, 92–5, 190, 200, 209

Yates, Frances 129

Zaretsky, Eli 221
Žižek, Slavoj 2, 174